D0844108

PÉTAIN THE SOLDIER

Pétain the Soldier

by

Stephen Ryan

South Brunswick and New York:
A. S. Barnes and Company
London: Thomas Yoseloff Ltd

© 1969 by A. S. Barnes and Co., Inc.

Library of Congress Catalogue Card Number: 68–25388

A. S. Barnes and Co., Inc.

Cranbury, New Jersey 08512

Thomas Yoseloff Ltd

18 Charing Cross Rd.

London W.C. 2, England

6904

Printed in U.S.A.

To Stephen and Rose Ryan,

My Parents

Acknowledgments

I should like to acknowledge my indebtedness to the New York State University Research Foundation, whose two summer grants made the completion of this book possible.

My thanks are due also to the staff of the James M. Milne Library, New York State University College at Oneonta, particularly to the ladies who have been in charge of the Inter-Library Loan Department. They patiently, diligently and intelligently pursued the many difficult requests which I made of them.

I am indebted also to Dr. William B. Fink, Chairman of the Social Studies Department of the New York State University College at Oneonta, who read the manuscript and made useful comments.

I would like to express my appreciation to my publishers for their expert and considerate handling of this volume. In particular, the editing of the manuscript by Mr. Leslie Bialler has been invaluable.

I should also thank Mrs. Hilda Mercun for her typing assistance.

Finally, my wife, Ethel Law Ryan, has contributed much, directly and indirectly, to the successful completion of this project.

Contents

PÉTAIN THE SOLDIER

1

The Early Days

In preparing a chronicle of a famous soldier the biographer looks first for a military background or tradition somewhere in the family which would explain the young man's career preference. In Pétain's story one looks in vain for military antecedents, for he came of simple, though respectable and solid, peasant stock, who had resided for centuries in the region which became, during the French Revolution, the Pas-de-Calais department in northern France. In a way difficult for most Americans to understand he had his roots in the soil of his native land, his part of France, the old province of Artois.

The only early military influence that we can find is in a friend of Pétain's granduncle, the Abbé Lefèvre. A veteran of Napoleon's armies, as a very old man he told his stories of the campaigns in Italy and under the Empire to the young grandnephew. Whether or not the Abbé's recollections, glamorized by time and the storyteller's art, fired his young listener with a desire to follow the flag and the trumpets, we do not know; but it is more likely that Pétain worked for admission to Saint-Cyr for much the same reason that Ulysses Grant applied to West Point: because it was a way for a man of modest means to get an education.

In some ways this allusion to an American military hero is not out of place. Both Pétain and Grant were military leaders of extraordinary ability to whom their respective countries owed much; but who, propelled to political power by virtue of a popularity resulting from their military achievements, found themselves in an element for which they were not at all suited. Also, only in France or the United States, among

13

the great powers, was it socially possible in the nineteenth and early twentieth centuries for a man of humble birth to become a high-ranking officer in the army. In France this could be done, as the careers of Joffre, Foch and Pétain attest; but in other European countries the commissioned ranks of the services were for sons of upper-class families. The career of Sir William Robertson, who rose from the ranks to become Chief of the Imperial General Staff in the British Army, was exceptional. In the France of the Third Republic careers were open to all men of talent, although it is unfortunate that men of lower class or bourgeois origin who became army officers tended to adopt the aristocratic contempt of republican institutions; thus in a sense they bit the hand that fed them.

Pétain's father, a farmer, was rather well off by local standards. The farmhouse in which Pétain was born, on April 24, 1856, still stands on the edge of the little village of Cauchy-à-la-Tour, as you approach the village on the road from Arras. Built of native chalkstone, as were most of the houses in Artois, the building was unpretentious but substantial. When Pétain was born the farm had been in the family for a century. He was named Henri-Philippe Benoni Omer Joseph but he used throughout his life the simple Philippe.

Before Philippe was two years old his mother died and his father, left with five young children, within two years married again. The stepmother, soon with children of her own, was not very affectionate toward the first children of her husband; Philippe spent a good deal of his childhood with his grandmother who lived close by. This lack of maternal affection may or may not have had an important influence on the formation of his character. However, he remembered this lack vividly enough to talk about it with friends some eighty-six years later at Vichy, in a conversation in which he described his stepmother as an unkind woman who practically forced him out of the house.[1]

Philippe's maternal uncle, the Abbé Legrand, took an interest in the boy and directed and financed his studies. At age eleven, when his half-brother Anthoine was born, he left home.

Legrand saw to it that he was admitted to the Saint-Bertin boarding school at Saint-Omer. In his eight years there Philippe was noted for his aloofness and solitary habits, but he was an excellent scholar and received a bachelor of philosophy diploma in 1875. He had by now determined upon a career in the army and set about preparing for the examination which would admit him to Saint-Cyr, the West Point of France.

In 1871, when Philippe was fifteen years of age and attending board-

---

[1] Général Bernard Serrigny, *Trente ans avec Pétain* (Paris, 1959), 222.

ing school, France had suffered the humiliating defeat at the hands of Prussia which cost her most of Alsace and Lorraine and her position as the Continent's foremost military power. Her material loss perhaps was not so great as the blow to her pride, but the lost provinces remained a symbol of her defeat—a constant reminder of her humiliation. It has been customary in France to speak of the men of Pétain's generation who chose the army as a career as being motivated by a desire for *revanche:* as officers they were said to have lived for and dreamed of revenge and the day when Germany would be brought to account; these men were supposed to have spent the next thirty years training and planning, with their "eyes fixed on the blue line of the Vosges."

How much of this is after the fact romanticizing and how much is a real factor in the history of France is a debatable point; probably there is a certain element of truth in it. Germany was the national enemy as far as the public and the army were concerned; certainly there were few people who thought in terms of a war with anyone else. Pétain may well have been motivated by a desire to recover the lost provinces; he did not divert his gaze to colonial adventures as did many other officers, and if his eyes were not exactly "fixed on the blue line of the Vosges" he did, as a professional soldier, think that any war for which he might be preparing undoubtedly would be with Germany.

To prepare for the military academy the nineteen-year-old Philippe chose the Dominican college at Arcueil and in October 1875 he presented himself at the home of its director. When the director expressed some surprise that the young man had appeared without his parents Philippe explained that he was quite alone in life. The transcript of his high grades from Saint-Bertin was an excellent introduction and reference, so the sympathetic head of the school accepted him without hesitation. After a year of study he entered the Ecole Spéciale Militaire at Saint-Cyr and completed the two-year course in 1878.

Pétain's graduating class of second lieutenants from the military academy, his "promotion," as each class was called, was nicknamed "Plevna" after the battle in Bulgaria in 1877 between the Russians and the Turks. The officers of a "promotion" were linked for life—helping each other at times, jealous of each other's career successes at times, but always members of the same group formed at the academy. All things being equal they would rise in rank at approximately the same pace under a system of army promotion where seniority counted as much as merit. In practice, of course, some forged ahead of the others.

In view of Pétain's well-known propensity for the defensive form of warfare the choice by his "promotion" of the nickname "Plevna" is perhaps significant. At Plevna the Turks, although cut off from their main armies, held off the Russians for months by digging strong field entrenchments from which repeated and costly assaults by the Russians were repelled. Although the Turks were finally forced to capitulate they demonstrated that well-entrenched troops with modern weapons, artillery and rifles, could inflict heavy losses on the attackers. The French army in the 1870's had little need of this lesson, having learned in the war with the Prussians the great strength of the defensive from a tactical point of view. The army regulations of 1875 reflected the lessons of 1870–71 in underlining the importance and strength of firepower and the need for caution in the face of enemy fire. The German regulations of that decade also reflected this concern, for their victories in the recent war often had been dearly bought and their ultimate victory was due more to faulty French leadership than to German tactical superiority.[2]

Pétain was a product of this decade and apparently the tactical lessons which he absorbed at Saint-Cyr, as well as his study of the war of 1870, and his adherence to the regulations of 1875, marked his judgment—happily for France in 1914-18 and perhaps not so happily in the 1930's. As a young officer he remained wedded to the principles of the regulations of 1875 when other officers were developing a reckless disregard for the strength of field entrenchments and modern firepower.

Pétain's first post was an ideal one for a young infantry officer. He spent the first five years of his army career as a second lieutenant in the 24th Battalion of Chasseurs Alpins stationed at Villefranche-sur-mer near Nice. The *chasseurs à pied* and *chasseurs alpins* were the élite troops of the infantry and Pétain was to spend some twenty years in chasseur units. He was strong, athletic and a good troop leader; a good shot and a tireless marcher and mountain climber.

In their off duty hours the chasseur officers at Villefranche made the most of the pleasures of the lovely Mediterranean coastal resort. It was, however, strictly forbidden for them to play roulette at the gambling casinos, a wise regulation some of them did not always observe. On a day off Pétain once ventured in civilian clothes into the casino at Monte-Carlo where he was tempted to place a bet. He won on the turn of the wheel and continued to play and continued in luck. His winnings grew until, just after placing a bet, he glanced up and to his dismay saw his colonel approaching. The young lieutenant maintained a calm front and moved around the table looking at it a little distrustfully, with the air of a curious sightseer; then with measured pace he sauntered to the exit and disappeared, leaving behind his bet and his winnings—some three hundred gold francs.

---

[2]Henry Contamine, *La Revanche, 1871–1914* (Paris, 1957), 44.

It was here too, in 1881, that Pétain met the girl who would one day be his wife, Eugénie Hardon, the daughter of friends he often visited at Menton. She was only four years old at the time. Some thirty-nine years later, in 1920, his little "Annie" became Madame la Maréchale, she for her second marriage and he for his first. She was with him for the rest of his life, faithful through the last sad days on the Isle d'Yeu and at his side at the end.

After five years on the pleasant côte d'Azur the young officer was promoted to first lieutenant and transferred to the less pleasant little garrison city of Besançon where he spent another five years with the 3rd Chasseurs battalion. He was not happy at his transfer, although it was mandatory after five years with the same unit. The amorous and handsome bachelor would miss the social life of his former post, but there were more important reasons for his reluctance to leave. His first command in the *chasseurs alpins* had been a demanding and rewarding experience for him; he enjoyed the physical challenge of the mountains and he had become attached to the men whom he had trained and led.

The role of his unit was becoming increasingly important in the 1880's, when the French establishment of a protectorate over Tunisia in 1881 had provoked an increase of tension with Italy who had hoped to acquire that North African possession for herself. In 1882 Italy signed the first treaty of the Triple Alliance with Germany and Austria-Hungary, a treaty aimed partly at France, and crack units of *chasseurs alpins* assumed an important role in the defense of France's frontier with Italy in the Maritime Alps. The chasseurs began wearing the beret and they were trained to operate in autonomous groups, supported by eighty-millimeter mountain guns. On the other side of the Alps the colorful *alpini* were the Italian answer to France's *chasseurs alpins.*

Pétain was considered a good officer by his superiors; their comments in his dossier are all commendatory in spite of his penchant for sarcastic remarks, often directed at them. He seemed to take a perverse pleasure in maintaining his individuality and independence by a lack of reverence for higher ranking officers, a quality not likely to win him advancement in a peacetime army. His promotions therefore were all made at the limit of seniority: he was a second-lieutenant for five years, a lieutenant for seven years, a captain for ten, finally being promoted to major in 1900.

Until 1899 promotions of commissioned officers in the army were made under the terms of the Soult Law of 1832, which provided that up to the rank of major two-thirds of the advancements in rank would be by longevity and one-third by selection on the basis of merit. Above the rank of major promotions were one-half on a merit basis and one-half according to longevity. The nominations for the promotions by selection were made by the *Commissions de classement,* made up of officers from the staffs of the army corps commanders or the Inspector General's staff and were entirely outside of civilian control.

The political upheaval and the loss of prestige to the army caused by the Dreyfus affair changed this, as it changed the status of the army vis à vis the Third Republic; after 1899 the *Commissions de classement* were abolished. Promotions of army officers were thenceforth the responsibility and prerogative of the office of the Minister of War, a civilian cabinet member responsible to the parliament, and although the War Ministry generally followed the recommendations of its army leaders the civilian government exercised a real, and not always beneficial, control of army commissioned personnel.[3]

For a Saint-Cyr graduate Pétain's advancement under either the old or the new system was slow. Participation in colonial campaigns was one way to achieve relatively quick promotion but service abroad did not attract him. Service in the colonies counted double for seniority purposes; for example, Joffre to some extent owed his high position and appointment to supreme command in 1911 to his years of service as an engineer officer in the colonies. Another way to improve one's chances was to win appointment to a two-year course at the War College, reserved for officers of talent, promise and high command potential. In 1888 Pétain was appointed to attend this army "holy of holies," but even that failed to improve his career. In later life the Marshal would joke about his slow advancement before 1914, saying, "I was an old lieutenant, an old captain, an old colonel; I've been old in all my grades."[4]

His first assignment after leaving the War College in 1890 was a two-year tour of duty as a staff officer in the headquarters of the XV Corps at Marseille. This staff duty was required of all officers of promise but Pétain did not like it. The routine and the paper work repelled him although he apparently did the work required of him well, so well that he was chosen by the corps commander, General Mathelin, to be his aide-de-camp. Mathelin noted of him: "Silent, cold, enemy of hasty decisions and always proceeding systematically,"[5] a description which could have fitted the man at any stage in his life.

---

[3] Raoul Girardet, *La Société militaire dans la France contemporaine* (Paris, 1953), 197.
[4] Jérome et Jean Tharaud, et al., *Album du Maréchal Pétain* (Paris, 1951), 8.
[5] Général Laure, *Pétain* (Paris, 1941), 7.

In 1892 he gladly left his staff position to command a company of chasseurs of the 29th battalion stationed at Vincennes, just outside of Paris; regulations required that he command troops in his grade of captain. After a year at Vincennes he moved into the city where he was on the staff of the military governor of Paris, then General Saussier who was also commander in chief-designate of the army. Most officers would have been delighted to obtain this post, but not Pétain. He criticized the red tape, and his superiors, whom he judged too immersed in daily routine, and even the dirtiness of the building in which he worked.

When Saussier was replaced by General Zurlinden as military governor Pétain continued on the staff and was pleased when the military governor's offices were moved to new quarters on the Boulevard des Invalides. He was given the responsibility for organizing the new offices and his work was done so well that the office of the military governor retained the same organization until the occupation of Paris by the Germans in 1940.

In the 1890's the Dreyfus affair, which had broken the army's privileged relationship with the Third Republic, was at its height. Pétain was an anti-Dreyfusard, although not a notably virulent one; he could hardly have been otherwise, given his background. Coming from a traditionally conservative peasant family, educated by the Jesuits at Saint-Bertin and the Dominicans at Arcueil, trained at Saint-Cyr and matured in the army, having lived since his eleventh year in a collective and authoritarian environment, he was conservative but not reactionary, Catholic but not a practising one (and certainly not "clerical"), contemptuous of politicians but not anti-republican.

In the conflict between the Catholic conservative elements of the army and the anti-clerical, left-wing politicians, which marred (or livened) the French political scene in the two decades before World War I, Pétain somehow managed to win few friends in either camp. He belonged to no clique, to no faction, and his lack of striking success in his prewar career was more an affair of temperament than a matter of politics or even entirely of military doctrine.

General Zurlinden liked the way Pétain worked and he chose him to be his aide-de-camp, a post that he continued to hold under Zurlinden's successor, General Brugère. But he still had to spend time in a line command in his grade of captain and he was transferred to the 8th Chasseur battalion at Amiens.

With the 8th Chasseurs Pétain helped the battalion commander to run the battalion and served with distinction. After the annual maneuvers, in which his unit distinguished itself, General Bonnal judged him as follows: "Unites the qualities of vigor, character, *coup d'oeil,* of decision and intelligence in the right proportions desirable in a future general officer *(grand chef)* ."[6]

The "future general," who in the next thirteen years managed to alienate enough people to limit his advancement to that of a regimental command, was assigned in 1900 as an instructor at the Firing School for Instructors at Châlons. Major Pétain had gained a certain reputation in the army as an expert on infantry rifle markmanship, particularly its tactical application. General Millet, who was once Pétain's instructor at the War College and was now Director of Infantry under the War Ministry, was concerned about the doctrine being taught at the school. It tended to emphasize the application of group firing: spraying the terrain with a hail of bullets aimed in a general way at the enemy with as much fire as possible, at the expense of individual, accurate marksmanship. The theory was that modern bolt-action magazine rifles fired fast enough so that individual accuracy was not so necessary as it had been. Pétain was an advocate of individual, accurate fire by infantrymen, something one would expect from an officer to whom the chasseur infantry had become a way of life; consequently the director of the school was not at all pleased with the theories of his new subordinate.

A new Director of Infantry at the War Ministry, General Lejoindre, supported the infantry rifle fire tactics to which Major Pétain was opposed. The latter therefore found himself in opposition to the official army doctrine. The director of the Firing School told his subordinate that his theories did not have official sanction and would have to be changed. The unorthodox instructor refused to comply and was transferred forthwith to the command of a battalion in the 5th Infantry Regiment. By that time promotions in the army were no longer made by the *Commissions de classement* but were controlled by the War Ministry and thus were more susceptible to politics, a system that was disliked by most officers. Pétain's refusal to comply with General Lejoindre's point of view, a gesture of independence toward the War Ministry which could harm his career, was a mark of character and perhaps of defiance. It was a point of honor for him not to relinquish or even to compromise on matters of principle.

The transfer to the 5th Infantry was not without its compensations, for that regiment was stationed in Paris and the girl whom Pétain had met as a child in 1881, Mlle. Hardon, now a young lady of twenty-four years, lived there. The two had seen each other frequently over the

---

6 Tharaud, 10.

intervening years and the affection which the soldier felt toward his little friend had grown into something more serious. But what had he to offer her? He was twenty-one years her senior; he had no income other than his army salary—hardly enough to live on—and his chances for advancement did not seem bright.

However, hardly six months had passed since his dismissal from the Firing School when his fortune changed. General Bonnal, then head of the War College, who had a high regard for Pétain's soldierly qualities and military proficiency from a practical as well as a theoretical standpoint, arranged to have him assigned to the College in 1901 as associate professor of infantry tactics. If attendance at the War College was reserved for officer-students who had shown evidence of high aptitude and were marked for high command, the assignment to teach there indicated that Pétain, in the minds of some of the army leadership, was a master of his profession.

He began to think that if he were going to marry at all it had better be now, since he was forty-five years of age. He therefore presented himself to the remaining family of Mlle. Hardon, her grandmother and stepmother, and asked for permission to court the young lady. The ladies refused to permit the match, largely on the basis of the disparity in ages. His lack of money and prospects also probably had something to do with their decision. Mlle. Hardon did not know for many years that her old friend had asked for her hand. Subsequently she married a physician, and had a son; but her marriage was unhappy and eventually ended in an amicable divorce.

It would be romantic to record that the disappointed suitor carried with him, in his lonely bachelorhood, the sad memory of a lost love, of the only girl who meant anything to him and who was lost to him. Perhaps something of the sort did take place for he did marry her finally in the twilight of his life; but he did not let his broken heart, if he had one, interfere with his love affairs with other women, and the evidence is strong that there were many of those. Soldiers are not poets, and Pétain was more likely to give a broken heart than to receive one.

His assignment to the important teaching position in the infantry tactics course at the War College came at a time when the army was going through a period of crises: a minor one in connection with a controversy over the best tactical methods to adopt for the army, and a major one provoked by the War Ministry's crude attempts to republicanize the army, to purge it of its strong Catholic, reactionary, bias. Major Pétain's appointment came during a period when his political and military opinions would have an important bearing on his career.

As an aftermath of the Dreyfus affair the victorious republicans, who had humbled the army and shown that its leaders could be as dishonest and as dishonorable as any Third Republic politicians, attempted to capitalize on their victory by weakening the politically reactionary influence of the army and the Church. The new minister of war in 1900 was General André, one of the few high-ranking generals— (the highest rank in the French army was the three-star divisional general; even Joffre did not rise higher than that rank until 1916) who could be counted upon as a strong supporter of the republic. General André conceived it as his duty to use the War Ministry's new power to control promotions in the army to further the advancement of officers who were preferably Protestants but who at least were not practicing Catholics, and to block or delay the promotions of the Catholic officers who were, or were deemed to be, enemies of the republic. Officers of aristocratic origin were of course prime suspects but outside of the cavalry they were not an important factor.

André's office staff had the ingenious idea of using their connections with the Freemasons, traditionally anticlerical and politically liberal, to set up a network which obtained information throughout the army from officers with Masonic connections, from local Masonic lodges in garrison towns, and from local prefects and other sympathetic authorities. The information thus secretly obtained was channeled through the Grand Orient Masonic lodge in Paris to the War Ministry, where a secret file on each officer was kept. Officers who attended Mass frequently, sent their children to Catholic schools, or whose wives were regular churchgoers, were duly marked down as suspect and therefore not eligible for promotion while officers who joined or helped the Masons or who otherwise manifested sound republican sympathies, were favored for advancement.

This was a deplorable and disgraceful episode in the history of France, as mean and vicious as the Dreyfus affair which preceded it; and before André was denounced and forced to resign in November 1904 it had caused considerable damage to the morale of the army. The most insidious aspect of it was the delation of officers by brother officers, when a careless word spoken in the mess could ruin a career; and men promoted during this period were, in the future, often suspect in the eyes of their fellow officers.

Pétain's appointment to the War College in 1901 was not evidence of his republican sympathies, because he had few, but rather of his refusal to get involved at all in political matters. He was not a churchgoer and that perhaps helped him. In the same year Ferdinand Foch, a devout Catholic whose brother was a Jesuit, was transferred out of the

War College because of his known clerical affinities (he returned to the College as its commandant in 1908).

Had Pétain wanted to exploit this situation the opportunity was there. General Percin, *chef de cabinet* of General André, respected his views on infantry tactics and particularly his theories on the importance of artillery and infantry liaison, and he offered to make Pétain head of the Firing School at Châlons—the school from which he had been dismissed for his unorthodox views. When Pétain objected that with the rank of major he would not have sufficient authority to do the job properly—the commandant of the school was normally a colonel—Percin offered to obtain a promotion to lieutenant-colonel for him. Pétain rejected the offer; as a matter of principle he did not wish to obtain advancement in this way, and as the event proved his decision was a wise one. The officers discriminated against under André's regime had long memories and Percin, for example, was relieved of his command in the early stages of World War I when the traditional officer corps again controlled the army.

Far from maintaining a discreet reserve during this critical period, as the situation became worse Pétain's anger grew. Although he had long since given up religion he now began to take an ostentatious interest in religious matters. When asked by an agent of André's office to supply the names of officers who attended Mass, Pétain replied with more than his customary glacial manner that he could not know them: since he was in the front row at the church he could not see who was behind him.

Many years later, when he was a colonel in command of the 33rd Infantry, a major whom Pétain knew had denounced him as a clerical during the period of the *fiches* was assigned to command a reserve regiment which would be working with the 33rd in the event of war. Pétain received the erstwhile delator correctly but without ceremony, then he terminated the interview by saying, "It was Colonel Pétain who received you. Pétain himself wants to have as little as possible to do with you." Then, turning, the colonel saw his embarrassed secretary, a young lieutenant, standing behind him and he roared, "You. Get the hell out of here."[7]

The lieutenant, Cary, who reported this incident affirmed that his colonel was not a clerical. Once on maneuvers on a Sunday the regiment found itself near a small village where there was only one Mass and that at noontime. But Pétain had an inflexible rule that all his officers should be at the table for lunch promptly at noon. The young

[7] Pierre Bourget, *Témoignages inédits sur la Maréchal Pétain* (Paris, 1960), 32.

officer, with some trepidation, requested permission to attend Mass, and the colonel, "as an exception," said that he would delay lunch for one hour, adding, "I envy you your faith."

This question of the man's religious predilection is of more than passing interest in a study of an important figure in the history of the Third Republic. The degree or denominational direction of an officer's, or a politician's, religious convictions was a matter of importance because it often could determine his political affiliation and thus affect his career. Although Pétain was born and died in the Catholic Church he apparently lived the greater part of his life as a nonbeliever. During the war he told one of his officers that long ago, when he was young, he had been a believer but that he was no longer one. He said that none of the faith of his childhood remained to him.[8] Yet he also told an English journalist, in 1917, while speculating as to why the French parliamentarians disliked him, that he was "certainly a Catholic" and respected his faith, although he was not *pratiquant* and had not been to Mass for thirty years.[9] It is safe to assume that Pétain's unpopularity with politicians during the war was not due to an excess of religious zeal, nor was his popularity after the war due to a reputation for anticlericalism. Religion was not an important factor in his life.

His position as instructor at the War College involved him in another controversy, this one of a technical nature involving infantry tactics. The development and adoption of quick-firing, breachloading artillery, the magazine rifle and smokeless powder, meant to some military thinkers that procedures regulating the action of infantry in combat and the relation of the artillery to the infantry needed drastic revision. To Pétain the increased firepower of both infantry and artillery meant that the strength of the defensive was greatly multiplied and that a sensible commander would expose his troops to enemy fire with the greatest caution; to him the regulations of 1875 expressed principles which were still valid. To other military thinkers the infantry regulations of 1884 and 1894—developed after the theories of Gilbert, Cardot and Bonnal among others, which prescribed a greater emphasis upon offensive action by the infantry in spite of and in the face of enemy fire, and which were in fact a return to the brutal and costly shock tactics of Napoleon—were doubly valid because, they reasoned, new weaponry favored the offensive and had rendered it more powerful.

Pétain was dissatisfied with the infantry regulations of 1884 govern-

8 J. R. Tournoux, *Pétain et de Gaulle* (Paris, 1964), 61.
9 C. à C. Repington, *The First World War* (New York, 1920), I, 549.

ing fire and movement, which held that the infantry could move forward under the heaviest fire against well-defended trenches and take
them. The new regulation of 1894 was no better. The infantry must
advance on the enemy, line after line in deep ranks, "the men elbow
to elbow." When the infantry did employ its firepower it should fire in
volleys on the command of an officer. (Pétain had opposed this official
doctrine vigorously when he was an instructor at the Firing School.)
Emphasis upon cover, the regulations said, should be avoided because
it weakened the cohesion of the formation; the assault should be made
with masses of men to the sound of bands and drums.[10]

What particularly distressed Pétain was the separation of the artillery from the infantry from a command point of view. In terms of
space such separation was inevitable and proper; he recognized that.
The new (1897) seventy-five millimeter field gun used by infantry
divisions, for example, fired accurately over six thousand meters. Therefore the artillery obviously could no longer be in the front line with
the infantry as it had early in the nineteenth century. Instead it must
seek shelter from enemy fire by taking positions farther in the rear;
its range was such that it could and should do so. But what disturbed
Pétain was that the artillery was removed from the infantry also in
terms of coordination and liaison; its primary function of supporting
the infantry was being lost sight of at a time when the infantry needed
strong support to counter enemy rifle and gunfire.

Artillery commanders, now technical specialists to an even greater
degree than ever before, were thinking in terms of tactical autonomy
for themselves. They argued that the observation of targets had become more difficult because with smokeless powder now in use there
no longer would be a cloud of smoke marking the enemy positions;
they felt that artillery specialists would have to choose their own
targets and control their own movement and fire. This trend away
from a close relation between the two arms disturbed Pétain and led
to his obsession with the idea of infantry–artillery liaison.

He also felt strongly that the trend toward offensive thinking in the
army was dangerous and impractical in the face of modern firepower.
Only the offensive could, in the final analysis, lead to victory; but one
should seek to defeat the enemy in destroying him on the battlefield
by utilizing strong defensive positions to shelter one's troops and
render their fire more effective. Then one could proceed to the attack
against a weakened adversary, a defensive-offensive combination or,
more simply, the "counterpunch" idea. This is as much an affair of
temperament as it is a technical matter; Pétain was above all a realist

---

[10] Eugène Carrias, *La Pensée militaire française* (Paris, 1960), 276.

who thought in material terms: to him the fact that bullets kill was the obvious condition with which a commander had to deal. Men like Foch, however, thought more in metaphysical terms; to Foch the will and morale of the commander was the vital condition in warfare and the material factors were of less importance.

The validity of Pétain's realism was borne out by the brutal lessons of World War I. He was the one commander who was prepared intellectually for the war and for whom the war held few surprises. His realism was again in evidence in 1940: the facts of France's complete military collapse and the absence of any obvious material factors which could help her meant to him a logical acceptance of the defeat, at least until such time as the material conditions should change. De Gaulle's quixotic movement from Great Britain, a country also apparently without the physical means to redress the balance, was to him another Foch-like escape into an unreal situation; and in fact he was right as far as his reasoning went. It was not de Gaulle's "voices" à la Joan of Arc or will to victory à la Foch which won in the end but the hard facts of American, Russian and British military hardware and manpower. Pétain, a brilliant tactician in his best days and usually a good strategist, perhaps erred in 1940 in underestimating the material factors.

In the late nineteenth century, as the defeat of 1870 receded in time, the military theorists of the French army began to look back to Napoleon as the great master in whose campaigns one could find all the secrets of the military art. This veneration of Napoleon's methods—or what they thought were his methods—cannot be overemphasized, as foolish as this might seem today. It is a curious example of nationalistic myopia that the "Little Corporal"—who had taken over a military organization already established and brought to a high degree of efficiency during the Revolution; who had access to a reservoir of manpower in the most populous country in Europe, made readily available through a system of mass conscription already established by the Revolution; who made disastrous strategic errors in his Spanish and Russian ventures; who, at the peak of his success, employed little art in his military tactics, substituting massed manpower for finesse; and who in the final analysis was defeated and died in exile—had become for many French military leaders the quintessence of the military art.

The trend of offensive thinking, which began not too unreasonably but which culminated, after 1911, in the absurd *offensive à outrance* doctrine, was largely due to an absence of protracted warfare in Europe between 1815 and 1914. The god of war must have been more pleased with the peace settlement of 1919 than with that of 1815. Military knowledge, to the extent that it is a science, needs a laboratory for experiment and observation; peacetime maneuvers and exercises on the map are not good substitutes for the real thing. Wars like the Franco-Prussian or the Crimean were limited in scope and taught few tactical absolutes. The four-year American Civil War could have been a valuable laboratory for a study of warfare under modern conditions but European soldiers paid little attention to it.[11]

The more recent Boer War and the Russian–Japanese War also taught valuable lessons which largely were ignored or misinterpreted by many French military leaders. The war in South Africa, to them, was just a colonial experience—and, they asked, had not the French officers conditioned in the Algerian and Mexican campaigns failed in 1870? To Foch the war in Manchuria confirmed his theory that modern weapons rendered the offensive more powerful than the defensive. To Pétain, who had studied the two recent conflicts in South Africa and the Far East, his own theories on the inviolability of fronts were confirmed; and even if, like Foch, he might have been looking for proofs of theories which he already held, the fact is that he was right and Foch was wrong.

Pétain's involvement in the pre-1914 discussions and disputes in French military circles regarding the relative merits of the offensive and the defensive was not a simple clear-cut opposition of views between himself and a ruling clique; not a single combat that in itself ruined his career, as is often maintained. The fact that the man who became one of the foremost leaders and the most popular military commander in France during World War I was going to be retired as a colonel in 1914 has required explaining, but the explanations often have been too simple, both by his partisans and by his enemies. Retirement as a colonel in a peacetime army, by a man who had never been on campaign in the colonies, is not exactly a mark of failure, as many retired colonels would protest.

The dialogue between the enthusiasts of the offensive and the proponents of the defensive went on from the 1880's to 1914 and it was only after 1911 that the former prevailed completely. Pétain's first appointment as an instructor at the War College was made by General Bonnal, a strong advocate, along with his friend Captain Gilbert, of the offensive. Since Pétain's views were hardly a secret his appointment by Bonnal indicates a certain openmindedness on the latter's part.

---

[11] Jay Luvaas in *The Military Legacy of the Civil War* (Chicago, 1959) demonstrates that the American experience was, for the most part, ignored by European military thinkers.

General Foch, who came to the War College as its commandant in 1908, gave Pétain glowing reports in his official dossier, yet the two men were often in disagreement on military doctrine.

Pétain was not the only instructor at the War College who emphasized caution in the face of modern firepower; his contemporaries de Maud'huy, Fayolle and Debeney, for example, taught there and also cautioned against an excessive devotion to the offensive. Debeney was at the College as late as 1913.

In 1885 Major Cardot had begun to teach an offensive doctrine at the War College (organized in 1878), a doctrine which scorned flanking maneuvers and the dispersed order and which stressed shock tactics and the moral factor in warfare. Captain Foch was his pupil. Throughout the nineteenth century Cardot, who became a general, exercised, as did his former pupils, an important influence on French military thinking. But the War College, in the twentieth century, was not a hotbed, or the origin, of the *offensive à outrance* doctrine.

Even less were the extravagant offensive theories a product of the Higher War Council (*Conseil supérieur de la guerre*) which was composed of the high-ranking generals who would command France's armies in the event of war. The Council, reorganized by War Minister Freycinet in 1888, was headed by France's senior general, whose title of Vice-president of the Higher War Council (its president was the Minister of War) made him the commander in chief-designate, or generalissimo, in the event of war. But the members of this Council, prospective army commanders, were usually not partisans of the growing cult of the offensive; Gallieni, Lyautey, Pau and Lanrezac, for example, thought that it was ridiculous. However, even though they would be France's foremost military leaders in wartime their control of military doctrine and personnel was limited in peacetime.

The *offensive à outrance* doctrine was largely a product of the Army General Staff, the organization of which to some extent is indicative of the political divisions in France and the civilian government's fear of military power. As reorganized in 1890 the Army General Staff was an extension of the War Ministry and subordinate to the War Minister. It in no way had the power that the German General Staff, answerable only to the Emperor, had in Germany; nor was its Chief of the General Staff intended to be the commander in chief in wartime. Yet its chief did, in peacetime, exercise virtual control of the army and it did, to a great extent, control doctrine and personnel; it was through this division of military power that the parliament intended that the military leaders should be controlled and their political aspirations, if any, should be curtailed.

The danger of a military takeover of the government seems a limited one in retrospect, largely because it did not happen and because the system was such that it could not happen; but the fears of Third Republic politicians were reasonable ones. Germany's military organization led to a military dictatorship after 1916, with disastrous consequences for that country. But the divided nature of the French command structure had disadvantages as well. The experienced general officers with demonstrated command competence were entrusted with the armies of France in the Higher War Council while the General Staff tended to recruit younger, brilliant but inexperienced theoreticians, too conscious of their intellectual qualities. Not only was the *offensive à outrance* doctrine impressed upon the army largely by the General Staff, through the authority of the Minister of War, but other important developments were to some extent their responsibility. For example, the prosecution of Captain Dreyfus was the work of the General Staff, over the expressed opposition of at least the head of the Higher War Council, General Saussier, and perhaps some of its members.

The *offensive à outrance* doctrine became firmly entrenched officially only after 1911 when the functions of the Chief of the General Staff and those of the Vice-president of the Higher War Council became merged in one office, held by General Joffre. This was done under the War Ministry of Messimy and it was the means by which the General Staff officers managed to gain control of the army. It was thought by the government that General Joffre, a former Mason, was safely republican, so the risk of combining the two posts seemed minimal. Therefore the army commanders, not at all in sympathy with the official military doctrine developed by the General Staff, found themselves at war in 1914 under a commander who was advised and influenced by the young General Staff officers, the "Young Turks" as they were called.

Even in the General Staff the evolution of the offensive-at-all-cost doctrine was not a clearcut development. The chief of the Operations Bureau of the General Staff for the five years prior to 1914, Colonel de Grandmaison, is generally considered the chief culprit in its adoption by the army; but the holder of the same post in 1902, Colonel Berrot, was opposed to it and advocated a form of warfare that, if followed would have saved France countless casualties in World War I. In three staff lectures Berrot attacked the theory of the offensive and said that in a war with Germany the French armies should go on the defensive at first, feel out the enemy and inflict upon him the heavy casualties which defensive tactics made possible, and only then take the offensive.

He stressed the strength of the defensive in the light of new weapons, particularly rapid-fire small arms and smokeless powder, and expounded the lessons of the Boer War and those of the American Civil War.

Berrot said that enormous armies would confront each other in the event of a European war, each unable to break through the other. Battles would take place on a vast front and would be of long duration. An equilibrium of forces would ensue, to be broken only by circumstances outside the control of the military leaders. All of this was a remarkably accurate forecast of World War I. His listeners took sharp exception to his theories, so strong even then was the cult of the offensive, and his views were not accepted.[12]

The merging of the two highest posts in the French military establishment in 1911 had the unfortunate effect of joining the tactical planning of the General Staff with the strategic planning of the Higher War Council. Before this time the *offensive à outrance* doctrine was confined to tactics, where it encountered the spirited opposition of Pétain and others at the War College and where it could do damage enough; but strategy, the formulation of the plans of campaign to be put into operation should war break out, was the task of the Higher War Council. As a result of the change in organization the members of the Higher War Council were shouldered aside in strategic planning and Plan XVII, with which France went to war in 1914, was the work of the General Staff. In fact the generals commanding the armies were kept in ignorance of the commander in chief's intentions until the war broke out and then they merely were given directions for the concentration of their respective armies.

At the last meeting of the Higher War Council before war broke out, on May 26, 1914, the only accomplishment of the council was the decision that each soldier should carry, as part of his field equipment, an individual tent-canvas. The high-ranking generals also discussed the adoption of rolling-kitchens for the infantry on campaign, but this question was left unresolved.

The current of the offensive, of the emphasis upon the moral values in warfare—the confidence and discipline of the commanders and troops—had been growing in the French army since the study of Ardant du Picq and Clausewitz was undertaken seriously in the 1880's, under the leadership of Cardot, Gilbert, Bonnal and Foch. But the grand plans of campaign which had succeeded each other since 1870 had not been greatly affected. The plans of campaign which had preceded Plan XVII had changed with the years, partly in response to the interna-

---

[12] General Palat, "Trois conférences à l'État-major de l'Armée en 1902," *Revue militaire française*, XXXII (May, 1929), 232–256.

tional situation—as for example, the attitude of Italy as a member of the Triple Alliance or the acquisition of Russia as an ally in the 1890's—and partly as a result of technological advances—particularly the growth of the railway system, which permitted the concentration of the armies in less time and therefore closer to the frontier. But all of these plans had been to a lesser or greater degree circumspect in that they had ranged, in the beginning, in the 1870's, from a defensive posture to the plans of the 1890's and the first decade of the twentieth century, which were defensive—offensive arrangements.

The defensive—offensive plans specified the concentration of the armies in strong defensive formations in northeastern France. They took advantage of the line of fortifications built by Séré de Rivières from Belfort to Verdun, the adoption of a waiting attitude to force the Germans to reveal their intentions and become committed to a line of action, and then the going over to the offensive at a time and place of the French high command's choosing. Some of the advocates of the offensive had never liked this tendency and during the 1890's Generals Cardot and Langlois had, in their writings, sharply criticized the advocacy by Bonnal and Gilbert of a defensive strategy at the beginning of a war with Germany; even Bonnal was more cautious in his strategy than in his tactics. Bonnal's influence in the adoption of a defensive strategy, as evidenced in Plans XIII and XIV, was continued by subsequent commanders in chief-designate, Generals Brugère, Hagron and de Lacroix, in their Plans XV, XV *bis* and XVI respectively; all of these were basically defensive in prescribing a "wait and see" attitude in the initial stages of a war with Germany.

Plan XVII was drawn up by the *offensive à outrance* theorists of the General Staff. It was a plan of concentration to put the French armies in positions ranged along the northeastern frontier, from Alsace to the Ardennes, from which they were to advance as soon as they were able against the enemy, without regard to anything that the enemy might do. The main idea was to drive through the enemy's center or wherever he might be encountered and impose the will of the French high command upon that of the German high command. As in the tactical offensive doctrine the commander was to break the enemy morale by the ferocity of his assault, so in the realm of grand strategy General Joffre would impose his will on the enemy commander by the very directness and single-mindedness of his drive.

The Germans also had developed a rigorously offensive doctrine, as apologists for the French planners have pointed out; but the German high command had drawn conclusions from their study of the Boer War and the Russian—Japanese War that were substantially the same as Pétain's regarding the inviolability of fronts. German planners recognized that modern weapons made frontal assaults extremely costly and yet they were impelled by temperament and strategic necessity to follow an offensive strategy; hence they evolved their extended order as opposed to the French close order, and their basic principle of fixing the enemy by fire and local pressure while enveloping his wing in a flanking maneuver: *festhalten und umfassen,* fix and envelope. This came at a time when the theorists of France, who scorned maneuver and flanking movements as a weakening of the offensive spirit in tactical situations, had taken over the strategic direction of French military policy to which they applied the same questionable reasoning as they had to tactics.

In his course in infantry tactics at the War College Pétain methodically and persuasively developed the thesis that "firepower kills" and demonstrated that the strength of the defensive was such that enemy positions defended with modern weapons could be taken only by the application of heavy fire power upon them prior to and during the attack. After leaving the War College for ten months' service with the 104th Infantry in 1903, he was brought back and continued his campaign for a revision of the tactics prescribed by the infantry regulations of 1894. In his dossier his superior noted: "He defends his views with a strong dialectic and an ardor which make him a champion. With regard to infantry fire techniques, notably, he has become one of two or three leading authorities in France."[13]

So strong and persuasive were his arguments that he became recognized as the leader of a school of thought and it was largely through his influence that the infantry regulations of 1894, which prescribed volley firing by riflemen and dense formations in the attack, were replaced by the regulations of December 1904, which prescribed supple and flexible formations in combat, with elements of the infantry advancing from cover to cover, supported by the fire of other elements, the whole operation being conducted with an eye toward terrain and any other factors which could influence the progression of the troops. It is unfortunate that this regulation governing the fire and movement of infantry in combat was not in use in 1914 but by then had been superseded by less practical and less sensible regulations.

In March 1907 a new commandant at the War College, General Valabrègue, took exception to Pétain's tactical ideas and had the newly promoted lieutenant-colonel transferred out of the College. Pétain requested that he be assigned to a post in eastern France—the more

13 Quoted in Laure, 15.

desirable units and military assignments were near the German frontier
—but by then he had incurred the displeasure of influential officers at
the War Ministry, partly through his independent attitude and partly
through his vehement, and sometimes sarcastic, opposition to the offensive-minded officers. Instead of the command in the east he was sent
to the 118th Infantry at Quimper in Brittany, which is about as far
west as you can go in France, a not too gentle suggestion that he be
more deferential in his relations with his superiors.

The new commandant at the War College, General Maunoury,
wanted Pétain back at the school to head the course in infantry tactics
but had difficulty in gaining the consent of the War Ministry. Pétain,
at Quimper, was aware of the dispute; he wrote to his nephew in
November 1907 that the War College wanted him back but since he
had a "bad press" at the Ministry he did not know what was going
to happen.[14]

Maunoury had his way and Pétain was recalled to the College as
head of the infantry tactics course; it was something of a victory to return as head of the course which he once taught as an assistant and a
victory for his school of military thought as well. The current of the
offensive had by no means swept all the older officers along with it.
The officer whom he replaced was unprepared and unhappy about
being removed and Pétain again made an enemy, one with friends at
the War Ministry. The same officer, who had been told abruptly that
Pétain was taking his place, had the satisfaction in June 1914, when
he was *chef de cabinet* for War Minister Messimy, of telling General
Franchet d'Espèrey, when the latter approached him about getting
Pétain promoted to brigadier general, that the controversial colonel
would spend the rest of his active career in his present rank.[15]

At the War College Pétain, as head of the important course in infantry tactics, was one of the leading authorities on infantry tactics in
the French army; his views on the importance and strength of the defensive in modern warfare were given wide attention in military circles. The proponents of the "offensive at any price" found in him their
leading antagonist.

Pétain's theories on the need for caution in the face of modern weapons did not by any means rule out the offensive as a form of warfare.
He recognized and taught that only the offensive can achieve victory;
one cannot win a war by standing on the defensive. But the offensive
should only be undertaken when conditions favor it—when the ad-

14 Bourget, 31.
15 Général Paul Azan, *Franchet d'Espèrey* (Paris, 1949), 77.

versary has been weakened by a judicious employment of one's fire-power and when the attacker is in a position to support the assault troops with an overwhelming concentration of firepower.

His greatest preoccupation in those years was to achieve in the army a close liaison between the artillery and the infantry. The main func-tion of the artillery was to support the infantry, but in order for this to be carried out properly the supporting artillery units would have to come under the command of the officer directing the attack. In his campaign to achieve closer liaison between the two arms Pétain found a supporter and active collaborator in General Percin, who once had favored him as commandant for the infantry Firing School.

Percin became in 1907 Director of Field Artillery Fire Instruction and his ideas closely paralleled those of Pétain. They worked together to get their policies accepted by the army, and even though their poli-tical theories would normally have held them apart—Percin was a noted "republican" general and had been close to General André—their common military ideas drew them together. This friendship con-tinued throughout the war, after Percin had been forced out of the army and Pétain had become a famous general. The idea of a close collaboration of the two arms was opposed by many artillerists, like Colonel Nivelle who would one day become famous for his unhappy failure on the Chemin des Dames. All officers who opposed Pétain and Percin on the question of the employment of artillery were not destined to failure, however; among them were Buat, Fayolle and Foch, the first of whom became a successful general and the latter two marshals of France. These men had to learn in the hard school of experience that, as Pétain said, "firepower kills."

The principle of artillery and infantry liaison, which became during 1914–18 the most important tactical development of the war, was tied in with the controversy regarding the strength of defensive tactics versus the idea that combat is a matter of will, élan and morale. If the attacking infantry was to be governed by a desire to overwhelm the enemy by the impetuosity of its attack, without regard to losses or the strength of the enemy positions, the artillery could not do much more than give it a superficial fire support.

Even the artillery officers did not foresee the paramount importance that artillery firepower would have in the coming war. The French army put all its reliance in the light fieldpiece, the famous "French 75" millimeter gun, and considered howitzers and heavy artillery un-necessary for the kind of war of rapid movement which they intended to wage. Consequently they found themselves in 1914 woefully short of the heavy artillery and guns with a high trajectory that trench warfare made mandatory. If in 1914–18 the infantry was still "queen of battles," heavy artillery became the king; and it was only in 1917 that the French high command received heavy guns in sufficient quantity to give their infantry the kind of support that German infantry had been receiving from their "big brother" since 1914. The great casualties which France suffered in World War I largely were concentrated in the first two years of the war, when the high command had to use the bodies of their hapless *poilus* in the place of projectiles.

Pétain and Percin had some success in getting the artillery regulations changed to provide a greater degree of coordination between the two arms but the artillery commanders in practice evaded the regulations. On the annual maneuvers it was noted that the artillery commanders in the majority of units were firing at targets of their own choosing instead of supporting the infantry. Jokes were current in the army about artillery officers: when asked upon what they were firing, they replied that they were firing "on the orders of my colonel," or, and this was as much an actual occurrence as a joke, artillery officers were told that the division commander did not care where they fired as long as they made a lot of noise. Percin eventually appealed to the Minister of War to end this anarchy but to no avail; and in 1913, after the *offensive à outrance* General Staff officers had gained control of army planning, the regulations were again changed to give the artillery commanders the autonomy that they wanted.

Even the lessons of the war were slowly learned. As late as October 1915, after the unsuccessful and costly Champagne offensive, Pétain, then an army commander after a series of rapid wartime promotions, wrote to Percin, saying, "I've been thinking . . . since the beginning of the war about the liaison of arms. The problem is resolved in the defensive. But what wavering [by the high command] there still is in the offensive! Anyway, the liaison of the arms is, from the tactical point of view, my principal preoccupation and it is to this tendency on my part, a tendency to which you are not a stranger, that I owe the few successes which I have obtained."[16]

One of Pétain's pupils at the War College made a note of his impressions: The Course attracted the elite of the army. When Pétain was scheduled to lecture the large hall would be full and as the lecturer entered, glacial and impassive as always, the hall was so still a fly could be heard. Pétain's strong personality dominated the room; he spoke without gestures or useless words. He had his own ideas and bowed to none other; his rules of combat were: the preponderance of

[16] Général Percin, *Le Massacre de notre infanterie, 1914–1918* (Paris, 1921), 89.

firepower and the fact that only a superior firepower could make movement on the battlefield possible.

To attack, he said, is to build up a line of fire against the objective. The attackers must maneuver closer to the enemy before making the final assault, and must not advance in the open against strong positions. The artillery must operate in close conjunction with the infantry.

He went on to say that the offensive is very important but is practical only when it has a powerful fire support to dominate and destroy the enemy. On the defensive he was opposed to the notion that it was dishonorable to relinquish an inch of terrain. If the defense of a position would cost more than it was worth, it should be abandoned. The defensive, scorned by many offensive enthusiasts in the army, was an important mode of warfare which sometimes would have to be employed, particularly when the commander wanted to spare his forces, to economize on manpower and material, or to gain time.[17]

In 1910, under the influence of General Foch, the French army established a Center for Higher Military Studies (Centre des Hautes Études Militaires) which admitted only young officers who had had the highest grades at the War College. The course was intended to teach the principles of strategy and its brilliant pupils were the potential leaders of the army. Out of the school, which was dubbed the "school for marshals," came the enthusiastic staff officers who were impregnated with Foch's "will to victory" and the idea that the moral forces in wartime and the will of the commander were more important than material factors. Pétain, to whom firepower was stronger than any metaphysical concept and whose concern was for the morale of the soldiers who would have to face the fire rather than the will of the commander, took the course in 1911. He was not converted to Foch's way of thinking.

His teaching days at the War College were over, and after a period of teaching general tactics at the Cavalry School at Saumur in 1912, he assumed command of the 33rd Infantry at Arras in 1913. In that year the offensive à outrance enthusiasts, whose school of thought had been expounded in two famous staff lectures in 1911 by Colonel de Grandmaison, Chief of the Operations Bureau and leader of the cult, imposed their doctrine on the army through new regulations sanctioned by the War Minister's decree, which committed the French

---

[17] Tournoux, 47. Also see Captain Charles de Gaulle, "Doctrine à priori ou doctrine des circonstances?", Revue militaire française, XV (March, 1925), 306–328, for a eulogistic account of Pétain's theories before 1914 as opposed to the doctrine of the offensive.

army to an exaggerated doctrine of a headlong offensive in all situations. This audacious formula was prescribed for large units, divisions and army corps, and was no longer limited to the regimental level. The offensive doctrine was reaching beyond the tactical level to the area of operations.

There was something contagious about the offensive at all cost doctrine: it appealed to dashing young officers, and some not so young; and those officers who might have been sceptical were made to feel that they were somehow lacking in initiative or imagination or even in courage. Pétain refused to be swayed by it and his regiment was trained according to his own methods. As he had said at the War College—and the General Staff officers knew that he had said it—if an adversary in wartime should try to apply the *offensive à outrance* doctrine against him he would know how to handle it.

The annual grand maneuvers usually ended in a spectacular attack which was viewed by high dignitaries, the military high command and government officials. These mock attacks were impressive and colorful but they displayed all the faults and weaknesses which later became apparent in the French army during the battle of the frontiers in 1914. In the autumn maneuvers of 1913 in Artois, Pétain's 33rd Infantry took part. The division, of which the 33rd formed a part, commanded by General le Gallet, ended its maneuver with the usual charge, in this instance against a village on a hill. There was no proper artillery preparation or support; three regiments advanced in line, on the double, with fixed bayonets—they were a colorful sight in their red trousers. Their flags were carried before them and they were accompanied by their regimental bands whose martial strains added the final touch to this magnificent but unrealistic scene.

After the maneuver the satisfied commanding general presided over a critique for his officers. When it was Colonel Pétain's turn to give his impressions he demonstrated the reason why he enjoyed a certain amount of unpopularity with some of his superior officers. He said, "I am sure that General Le Gallet intended, the better to impress you, to present a synthesis of all the faults that a modern army should not commit." There was a shocked stillness, then the grave colonel went on to say that first you must crush the enemy by artillery fire, then you can proceed to gather your victory.[18]

Taking part in the demonstration was young Lieutenant Charles de Gaulle, just out of Saint-Cyr. In the 1920's and 1930's when Marshal Pétain was the most eminent and popular military figure in France, de Gaulle, a very ambitious officer, let it be known that he had chosen

---

[18] Tournoux, 51, quoting a witness.

Pétain's regiment because of his admiration for its colonel. Perhaps he did so, but in 1909 he had already served in the 33rd Infantry for a year. At that time Pétain was still at the War College. By the military law of March 1905 appointees to the national military academy had to spend a year in the ranks before entering the academy and de Gaulle spent his year in the 33rd, two years before Pétain's appointment to command that regiment. In 1912 he merely was returning to the unit in which he had once served.

In the spring of 1914 Pétain had apparently reached the end of his career. Perhaps it would be appropriate to say that he was nearing the end of his first career, because in his long lifetime he experienced three. His first career was ending on a controversial note; his second career would be enormously successful; and his third again would be a controversial one.

2

1914

In 1914 Europe entered into a war of unexpected and unprecedented proportions, a cataclysm which shook the brilliant European civilization to its foundations, a war the effects of which have not yet ceased to reverberate in all parts of the world. To no country was this gigantic conflict more of a national crisis than to France, upon whose soil the most important campaigns were to be fought. The man who in a few years would command the French armies on the western front was, at the beginning of 1914, an obscure and aging colonel, preparing for retirement.

Pétain was in command of the 33rd Infantry Regiment stationed at Arras; he was fifty-eight years old and apparently at the end of a not particularly distinguished career. His military theories ran counter to the official *offensive à outrance* doctrine and his forthright, and often tactless, opposition to the audacious theories of the young enthusiasts who dominated the staff planning of the high command had blocked his advancement.

Pétain was a rare individual, a man who forthrightly—and perhaps too brusquely—followed his professional judgment and refused to compromise his convictions—although to follow this course would, as he knew, deny him the higher rank which he might otherwise have achieved.

There are not many people who have the moral strength to act that way. It might be argued that since he had no family he had less need than most men to mask his heretical opinions, less need to achieve material success; but the responsibility which dependents bring is more often a rationalization of conduct than the reason for it. It is ironic that many years later, after the fall of the Vichy government, Pétain should have been depicted as a scheming, power-hungry man who plotted his country's downfall for his own selfish ambitions. Such a reversal of character in one lifetime, although not impossible, strains the credulity of the observer.

Early in 1914 General Franchet d'Espèrey, the commander of the corps of which Pétain's unit formed a part, and a man destined to be one of the best commanders that the first World War produced, attempted to raise Pétain to higher rank. A vacancy had occurred at the head of the 3rd Brigade, whose headquarters were at Arras, and the corps commander named Pétain to fill the vacancy of brigade commander, although he was still a colonel in rank. Shortly thereafter he replaced Pétain at the head of the 3rd Brigade by the general commanding the 4th Brigade, and in exchange placed Pétain at the head of the 4th Brigade, stationed at Saint-Omer. The commanders of the 3rd and 4th Brigades, whom Pétain replaced successively, were general officers, yet Pétain remained a colonel.

In June Franchet d'Espèrey attempted to get Pétain promoted to brigadier-general so that he might be retired as a general of division (equivalent to an American major-general). D'Espèrey took the matter up with the *chef du cabinet* of Minister of War Messimy and was told, formally, that Pétain would never be promoted to general of division. It was therefore officially understood that Pétain should remain a colonel until his retirement promotion to brigadier-general.

Near Saint-Omer Pétain negotiated for the purchase of a small house, to be ready for his retirement. As a boy he had attended a boarding school in Saint-Omer for eight years and his birthplace, Cauchy-à-la-Tour, was only twenty miles distant. The region was home to him.

For a man of fifty-eight years Pétain was in excellent physical condition. He was of medium height, erect and trim. He was bald, fair and blue-eyed, with a long mustache. He was still considered handsome and had a reputation for amorous adventures. He was reputed to have had at least one mistress in every garrison town in which he had been stationed, perhaps finding in the sex life of a bachelor a variety which compensated for its lack of regularity. He once remarked, late in life, that he had had but two passions in his lifetime: women and the infantry. On maneuvers the colonel could march with the best of his men (had he not been an officer of chasseurs for twenty years?) ; he was a good horseman and a crack shot. After the war, in the course of a routine medical examination, the doctor who examined him, not knowing who he was, is supposed to have remarked that it was easy to see, by his good physical condition, that he had not served in the war.

Throughout his career, from garrison to garrison, Pétain had lived in hotels and furnished apartments. His possessions, apart from his small library, could be put together in a few bags, and the outbreak of war in August 1914 constituted less of a break in his personal life than it did for most Frenchmen, even for most army officers. He was as ready as a man could be, by training and by temperament, as well as physically and mentally.

On August 2 a general mobilization took place in France and, unlike 1870, the mobilization proceeded with considerable efficiency. Within fifteen days France had four million men under arms, actually more than they could effectively use in the early campaigns. Many men were returned to their homes, temporarily, in order to ease the burden on the overcrowded replacement depots. Pétain had six thousand men under his comand—Pas de Calais men from the Saint-Omer region—in the 4th Infantry Brigade. They comprised two regiments, the 110th (Lt. Col. Lévi) and the 8th (Col. Doyen).

Both of these regiments were of the "active" army, the first-line troops which the French high command thought were alone capable of waging the important first battles of the war. Each regiment had a nucleus of regulars, but a larger proportion were conscripts of the classes of 1911, 1912 and 1913 (twenty to twenty-three years old) currently undergoing their military service. To them were joined, upon mobilization, men from the active reserve: men from the classes which had most recently completed their training and had been released to civilian life.

Not only was Pétain in command of a brigade that had known him for only a few months, but a large number of the men had never been under his command at all—not even for the annual maneuvers in which the reserves participated. Commanders normally came into contact with the reserves assigned to their units when the active reserves joined their regiments for their annual training, but Pétain had not been in command of the 4th Brigade during the 1913 maneuvers. In addition, his two regimental commanders were influenced by the *offensive à outrance* doctrine which they knew was the prevailing theory among the staff officers in Joffre's entourage. Pétain later told a friend that in August 1914 he was not at all satisfied that he had his brigade firmly in hand.

Prior to 1914 it was believed by both French and German military leaders that a modern war must of necessity be of short duration and that the opening engagement would be a giant battle which would decide the issue. It was felt that a modern European society could not for long sustain the extraordinary demands of a twentieth-century war —economically and financially—nor could civilian morale be counted upon in a protracted struggle. For Germany the emphasis on the necessity for a quick war was doubly important because of her strategic position; the Franco-Russian alliance threatened her from east and west. A two-front war was the nightmare of German General Staff planners; they had to knock out one of their adversaries quickly so as to be able to throw their whole weight against the other. Russia would be the slowest to mobilize, therefore France must be the first target, for the lightning blow. There was less reason for France to stake all on the first throw and her plan to do so, imbued as she was with the offensive spirit, was evidence of poor judgment, if only for the very reasons which led Germany to seek a quick decision.

In criticizing the French strategy of 1914 one must keep in mind that the Russian alliance, as modified in 1913, called for an immediate offensive action by both countries in the event of a war with Germany. This agreement covers the French high command for its line of action in August 1914, although the intention to go on the offensive probably preceded the Franco-Russian military agreement of 1913 rather than followed it. In 1939 France had a similar agreement with Poland but her feeble pecks at the German "West Wall" while Poland was being overrun indicates that a military philosophy can take precedence over treaty arrangements.

Since the outcome of the war, both sides thought, was to hinge upon the opening blow, the initial disposition of the armies, in terms of time and space, became of vital importance. Speed and precision in mobilization and concentration were the objects of detailed and careful study. For the French, their Plan XVII, a design for concentration rather than for operations, was calculated to put the armies in positions from which they could be thrown against the Germans in a combination of overwhelming blows.

The French armies were formed south to north, from the Swiss border to the Ardennes, numbering One, Two, Three, and Five respectively, with the Fourth Army concentrated behind the Third and Fifth Armies. The right wing of the French Army, comprising the First and Second Armies, was to invade Alsace from the south and strike toward Sarrebourg and Morhange. The left wing too was to take the offensive but its operations were contingent to some extent upon the actions of the Germans with regard to the neutrality of Belgium and Luxembourg. The possibility of the German invasion of Belgium was foreseen, although it was thought the enemy main thrust would be limited to the right bank of the Meuse, in which case the Fifth Army, covering the French left flank, would move to meet the threat, with the Fourth Army moving up on a line between the Fifth and Third Armies. The Fifth Army, commanded by General Lanrezac, and in which Colonel Pétain commanded a brigade, thus became involved in the most crucial battles of the early days of the war, for upon it fell the brunt of the German encircling maneuver.

In later life Pétain strongly criticized the French decision to undertake an immediate offensive at the outbreak of the war. He pointed out that by force of circumstances Germany was compelled to attack very quickly in 1914 and in that sense she did not have the operational initiative. But fortunately for the Germans the French armies preceded them by several days in taking the offensive; and the French attacks were made in the east and center, so that the German attack through Belgium became in a sense a counter-offensive—with all the advantages of the counter-punch—and the Germans obtained from this circumstance advantages which they had not, Pétain felt, entirely foreseen.[1]

The Schlieffen Plan[2] had been formulated by Graf von Schlieffen, Chief of the German General Staff, in his memorandum of 1905 and put into operation, with modifications, by his successor, von Moltke, in 1914. Unlike the French Plan XVII the Schlieffen Plan was a plan of operations as well as of concentration of the armies, and the line of action to be taken by the commanders of the armies in the campaign was carefully outlined for them to follow. Like the French plan, however, Schlieffen's brainchild was audacious and, as the event proved, quite beyond the capabilities of the German army to execute to completion.

Schlieffen viewed France as a great fortress with her most accessible frontier, the eastern, almost impregnable to frontal assault by virtue of her fortifications there and the nature of the terrain on that frontier. A quick victory in Western Europe, vital to German plans of avoiding a prolonged two-front war, required that Germany sweep around the French line from the north by way of Belgium and flank the French positions from the west. This meant that the bulk of the German army would be concentrated in its right wing, with the left wing in Alsace-Lorraine left weak—too weak to hold back a determined French offensive into southern Germany. The right wing was to ex-

---

[1] General Chauvineau, *Une Invasion est-elle encore possible?* (Paris, 1939), Pétain's preface, x, xi.

[2] See Gerhard Ritter, *The Schlieffen Plan* (New York, 1958).

ecute a gigantic wheeling movement through Belgium and the Netherlands in order to penetrate into the heart of the French fortress through its northern gate and to encircle its "garrison" from the west. A maneuver of such enormous proportions required that the bulk of the German army be employed in its execution, which meant taking risks in Alsace-Lorraine as well as on the Russian front in eastern Europe.

Von Moltke quite properly modified the plan so that a larger proportion of the German army was deployed on the left wing and on the eastern front. It should be pointed out, however, that the strength of the right wing envisaged by Schlieffen was not reduced in absolute terms but in relative terms only; Moltke's' right wing was as strong as Schlieffen planned it should be, and in fact numbered as many army corps as could properly be deployed across the Belgian plain and be supplied on its march deep into France. On this point Ludendorff and other members of the General Staff were agreed. Moltke further modified his predecessor's plan by refraining from the invasion of Holland, certainly a wise decision on his part.

As it developed, in August 1914 the Germans on the right wing were exhausted by hard marching and could not be supplied or reinforced adequately because of the destruction of the railway system by the Belgians. The bulk of the German motor transport was employed in the attacking armies on the right but it was not sufficient for the task. On the other hand the French high command, operating on interior lines with an excellent railway system, rapidly transferred large numbers of troops from the east to the west to form a new army, the Sixth, to threaten the right flank of the German advance and to force it eastward, instead of west of Paris.

Schlieffen himself, as his memoranda and notes show, was not certain that his right wing could execute the maneuver required of it in the region of Paris and he left quite unclear how the problem would be resolved. He even envisaged the possibility, should events prove it necessary, of his marching-wing wheeling inward east of Paris instead of enveloping that strongly fortified position. This is in fact what von Kluck was forced to do. And the German attacks in Lorraine, far from undermining Schlieffen's conceptions, served to keep pressure on the French right to hamper its deployment of troops eastward.

But in the early days of August the ordinary soldiers on either side could not be aware of the exact nature of the master plans which were deciding their destiny. Colonel Pétain was concerned with keeping his unit in fighting trim as it moved into position, as part of the Fifth

Army, on the left flank of the French concentration on the frontiers.

General Lanrezac, Fifth Army commander, who was responsible for the security of the French left flank, had never been a partisan of the *offensive à outrance* theory, of which, in fact, he spoke quite openly in terms of contempt. He very early in the campaign began to distrust the intentions, and even the competence, of the French high command. He was particularly concerned about the security of his left flank and strongly suspected that the Germans would advance in great strength on the left (west) bank of the Meuse. He repeatedly warned the high command of the threat, requesting permission to move his army northwestward to forestall the enemy envelopment, a permission which was not at first forthcoming.[3] G.Q.G. was satisfied that the Germans did not have the numerical strength (assuming their exclusive employment of active army troops in the assault armies) to extend their line west of the Meuse. When at last on August 15 Lanrezac received the order—even then somewhat equivocal—which he had been soliciting for eight days, and hurried his army northwestward to take up positions in the angle formed by the Sambre and the Meuse, the delay had given the Germans a great start and to some extent compromised Lanrezac's deployment to meet them.

The staff officers at headquarters rather hoped that the enemy would advance in force on the left bank of the Meuse, an action that would mean that his center would be weakened for the attack which they intended to launch against it. They were understandably reluctant to modify their plans because of an unforeseen German maneuver, real or imaginary, in a manner that would yield the initiative to the enemy at the outset of the campaign.

It is apparent that Joffre and his staff felt that the German operation through Belgium west of the Meuse was not likely, for according to their calculations the enemy had at his disposal twenty-one army corps, which would not give him enough effective strength to maneuver on so grand a scale without seriously weakening his line elsewhere. They were not aware of an additional thirteen corps of reserves incorporated with the German active armies. French General Headquarters had made its plans in accordance with the information it received from its Intelligence Bureau: twenty-one German army corps on the Franco-Belgian border, the rest in Russia. Under these conditions the extension of the German right wing seemed to be limited. "If the Germans passed the limit [of the extension to the

[3] General Lanrezac, *Le Plan de campagne français* (Paris, 1920), 55, 56; Fernand Engerand, *Le Secret de la frontière* (Paris, 1918), 510–512; Anon. "Le Plan XVII," *La Revue de Paris*, II (March 15, 1920), 343–347.

north] so much the better for us . . . the front against which we will strike will be that much less solid."[4] With only twenty-one or twenty-two army corps at its disposal the German high command would have to stretch its line to a dangerous thinness in order to execute the Belgian maneuver. This would give Joffre the chance he wanted.

On August 17 a captured German aviator revealed the startling intelligence that there were two German armies operating west of the Meuse and he gave the exact composition of von Bülow's Second Army, with its four active army corps and three reserve corps. This was the first intimation that the Germans were using reserve units as first-line troops. He also told them that north of the German Second Army the First Army (von Kluck) was passing between Liège and the Dutch border. Maps found in the captured airplane confirmed this information. General Franchet d'Espèrey, in whose corps area the airplane had been downed, immediately sent the papers and the aviator on to higher headquarters. He was told later that when the information got to General Headquarters a "very great *(gros)* personage" cried, "It's an asininity; the First Army is in Russia." Two days afterward it entered Brussels.[5]

In August 1914 the Germans used in the campaign on the western front thirty-four army corps, of which twenty-one were of the active army and thirteen of the reserves. This amounted to 1,700,000 men. Opposed to them, in the first battles, were twenty-one French army corps with 1,300,000 men and added to these were the Belgian army and the 100,000 man British army of regulars. French army corps were all of the active army. It appears that the greatest error of the French high command was its calculation that the Germans would not use reserves as first-line troops.

It would be a misconception to conclude that French active units were composed of regular, professional soldiers. As noted previously, only a very small nucleus of Pétain's command, as in the other units, were regulars. The rest of the troops, even in active formations, were far from being highly trained specialists. The conscripts were largely from the classes of 1912 and 1913, called up together in October and November 1913 under the provisions of the new Three Year Law, and in August 1914 they had had only nine or ten months training. The class of 1911, still in service at the outbreak of the war, had a year and ten months training. Joined to them upon mobilization, to fill out the active regiments, were the three classes, 1910, '09, and '08, which had

[4] Anon., "Le Plan XVII," *op. cit.*, 346, 347.
[5] Maréchal Franchet d'Espèrey, "Le Ier corps d'armée en aout et septembre 1914," *Revue des deux mondes,* LII (July–August 1939), 33, 34.

most recently completed their two years of training. Additionally, one regiment entirely of reserves was added to each active division upon mobilization. So a French active division was not at all equivalent to a regular army division in the American sense or, for example, to a division in the British Expeditionary Force in 1914.

The French military leaders had little confidence in the combat value of reserve divisions because they were officered almost entirely by reserve officers, commissioned and non-commissioned, leaders without extensive training in combat techniques and without the habit of command. Also, the men in the reserve ranks were older than the men of the active army; they were usually men with families, and they had been separated from the army from one to ten years, depending upon their ages. Even the active divisions often showed that they were not on a par with their German counterparts when hostilities began. German soldiers, though no braver than French soldiers, were better trained and had the benefit of better leadership. German officers, commissioned and non-commissioned, were of a higher quality, from the standpoint of technical proficiency, than those of the armies they faced. Add to this national characteristics such as the German habits of command and obedience compared to a Frenchman's inclination to an individualism sometimes bordering on anarchy, and you have, although these things are difficult to evaluate, some of the reasons why the Germans quite early in the war established a military superiority over the French.

Left wing political leaders in France continually and often bitterly criticized the high command's preference for active units and its prejudice against reserve formations. The politicians often claimed that reserve units performed as well as the active units during the war, but generally speaking such was not the case. French officers had difficulty enough in 1914 with their active troops and had reserve units been used extensively the defeat on the frontiers might well have been of graver proportions.

But in early August the soldiers who were to do the fighting, as they moved into their concentration areas along the frontier during an August heat wave, were beginning to realize that war was mostly marching and weariness, dust and sweat and sore feet. The Fifth Army covered the left flank of the French concentration and the I Corps was on the left flank of the Fifth Army, which put Pétain's unit on the extreme left of the whole French army, on the flank which the Germans intended to turn. The mission of the I Corps was to guard the Meuse from Mézières to Givet, a strip of French territory which, like a little spine, extends into Belgium, and of which Givet forms the tip. From its positions along the river I Corps was ready to debouch toward the east in accordance with General Joffre's initial plan. The German invasion of Belgium on August 4 relieved the French of the necessity of avoiding Belgian territory and enlarged the importance of I Corps' mission.

On August 10 Pétain's brigade left its concentration cantonments at Bourg-Fidèle and marched northeast toward Revin, on the Meuse. The hurried march under a broiling sun was a difficult one for the untried soldiers, particularly for the reservists who had been civilians but a week before. There were large numbers of stragglers and many men collapsed from the heat. Pétain's 110th Regiment reached Revin on schedule but the 8th was slow, and its colonel received a blistering reproof from the 4th Brigade commander. Pétain earned a reputation for severity—and even, by his own admission, of brutality—on those early marches.

The young French soldiers were tough and willing but the forced marches took their toll. Their uniforms were hot and their equipment too heavy for the exertions demanded of them during this period when the war was one of movement. On their backs were model 1893 packs each containing a change of linen, a jacket, a brush, a full toilet article kit, one day's provisions and six hardtack biscuits. On top of each man's pack was a rolled blanket or tent canvas, a pair of shoes, a mess kit, and topping it all the metal mess-tin that the soldiers called their "monkey cup." The French soldier had to carry cooking equipment that his German counterpart was spared in 1914; German infantry units were fed on campaign by highly mobile rolling kitchens while the French were not. On the left side of the French pack was fastened an entrenching tool and on the back was a shallow metal pan. Over the shoulder was slung a haversack for carrying bread, "le quart" (a quarter-liter drinking mug) and a two-liter canteen. Shoulder straps supported the waist belt which held three or four ammunition pouches containing cartridges. The regulation rifle, the Lebel model 1886–1893, the use of which was the reason for the soldiers's existence, completed the burden. The whole weight came to fifty-five pounds.

Much has been written to criticize the bright red trousers worn by the French soldiers early in the war and the fact that these made excellent targets. It should be noted that the equipment on the soldier's back, particularly the shiny metal containers which came up as high as the back of the man's head, also made of him a highly visual object. A young German infantry platoon leader, Erwin Rommel, related how he saw in August 1914, a French unit moving through a grain field, invisible except for "the sun's reflection on bright cooking gear piled on top of the tall French packs." He and his men fired at will on the enemy column which dispersed without ever knowing where the hostile fire was coming from.[6]

Not only were German soldiers more sensibly accoutered but their uniforms had been since 1910 a neutral grey color. The French red trousers were somehow supposed to fit in with the national self-image of military dash and spirit. They were worn only by the line infantry; the chasseurs and the artillery and engineers wore dark blue, not the best camouflage but better than red. Actually the French high command had been experimenting for years with a low visibility cloth color and had decided on a bluish-grey. Uniforms of this color were already being produced in 1914 and some were in army warehouses, but it was 1915 before all the French infantry received the new issue.

Although Lanrezac did not receive the order to move his army northward until the fifteenth he was already, on the twelfth, in response to reports that strong German cavalry forces had uncovered the front Givet-Namur, moving advance elements into Belgium to cover the Belgian Meuse from Givet to north of Dinant. This extension of his forces, entrusted to I Corps, was on his own initiative and it gained a few precious days. The Corps had orders to be in the region of Phillipeville, west of Givet-Dinant, by August 14 and, in liaison with Sordet's cavalry corps operating in Belgium, its mission was to counter any enemy attempts to cross the Meuse between Givet and Namur.[7]

As Pétain's troops marched into Belgium as an advanced guard they were received with enthusiasm by the population, who could not know that within a few days all the French soldiers would be gone and would not be seen again for over four years. They were plied with cakes, beer, wine mixed with water (not the soldiers' own recipe), and cigars.

Colonel Pétain apparently was as surprised as anyone that the Germans should have invaded Belgium. In Olloy-sur-Viroin on the evening of August 13, lodged in the home of M. Chot, a professor of his-

[6] General Field Marshal Erwin Rommel, *Infantry Attacks* (Washington, 1956), 11.

[7] For the August campaign of Pétain's unit see Pierre Bourget, *Fantassins de 14 de Pétain au poilu* (Paris, 1964); Commandant Larcher, "La Campagne du Ier corps en Belgique," *Revue militaire française,* Vol. 37 (Paris, 1930); Larcher, "Le Ier corps de la Belgique à la Marne," *Ibid.,* Vol. 41 (Paris, 1931); Ministre de la Guerre, *Les Armées françaises dans la grande guerre,* Tome I, vol. I (Paris, 1922); Général Paul Azan, *Franchet D'Espèrey* (Paris, 1949), 79 *et seq.*

tory from Brussels on summer vacation, in response to a question of his host Pétain explained that French military planners had never seriously believed that Germany would risk adding England to her list of enemies by violating Belgian neutrality. The colonel was so ignorant of Belgian geography that he asked Chot if they were in Belgian Luxembourg and was told that the province in question was 45 kilometers to the east. One of Pétain's staff officers explained that they had had two staff maps but had lost them. Perhaps this incident illuminates some of the difference between German and French soldiers: one can hardly imagine Lieutenant Rommel losing his maps.

On the morning of August 14 the 4th Brigade reached the vicinity of Florennes, some fourteen miles west of Dinant. Despite his fatigue Pétain made an afternoon inspection of his positions and, upon finding that two battalions of the 8th had failed to post guards, he punished the two commanding majors with eight days' arrest. At 7:00 P.M. he was hurriedly summoned to division headquarters where he was given the corps commander's order to get to Bioul before 3:00 A.M. The night march began at 10:00 P.M. and the troops, already tired from lack of sleep, fell asleep at every halt. Many of them had to be hit with sticks to get them to rise. The fifty-eight-year-old brigade commander walked instead of riding his horse for fear of falling asleep, putting his arm through a stirrup strap to hold himself up. In less than twelve hours the 4th Brigade marched some twenty-seven miles, racing the Germans to the Meuse below (north of) Dinant, each soldier still carrying over forty-five pounds although by now the men were throwing away their equipment.

From the 15th to the 18th of August Pétain and his men received their baptism of fire. Pétain commanded one regiment of infantry, his 110th—the 8th had been temporarily put under General Mangin's command—plus a half squadron of cavalry and a group of corps artillery. His mission was to hold the Meuse at Anhée (the sector Houx to Yvoir). The combat there was light and consisted mainly of artillery fire and small fire fights as elements of the German Third Army (Hausen), pushing westward north of the Ardennes, probed the French positions on the river line.

On the 15th a battle had taken place at Dinant a few miles south of Pétain's position, and when units of the 148th Infantry, who had taken part in the battle, marched past Pétain's command post he interrogated officers and noncoms on the effect of German fire, their employment of artillery and machine guns, and gathered whatever information on enemy methods that he could. This is important for an understanding of Pétain's future success; he looked for firsthand

information from combat soldiers, the infantrymen, in order to improve his own plans, a happy contrast to those staff officers who made
plans with pins on a map and to the commanders who accepted such
plans.

Pétain's prewar theory of liaison between artillery and infantry was
still an important concept to him. He noted in his *journal de route*[8]
on August 18 that he had made pressing requests to the artillery to
have them occupy, with small elements, the forward lower slopes in
support of his troops holding the river line. The artillerymen did not
like it. Pétain took Colonel Clément of the 27th Artillery Regiment
to inspect the position of Haut le Wastia held by the 1st Battalion
of the 110th and a half-company of engineers. Pétain noted that once
the artillerymen understood what he wanted they went ahead with
good grace. He knew that three days previously, at Dinant, his old
regiment, the 33rd, had suffered serious casualties because of lack of
artillery support (including the fact that the French artillery had fired
on their own men by mistake). Lieutenant Charles de Gaulle was
wounded in the leg in that action.

In the afternoon he returned to the artillery positions in the valley,
still checking up, and then made a tour of the infantry positions on
the left bank of the Meuse. He found too many troops in the front
line but not enough stationed in readiness in secondary positions.
The positions which they held were satisfactory to him but not the
distribution of the troops. There were too many troops in the front
line, constantly on the alert; he noted ". . . impossibility for this line
to be reinforced or to be retired easily. Consequence: great expenditure in men and great fatigue." He ordered for the next day not a
change in positions but a different distribution of forces.[9]

This was a forecast of his successful method of 1918: a covering
force in the front line to engage the enemy and force him to deploy
and then a strong position of resistance in the second line on which
the enemy attack would break and from which counterattacks could
be launched. These plans and procedures were made on the battlefield, a school of experience which unfortunately was not required of
all high-ranking officers.

Behind the cover provided by the I Corps on the Meuse Lanrezac
moved the rest of the Fifth Army to the north to take up positions on
the Sambre. He intended to attack on August 23 in conjunction with
the British Expeditionary Force which had come up on his left, and
also in conjunction with the major attack on the right bank of the

---

[8] See Bourget, *op. cit.*, 110–113.
[9] *Ibid.*

Meuse by the Fourth Army (de Langle de Cary) on his right (the Fourth Army had moved up into the positions vacated by the Fifth).

Joffre had judged the time ripe for his attack against the German center. With the Germans moving in great strength through Belgium he felt, logically enough, that a powerful offensive by his Fourth Army through the Ardennes against Neufchâteau and his Third Army (Ruffey) toward Arlon, would hit the enemy enveloping maneuver on its flank. The Germans in effect were making a flank march across Joffre's front and a strong thrust in the center by the French offered the possibilty of cutting off the enemy right wing. To think otherwise at this time was to relinquish the initiative to the Germans before the campaign had developed and to concede the loss of the "battle of the frontiers" before the issue had been decided on the battlefield.

The French offensives of August 20–23, from Lorraine to Belgium, were complete and costly failures. The First and Second Armies, attacking toward Sarrebourg and Morhange respectively, were repulsed with heavy losses. In the center the Third Army was unable to penetrate the German lines and was forced back. The most important failure was that of the Fourth Army in the Ardennes, which encountered the German Fourth Army and was defeated with heavy casualties. This battle was the decisive one because when the Fourth Army stumbled back in retreat the right flank of Lanrezac's Fifth Army was exposed, making his position untenable and his retreat inevitable. With the left wing army falling back and the Germans threatening it with envelopment, the entire French Army had to fall back.

If the attack by the Fourth Army had been successful the whole German plan of operations would have been jeopardized and the security of the German right wing imperiled. The failure of the French Fourth Army meant victory for the Germans in the "Battle of the Frontiers." This defeat in the Ardennes had serious consequences for two wars because the 1914 "sound drubbing" there, as General Weygand later put it, convinced the French for the future that the area was very difficult country, so that they were not so alert to a German penetration there in 1940 as they might have been.[10]

In the battle on the Sambre, on August 22, Pétain's command, along with the rest of the I Corps, was pulled out of its positions along the Meuse and moved to the north to attack Bülow's Second Army, which had crossed the Sambre and was attacking the rest of the Fifth Army.

[10]France, *Commission chargée d'enquêter sur les événements survenus en France de 1933 à 1945,* VI (Paris, n.d.), p. 1600, General Weygand's testtimony.

But the French attack never took place. Elements of Hausen's Third Army succeeded in crossing the Meuse in their rear and I Corps had to retrace its steps to attempt to throw them back. On August 23 Pétain was ordered to cover the rear of I Corps as it moved to contain the German penetration at Dinant and Onhaye. With his rear threatened by the German bridgeheads across the Meuse and with the knowledge that the French Fourth Army had failed to debouch from the Ardennes and was instead in retreat, Lanrezac had no choice but to order a retreat. On August 24 he gave the order "marche rétrograde générale."

On the same day Pétain's 4th Brigade was reformed and he had both regiments again under his command. Also on the same day General Joffre reported in a telegram to the Minister of War that the French armies were checked on all fronts and were in retreat, "condemned to a defensive" as he put it. He attributed the reverses to a lack of offensive capabilities on the part of his troops.[11]

Joffre's criticism of the combat value of the French soldiers was not entirely fair. The fact was that their training had been inadequate and was based on faulty military doctrines. Some officers before 1914, Pétain among the more articulate of them, had criticized the methods and tactics in which the army was being indoctrinated but these officers were a minority. The test of combat in 1914 proved them correct.

It was quickly noted by commanders that their losses were excessive and defeats numerous because their men had little knowledge of cover and concealment, individual rifle markmanship, use of terrain, or how to advance in extended order. Their officers were given to ordering wild rushes in dense formations, attacks which were quickly broken by the enemy firing from concealment and entrenched positions with machineguns and well aimed rifles. The failure of their attacks—often made with great courage—and their staggering losses soon demoralized the French infantry. German heavy artillery outclassed the light French 75 and liaison between artillery and infantry on the French side was almost nonexistent. Pétain's pre-1914 theories had been proved sound but the price paid for the knowledge was high.

It is a curious fact that the Allied propaganda, throughout the war and even after, pictured the Germans as automatons who advanced to the attack in dense formations, shoulder to shoulder, to be mowed down by allied marksmen, and who succeeded in gaining ground only by means of superior numbers and disregard of losses. The soldiers of the democratic countries were pictured as men trained to fight as

---

[11] *Les Armées françaises* . . . , Tome I, Vol. II (Paris, 1925), 12, 13.

individuals, to advance in lines of skirmishers, who inflicted greater casualties than they received. The fact is that this picture is just the opposite of what really happened, not only in 1914 but throughout the war.

The French high command made belated efforts to correct the effects of years of faulty training. On August 16 and 18 instructions were sent to all commands giving orders to discontinue the practice of assaulting fortified positions without waiting for artillery support. The troops must no longer be exposed too hastily to enemy fire; attacks should be prepared, artillery cooperation assured and frontal attacks avoided. Numerous and dense lines of infantry should not be thrown forward, they said, against entrenched positions.

It became evident that the French infantryman was not a marksman. His rifle fire was often poorly aimed and usually too high for practical effect. His German counterpart was trained to fire slowly and deliberately, aiming carefully, and his training before hostilities began taught him the value of entrenching himself at every opportunity, to avoid the effects of modern firepower.[12] The Germans attacked in lines of skirmishers, against positions which had been "prepared" by their artillery,[13] a method sharply in contrast to the French attacks in massed formation which was, according to Lieutenant Rommel who knew from firsthand contact, their "usual" practice as late as June 1915.

In terms of life and limb the French paid dearly for poor training and poor leadership. In the initial battles of 1914 France left one-third of her effectives in casualties on the frontier—one-third of the army and the best part of it too. In 1915, in France alone, the French Army had 1,350,000 men killed, wounded, and prisoners, as against German losses of 550,000.[14] This disproportion in casualties was a result of what Joffre called his "nibbling" strategy.

Colonel Pétain had little time to reflect that his prewar theories and predictions had been vindicated. His 4th Brigade was in retreat to the southwest and his principal task was to keep it intact and to maintain march discipline. On August 29 General Franchet d'Espèrey personally brought Pétain the news that he had been nominated for pro-

---

[12] Les Armées françaises . . . , Tome I, Vol. II, 23–25, Vol. III, p. 1323; Col. Alléhaut and Commandant Goubernard, "A propos d'un jugement allemand," Revue militaire française, Vol. 17 (Paris, July 1925), 38; Rommel, op. cit., 2, 10, 17, 29, 59, 68; Abel Ferry, Les Carnets secrets (1914–1918) (Paris, 1957), 247.

[13] Général Lanrezac, Le Plan de campagne français (Paris, 1920), 176.

[14] Charles de Gaulle, France and Her Army (London: n.d.), 93, 99.

motion to brigadier general and that he would be given command of a division. Pétain's ironic comment in his journal was, "Are they already reduced to revolutionary procedures?" His irony perhaps would have been deeper had he known at the time that in the first month of the war, before the battle of the Marne, the commanders who were summarily removed from their commands numbered two army commanders, ten army corps commanders, and forty-two divisional commanders; thus more than a third of the commanders of large units, not to mention officers of lesser rank, had been dismissed.

These dismissals were not in all cases justified if military competence alone were the criterion. In some instances a commander was relieved more as a scapegoat for the high command's shortcomings than for demonstrated incompetence; and in other cases political motivation seems to have been at least part of the reason for an officer's downfall. Colonel de Grandmaison, chief exponent of the *offensive à outrance* gospel, was supposed to have said, at the beginning of the war, "At last we are going to get rid of General André's clique," which meant that those officers suspected by their colleagues of having benefited in promotions over the past ten years by virtue of their republican sympathies were now, with the high command in complete control of the army for the first time since the Dreyfus Affair, to have their performance under close scrutiny.

Among the high-ranking officers dismissed was the commander of the Fifth Army. So bitter was Lanrezac at what he considered to be errors of judgment made by the high command that he made no attempt to hide his contempt for the commander in chief and his staff officers, particularly the latter. This, in addition to some undiplomatic conduct with regard to the British army which was supporting him,[15] caused his dismissal by Joffre, after he had executed a skillful retreat which saved the Fifth Army and perhaps the whole French army.

In 1924 Marshal Pétain, as head of the French army, had the satisfaction of officially vindicating his old commander when he decorated Lanrezac with the Grand Cross of the Legion of Honor for his part in the 1914 operation. In presenting the award at the decoration ceremony Pétain used words which amounted to an official criticism of Joffre and his leadership in 1914:

---

[15] As an indication of his attitude toward the British, when Field Marshal French, B.E.F. commander, who spoke no French, asked Lanrezac through an interpreter, on their first encounter in Belgium in August 1914, if he thought that the Germans would cross the Meuse river when they reached Huy, Lanrezac, who spoke no English, snapped back, "What does he think they will do when they get to the Meuse, urinate in it?"

The eminent services that you have rendered to the country have not been forgotten. The maneuver-in-retreat that you directed will remain as an example for this type of operation. We all have had the impression that in executing it you preserved your troops from a complete encirclement and saved your army and, at the same time, France.[16]

This added another reason for the hostility which by that time Marshal Joffre had developed toward Pétain, a hostility which was reflected in Joffre's memoirs published in 1932.

On the evening of August 28, 1914, in the little village of Tavaux, Pétain was billeted in the home of M. de Forceville, who gave his guest the general's stars which had belonged to his father-in-law, General de Sonis, a hero of the war of 1870. On the morning of the 29th he was surprised to find that during the night Mme. de Forceville had sewed her father's stars on his tunic while he slept, a kind gesture which would bring good fortune to the new general.

He had need of good fortune that day for he was going into his first offensive action of the war, the action called the battle of Guise. In this battle the Fifth Army turned on the advancing Germans and gained a small victory, perhaps gaining a small breathing spell for themselves and the British on their left but hardly more. Pétain prepared to attack with his 4th Brigade, as usual personally supervising the preparations, leaving as little as possible to chance. His superior, Franchet d'Espèrey (who soon would take command of the Fifth Army), approached Pétain before the attack, and knowing Pétain's meticulous approach to battle plans—particularly regarding artillery support for his precious infantry—asked him somewhat facetiously if he were satisfied with the artillery preparation and what the former professor of infantry tactics thought of the maneuver in progress.

Pétain dryly conceded that the artillery preparation was as good as their means permitted but he regretted that the German artillery fire had not yet been neutralized. Leaving Pétain, d'Espèrey personally went to a group of artillery and ordered them to move forward, closer to the front line.

The attack began in the evening, about two hours before sunset. If anything went wrong the darkness could cover a retreat. The conduct of this attack, under the eyes of the corps commander, was an illustration of many of the faulty tactical techniques of some French commanders as well as an illustration of the methods which had helped earn Pétain his promotion.

---

[16] *Revue militaire française,* Vol. 20 (May, 1926), 280, quoted by the reviewer of a book by Fernand Engerand, *Lanrezac* (Paris: Editions Bossard, 1926).

The First Division attacked first, its two brigades on either side of the Guise highway. The 2nd Brigade advanced in close order with flags waving and drums and bugles sounding the charge. Their band was prevented from playing only because its members were filling their secondary function—soon to become their primary one—of acting as stretcherbearers for the wounded.

The 1st Brigade also advanced in close formation with flags flying but in addition they had two regimental bands playing the Marseillaise, the whole performance resembling, not by accident, a maneuver of the Napoleonic era. The commanders thought that the panoply of a bygone era might bring out the martial qualities in the soldiers whose morale had been affected by defeat and retreat. Having talked so much of the *furia francese* in the years before 1914, when war seemed a simple art when you knew its secret, they now tried to find it. In a short time enemy shellfire forced flags and bands to take cover.

As the troops advanced up the slopes they suffered heavy losses, particularly among the officers, who stood out in their black tunics and red trousers. The attack began to break down in disorder; units became dislocated and mixed together, the forward line broken and ragged. When the higher officers had lost control of their units d'Espèrey ordered Pétain's brigade to attack on the left flank.

With a half hour left of daylight the 4th Brigade moved forward. Pétain's troops advanced in open order, with the battalions echelonned, the whole line open and flexible, taking advantage of terrain features and offering as little exposure to enemy fire as possible. Pétain personally led the 110th Infantry, his leading regiment in the attack, although he was now a general. Night fell before he could accomplish much and in the darkness some of his units went astray. He spent most of the night collecting his units and organizing them for a renewal of the attack in the morning, with the flames of burning farm buildings adding a garish touch to the scene.

On the 30th d'Espèrey ordered a renewal of the attack by his First Division, plus Pétain's brigade; but before the operation could begin the order came from Lanrezac to break contact and resume the retreat. Pétain covered the retreat of the I Corps with his brigade plus an additional regiment of infantry, three groups of corps artillery and three companies of corps engineers. On September 1 an automobile with his baggage met him at Roucy and he took leave of the 4th Brigade. The next day, north of Fismes, he assumed command of the Sixth Division.

The Sixth Division was in poor condition and its former commander, General Bloch, had almost lost control of it. During the battle of Guise elements of the division had panicked and abandoned their positions. Their march discipline was gone; they were more like a disorderly mob than a military formation. Bloch was sent to Limoges, the station for dismissed officers without commands, and Pétain shortly after assuming his new post relieved one regimental commander of his command. Both brigadier generals of the division were senior to Pétain in rank and one of them, General Hollander, complained to his new superior about serving under an officer who was his junior in rank. The question became academic on the next day when Hollander was seriously wounded. The other brigade commander, General Lavisse, the brother of the historian, apparently was less disturbed by the new arrangement, particularly as Pétain took the division in hand and whipped it into shape for the battle of the Marne.

The undisciplined state of the Sixth Division was not a unique condition for French units in those summer days. One of the biggest problems facing the commanders was keeping order among the troops. Men had been throwing away their equipment since the beginning of the campaign, breaking ranks for foraging, pillaging, looting, and common malingering. Throughout the war, in fact, the French soldier showed a marked disrespect for civilian property. Abandoned homes were particular targets for the looters and sometimes entire villages were put to the sack. Buildings and even churches were despoiled and often subjected to wanton destruction. In many cases the German invaders could hardly have been more destructive.[17]

Men of the Sixth Division felt an iron hand when their new commander took over. The good soldiers among them were satisfied that they now had a real leader. He kept after them, imposing his physical presence upon as many units as he could cover. An incident, recounted by an artillery officer who observed it, is an example of the control that the General exercised. As the division, hot, thirsty and hungry, crossed the Marne at the Verneuil bridge, some of the men abandoned the column and wandered out into the fields on both sides of the road to shake the plum trees for the fruit. Suddenly there were several shots and Pétain rode among them on a big horse, firing his pistol in the air and angrily ordering the men back into the ranks. The startled

---

[17] See Maréchal Fayolle, *Cahiers secret de la Grande Guerre* (Paris, 1964), 100, 136; also Lieut.-Col. de Thomasson, *Le Revers de 1914 et ses causes* (Paris, 1919), 204, 205. Some American soldiers were shocked in 1918 at the French soldiers' pillaging of their countrymen and at the resigned attitude of the civilians to such conduct; see James G. Harbord, *The American Army in France, 1917–1919* (Boston, 1936).

soldiers scurried back to their places without waiting for a second order.

This kind of leadership inspired confidence and the morale of the division was restored as the new general officer shook up the officers and demanded an iron discipline. Under the stern control of this commander, who would not hesitate to take the strongest measures against soldiers and officers who failed in the performance of their duty, the division recovered its combat value and took part with signal success in the battle of the Marne. It would not be the last time that Pétain would have to deal with broken morale; the same need would arise in 1917 and again in 1940.

3

Marne, Aisne, Artois, and the Champagne

On September 6 the French armies turned to face the Germans on the Marne and defeated them in a decisive battle: decisive because the whole German scheme rested upon the rapid conquest of France with the conquest of Russia following. Defeat on the Marne meant a two-front war for a besieged and blockaded Germany, one that they could prolong but could not win. The 1917 elimination of Russia came too late, for the mobilization of the British Empire and the entry of the United States into the struggle tipped the balance against them.

The French high command had a numerical superiority over the Germans on the eve of the battle of the Marne. The German forces in France consisted of seventy-four divisions of infantry and ten of cavalry, of which two divisions were detached to besiege Mauberge and twenty-six divisions of infantry and two or three of cavalry were operating in Alsace-Lorraine, leaving forty-six infantry divisions and seven or eight cavalry divisions available for the battle. To meet them Joffre had eighty-five infantry divisions and ten cavalry divisions, of which eleven territorial divisions had missions away from the field of battle and twenty-three infantry divisions and two cavalry divisions belonged to the First and Second Armies in Alsace-Lorraine, leaving fifty-one infantry and eight cavalry divisions ready for the battle, plus six British divisions.[1]

The French army was weary and somewhat demoralized but the fact that it was still intact and able to do battle after its defeat on the

---

[1] France, Ministère de la Guerre, *Les Armées françaises dans la grande Guerre,* Tome I, Vol. 2, 811, 818.

frontiers and its long retreat is an indication that its discipline, its morale and its leadership were strong. An interesting comparison can be made between 1914 and 1940; in the latter campaign those three qualities were deficient.

On September 4 Joffre asked Franchet d'Espèrey, now in command of the Fifth Army, if he would be able to take part in an offensive on the 5th or 6th. D'Espèrey replied that his army could fight on the sixth but that the situation would not be "brilliant." Actually the Fifth Army played the leading role in this decisive battle.

Pétain's Sixth Division, recovered from the breakdown in morale which it had suffered during the battle of Guise, took a prominent part in the battle of the Marne, in a decisive sector; its commander utilized his talent for organizing an attack in detail, with a close cooperation between infantry and artillery. On the evening of the 5th a laconic order was received to prepare to attack on the following day as part of a general attack which would get under way at 6:00 A.M. At midnight Pétain received more precise instructions and much of the night was spent in preparation.

Pétain's order to his division was: "The attack of the Sixth Division will begin at 6:00 A.M., but the infantry must not debouch from its positions until the artillery preparation has been judged sufficient and until the order to advance has been given by the general commanding the division";[2] that is, by himself. He had learned from experience that brigade, regimental and battalion commanders tended to expose their men too hastily and too rashly to enemy fire, in poorly prepared attacks; and he intended to prevent a premature and reckless commitment of his troops by his subordinates.

On the morning of the sixth his divisional artillery, reinforced by part of the artillery from another division, went into action and spent several hours methodically pounding the enemy positions. In the afternoon the infantry moved forward, with the divisional commander accompanying the forward elements. Pétain directed the attack on horseback so as to be able to move quickly from one critical point to another and also to be more visible to his men. In the early days of the war this practice was common enough but it soon became an outmoded custom.

The attack went well although losses were heavy. In front of the Sixth Division was an élite German division, the Sixth Brandenburg, and one brigade of Pétain's division lost 600 men in an hour while taking the Châtaigniers farm. However by evening, thanks largely to effective artillery support, Pétain had driven the enemy back beyond

---

[2] Quoted in Henry Contamine, *La Révanche, 1871–1914* (Paris, 1957), 240.

Montceau-les-Provins so that an infantry brigade of the neighboring XVIII Corps could occupy the village which was in flames and abandoned.

During the next few days the Sixth Division, as part of the whole French forward movement, pursued the enemy northward. The Germans were pulling back to strong defensive positions along the Aisne. On September 13 Pétain ordered his two infantry brigades to attack across the Aisne canal (which extends from the Aisne to the Marne) in the direction of Brimont. Brimont was a wooded range of hills topped by an old fort, a position of considerable natural strength further developed and entrenched by the Germans as a bastion for their line along the plateau of Craonne. Pétain's attacks failed to reach their objectives and in fact his units were sometimes reduced to desperate holding operations in the face of determined German counterattacks.[3]

For weeks Pétain's division continued its costly and fruitless assaults. In spite of meticulous planning and carefully coordinated artillery support he was unable to take the Saint-Marie farm, two kilometers from Brimont, let alone Brimont itself. At one point General Lavisse advised his commander that, with one regiment reduced to 1200 men and under heavy pressure, he must pull back; but Pétain ordered him to hold on even if it meant sacrificing his two regiments, because this action was vital to the operations of the Fifth Army. The Fifth Army was attempting to drive the Germans out of the region north of Rheims, to disengage the city which was under the German guns, and to prevent the enemy from consolidating his position on the heights of Craonne; but the terrain and the enemy were too much for them.

These battles before Brimont were a hard school of experience for the Sixth Division commander. At one point, when a staff officer ventured to remark to his coldly aloof superior that it might take days to gain their immediate objectives, Pétain snapped back, "Or several months." His pessimistic appraisal was far short of actuality, for it was years before the French moved out of these positions. Their greater attack in the same sector in April 1917 fell short of expectations by far; it was May 1918 before they moved out of the positions occupied by Pétain in September 1914, and then it was to retreat before a great German breakthrough. Not until October 1918 did French troops take the positions so bitterly contested in the first months of the war north of Rheims.

---

[3] Pierre Bourget, *Fantassins de 14 de Pétain au Poilu* (Paris, 1964), 204, 228–236; Ministère de la Guerre, *Les Armées françaises* . . . (Paris, 1931), Tome I, Vol. 3, 224, 225, 846–850, 872–876, 904–911.

On October 16 Pétain wrote to his superior, corps commander General Hache, telling him that conventional tactics were not the answer; his own carefully planned attacks which broke on the German defenses proved that. He said that the campaign had assumed the character of siege warfare and that they must revise their methods accordingly. Generals Castelnau and Dubail, Second and First Army commanders respectively, were, by September 1914, coming to similar conclusions regarding the siege character of the war. But the French high command could not fully accept the logical consequences of this line of thinking. With the Germans in possession of a large part of French territory, not to mention the obligations of France to her hardpressed Russian ally, the nation expected that the army should make the maximum effort to throw the enemy back and win a victory in the classical fashion. There were enough influential officers with a Napoleonic orientation, the *offensive à outrance* theorists, to keep pressing for such a victory. More than two years, with millions of casualties, would pass before those who were responsible for France's war effort would accept the realities which were in fact imposing themselves on the battlefield.

The situation was made doubly tragic by the fact that commanders, seeking the causes for their failure to break through the German defenses, tended to list among the reasons for their lack of success that of a "lack of offensive spirit among the combat troops."[4] General Franchet d'Espèrey, as Fifth Army commander, could hardly be blamed for reaching this conclusion when this was the substance of reports made to him by his subordinates; but Pétain knew better.

The very high casualties which the French army suffered in the first months of the war—955,000 men from August to December 1914—is testimony enough to the combat qualities of the troops, even allowing a small percentage of that figure for prisoners. The other reasons given by d'Espèrey for the failure of his army's attacks were: tactical errors, that is, failure to carry out properly the original orders; lack of cooperation between corps commanders; poor employment of heavy artillery; and "psychological" errors—the tendency of combat units to seek an alignment on each other.

His criticism of the employment of heavy artillery was not quite fair to his commanders inasmuch as they often had very little heavy artillery to employ; and when they did have big guns they did not have sufficient ammunition for them. The French army was paying

---

[4] See Franchet d'Espèrey's note of October 18, 1914, to his army Corps commanders, listing reasons for the failure of the offensive, in *Les Armées françaises* . . ., Tome I, Vol. 4, 497.

for its prewar theories which relied upon the 75 millimeter field piece as the artillery weapon par excellence—as perhaps it would have been if the war had been one of movement and quick victories in open country as the French had anticipated. But for trench warfare, a "war of siege" as Pétain put it, the light artillery piece had little effect, either for demolishing the entrenchments of the enemy or for long-range counterbattery fire to silence the enemy guns. Its trajectory was too flat, its range too short, and its explosive effect too light. French troops found themselves outclassed by the Germans, who were more liberally supplied with heavy artillery and better trained and equipped for the observation and communication which the indirect fire of heavy artillery required. In September 1914 General Joffre stripped the fortified places of Verdun, Toul, Epinal and Belfort, as well as coastal defenses, of their heavy artillery and ammunition to use in his field armies but there was still an acute shortage of both guns and munitions, for which the French infantrymen paid dearly.

D'Espèrey's criticism of the "psychological" error of units seeking to align themselves upon neighboring units is an interesting commentary upon how quickly the realities of combat shook the prewar theories of offensive at all costs without regard to the security of one's flanks. Already, in October 1914, the linear psychology of trench warfare had imposed itself.

None of these criticisms by d'Espèrey, well-intended as they were, got as close to the heart of the problem as did Pétain's observation that conventional tactics would have to be abandoned in the face of the new character of warfare. The strength of the defensive was such that only siege tactics, unglamorous and protracted as they would have to be, were appropriate.

On October 20 Pétain was ordered to report to General Foch, Joffre's assistant commanding the armies in the north, to take command of an army corps. On October 22 he assumed command of the XXXIII Corps with headquarters at Aubigny near Arras. This was country that he knew well; he would be fighting over terrain which he had studied and used for maneuvers when he was in command of a regiment. He arrived while his new command was under heavy attack with the enemy making a determined effort to take Arras, but within a few days the attack was repulsed.

Winter had set in, the first in the trenches. The men were unprepared for this kind of a war and were thoroughly miserable. Pétain did what he could to make life easier for his troops. He permitted them to go on leave to Amiens, he arranged for entertainers to come from Paris, and he organized the first French army theatre. Perhaps

his greatest contribution to the welfare of his troops was to put a stop
to the countless minor attacks which some commanders felt that they
had to undertake. His intention, as he explained to his superiors, was
to avoid wasting effectives in unimportant attacks in order to save
them for large-scale operations which offered worthwhile results.

He did not, however, believe in pampering soldiers. He was ruthless in removing incompetent officers and equally ruthless in dealing
with men who were guilty of infractions of discipline. In November
he relieved two generals, Drude and Trafford of the 45th Division, for
manifest inactivity and incompetence. As trench warfare and weather
conditions took their toll of morale, cases of self-inflicted wounds
among the men began to mount and at one time there were forty men
in one unit incapacitated by such wounds. Pétain at first indicated
that he was going to have twenty-five of them shot but on the next
day he directed instead that they should be tied up and left out in
the open in front of the trenches closest to the enemy for one night.[5]

From December 16 to 28 the XXXIII Corps was engaged in an
offensive conducted by the Tenth Army in the region of Arras. It was
Pétain's plan for the attack which was adopted by General de Maud-
'huy, Tenth Army commander. Although carefully planned and well-
supported by artillery the attack yielded no appreciable results, due
to determined German resistance, the nature of the terrain and bad
weather. With men up to their stomachs in mud and water the attack
was discontinued and the rest of the winter passed without serious
military activity on the Arras front.

In January 1915 Joffre wrote to his commanding generals, "The
present war has by no means weakened the principles which are at
the base of our offensive doctrine, but, because of the new form which
it has taken, operations are characterized, in time and in space, by a
slower and more methodical development. This is a consequence of the
force of fire power and the strength of defensive organizations. . . ."[6]

The French high command planned its first important offensive of
1915 in Artois, under the direction of General Foch, since January
officially the commander of the Northern Army Group. The attack
was to be made by the four army corps of the Tenth Army under
d'Urbal (who had replaced de Maud'huy early in April). Pétain felt
a certain disappointment that he had not received the command of
the army himself when de Maud'huy was replaced, but his own rise
had been very rapid and he was considered by his colleagues and

[5] Maréchal Fayolle, *Cahiers Secrets de la Grande Guerre* (Paris, 1964), 79.
[6] *Les Armées françaises* . . . , Tome II, 401.

superiors to be one of the best of the officers who had risen to high command during the war. They noticed his energy, and his knowledge and understanding of the kind of war in which they were engaged, although they also remarked on his cold severity toward his men and officers. But the benign, ear-pulling, father-image general officer was more likely to sacrifice his men in operations of dubious merit than was the strict, impersonal Pétain who looked for obedience and not affection.

His disappointment at not receiving the command of the Tenth Army was dissipated in a few weeks when he was notified of his promotion to divisional-general à titre exceptionnel. He now would wear three stars on his shoulder instead of two; this was, in 1915, the highest rank a French officer could achieve short of the seven stars of the marshalcy, and in 1915 there were no marshals in the French army. He remained in command of a corps for the time being because his XXXIII corps was counted upon to play a major role in the forthcoming offensive.

The plan of operations for the Arras offensive, which was launched on May 9, 1915, was one which had been drawn up for the Tenth Army by Pétain and his staff, submitted to d'Urbal and Foch and accepted, in its main lines, by them. This battle was a local, tactical success for Pétain's corps and was, in fact, the first sizable success for the French army since the Marne; but strategically the operation was a failure. It could not even be judged successful from the point of view of lessons learned because the Germans learned as much from their near-defeat as the French did from their near-victory.

The key to Pétain's success was his meticulous attention to every detail of the operation. He visited every front-line battalion and toured the trenches; a three-star general in the frontlines was an unusual sight in World War I, or perhaps in any modern war. He talked to most of the officers and many of the noncoms who would take part in the attack and questioned them to see if they knew their roles. He did not neglect the other branches, the engineers and the artillery—particularly the latter. Without proper artillery preparation and support the attack could not succeed. The corps commander inspected every battery and had each fire one round to make certain that it was zeroed in on its assigned target. So zealous was his attention to this aspect of the operation that his soldiers joked that "the general has pointed all the cannons himself."[7]

The army corps on Pétain's flanks—the XXI Corps on his left and the XX Corps on his right—were not so well prepared. The XXI Corps

[7] Général Serrigny, Trente Ans avec Pétain (Paris, 1959), 22.

had been in the line for a long time but had not worked out as meticulous a plan of attack, and the XX Corps had only just entered the line on Pétain's right a short time before the offensive. The latter corps had no time for its infantry to study the terrain; it hardly knew where its objectives were; and the artillerymen did not have enough time to sight their guns properly.

On May 9 the attack began and Pétain's corps completely shattered the German line. Within several hours the 77th Division and the Morroccan Division penetrated to a depth of two and one-half miles, on a seven-mile front, and at some points had passed Vimy Ridge. The enemy defensive organization was broken; resistance became local and scattered and the German artillery began firing blindly and haphazardly. The German headquarters twenty miles away at Lille began making preparations for a possible withdrawal.

However, the army corps on Pétain's left and right flanks made no headway and in fact were thrown back with heavy losses. His leading units found themselves isolated and unsupported; the Germans recovered and reacted vigorously by massing all available reserves from other parts of the front to stop the XXXIII Corps' advance and then to push it back. Pétain called for reinforcements from Tenth Army to exploit his breakthrough but Army headquarters was apparently as surprised as the Germans at the success and less prepared to react to it. The only reserves available were one brigade of infantry and it was too far behind the front to intervene at the critical moment.

The Germans reorganized their front, brought up their reserves, and with the Tenth Army checked elsewhere the opportunity for further success no longer existed. But d'Urbal and Foch were fascinated by the tactical victory of May 9 and, against Pétain's advice, they persisted in prolonging the offensive with a series of attacks lasting until June 28, finally bogging down in a sea of liquid mud. These attacks were characterized chiefly by a lack of surprise, foul weather, and heavy losses, and when the high command mercifully but belatedly suspended them in June it was acknowledged that the Arras offensive was a strategic failure.

In the Artois battle the French Tenth Army lost, from May 9 to June 18, 102,500 men according to the figures compiled in the official history—a source often prone to minimizing French losses. The Germans facing them lost 50,000 men according to their own account and 80,000 according to General Joffre. The persistance of the French high command in the attacks long after they had ceased to have a chance of success was to a great extent due to Joffre's "nibbling" policy, designed, in theory, to keep the Germans from reinforcing the Russian front. Of course he hoped also to effect a breakthrough if he could do so, but in general his whole policy throughout the first eight months of 1915 was one of attacks for the sake of attacking, to wear the Germans down through attrition and to contain their reserves. The fact that the French high command was completely unprepared on May 9 to exploit the breakthrough at Arras indicates that they did not expect a breakthrough to occur; the lack of available reserves was not merely a mistake in staff planning.

Throughout May and June Pétain protested to his superiors that all chance of a strategic success was gone and that the attacks were useless and costly but he was ordered to continue them. A colleague during those bitter spring days, General (later Marshal) Fayolle, recounts how one day in June Pétain came to his headquarters and furiously let off steam. He said that d'Urbal and Foch were crazy; " 'attack,' says Foch, without regard to the state of preparation. 'Attack,' echoes d'Urbal." He and Fayolle regretted the loss of thousands of men to gain parcels of useless terrain.[8]

Pétain's breakthrough on May 9 caused the Germans to alter their defensive organization along the western front. They constructed their lines in greater depth so that they could no longer be taken in one assault; they built their secondary positions, wherever possible, out of range of the French artillery so that attackers would face an unbroken second line should they break through the first. This system cost the French dearly in the September 1915 Champagne offensive. On the other hand Pétain's striking initial success gave the French high command the idea that this could be repeated on a larger scale, which led them to plan the abortive Champagne offensive accordingly.

One tangible result of the Artois campaign for Pétain was that on June 22 he was promoted to command the Second Army. As Joffre put it, he "had climbed to the top of the tree in less than a year."[9] The fact is that Pétain was not yet at the top; it would be almost two years before he would take command of all the French armies on the western front, two dreary years of frustrated offensives and desperate defensives, and hundreds of thousands of additional grief-stricken French families mourning their dead.

The abortive campaign in Artois in May and June 1915 had a considerable influence on Pétain's thinking with regard to the form operations should take on the western front. Prior to the attack he had not given up hope that the war could be won in the near future

---

[8] Fayolle, *op. cit.*, 111.
[9] Marshal Joffre, *The Personal Memoirs of Marshal Joffre* (New York, 1932), 335.

by using conventional methods. In letters to his niece and nephew, in November 1914 and in January and May 1915, he indicated that a breakthrough could be achieved in the trench-war and that the German armies could be brought to terms.[10] But the inconclusive results of the recent battles, in which he and his men had done all that the intellect and the will could do, confirmed his growing feeling as to the uselessness of that kind of operation.

His attitude was expressed in his memorandum of June 29, 1915, to the high command, entitled "Note on the operations in the Arras region," in the following terms: "The present war has taken the form of a war of attrition. There is no longer the 'decisive battle' as formerly. Success will come in the final analysis to the side which has the last man." He went on to say that the expenditure of troops should be limited as much as possible, to save them for the decisive moment which would come after the Germans had made their last effort.[11] This is of course how the war actually did turn out even though the high command did not follow his advice as to the husbanding of manpower for the "decisive moment" in 1918. Providence came to their rescue in the form of large numbers of Americans.

The pessimistic tenor of this memorandum was viewed with disapproval by the high command, the staff officers of which were still influenced by the *offensive à outrance* doctrine. Grandmaison had been killed on the Aisne early in the war, along with other victims of his military philosophy, but the staff thinking was still impregnated with his ideals. A leader of the "Bergsonian" entourage which surrounded General Joffre—the 'Young Turks' prided themselves on their adherence to Henri Bergson's philosophy, as they understood (or misunderstood) it, of action governed by intuition rather than by the intellect—was a young officer, Maurice Gamelin, who was destined in 1940 to preside over a fiasco greater than any mistakes that Joffre made.

Joffre had had the idea, after Pétain's incomplete success at Arras in May, of bringing him to General Headquarters as his assistant. He sent Gamelin to see him to get his personal opinion as to what form future operations should take. Shortly thereafter Pétain presented his recommendations to the high command for the careful attacks, limited in scope, which seemed to him the best answer to conditions as they then existed. This policy was little to the liking of General Headquarters and he was not given the appointment. Later General de

10 In Pierre Bourget, *Témoignages inédits sur le maréchal Pétain* (Paris, 1960), 37–44, the three letters are reprinted.
11 Général Laure, *Pétain* (Paris, 1941), 49.

Castelnau was made Joffre's assistant, although for the time being he was made commander of the Center Group of Armies, and Pétain was given command of Castelnau's Second Army.

Perhaps if Gamelin and Joffre had any idea of Pétain's opinion of them he would have received no promotion at all. Some thirty-three years later, in 1948, Joseph Simon, the director of the prison in which Pétain was kept, asked him what he thought of Gamelin. "Gamelin?" Pétain said, "He was always considered the repository of Joffre's military thought. The unfortunate thing is that Joffre didn't have any."[12]

His promotion put him in an important position for a major offensive. His Second Army was to play a key role in the projected September offensive in the Champagne region and a repetition of his initial Arras success was hoped for by the high command. By the same token the Germans sought to avert a recurrence of an event which must have shaken them, for the French General Headquarters received intelligence reports that the attention of the enemy was attracted toward Pétain, in whose movements they sought a clue to the next French offensive. To offer a false scent to German Intelligence, Joffre had Pétain pretend to study a plan of operations for the Haute-Alsace, and a simulated headquarters was set up for him at Belfort. He also made an ostentatious tour to Nancy with two members of his staff.

The party stayed at Nancy for two days, attempting to give the impression that there would be an attack in that region. Pétain was seen a lot and talked a lot, the latter an activity to which he was not accustomed. One member of the party, Captain Tournes, had been married in Nancy and his wife lived there. Tournes told his wife and mother-in-law "in strict confidence" that an attack was imminent. Lt. Molinier was detailed to circulate in the city's night life, meet women, and drop information—an assignment which he found not uncongenial. All three returned from their trip satisfied, for different reasons.

But Pétain was not at all satisfied with the plans for the forthcoming offensive, in which he was supposed to play a key role. On July 25 he reported to Castelnau's headquarters (the Second Army was part of Army Group, Center, and Castelnau was in overall command of the operation) and was told of Joffre's expectations. It would be a new edition, on a bigger scale, of the May 9th operation; that is, to make a breach in the enemy line and to pass on to a war in open country. Pétain pointed out that conditions had changed since May 9; now the enemy had constructed a line of secondary positions along the whole front, situated about four miles behind the first line, and

12 Pierre Bourget, *Fantassins de 14 de Pétain du Poilu* (Paris, 1964), 25.

out of range of the greater part of the French artillery. He said that they could no longer hope to force the enemy to retreat by attacking in force on a wide front. Castelnau listened sympathetically but plans went forward, throughout August, for an offensive on a grand scale with ambitious objectives.

Joffre and Castelnau believed in the possibility of a breakthrough of the enemy front, with a return to conditions of open warfare, by means of an *attaque brusquée*, an abrupt and all-out attack. Pétain's proposals for a slow, methodical, well-prepared attack aimed at limited objectives, in a series of steps, calculated to economize on lives and to keep morale at a high level, were not accepted by the high command. Joffre and his staff looked for a big and vigorous attack, with wide and deep objectives. They expected to gain six or seven miles in twenty-four or forty-eight hours and planned to push reserves quickly into breaches made in the enemy front. They thought that Pétain's proposals were unnecessarily cautious and in any case would require more matériel than France had available in the summer of 1915.

But the heavy losses of the first year of the war had caused great uneasiness in France and the government felt increasingly reluctant to give a blank check to the high command for an expenditure of the nation's manpower. The great losses during 1914 could be accepted as part of the price one had to pay to stop the attempted German conquest of the homeland, but the hundreds of thousands of men being lost in 1915 as a result of Joffre's "nibbling" strategy were more difficult to rationalize.

President Poincaré visited Pétain at Second Army headquarters on July 6, 1915, and discussed the Arras offensive and the military situation in general. Pétain told him that it was not true that if there had been reserves ready for exploitation at Arras on May 9th a decision would have been gained, although the high command thought otherwise. He advised that if he had advanced any farther he would have been dangerously exposed to counterattacks, in view of the failure of the army corps on his flanks to advance.

This was disquieting news to the President of the Republic, inasmuch as the high command was staking much of the success of the forthcoming offensive on that very hypothesis. They hoped that Pétain would provide them with a similar breach in the enemy line, into which they planned to throw masses of infantry and cavalry, which would be held ready in close proximity to the front. He went on to tell Poincaré that he was against any new offensives at the moment, feeling that they should conserve their manpower and at the same time amass a huge quantity of heavy artillery and munitions, which the achievement of victory would require.[13]

On August 14, 1915, Poincaré, Premier Viviani, and Minister of War Millerand visited Joffre's headquarters at Chantilly where the latter briefed them on the forthcoming Champagne operation. When Poincaré expressed some misgivings, reporting that "several army commanders" had voiced objections to him, Joffre replied that an offensive was necessary because of the Russian alliance. This was the stock reason, or excuse, offered for the series of abortive offensives undertaken throughout 1915. Poincaré then said, "No, no, General. The questions of alliance are governmental matters and not military. Base your opinion in this matter solely upon a strategical point of view. The rest we will take care of, the ministers and I." Joffre replied, "All right then, from a military point of view; I cannot stay on the defensive. Our troops would little by little lose their physical and moral value."[14]

General Joffre's theory that troops must be continually blooded to keep them fit, if that was his theory, was carried to an extreme when his offensives devoured whole units. The simplest *poilu* could have told him that dead soldiers do not win battles.

President Poincaré felt that it was Joffre's secret hope to achieve a "great decision" in the next battle to recover from the Arras failure, where the French high command had hardly added to its prestige. If that was the General's motive he was to be disappointed, for the September operation, although meticulously prepared and executed, lavishly supplied with heavy guns and munitions, ended in yet another failure. As Pétain had predicted, initially they were successful but the attack broke down on the second positions.

Pétain's instructions to his Army on September 5, 1915, for the conduct of the battle illustrates his method of attack: he insisted upon a strong artillery preparation, so that the assault troops would have before them only a shaken and disconcerted enemy. A close relationship between the commanders of artillery groups and colonels of infantry regiments was indispensible for the designation of objectives. At the moment of the assault all batteries would go into action; counterbatteries would continue their fire on the enemy second positions; and a certain number of batteries would have the special mission of shelling the enemy communication trenches and routes of

---

[13] Raymond Poincaré, *Au Service de la France* (Paris, 1930–33), Vol. VI, 311, 312.
[14] Poincaré, VII, 36, 37.

access. Field artillery and howitzers would concentrate their fire on the successive lines of trenches which formed the first position, in such a manner that their fire constituted a rolling barrage in front of the infantry, keeping pace with its advance. For the latter, a close liaison between infantry and artillery would be necessary and a special surveillance would be maintained by the aviation and balloons.

In actuality the weather on the day of the attack was too poor to permit air or ground observation but the attack had been so well planned that the operation went like clockwork, in taking the first enemy position. It was on the second positions that the attacking formations broke. The positions there, out of range of most of the French guns and emplaced on the reverse slope of hills, were relatively unaffected by the artillery preparation. Even the barbed-wire entanglements were still intact. Some of Pétain's troops, suffering heavy casualties in the process, did occupy small sections of the enemy second line but they could not hold their gains. After three days of beating against the second line he told Castelnau that they must halt the attack, to "prepare" methodically and destroy the second line just as they had done for the first. Pétain also warned that when they had penetrated the second line they would be faced by a third, and more fresh troops would be needed.

Castelnau disregarded his objections and ordered that the offensive continue and the enemy second position be pierced "at any cost." Pétain disregarded the order and ordered the Second Army to stop their attack and to "prepare" the second line with artillery fire. His order was never delivered, for on the afternoon of the 28th Joffre personally came to Pétain's headquarters and persuaded, or ordered, him to continue the offensive for a few more days.

On the 30th Castelnau stopped the operation, in order to reorganize the attacking units and to make the necessary preparations for breaking the enemy second line. The new attack was planned for October 5 but it did not take place on the scale originally contemplated. On October 4 Joffre went to Pétain's headquarters and the two were closeted in the latter's office for half a hour. Pétain once again told Joffre that the Germans had too much strength in front of the French for his troops to effect a breakthrough. To continue attacking on the present scale they would need more men and munitions, and Joffre agreed that they did not have them. The operation of October 6 and 7 failed with heavy losses and the commander in chief decided to dig in for the winter.

It is difficult to arrive at a reliable figure for the losses in the

Champagne offensive of the French Second and Fourth Armies which took part in it. The official figure given is 191,797 casualties[15]—probably much too low. Jean de Pierrefeu gave a figure, for the whole French front during the period September–November 1915, of 410,000 casualties.[16] Since the official history tried to minimize losses in order to defend the high command, and Pierrefeu was attempting to prove the incompetence of the high command, the truth probably lies somewhere between, perhaps 200,000–300,000.

The problem of an accurate figure for casualties for each offensive or campaign will probably never be resolved. Military commanders of any country are understandably prone to minimize losses when they can and casualty figures rarely include losses due to illness, disease, or accident, which often are very heavy. However, de Gaulle's figure of 1,430,000 French casualties for the year 1915[17] is reliable enough to give a picture of what was happening to France in that period. In a nation of only-son families the cumulative sadness which those figures represent goes far to explain much of France's subsequent history.

The lessons of the Champagne operation were of significance and Pétain's exposition of them in his November 1, 1915, report outlined a line of conduct which greatly influenced future operations. Of the battle itself he said: it "demonstrates the difficulty, if not the impossibility, under present conditions of armament, method of preparation, and of the forces which oppose us, to carry in one bound the successive positions of the enemy." He said that the taking of the first position required considerable preparation, then after taking it he could not pass to the attack of the second until after a new and long preparation; if he succeeded in taking the second position he would find himself faced by a third. The reports from Generals Foch and Castelnau of that period follow substantially the same line of thinking.[18]

Pétain's report continued, illustrating a conception of the situation which was entirely his own: the attrition of men and materials in long and costly attacks would not produce a definite setback to the enemy if, after the second hammerblow, the enemy still had fresh troops to oppose to one's offensive. The enemy therefore should not be attacked in depth until after he had been exhausted by a process of attrition which would use up his reserves. He recommended that the war be conducted in two phases: first, the wearing down of the

[15] *Les Armées françaises* . . . , Tome III, 539.
[16] Jean de Pierrefeu, *L'Offensive du 16 avril* (Paris, 1919) , 142, 143.
[17] Charles de Gaulle, *France and Her Army* (London, n.d.) , 99.
[18] *Les Armées françaises* . . . , Tome III, 563–566.

enemy; second, the attempt at a decision. The first would be accomplished by proceeding all along the western front to wear the enemy down by the "conquest of objectives very limited in depth." During this phase one would not seek a breakthrough but rather to weaken the enemy by attacks with limited objectives, attacks which would not be pushed to the limit of the attacker's powers as had been done in the past. These attacks would be made with less reliance upon manpower but with a formidable bombardment by artillery and with the employment of all the engines of destruction known, including poison gas and mines (flamethrowers and tanks did not come into use until 1916 and 1917 respectively).[19]

After the enemy had been sufficiently weakened, one could proceed to the decisive effort; that is, major attacks at a number of decisive points, while at the same time the "wearing down battles" would continue all along the line. (This foreshadowed Foch's strategy of 1918.) Pétain pointed out that the breakthrough was not the aim but rather the means by which one could succeed in giving battle in open country, on the enemy's flanks. This is an important point, for the trend of high-command thinking had been to achieve a breakthrough at whatever the cost, so much so that a breakthrough seemed to become an end in itself, as if that would terminate the war. But what assurance had the French now that they could win a war in open country? They had not done so in 1914. The Germans were not notoriously lacking in proficiency in a war of movement. Pétain went on to emphasize the need for more guns and munitions, in quantities sufficient to overwhelm the enemy.

General Joffre was not in accord with all of these conclusions, for in his memorandum of December 27, 1915—apparently in answer to Pétain's recommendations—he said that one could not and should not fix in advance the line upon which one should stop in an offensive, for "that would tend to limit in advance the results of a well prepared operation and to deny oneself any unforseeen advantages."[20]

Joffre's method, under the conditions then obtaining, was bound to incur heavy losses with little appreciable result. In the Champagne battles there were many instances of units advancing too far; with no flank support they were wiped out. Joffre's thesis perhaps would have been correct if there were a chance of realizing a decisive victory by employing his method, but to incur such losses for the possible acquisition of a few square miles of muddy real estate was not realistic,

---

[19] *Ibid.*, III, 576, 577. See also Capt. de Gaulle, "Doctrine à priori ou doctrine des circonstances?" *Revue militaire française*, XV (March, 1925), 320.
[20] *Les Armées françaises* . . . , Tome III, 578.

and was, in terms of manpower, ruinous. That was really the essence of the thinking of Pétain and Joffre: one was economical of personnel; the other was heading toward a possible bankruptcy of the manpower bank.

Joffre and his staff were still applying classic rules of military science to a situation which called for totally different concepts. The strength of defensive weapons had driven men below ground where they would stay until the next swing of the pendulum when offensive weapons would again come into their own. Open warfare was out of the question; the principles of siege warfare applied and a Vauban was needed, not a Napoleon.

Pétain later described the World War I situation with this stark simplicity: a human being could "no longer run when, entangled in the brambles of an artificial net [barbed wire], he has received in the head or in the spine a metal projectile fired from an invisible weapon. No patriotic enthusiasm, no moral ardor, can hold up before this fact."[21]

On December 2, 1915, a governmental decree created the post of Commander in Chief of the French Armies, and Joffre was given the command. He thus took over direction of the French forces in Macedonia as well as those of metropolitan France. The reason for this enlargement of Joffre's powers was not that he was highly thought of by the government, for he was not. But the French government hoped for a unity of command for the allied armies, under French leadership, and they wanted to augment Joffre's authority for that reason. The famous "victor of the Marne" was the only allied military leader with sufficient moral authority and prestige to effect this. Joffre was more highly though of abroad than he was at home.

Another reason for the appointment was that Joffre was opposed to the dispatching of troops to Salonika; he was opposed to diverting any strength from the western front. It was hoped that by enlarging his responsibilities to include the Macedonian front he would be more amenable to sending troops there.[22]

Minister of War Gallieni approved the appointment but insisted that Joffre be required to rid himself of some of the "Young Turks" in his entourage. This request apparently had little effect but it does indicate some of the disenchantment which the government felt toward the conduct of the war by the high command.

Joffre put his exhausted western front armies on the defensive for

[21] General Chauvineau, *Une Invasion est-elle encore possible?* (Paris, 1939), Pétain's preface, p. xi, in which he referred to the first World War.
[22] See Mermeix, *Joffre* (Paris, 1919), Chap. 7; also Poincaré, *op. cit.,* VII, 304.

the winter and planned, in thinning out his front, to accumulate reserves in the rear who would undergo extensive training, in preparation for the contemplated offensives of 1916. His choice of the officer who would direct this training was General Pétain, for despite their differences Joffre considered his Second Army commander to be the foremost expert on infantry tactics in the French army.

The next few months were probably the most pleasant of the war for Pétain. His headquarters at Noailles was in peaceful surroundings and his duties as director of training undemanding. There was time for horseback rides through the nearby forest and even trips to Paris. He would need all the rest which this interlude offered, for in February 1916 his repose was shattered by the greatest battle in history: Verdun.

4

Verdun

The night of February 20–21, 1916, was a quiet one in the Verdun area, with a light snow falling on the French outposts huddled in their forward listening posts. In the early morning the snow stopped and the weather cleared, with the temperature dropping below freezing. The night was unusually still and the veteran *poilus* on outpost duty stirred uneasily as they peered into the darkness, while behind the German lines masses of infantry and heavy artillery, who for weeks had been taking up prepared positions according to careful plan, put themselves in a state of final readiness. Toward 7:30 A.M. the German bombardment began, increasing in intensity and extending its coverage until it put the whole front of Meuse-Ornes—north of Verdun on the right bank of the Meuse—under its blanket of high explosives and gas. Its unprecedented intensity left little doubt in the minds of the defenders at Verdun that the expected offensive had begun—a drive which was to last throughout the greater part of 1916 and would consume in casualties over half a million French and German men.

The French high command had had considerable indication of an impending German attack on Verdun—warnings which could not be ignored but which left uncertainty as to the seriousness of the enemy intentions in that area. It was thought likely that the Verdun attack would be diversionary in nature, with the main blow falling elsewhere—perhaps in the Champagne region. For that reason the French reserves were not concentrated to meet the attack but were instead oriented toward the approaches to Paris and also toward the point of junction with the British army in Flanders, for these two areas seemed to offer the Germans the most profitable objectives.

An additional reason for Joffre's refusal to let his attention be wholly drawn to Verdun was the allied plan for a combined Franco-British spring offensive on the Somme. In order to carry out the original plan the French Commander in Chief was determined to retain the initiative. General Foch had been designated to direct the French participation in the Somme operation with three French armies including Pétain's Second; and the allied military leaders had high hopes for a major success. The German high command were aware that an allied offensive was in the offing and their own attack at Verdun in February was designed in part to anticipate and forestall the allied spring drive. So eager were the German planners to precede the allies that they accepted the handicap of February weather conditions, which hampered and delayed their operation.

Joffre was reluctant to accept the fact that a major battle at Verdun would absorb the greater part of his army during 1916 and his reluctance continued even after the battle was joined. This attitude on the part of the French high command was reinforced by their opinion that little strategic advantage could accrue to the Germans by an attack on Verdun, particularly if the attack were confined to the right bank of the Meuse as it initially was.

Verdun, ancient citadel of northeastern France, was a bastion upon which the right flank of the French western front positions rested, short of the Vosges mountains. The river Meuse ran directly through the Verdun fortified area, dividing it into two parts; the right or east bank formed a salient in the German line, a fact which contributed to the weakness of the French position, but was the posture in which it found itself after the stabilization of the front in 1914. To add further to its vulnerability the forts of the Verdun defense complex had been systematically stripped of their artillery, munitions and personnel in 1915 to provide desperately needed heavy guns to the armies in the field.

The impetus of the initial German drive on the northern face of the Verdun salient drove the French defenders back in a retreat which raised fears that an evacuation of the right bank would be necessary. Joffre hastened to send his assistant, General de Castelnau, to the area with full powers to act for him. Castelnau, arriving on the scene, gave orders for the defense to be conducted on the right bank of the Meuse with no thought of withdrawal across the river. This command reflected the thought of G.Q.G. staff officers who had come to think that any positions, no matter what their strategic value, should be defended à outrance (a corollary of the offensive à outrance doctrine); but the orders condemned the French army at Verdun to a costly holding operation in a narrow salient, with no room for maneuver and with a river at its back.

Pétain and his Second Army headquarters had already been alerted, on the evening of February 24th, to take over the defense of the Verdun sector on the left bank of the Meuse. Castelnau telephoned G.Q.G. on the 25th and recommended that Pétain assume command also of the battle raging on the right bank, a proposal which Joffre later said was the "solution that . . . saved Verdun."[1]

The conditions under which he received the news of his new and awesome responsibility are described in different terms by three participants in the events. Pétain records[2] that he had considered it highly likely that he would be called upon to take over the Verdun front, since he was available, with his staff, at Noailles and the magnitude of the battle that was developing seemed to require the commitment of a new army into the line. He was therefore not at all surprised on the evening of the 24th to receive the order to send his headquarters to Bar-le-Duc and to report personally to Joffre on the morning of the 25th; and in fact he had, he said, on his own initiative already taken measures to carry out the anticipated command.

Joffre's memoirs[3] record that the commander in chief telephoned Pétain at the latter's headquarters at 11:00 P.M. on the 24th and told him to take command of all the forces on the left bank of the Meuse at Verdun and to move his headquarters to Bar-le-Duc. In these two accounts there is no conflict.

But Pétain's staff officer, Captain Serrigny, has a different story to tell.[4] According to Serrigny the order to Pétain on the evening of the 24th came in the form of a telegram signed by Joffre and also came as a surprise. The Second Army commander had gone to Paris at four o'clock that afternoon and had not left word where he could be found, since the news from the front was not of a particularly significant nature. Serrigny went to Paris looking for him and, through luck (and a knowledge of Pétain's habits?), he finally found his superior at 3:00 A.M. in the Hotel Terminus at the Gare du Nord. At first the woman who ran the hotel vigorously denied that the general was there but when she was informed of the gravity of the situation she took him to Pétain's room. On the threshold of the door Serrigny recognized

[1] Marshal Joffre, *The Personal Memoirs of Joffre,* trans. Col. T. Bentley Mott (New York, 1932), II, 446.
[2] Maréchal Pétain, *La Bataille de Verdun* (Verdun, n.d.), 45.
[3] Joffre, *op. cit.,* 441.
[4] Général Serrigny, *Trente ans avec Pétain* (Paris, 1959), 43–45.

the general's yellow boots; there was also a pair of ladies' shoes. Pétain appeared at the door scantily dressed and annoyed at the intrusion, but after he learned the nature of his aide's errand he instructed Serrigny to find a room in the hotel and in the morning they would leave together.

Their sleep was brief; they were up at 7:00 A.M. and by 8:00 A.M. Pétain reported to Joffre's headquarters at Chantilly. The atmosphere among the staff officers at G.Q.G. was one of anxiety and agitation, as bad news and rumor from Verdun continued to come in; but Pétain found Joffre his usual calm and optimistic self. Whatever else might be said of Joffre's military ability he did furnish, as he had on the Marne in 1914, an indispensable element of unruffled sangfroid which, in moments of crisis, was of inestimable value to the French army. Of course a cynic might argue that if his military competence were higher the crises might have been fewer and less critical.

By 10:00 A.M., after Joffre had given him what little information he had on the battle situation, Pétain was on his way to Souilly, a village on the Bar-le-Duc–Verdun road about eleven miles from Verdun, where he was to meet Generals Castelnau and de Langle de Cary, the latter in command of the Center Group of Armies which included the Verdun sector. Because of the condition of the roads, it took nine hours for him to make the trip by automobile, with a brief stop for dinner. Snow and ice covered the rutted road and as they approached the front the military traffic increased so that in spite of the urgency of his mission his vehicle was slowed at times to a speed of two miles per hour. The General had had little sleep the previous night and the cold and bumpy ride was an arduous one.

Stopping briefly at Souilly, where he was unable to gather little precise information as to the progress of the battle, he proceeded to Dugny, south of Verdun, the command post of General Herr, who was the commander of the Fortified Region of Verdun. Here confusion reigned; the unfortunate Herr was overwhelmed by a disaster not of his own making and he and his staff apparently were on the verge of losing control of the situation.

Pétain calmly gathered what information he could out of this hectic atmosphere. He already had a good idea that things were not going well from observing the disorder on the roads as he came from Souilly to Dugny. Men, guns, horses, and truck convoys made their way with difficulty toward Verdun through the darkness on the icy roads on which horses slipped and fell and trucks skidded, while toward the south streamed the ambulances and crowds of refugees fleeing the guns of the enemy. Mixed with all of these were crowds of disorganized soldiers, stragglers who had lost or abandoned their units and were making little effort to find them.

Pétain had seen enough combat and knew enough of frontline combat psychology so that he was not overly dismayed by this "rear echelon" view of a battle in progress. For every malingerer milling in disorder he knew that there were ten good soldiers doing their best at the front; and the snarled traffic, delayed infantry columns, and cursing, struggling artillery men with their guns and horses were images of an army making a great effort, which needed only a firm hand and a competent authority to organize it. An army engaged in a difficult battle usually appears in worse disarray from the rear than it does at the front.

He did learn one piece of bad news at Dugny which had grave consequences for the future of the Verdun campaign: Fort Douaumont, the most important fortification in the Verdun fortified system, had fallen to the enemy without a shot being fired in its defense. The French troops fighting on either side of the fort, relief troops belonging to the crack XXth Corps thrown hastily into the battle, were supposed to assure the defense of the fort but through a command mixup, always possible in the confusion of a battle such as this, they had not received the order to do so. The commanders of these units flanking the fort were going by old regulations no longer in effect, which specified that fortress troops held the forts and that field troops acted independently. They assumed, if they thought about it at all in the heat of battle, that a permanent garrison or some other designated unit was installed in the place when in fact it was occupied by only a few Territorials who were surprised and captured by a handful of enterprising Germans.

The Douaumont blunder was one of the most tragic of the war, one that cost the French dearly. If ever soldiers had reason to blame their commanders for inept leadership surely the French army of World War I had such justification.

Fort Douaumont was the best and most modern of any French fortifications. Situated in a commanding position northeast of Verdun it could dominate the approaches of the Germans, and in their hands could and did dominate the defensive positions of Verdun. Massively constructed of cement and steel it was impervious to the fire of the heaviest guns.

It had been built as part of the system of fortifications constructed in northeastern France by General Séré de Rivières after the war of 1870 and had been strengthened and modernized several times since then. But the mystique of the offensive which so heavily influenced the policy planners of the French army in the years before the war led the French high command to downgrade the importance of these fortifications—defensive in concept as they seemed to be—although it was the existence of the fortified line Verdun—Belfort which forced von Schlieffen to plan the hazardous march through Belgium at the outset of the war.

The criticism of the fortifications so well planned by de Rivières began with Captain Gilbert in 1892 with his publication of several military studies. Gilbert was a forerunner of the *offensive à outrance* school and he was firmly opposed to anything that detracted from the idea of the offensive. He said that only battle in open country could decide a military issue and he cited the fate of Metz in 1870 as an example of the uselessness of "entrenched camps." Permanent fortifications, Gilbert taught, ruined the offensive spirit of the army and its commanders, immobilized too many people, hampered maneuver and condemned the army to "ataxy" and dispersion.[5] Gilbert's influence on the young army officers of his day was considerable and his contribution to the scorn of fortifications which had developed by 1916 was a significant one.

The 1914 campaign seemed to prove the ineffectiveness of fortifications; the fortified places of Liège, Namur, Maubeuge and Manonvilliers fell to the enemy with seeming ease. But these forts were not as strong or as heavily armed as were the forts of Verdun. Furthermore, they were isolated positions having no support from the field armies, while this was not the case for the forts of Verdun. So little regard did the French G.Q.G. have for the Verdun position that in the retreat of August and September 1914 Joffre gave General Sarrail, whose Third Army included the Verdun area, permission to retreat as much as eighty kilometers south of the place, with no provision for its defense. Happily for France and the allied cause Sarrail ignored the directive, hinged the right of his army on Verdun and moved his left back some twenty-five kilometers so as to face west instead of north; he thus flanked the German armies plunging southward, an action which made the battle of the Marne possible.[6]

In 1915 a parliamentary Army Committee went to Verdun on an inspection tour. General Dubail, comander of the Eastern Army Group, met them and in response to their inquiries the general said that the experience of Liège and Namur had demonstrated the feeble-

[5] See Fernand Engerand, *Le Secret de la frontière* (Paris, 1918), 54.
[6] See Général Percin, *1914—Les Erreurs du Haut Commandement* (Paris, 1920), 140–145.

ness of fortified places in the face of modern artillery whose power and great range could readily crush the fixed targets which forts and fixed batteries constituted. The military governor of Verdun as a fortified place, General Coutanceau, disagreed with Dubail but his superior silenced him brusquely in front of the parliamentarians.

When Pétain returned to Souilly on the night of February 25 he carried the news of the fall of Douaumont to his superiors, de Langle and Castelnau. The latter felt that there should be no time lost in getting the defense of Verdun organized and he took a notebook from his pocket and scribbled the order which made Pétain commander of the Verdun operation officially, an order which went into effect immediately. Pétain's first act was to telephone to his subordinate commanders on the right and left banks of the Meuse to inform them of his accession to command and then, after a meager supper, worn out from travel and lack of sleep, he spent a chilly night in the house of the local notary, which he had made his personal quarters.

On the morning of the 26th, his first day as commander at Verdun, he awoke feverish and coughing. A doctor diagnosed his illness as double pneumonia and the General spent the next five or six days in bed. His illness was kept a secret and he directed the battle from his bedroom, to which his staff reported and from which orders emanated, a system of command far less glamorous than that described in the official communiques but probably effective enough. Under trench warfare conditions commanders above the army corps level could exercise little personal control of operations and their activity—or lack thereof—would often have little direct effect on the outcome of an operation in progress.

The new commander ordered that the remaining forts be manned and armed, and held at all cost. He then set about organizing a coherent plan of defense for the whole sector. He prescribed a solid line of resistance to be held at all cost: in the north it rested on the right bank, on the approaches to Thiaumont and Souville, and went as close as possible to Douaumont; to the east, it rested on the line of Forts Vaux, Tavannes and Moulainville, and extended along the crest of the Heights of the Meuse overlooking the plain of Woevre. On the left bank the "principal line of resistance" was based on the line Cumières, Mort Homme, Hill 304 and Avocourt—all names to become tragically familiar in the weeks ahead. Ahead of this "principal line of resistance" extended his "advanced line of resistance"—a line which, unlike the main line, was not necessarily continuous and was not necessarily a line to be held at all cost, but was designed instead to break and canalize the German advance and to give the commander a certain amount of room for maneuver. In the rear of the main line was a third line consisting of redoubts for reserves and reinforcements and serving as a base for counterattacks.

This defensive system, as elastic as the limited depth of the terrain permitted, to some extent foreshadowed Pétain's defensive method of 1918 and was a departure from the prevalent French military psychology which prescribed holding tenaciously to all forward positions in a defensive battle without regard to their relative tactical value. However, during March—when the Germans extended the area of their offensive in new and powerful attacks to include the left bank, and the defenders were pressed back—the battle entered a critical stage; then the commander encountered the defects of his "elastic defense" method when applied to a limited zone of battle where there was no space for maneuver. On March 31 Pétain was compelled to change the designation of his first line to that of "principal line of resistance" which would be held at all cost, with the second line becoming the "support line" to serve as a point of departure for counterattacks. He had found that the front-line commanders had come to think of the first line as a line destined to be relinquished, step by step, but the lack of depth in the terrain around the beseiged Verdun now precluded such a conception.[7]

The basic strategy involved in the defense of Verdun was a matter of considerable concern to Pétain. As has been shown, he was not of the school of thought which attached an exaggerated significance to every foot of terrain held by his troops. In some ways he was not the ideal commander for a defensive operation like that of Verdun because he questioned the strategic value of the place. If left to follow his own policy he probably would not have attempted to hold the right bank in the first place. It was not worth the high price in men and material which the French were forced to pay to keep it.

Verdun in a curious way epitomizes the effect upon military operations which public opinion exercised in World War I. Each government among the major warring powers needed the total commitment of its people to the prosecution of the war effort and therefore any appearance of a repulse on the battlefiield was to be avoided at all cost. This had the effect of tying the hands of commanders in the field who sometimes might have preferred to maneuver in retreat rather than hold positions to the death—positions which often had little or no strategic or even tactical value. In this sense terrain became

[7] Ministère de la Guerre—État Major de l'Armée—Service Historique, *Les Armées françaises dans la grande guerre* (Paris, 1922–37), Tome IV, Vol. 1, 359, 446, 486.

the object of the commanders' attention rather than the enemy armies, a concept which is the negation of military science. The commanders themselves were partly to blame for this situation because of their concern that the appearance of retreat would cause damage to their reputations or to their careers.

The awkward salient of Verdun was a weak enough position in itself, but cut off by a large river as it was from the bulk of the French armies it constituted little value defensively and was hardly a threat to the Germans offensively. As had been seen, Joffre was willing enough to relinquish Verdun in August 1914 and it was still in French hands in 1916 only because of the independent action take by General Sarrail at that time. The weakening of the defenses there in 1915 by the wholesale removel of heavy armament for use by the field armies was in line with the high command's feeling that the area held little strategic value. This is not to say that they were willing to give it up cheaply any more than any other front-line position, but Verdun was not considered of primary importance. It only became vital in the minds of both German and French leaders when they had, unwisely on both sides, propagandized their respective efforts there with an eye toward public opinion at home and in neutral countries.

It was not only the French military high command who, before February 1916, had not considered Verdun a position to be held at all cost; the French civilian leaders also showed no evidence of considering the possession of the place a matter of vital concern. The parliamentary Army Committee mentioned above which inspected its defenses in 1915 were not concerned so much with the adequacy of the Verdun defenses as they were with the facility with which the place could be evacuated in the event of a retreat. They were primarily interested in finding out if preparations in the way of pontoon bridges and railway construction had been made for the evacuation of troops and field artillery and other material if the enemy should take the place. The commanders whom they interviewed assured them that all measures had been taken to assure the security and success of such a withdrawal.[8] The danger of an exposed Verdun on the right bank of the Meuse therefore was foreseen in the summer of 1915, and its evacuation was considered a possibility by both civilian and military authorities.

The President of the Republic himself had considered the evacuation of Verdun an eventuality which was not cause for undue alarm. At a meeting of the Council of Ministers on July 29, 1915, Verdun and its defenses were discussed, in connection with the proposed in-

---

[8] Mermeix, *Joffre* (Paris, 1919), Chapter 10.

spection of the place by the Senate Army Committee. President Poincaré explained to the Council that there were no longer any fortified strongholds of the Verdun type because the war had demonstrated their inefficacy. "If Verdun were invested," he said, "It would be necessary to evacuate it with its material."[9] At this date at least the government did not feel that the possession of Verdun was vital to French morale.

However, since Pétain had been appointed to command at Verdun with orders to hold the place, he was bound to do everything possible to implement the will of the military high command and the government, and these authorities were increasingly bound by their public statements that Verdun would not fall. After March 3, 1916, confidence began to grow in France with regard to Verdun. President Poincaré and General Joffre made a visit to Pétain's headquarters at Souilly. So struck were they by his organization of the defenses and the achievements of his troops that they became very optimistic in their appraisal of the operation. This disturbed Pétain, who was not at all complacent about his chances of success and who was in any case dubious about the advantages of holding Verdun if the defense should cost too much. He therefore attempted to temper the optimism of Poincaré and Joffre by pointing out some of the difficulties and dangers confronting the French forces.

When Poincaré said to Pétain that under present conditions the General should certainly not contemplate a retirement to the left bank he replied, with deliberate coldness, that the great captains of history best showed themselves great by wise retreats. He continued, "I do not know if I will be obliged to abandon Verdun but if the measure appeared necessary to me I would not hesitate to consider it." This lesson in military history and strategy was lost on the President, who replied, "Don't think of it, General. It would be a parliamentary catastrophe."[10]

This remark of Poincaré's illustrates the political importance of Verdun and demonstrates also that the "fixed line" mentality of World War I was a civilian phenomenon as well as a military one. Public opinion in the warring nations was too important a factor to be ignored by their leaders, a situation about which a Napoleon or a Frederick the Great had had less need to be concerned.

The defense of Verdun had become a matter of national morale for France (and for Germany too but less vitally) and for that reason it had to be held to the death. There were also military factors to be

---

[9] Abel Ferry, *Les Carnets secrets (1914–1918)* (Paris, 1957) , 107.
[10] Serrigny, *op. cit.,* 63.

considered, such as the guns and munitions on the right bank, which could not be evacuated in the event of a German victory there because of a lack of adequate bridge facilities over the Meuse. When the French high command decided to fight it out for the possession of Verdun, great quantities of guns and munitions were moved into the area, much of it onto the right bank, and if the German drive should succeed in forcing the defenders out of the salient most of this valuable material would be lost. At that time the French army was in need of all categories of war equipment, particularly artillery and shells, and if the immense stocks of these accumulated on the right bank should be lost the effect upon future operations could have been quite serious.

There was some justification for the French high command decision to hold Verdun. No parcel of land is worth the nearly 400,000 casualties[11] which the French suffered there but it must be remembered that the French army was fighting on French soil and that seven departments of northern France, her richest ones, with a population of 2,-000,000 people, were already in the hands of the enemy. Could they give up more territory? This is the question which critics of French strategy must answer and one must consider that France did not have enormous expanses of territory, as did Russia, which could be traded for time and space to maneuver.

Pétain undoubtedly was correct in his view that little strategic harm would result if Verdun were relinquished but he also knew that the loss of the city and its defenses would constitute a moral and, to some extent, a material loss which his superiors had decided to avoid at all cost. He therefore devoted himself to a stubborn and even brilliant defense of an outpost which had become a symbol.

Among his principal concerns was the question of communications between Verdun and the interior. The huge amounts of men, guns, munitions and supplies of all kinds which the French army poured into the defense of Verdun required the organization of an adequate communication system. In this respect the Verdun sector had been gravely lacking and one of the reasons for the choice by the Germans of this point of attack was the fact that they controlled good means of communication to the Verdun area, while on the French side communications, both rail and road, were inadequate.

The two main rail lines to Verdun were unusable, one cut off by

---

11 The official casualty figures for the Second Army at Verdun, from February 21 to December 31, 1916 were 378,777 men (61,289 killed, 216,337 wounded, and 101,151 missing). A substantial number of the missing were dead.) See *Les Armées françaises . . .* , Tome IV, Vol. 3, 509.

the German lines at the Saint-Mihiel salient and the other under the fire of enemy guns as it passed Aubreville. This left the little narrow gauge railway called the "Meusien," sufficient only to carry some part of the food supplies, and the road from Bar-le-Duc, which was never intended for the traffic it was now called upon to sustain and which, in the spring thaw, soon degenerated into a muddy track.

The fate of the battle of Verdun and the security of the Second Army depended upon the route from Bar-le-Duc and this problem, next to his concern about his artillery, caused Pétain the most anxiety. Fortunately he had an officer, a Major Richard, in peacetime an engineer, who proved invaluable in keeping the road open and the traffic moving on what came to be called the "Sacred Way."

As the unpaved road thawed it became almost impassable because of the mud and holes. It could be repaired by work crews but the problem was that the traffic could not be interrupted even for a short time. Major Richard found that by digging into the fields adjoining the road they would find calcareous stones and pebbles which could be spread on the road to cover the mud and holes. They had no rollers and could not have used them if they had because their use would have blocked traffic. Richard proposed that teams of Territorials, older reserve troops generally employed in non-combat assignments, be posted along the road, armed with shovels, and given the task of continually throwing spadefulls of the gravel on the roadway. The passing vehicles would, with their weight, act as rollers.

This method worked well—so well that a force of 450,000 men and 140,000 animals (horses and mules) at Verdun was kept up to strength and supplied, and enormous quantities of guns and munitions were hauled to the front. Wounded men and worn-out troop units were brought back from the battle as reinforcements rolled forward, in an uninterrupted stream which attained the rate of one vehicle every fourteen seconds.

The crude road material played havoc with the hard rubber tires which the trucks at that time used and the engines of the overworked vehicles suffered frequent breakdowns. To meet this need repair shops worked around the clock for months repairing and replacing truck parts and engines, while hydraulic presses at Bar-le-Duc and Troyes turned out new rubber tires. When a vehicle broke down it was simply pushed off the road while teams of mechanics operated along the vital highway putting the broken-down vehicles into operation.

The drivers, 8500 of them for 3900 trucks, spent long and dangerous hours at their task, performing an unglamorous but vital function. Many of them fell asleep over their wheels, adding to the hazards of the precarious roadway, but the steady stream of vehicles was maintained.

As always, the question of artillery was uppermost in Pétain's mind, and at Verdun this was a particularly vital point as the enemy high command had massed an overwhelmingly superior quantity of heavy guns to support their offensive. In his daily conferences with his subordinate commanders he insisted that they give a report on the effectiveness of their artillery organization before taking up anything else. His emphasis on this vital question, weighted by his requisitions to the high command for more heavy guns, made itself felt at the front where the French soldier had been accustomed, but not reconciled, to German artillery superiority. He repeated constantly that the artillery had to give the infantry the impression that it supported them and was not dominated by the enemy.

General Bazelaire, commanding the left bank sector, was ordered to direct his artillery fire to the northeast in order to enfilade the German attacking lines on the right bank. The enemy was badly hurt by this fire, which gradually increased as the French rapidly increased their strength in guns. The German high command began to realize that their drive would have to include the left bank if they were to take Verdun.

Heavy artillery groups were kept under the immediate control of the commanding general rather than under the corps commanders, so that Pétain could move them immediately to any part of the battlefield. In this way concentrations of fire could be developed at any point where the Germans threatened to break through. Pétain's artillery commander, General Darde, was not up to the highly demanding task which the operation required and was too old to learn new tricks. Darde dined at the commanding general's table, as befitted his rank and the importance of his position, and Pétain, normally tolerant and certainly accustomed, after years of army service, to all varieties of personal manners, unaccountably took constant offense at Darde's eating habits. After a few weeks General Darde was relieved of his command and sent to the interior, where presumably he could pick his teeth in peace.

The forts of Verdun, rearmed and garrisoned, formed the backbone of the defense. One of the important staff officers involved in this was Major Bunau-Varilla, the same individual who was involved in the acquisition by the United States of the Panama Canal Zone, now in his sixties and director of the water service. He had previously rendered great service to Pétain's Second Army in the Champagne offensive of September 1915 when he found and developed wells to pro-

vide water for the great concentration of troops. The Verdun forts,
particularly those of the Heights of the Meuse, needed water, because
in their original planning they were to get their water from the Woevre plain, now behind enemy lines. Bunau-Varilla solved the problem
by pumping water for a distance of several kilometers through flexible
canvas pipes. Several weeks later he was wounded when he went to
inspect one of his conduits broken by the enemy shellfire and his leg
had to be amputated.

Pétain thought, from the beginning of the German offensive, that
the enemy had committed an error in his original planning by not
extending his offensive to the left bank, between the Meuse and the
Argonne forest. Had he done so Verdun might well have fallen in
February as the Germans intended. The French defenders did not
have available the reserves, in the early days of the battle, to "feed"
both the left and right bank fronts. A substantial advance by the Germans on the left bank would have permitted the enemy to bring their
artillery to bear on the right bank defenders, thus rendering their
positions untenable and would also have compromised the vital and
solitary communication artery from Bar-le-Duc to Verdun. Upon his
accession to command Pétain made it his principle concern to
strengthen the left bank positions, hoping with each day that he would
have time to complete his preparations.

When the Germans made a powerful attack on the left bank on
March 6 they drove in the French front at its eastern end along the
Meuse. Suffering great losses under the staggering artillery bombardment which pulverized their positions, the French defenders finally
held. The main positions from the hill known as Mort Homme to
Avocourt were still in French hands although under great pressure
from the attackers who were driven forward by the German high
command, desperately trying to keep its promise to the Kaiser and
to the German public, who had been assured for weeks that Verdun
would fall.

To say simply that the French defenders "held" gives a false impression of what actually took place in the battles of the Verdun campaign. What usually happened was that the preliminary German
artillery bombardment would obliterate the French forward positions
and annihilate the defenders. The French command would rush in
reinforcements, who even before reaching the forward positions would
suffer heavy losses in moving up through the enemy artillery barrage
on the rear areas. The survivors of the approach march would fight
desperate actions from demolished trenches and shell-holes until concentrations of French artillery fire and sustained machine gun fire

would inflict heavy casualties on the attackers and drive them to earth.

It would be of little value to discuss tactics, maneuver or nuances of military science in the defense of, or the attack on, Verdun, because there does not seem to have been any. The battle area was a great abattoir where hundreds of thousands of men were jammed into a compressed space, writhing under a constant rain of artillery shells which reached, on the French-held positions, an average of 80,000 explosions per day. For many months both sides were subjected to an artillery storm that pulverized trenches and dugouts, made movement above ground in the "death zone" almost impossible, and which would have denuded the stricken area of all life had the two opposing commanders not continued to feed a steady stream of reinforcements into what the German soldiers called the Verdun "sausage grinder" and the *poilus* called the "furnace."

The environment of screaming shells, earth-shaking explosions, terror, hunger, thirst, death, gas, mud, human filth and decomposed bodies was a nightmare to those who endured it. It was an artificial hell, a somber and savage landscape where only the rats were happy, and the morale of the men upon whose nerves and sinews the country depended to hold Verdun was a major problem. In order to maintain the combat value of his divisions Pétain initiated what he called the "noria" system, named after the apparatus for raising water from a well, which consisted of a revolving chain of buckets which are filled below and emptied when they come to the top.

His policy was to relieve divisions before they became completely worn out, a policy in marked contrast to the prevalent method. He maintained a system of rotation by which divisions were withdrawn from the line after a period determined by their losses sustained and were replaced by fresh divisions. When a division in the line reached its limit of wastage and fatigue it was replaced by a fresh or rested division. Army corps headquarters, with corps artillery and services, remained in place. As a rule of thumb, when a division had lost fifty per cent of its effectives—and sometimes that figure was reached in forty-eight hours although eight days was more normal—it was entitled to relief. After rest and refitting, usually in a rest area near Bar-le-Duc, its ranks filled out with replacements, the division could be used again, often at Verdun for a second or even a third time. As a concession to the unfortunates who returned to Verdun for another tour of duty such divisions were never employed in exactly the same area where they had previously fought—it was feared at headquarters that the troops could not bear the anxiety of such a revisit.

This system worked well and the French army probably could not have endured the battle without it; but in this way Pétain drew over sixty divisions—two-thirds of the French army—through the Verdun furnace, and General Joffre began to worry about the effects this would have on his planned participation in the battle of the Somme. The French and British high commands had hopes for a great success on the Somme but if French participation were reduced—as it eventually was, from forty to fourteen divisions—due to their Verdun commitments and losses, France would not be adequately represented, Joffre feared, in what might be the decisive victory.[12] Joffre need not have worried; victory was a long way off and by no means assured.

The German method on the Verdun front was in contrast to Pétain's. The enemy left most of their attacking divisions in line, making good their losses with replacements sent to them on the ground they occupied; by May 1 the French had used forty divisions at Verdun to the German twenty-six.[13] The German method had the advantage of eliminating the technical and administrative problems arising from replacing large units during an engagement while Pétain's noria system had the effect of conserving the combat value of all divisions engaged and tended to reduce deterioration of morale in troops exposed too long to Verdun. He had reason to worry about his men; the majority endured their exposure to the battle with resignation and often with courage, but there were many instances of breakdowns in morale and breaches of discipline. Joffre grumbled to Pétain that the German troops seemed to stand prolonged exposure to the battle without apparent serious strain to their morale and he asked why the French soldiers could not do likewise. But Pétain was more concerned with conditions as they were rather than in speculation as to why they existed; if French troops were more impressionable than their German counterparts it was a fact that he had to deal with. In any case the German soldier enjoyed better leadership and better and more numerous heavy artillery.

On March 20 the Germans renewed their assaults on the left bank, this time on the western end of the French positions, attempting to break through along the edge of the wooded heights of the Argonne. This time they made a rapid and substantial advance, capturing Avocourt and the Malancourt forest. This breakthrough was an unpleasant surprise to Second Army headquarters; troops were rushed in to reinforce the line and at great cost some of the lost territory was recovered, thus easing a serious threat to the French flank. The defeat at Avo-

---

[12] Joffre, II, 453.
[13] *Les Armées françaises . . .*, Tome IV, Vol. I, 641.

court and Malancourt was due to treason on the part of the defenders. Before the attack there had been local negotiations between the French and German soldiers and the French surrendered their positions and themselves without a fight, as an inquiry later showed.

Almost the whole of a brigade of the Twenty-ninth Division was captured, including the brigade commander, whose command post was surrounded before he knew that his brigade was under attack. This incident was reflective of a serious decline in the morale of the French troops at Verdun, which was a source of constant concern to Pétain, a concern which he was unable to communicate to the high command without being labeled a pessimist. The staff officers at G.Q.G. had been trained in a school which was concerned with the morale or "will to victory" of the commanders in battle, not the executants.

Throughout April the Germans kept up the pressure, attacking the whole Verdun area on both sides of the Meuse. The French defenders were able to hold them on the principle line of resistance but the issue continued in doubt. However, the continued resistance of the Verdun defenders, and the official communiqués, gave the public the impression that the danger was past. To some extent G.Q.G. shared this optimism and there began to grow a divergence of views between Pétain's headquarters at Souilly and the commander in chief's headquarters at Chantilly. We have mentioned Joffre's increasing reluctance to send more fresh troops to Verdun at the expense of his projected Somme enterprise. He viewed with alarm a "noria" system which was costing him two divisions every four days in April to be increased to two divisions every three days in May. Not only did he begin to resist Pétain's demands for fresh troops but he became increasingly reluctant to send artillery and other munitions on the great scale which Pétain had been requesting and receiving. He also began to object to his Second Army commander's continued defensive attitude; Joffre complained that with the enormous amounts of men and guns at his disposal Pétain should take the offensive.

The latter thought that the plans of G.Q.G. were unrealistic. The French forces at Verdun, he felt, were in no condition to take the offensive; they were still barely holding their own. On a larger scale he thought that France was in no position to mount a major offensive on the Somme or anywhere else in 1916; he wanted the British and the other French allies to make the major efforts for the rest of the year. The single combat of France with Germany at Verdun was all that should be expected of France that year. This attitude, which was in fact in conformity with the balance of forces on the western front, was less evidence of a pessimistic approach than it was of a realistic appraisal of the facts and of a patriotism which viewed with alarm the heavy losses which France had been incurring for almost two years. Pétain pointed out to Joffre that divisions returning to Verdun for the second time had their ranks filled out with young recruits of the class of 1916, inexperienced in combat and not equal to the demands of the Verdun front. Joffre may have argued that this reasoning was more sentimental than realistic but it was Pétain who had to stand, as he often did, on the front steps of his headquarters at the Souilly town hall, watching these young men going up to the front, and then seeing the survivors return, with staring eyes, mud-caked and hunched under the burden of their experience. Pétain hid under a glacial exterior the grief that he felt for his beloved *poilus*.

His defense of Verdun had made him a national figure and he had proved himself, since 1914, to be one of the most able of the French generals. He was popular with the country and with the army, and in March 1916 Premier Briand wanted to promote him to command an army group. The Center Group of Armies was commanded by General de Langle de Cary who would reach the legal age limit on March 30; Briand thought that Pétain should replace him.[14] Before approaching General Joffre with his proposal Briand sounded out President Poincaré on the subject of Pétain's promotion. Poincaré objected that a change of command should not be effected in the middle of a battle but Briand said that his intention was only that Pétain should take the new command when the battle was over. He took his request to Joffre who had no good reason to oppose the promotion and who also felt that with Pétain removed to a higher post perhaps the additional responsibilities would quiet his demands for the Verdun front. At the end of March de Langle de Cary retired and the Center Army Group was put, temporarily, directly under G.Q.G. and was reserved for Pétain.

Poincaré's objections to Pétain went deeper than he leads us to believe in his memoirs. The President made a habit of frequent visits to the headquarters of the various army commanders, particularly to those commanding in important sectors. Ambitious and tactful generals generally made those visits as pleasant and as reassuring to the chief of state as possible. When Verdun captured the attention of the world Poincaré naturally took a personal interest in the direction of the battle and the presidential train went several times to Souilly. Much to Poincaré's dismay the suddenly famous commander of the Second Army was not at all impressed by the dignity of the chief of

14 Poincaré, VIII, 98, 153.

state's office and Pétain's caustic comments on the conduct of the war, on matters sometimes outside of what Poincaré considered to be a general's province, offended the President. The one-time colonel of infantry, who had once ruined his chances of promotion with his ironic and sarcastic comments at his superiors' expense, had not mellowed with age. The war had saved him from obscurity but he had no intention of compromising with what was, in his eyes, an inept hierarchy. The President could hardly be blamed for his dislike and distrust of Pétain for the latter's frankness bordered on rudeness and sometimes went beyond the bounds of propriety.

On one occasion, during a dinner in the presidential railroad car, the conversation between Pétain and the President concerned itself with the deplorable shortage of artillery munitions, a discussion which led to references to a lack of organization in the interior of the country. Pétain was led to remark that the proper coordination of the governmental machinery only would be possible through the exercise of a dictatorship by the chief of state. "But General," said the astonished President, "What do you do with the Constitution?"

"Personally I don't give a damn about the Constitution," was Pétain's reply, with no hint of a smile on his expressionless face to soften the remark.[15] His bitter words are better understood when one realizes that the terrible casualties suffered by the French army in the first years of the war were due in large measure, as Pétain often said, to a lack of heavy artillery, but the President had a right to feel that the words were out of place.

A more famous Pétain remark was his comment to Poincaré, on another occasion, that no one was better placed than the President to know that France was neither governed nor commanded. "But you are joking, General," said Poincaré, greatly offended. "Not at all," said Pétain. This exchange, which soon became well known, was vouched for by Pétain himself when questioned about it by an English journalist.[16]

People who knew him insisted that the author of these remarks was not really the ogre he pretended to be and that this was his way of joking. There is no doubt that his outrageous comments were an expression of his sense of humor but along with it there went a contempt for politicians that most French professional army officers of his generation shared.

In some of these incidents there was no humor at all. Poincaré once sat in on one of Pétain's daily conferences with his sector commanders

15 Serrigny, 81, 82.
16 C. Repington, *The First World War* (New York, 1920), II, 84.

at Verdun. The battle was at its peak and the session was an anxious one: the commander received their reports, questioned each one in turn and gave instructions for the day. Before dismissing his subordinates, he asked Poincaré if the latter wanted to say anything to the officers before they went back to the front. The President remained silent and a moment of stillness hung over the room, then Pétain turned to his generals and said, "The President of the Republic has nothing to say to you." It was something that the officers concerned never forgot.[17]

Other high ranking officers carefully hid their animosity when they came into contact with the army committees of the Chamber and the Senate, or other parliamentarians and ministers; otherwise they would have found their careers in jeopardy. Pétain felt that this kind of thing went too far when generals gave overly-optimistic appraisals of the military situation or forecasts of military operations; he owed his reputation for pessimism, in part at least, to the calculated manner in which he told the government leaders, with sometimes brutal frankness, the harsh realities of France's military situation. When members of parliament, visiting Verdun, would ask him if the Germans could take the place he would reply, "I hope not."

General Joffre, in his memoirs, recorded that he promoted Pétain to command the G.A.C. (*Groupe d'Armées du Centre*) in April to get him away from Verdun where his requests for divisions, guns and shells threatened to delay and hamper the Somme Offensive. Granted that Joffre, as commander in chief, was the final authority in promotions of this nature, the civilian cabinet kept a close eye on the promotions of generals, particularly army and army group commanders, and we have seen that it was on Briand's initiative that the G.A.C. command was reserved for Pétain. Joffre's prestige had been diminishing, as far as parliament was concerned, throughout 1915 and his failure to foresee or prepare for the German attack on Verdun had cost him much of his remaining political support.

Pétain's Second Army at Verdun had not been part of an army group but had answered directly to G.Q.G., testifying to the importance which the French high command attached to the Verdun defense. On April 28 Pétain was appointed to head the G.A.C. and on May 2 he assumed his new command, with headquarters in the town hall at Bar-le-Duc. The Second Army was placed under the command of one of Pétain's corps commanders at Verdun, General Nivelle, but it no longer was under the direct command of G.Q.G. Second Army

---

[17] George Loustanau-Lacau, *Mémoires d'un français rebelle* (Paris, 1948), 36, 37.

now was part of G.A.C., Pétain's army group, and the battle of Verdun was still his principal preoccupation although his responsibilities also included three other armies and a wider front.

Joffre apparently hoped that the demands of the Verdun front could be met by the forces available to the Center Army Group and Pétain's command therefore could live off itself; in this way the commander in chief could proceed with his Somme preparations without further nagging from Pétain for reinforcements. He thought, with some justice, that the Somme offensive would force the Germans to relax their pressure on Verdun. He thought too that with Nivelle, a dynamic and enthusiastic officer, in immediate charge of the Verdun operation there would be more offensive action on the part of the French forces there. In these hopes he was disappointed, for the time being, largely because his Somme operation was delayed until July; and although he tended to blame Pétain for his Verdun problems the Germans were the real authors of the difficulties there.

In May and June the Germans redoubled their assaults on both banks of the Meuse. Their purpose obviously was to force a French withdrawal from the right bank, thus gaining an important moral victory and capturing enormous stocks of guns and other material. They also hoped to force the French high command to give up its plans for the Somme offensive, an operation which the Germans knew was being prepared. The masses of men which the German high command hurled against the French defenders suffered very high casualties; now for the first time at Verdun the attackers were losing more men than the defenders, under the massed firepower—particularly in artillery—which the French had organized. It is in this period that the Germans began to suffer their worst losses at Verdun.

The German motives for the Verdun offensive are open to question. The German historical attitude, derived from General Falkenhayn's postwar writings, is that the intention was to bring France to battle at a point from which she could not withdraw without loss of prestige and to which she would commit all her resources in men and materials, thus bleeding her to death. The French official history takes the same view, and we have seen that General Joffre had, prior to February 1916, discounted the possibility of a major enemy operation in the Verdun area because, as he put it in his memoirs, "from the point of view of German strategy, Verdun had no justification."

Pétain thought differently; to him the Germans attempted to establish, after the fact, a limited motivation for their undertaking in order to cover up a defeat. He reasoned that attrition could not have been the only aim as such an objective would also work against them; and

there was always the possibility that the allies of France would com-
mence an offensive on another front to disengage the Franco–German
single combat, which was in fact what happened when the British
opened their July 1916 offensive on the Somme. He believed that the
enemy plan envisaged an enveloping movement designed to trap the
defenders of the city, exposed as it was in a salient on the right bank
of the Meuse, thus winning at least an important tactical victory and
a moral victory as well. Whatever had been their original intentions
it is obvious that the German attacks throughout May and June were
desperate attempts to win a victory and not simply to wear out the
French army.

Pétain went daily to Nivelle's headquarters at Souilly during this
period. The latter attempted to comply with Joffre's directives that
the Second Army cease its requests for fresh troops but found that
the attrition of his units were such that he needed reinforcements on
a scale greater than had Pétain. The G.A.C. commander supported
Nivelle's requests for more men and guns, and it was he who had to
relay them to the high command and bear the brunt of Joffre's displeasure, although in some instances he requested less from General
Headquarters than Nivelle declared necessary. On June 6 the Germans took the fort of Vaux and a few weeks later they reached the
approaches of the fort of Souville.

Pétain considered the situation desperate and on June 23 he telephoned G.Q.G. and told them that if reinforcements in men and
munitions were not forthcoming he might have to evacuate the right
bank. This threat stirred Joffre to send four fresh divisions and the
German advance was stopped. This telephone call of June 23, according to Pétain's chief of staff, was a means Pétain employed to get
what reinforcements he thought were necessary to conduct a successful
defense of Verdun and was not evidence of a failure of nerve or of
extreme pessimism.[18]

Another witness, Lieut.-Col. Pineau, a staff officer with the Second
Army at Verdun on June 23, later told the writer Henry Bordeaux
that on that day Pétain had been as calm as ever. He had said to the
assembled staff officers, at the daily "report": "Gentlemen, you mustn't
worry. We have not been lucky today but we will be tomorrow.[19]

---

[18] Serrigny, 95. Serrigny had been G.A.C. chief of staff since May 20, 1916.
He agreed with Joffre's thesis that the Verdun Second Army should live on
its own effectives and that the Somme offensive should be the means of disengaging Verdun, and he had many arguments with Pétain on the subject,
but as an eyewitness of the June 23 events he records that Pétain was not
so desperate as his call to G.Q.C. would indicate.
[19] Henry Bordeaux, *Histoire d'une Vie* (Paris, 1959), Vol. VI, 30, 31.

Pétain took the tack of encouraging and covering for his subordinates but was not afraid to growl at General Headquarters and frightening them a bit to get what he wanted. However, he gained a poor reputation with the "Young Turks" on Joffre's staff. Joffre had further grounds for displeasure when, on June 25, Pétain complained to the Minister of War, General Roques, who visited his headquarters, that the artillery at Verdun was insufficient and that the situation was still precarious. When Joffre was informed of this interview he complained bitterly about his subordinate going over his head. Joffre's postwar memoirs reflect his anger at Pétain; he claimed that General Nivelle was the true savior of Verdun, not Pétain.

Pétain did not consider the Verdun operation to be more important than that of the Somme. In fact he continually requested G.Q.G. to advance the date of the Somme offensive so as to relieve the pressure on Verdun. But he did think that the Somme battle should be primarily a British enterprise and that France should limit her participation in it. His focus was on Verdun, a narrow view perhaps, while Joffre was attempting to see the larger picture; but Pétain did not expect a great success for the allied arms on the Somme and in that view he was proven correct. He looked upon the operation solely as a means of winning the battle at Verdun.

Nivelle was acutely aware of Joffre's desire that the Second Army take the offensive at Verdun and soon after assuming command he began to prepare a plan for the recapture of Fort Douaumont. Pétain felt that the French forces were in no position to take the offensive yet but he supported Nivelle, knowing that this was what Joffre wanted, by procuring troops and guns for the operation. On May 22 the attack took place and in two days failed with heavy losses. Another carefully planned attack on July 15 also failed.

However, by October 1916 the German reserves were being absorbed by the Somme offensive and Nivelle was able to recapture Fort Douaumont. For the purpose Pétain had been able to procure two immense 400 millimeter mortars whose shells penetrated the thick exterior of the fort. Added to these were great quantities of heavy and field artillery, and six divisions of infantry (three in the first line of attack and three in the second). On December 15 another powerful attack recovered most of the territory lost to the Germans since February. It was the end of the battle of Verdun.

The success of these two relatively small operations, against a front then weakly held, assumed an importance out of proportion to its real significance; for the generals who carried out these attacks, Nivelle and Mangin, proclaimed that they had proven that the enemy front could be broken by a quick and brutal attack and that all that was needed was then to push reserves through the breach to exploit the victory. The fact that in two short operations they had recaptured much of the ground which the Germans had spent the better part of a year in taking gave an undue prominence to their views, and their line of thought with its emphasis on the *attaque brusquée* became known as the "Verdun school." Opposed to this was the so-called "Somme school," which emphasized a heavy preparation by artillery with the infantry occupying successive positions methodically.

The disappointing lack of conclusive results on the Somme had dimmed any luster that the latter undramatic school of thought might have had, whereas the former, with its dazzling promise of quick success, appealed to war-weary France. Accordingly, when in December 1916 Joffre was forced to resign, Nivelle was named to succeed him as commander in chief. Nivelle brought with him the conviction that he could in one bound succeed in breaking the enemy lines, in one or two days, using the methods which had been successful in the last Verdun attacks. In effect the French army was returning to the 1914 *offensive à outrance* theory, a line of thinking that had once bent the army but had not quite broken it. This time something would crack.

Prominent members of the French parliament had been after Joffre's scalp for a long time and in December 1916 he was "promoted" to the position of technical counselor to the government, a position which he soon found carried with it no authority. He therefore tendered his resignation. He was made a Marshal of France, the first to be appointed by the Third Republic, and, in the words of General Fayolle, ". . . put in a niche surrounded by incense."

Joffre and Poincaré were largely responsible for the appointment of Nivelle to command the French armies, the former because he thought, before his resignation, that he would be able to dominate the G.Q.G. from his new position by appointing a man of secondary stature, and the latter partly because he was intrigued, as were most political leaders, by Nivelle's calm assurance that he possessed the key to victory. Also, Nivelle was a Protestant and therefore was acceptable to anticlerical politicians, and he spoke fluent English due to his English mother, a fact which was supposed to increase the cooperation, and perhaps even the subordination, of the British armies.

The French government could not see any other choice. Foch was in partial disgrace after the failure of his Somme hopes; Fayolle was too old and too Catholic; de Castelnau was also devoutly Catholic, aristocratic, and tainted by his long association with Joffre; and

Franchet d'Espèrey was considered a political reactionary as well as a Catholic. Pétain was thought by Joffre to be too cautious and pessimistic; Poincaré had conceived an active dislike for him, and many other leading politicians distrusted the hero of Verdun. Nevertheless Pétain had thought himself a strong possibility for the post, which many people expected would soon be vacant, and in November 1916 his chief of staff, Colonel Serrigny, according to his own account, had been preparing a plan for a new organization of the General Headquarters in the event that his chief should attain the high command. Although Pétain was raised a Catholic he was not a church-goer and was not "clerical," but his obvious contempt for politicians repelled them. Besides, no one could compete with Nivelle's glittering promises of a swift victory; Pétain's realistic appraisal of the military situation was the antithesis of Nivelle's.

Nivelle, as commander of the Second Army, had been engaged in the planning of his highly successful attack of December 15, 1916, north of Douaumont, when on the night of December 11 or 12 he was called to Paris and he left immediately. Pétain, as his chief, learned of Nivelle's departure at four o'clock in the morning and he realized that his former subordinate was now to be commander in chief of the armies. His reaction was instant and characteristic. He immediately called for his automobile and by 5:00 A.M. he was on his way to Souilly to take personal command of the operation. For the next few days he could be found working at the 3rd Bureau (Operations) at Second Army headquarters.

On December 15 Nivelle arrived at Souilly to reap the laurels for the day's victory. He and Pétain, with their respective chiefs of staff, lunched together. During the meal Nivelle turned to his assistant, Lieut.-Col. d'Alençon, and, referring to the tactics used in the successful attack which had just driven the Germans back two miles beyond Douaumont, said, "Eh bien, d'Alençon, we now have the formula. We will defeat the enemy with it."[20]

Serrigny murmured something about the hazards of formulas in wartime while Pétain remained silent. Nivelle's "formula" would cost France dearly.

---

[20] Serrigny, 112, 113; Bordeaux, VI, 9, 67. D'Alençon might more properly be referred to as Nivelle's *chef de cabinet*, since he was not Chief of Staff of the French army.

5

The April 1917 Offensive

The French offensive on the Aisne in April 1917 marked a turning point in the fortunes of France in World War I, and thus of the allies as well, for several important reasons. Its lack of success wrecked the career of its commander, General Nivelle, and propelled Pétain, unpopular with President Poincaré, to command of the French armies on the western front; this fact in itself denoted a drastic change in methods, both strategical and tactical. It was so costly in casualties and in ruined hopes that the French army was almost put out of action by the resulting serious mutinies and a large part of the French nation was plunged into the gloomy pessimism and defeatism of 1917. As an aftermath of the offensive the French civil government took an increased control of military operations; thus the period during which the military leaders enjoyed considerable autonomy in matters affecting their own métier ended, being replaced by the "war is too important to be left to the generals" phase. Few other campaigns in World War I gave rise, in France, to so many postwar recriminations, self-justifications and polemics.

The spring offensive for 1917 was planned by Joffre during November and December 1916. At the Chantilly conference of mid-November 1916, the representatives of the allied armies agreed on an offensive on all fronts for the month of February 1917. February was really too early in the year for optimum weather conditions but the allied military leaders were eager to launch their 1917 operations before the Germans could begin their own; in 1916 the surprise German offensive at Verdun in February had upset allied calculations and consid-

103

erably modified the planned French participation in the Somme offensive of that year. As a matter of fact the 1917 allied offensive on the western front did not take place until April and even at that later date weather conditions were so poor as to contribute seriously to the French failure.

It was agreed between Joffre and Haig that the British would attack first, between Bapaume and Vimy, and thus, hopefully, would draw to themselves a large part of the German reserves. The French would then attack between the Somme and the Oise. The Russian and Italian armies would cooperate by undertaking large-scale offensives on their own fronts.

Joffre planned that the main French effort would be made by his Northern Army Group, with four armies attacking on a twenty-six mile front north of the Oise. Fifteen days after this operation began one army, the Fifth, from Pétain's Center Army Group, would go on the offensive to the southeast of Laon. It was hoped that the success of the operation in the north would draw off the German forces from Pétain's front and his subsidiary attack would profit thereby and would take advantage of, and add to, the enemy's confusion. It was hoped also that the menace of encirclement would induce the enemy to withdraw from the large salient in the Soissons region.

Since the beginning of November Pétain's staff had been studying a limited offensive on the Fifth Army front, an operation which would seek the element of surprise and would limit itself to a depth of advance which could be thoroughly "prepared" by French artillery. However by the end of November these plans clashed with the more ambitious proposals of Joffre's headquarters. Joffre desired Pétain to aim at a breakthrough north of the Ailette.

Pétain protested this extension of his more modest plan. His line along the Aisne faced the heights of the Chemin des Dames, a rugged watershed between the Aisne and the Ailette. The nature of the terrain was such that he believed that a breakthrough was not feasible, largely because his artillery would be ineffective against the German second positions. Inasmuch as Nivelle's offensive, made with greater resources in guns and men, failed to penetrate these positions in April 1917, his objections were justified.

Pétain proposed that he attack in a more northeasterly direction, thus avoiding a direct assault on the most formidable of the Chemin des Dames positions.[1] Before the question could be resolved between Pétain and Joffre's staff, Joffre was replaced as French commander in

[1] See Général Bernard Serrigny, *Trente ans avec Pétain* (Paris, 1959), 104–106.

chief, in mid-December, by Nivelle. The new commander in chief changed the entire plan of his predecessor in such a manner as to lessen the importance of the attack north of the Oise and to make the attack on the Chemin des Dames, on Pétain's front, the main effort. The idea was to crash through the Chemin des Dames defenses with a short and crushing offensive, supported by masses of men and artillery, then sweep northward across the Ailette on to the plain of Laon and to take the latter city within two days. What Pétain had considered impractical as a subsidiary operation now became the main effort upon which Nivelle staked everything in order to break open the German defenses and to shatter the enemy's main forces in France. This, Nivelle planned, would be the decisive battle of the war.[2]

The new orientation of the projected French spring offensive for 1917 met with Pétain's immediate opposition. The plan itself, as a map exercise, looked very attractive. The French and British between them, in converging attacks, aimed at pinching off the huge German salient between Arras and Soissons. But the Chemin des Dames obstacle, directly in the path of the French advance, was a position of imposing natural strength. Pétain had already, as commander of the Sixth Division, in September and October 1914, repeatedly and vainly attacked in this region. Nivelle, as an artillery officer, had never had this experience, nor, of course, had Joffre.

Pétain was a first-rate infantry officer and had held front-line combat commands—down to the regimental level although he was a brigade commander—in the early weeks of the war. No other commander in chief of any army in World War I had this educational experience. Both Foch and Haig had been corps commanders, relatively far removed from the front, in 1914. Of other commanders only Ludendorff had been in close contact with the front, during his attack on Liège in August 1914, and his tactical directives throughout the war were of a high order.

On Christmas day, 1916, Nivelle and Pétain together reconnoitred the front of the projected attack, and Pétain reiterated his disapproval of the plan, noting that the configuration of the terrain rendered impossible the speedy breakthrough envisaged by Nivelle. The Fifth Army artillery commander, General Fetter, advised Nivelle frankly (a frankness which later cost him his command) that from a technical point of view the operation appeared very hazardous,

2 See Ministère de la Guerre, État-major de l'Armée—Service Historique, *Les Armées françaises dans la grande guerre* (Paris, 1931), Tome V, Vol. I, 161–163 for Nivelle's plans and his letter to Haig explaining them.

because conditions were such that he would be unable to soften the German second positions with his guns prior to and during the attack.

The area between the Aisne and the Ailette is a rugged wooded mass of steep hills. Along the plateau which crowns the heights, from the farm of la Malmaison to Craonne, runs the Chemin des Dames, so named after the daughters of Louis XV for whom the road was built to enable them to get to their chateau of la Bove. The terrain is so broken and rough that even infantry would have difficulty traversing it, let alone the artillery which would have to accompany any appreciable advance. In addition to the natural defensive characteristics of the massif there were many large underground stone quarries, called "creutes" in the neighborhood, which the Germans had developed into shelters for reserves. The entrances to the quarries were for the most part safely out of sight of French artillery observation.

The heights constituted a formidable barrier but even beyond them further difficulties existed. The valley of the Ailette, two miles wide, was very marshy in the early spring and was a serious barrier to the passage of artillery. And north of the Ailette lies further high ground, before the plain of Laon is reached. In addition to these handicaps there were few roads running from south to north in the region, making transport for the proposed operation a problem.

Nivelle was determined to proceed with the attack in spite of the difficulties but he could not put his old chief, Pétain, in command of an operation in which the latter had no confidence. Therefore he chose General Micheler, Tenth Army commander, to conduct the main attack with the Reserve Army Group comprising the Sixth, Tenth and Fifth Armies, the latter army having been removed from Pétain's command. Pétain retained command of the Center Army Group but would take part in the offensive only to the extent that his Fourth Army would advance, in a subsidiary role, on the right flank of the attack, extending it east of Rheims (toward Moronvilliers).

Nivelle undoubtedly was relieved that Pétain had given him an excuse to do what he wanted to do anyway: sidetrack his former commander. He confided to General Fayolle in late December 1916 that he did not want Pétain because the latter was not "offensive" enough but that he could not find a way to get rid of him.[3] Pétain's vigorous objections to the operation provided an excellent reason and both of them must have known it.

Nivelle and Pétain represented two divergent points of view and there was no reconciling their differences. Pétain felt that a break-

---

[3] Maréchal Fayolle, *Cahiers secrets de la grande guerre* (Paris, 1964), 196.

through on a large scale was impossible, given the equilibrium of the opposing forces on the western front in 1917, and he wanted to conserve French forces while wearing down those of the enemy. He felt that given an adequate preparation, mainly with massed artillery fire, his troops could always take the enemy's first line and sometimes the second; but that a real advance beyond that, beyond the range of his artillery, was not possible. His men would be halted before the enemy positions which still would be intact and could go no farther until an artillery preparation against the new line could take place. But this would take time and in fact would be an entirely new operation; the guns would have to be moved forward into new positions, over ground devastated by their own fire, and the work would have to begin again. By that time the enemy would have massed his reserves at the threatened point and the opportunity would be gone.

Pétain therefore thought in terms of limited offensives, aimed at taking the enemy's first positions, always possible with adequate artillery preparation, but he would not try to push his advance beyond that point. By means of many such limited operations he hoped to wear out the German army, to use up its reserves. The enemy army was his objective, not the terrain it occupied. Inasmuch as the terrain in question was French soil it is hardly surprising that Pétain's countrymen were inclined to try Nivelle's method, at least until it failed.

Nivelle had made his conceptions known shortly after his assumption of overall command, in his "Instructions" of December 26 and 28, 1916, to the French armies on the western front. These "Instructions" were clearly aimed at refuting Pétain's strategy and at counteracting its influence. Nivelle declared in the "Instructions" that "certain commands" had adopted a defective method of attack in which they had limited the depth of the terrain to be conquered, had chosen objectives which were not sufficiently distant, and had lengthened the amount of time separating successive operations. He proposed that the enemy lines be broken in a short and powerful offensive, an affair of twenty-four to forty-eight hours: in it the enemy's positions would be taken as far back as his heavy artillery, his line would be shattered, and battle would then take place in open country against the enemy's disorganized formations.[4]

Nivelle's December 1916 "Instructions" also outlined an interesting tactical procedure which intended that the infantry should recover its preponderant role on the battlefield. Instead of the artillery conquering each position, point by point, and the infantry following it

---

[4] *Les Armées françaises* . . . , Tome V, Vol. I, 161–163, 174–179, 192, 193; see also Jean de Pierrefeu, *L'Offensive du 16 avril* (Paris, 1919), 17–20.

up, now the infantry would maneuver and penetrate as quickly as possible, bypassing strong points which would fall when flanked. This is precisely what the Germans did, with considerable success, in their great breakthroughs in the spring of 1918. But the difference lay in the element of surprise: Nivelle's April 1917 offensive was preceded by a bombardment of six days duration which gave the Germans every opportunity to reinforce the front of the attack, even if the operation had not been one of the worst-kept secrets of the war in other respects; on the other hand the German method in 1918 depended upon a strict application of the element of surprise, the attacks themselves being preceded by a bombardment, well planned and very powerful, of only a few hours duration. Of course the German breakthroughs of 1918 were not followed by the defeat of their opponents' armies in open country and it is highly unlikely that Nivelle could have achieved his objective in 1917 even had he succeeded in breaking through.

Throughout January 1917 Pétain was occupied with preparing for his relatively small part in the forthcoming offensive. He was not yet particularly alarmed at the way things were going because he expected that a moderate success might be achieved, though nothing like the decisive victory hoped for by Nivelle. But in February and March the Germans executed their maneuver "Alberich," a strategic withdrawal from the great salient they had occupied between Arras and Soissons. This changed the whole face of of the French plan. It had been expected that the British and the French Northern Army Group (Franchet d'Espèrey) would attack the northern face of the salient but the German withdrawal to prepared positions, the "Hindenburg Line" (*Siegfried Stellung*), rendered that part of the plan inoperative, thus putting almost the whole of the burden on Micheler's Reserve Army Group facing the Chemin des Dames. The Germans had greatly shortened and strengthened their front and had gained additional reserves through the divisions thus released. Nivelle's plan was falling apart; the exposed German situation in the big salient had been one of the chief reasons for the original proposal for the offensive in that area. What had been a subsidiary operation for Joffre, against the Chemin des Dames, now was not only the principal French operation but was almost the only one.

Nivelle's problems did not end there. The Russian revolution on March 12 was followed by the abdication of the Czar. War weariness and pacifism weakened the Russian army, so that General Alexeiev had to inform his French allies that his forces were incapable of large-scale operations and that he could not take part in the concerted operations agreed to at Chantilly in December. He hinted that perhaps the French should change their plans. General Cadorna of Italy also indicated that he would not be ready. The whole Chantilly plan for concerted action had vanished.

Nivelle also had problems on the home front. His sponsor, Briand, had resigned as President of the Council on March 17 and was succeeded by Ribot. Painlevé, the new Minister of War, had misgivings about the planned operation. He was the one politician to whom Pétain was close and the latter was vehement in his denunciation of the offensive, particularly as the unfavorable conditions developed.

He and Painlevé had become friendly in the spring of 1916 when the latter was Minister of Inventions and had gone to Verdun to confer with Pétain about an idea for new tracked vehicles, later called tanks. The two reached agreement, after several hours argument, and out of this grew a relationship of mutual confidence and understanding,[5] unique to Pétain because of his reserve and even suspicion where politicians were concerned. He usually made parliamentarians feel that they were not welcome at his headquarters and they tended to avoid him. Painlevé apparently found his honesty refreshing and was attracted to his strategical and tactical ideas, unglamorous but sensible.

General Micheler, who commanded the Reserve Group of Armies (G.A.R.) that would have the principle role in the offensive, had become increasingly uneasy about the grandiose expectations of his superior, Nivelle, and of his subordinate, General Mangin, who commanded the Sixth Army and who enjoyed the close confidence of Nivelle. He began to speak quite openly of his lack of faith in the operation, apparently to everyone but Nivelle. On March 28 Painlevé summoned Micheler to Paris, to discuss the offensive, and found him opposed to Nivelle's plans and of the opinion that a breakthrough could not be achieved. He did, however, feel that some kind of offensive action should be taken, in order to retain the initiative, and he did not recommend, in answer to a direct question, that the offensive be abandoned.

On April 1, 1917, Painlevé visited Pétain's headquarters and spent most of the afternoon talking to him. Pétain was more emphatic than Micheler in his opposition to the offensive and he convinced the War Minister of the danger of disaster. He was aware that great stocks of artillery shells had been gathered for the preliminary bombardment

---

[5] Paul Painlevé, "Le Maréchal Pétain au Maroc," *Les Annales Politiques et Littéraires* (August 2, 1925), 121. According to this article Pétain was very influential in the development of French tanks during World War I.

but the plans were to pound all the German positions all the way back to the fourth position and such a scattering of shellfire over an immense acreage would only succeed in sprinkling the German defenses. There would not be enough concentration of artillery fire on the vital first two positions.

In answer to Painlevé's question as to what should be done, the general said that any idea of a breakthrough should be definitely abandoned and all guns now trained on scattered targets should be trained on the first two German positions. The attack still would be a costly one and its success would be limited to taking the first two German positions but it would hurt the enemy and it could be a tactical victory.[6]

On the following day Pétain and Franchet d'Espèrey (Northern Army Group) had dinner with Painlevé in Paris. The Minister of War had intended to invite Ribot, President of the Council of Ministers, but Pétain objected that it would appear that he was engaged in a campaign to undermine Nivelle if he should meet the Premier directly. After dinner Painlevé called to his house two members of the cabinet, Albert Thomas (Armament) and Admiral Lacaze (Navy) and Pétain repeated to them his objections to the operation. He said that they risked using up all the French reserves in a single battle, that they certainly would be unable to penetrate the German second and third positions, and that it was foolhardy to count on the strategic exploitation of a breakthrough.[7]

Thomas was upset by Pétain's views and objected, "But then are we not going to end the war?"

Pétain replied, "No, we are not going to end the war but isn't that better than ending it by a defeat?"

Thomas's anguished question was significant for it seems that Nivelle owed his position, in part at least, to his promises to a war-weary France of a quick victory. The country was tired of the war and even before the April 1917 disaster there were signs that civilian morale was low. The lassitude extended to the army and worried commanders already saw the germs of indiscipline.[8] The French nation, military and civil, was near to a crisis in morale before Nivelle's grandiose scheme; the appointment of Nivelle, and his plan to end

---

[6] Brig.-Gen. E. L. Spears, *Prelude To Victory* (London, 1939), 345, 346.
[7] Serrigny, 119; Raymond Poincaré, *Au Service de la France* (Paris, 1932), IX, 99, 106, 107.
[8] See Fayolle, 191; also Spears, 66, 68, 102, 103. Nivelle told the British liaison officer that they must win the war in 1917 because he did not think that the French army could last for another twelve months.

the war quickly, were answers to what the nation wanted. The morale of the army was near a breaking point even without Nivelle's failure; he was merely the occasion for it.

By the next day, April 3, Ribot had been informed of Pétain's statements of the night before and he passed them on to President Poincaré. Pétain informed Nivelle of what had taken place so as not to appear to be conspiring in secret against the commander in chief but Nivelle was angry at what he considered an unwarranted governmental interference in military matters and at the Minister of War's communicating with his subordinates. Since he was doing the same thing in going over Micheler's head to confer with Mangin his complaints sound somewhat hollow.

On the same day Painlevé had Nivelle come to Paris to confer with himself, Ribot and three ministers—Thomas, Lacaze and Maginot (Colonies), the latter a friend and supporter of the general. Nivelle was bitter about his subordinates' complaints but in response to Painlevé's questioning he assured the ministers that his plans would lead to a quick breakthrough, within forty-eight hours, followed by a strategic exploitation. This attack was not going to be another Somme, he promised; it would not be a costly battle of attrition.

On April 5 at a War Committee meeting Painlevé alarmed the government leaders by describing Pétain's and other officers' objections to the offensive and by declaring that under the influence of the "Young Turks" there was a danger of throwing not only the attacking armies but also the reserves into an abyss. With the entry of the United States into the war imminent one should hold on until the American forces arrive; this was no time for a "va tout," he declared. It was decided that the War Committee, Poincaré, Ribot, Painlevé, Thomas and Lacaze should meet the next day with Nivelle and the army group commanders (Micheler, Franchet d'Espèrey, Pétain and de Castelnau) for a showdown.

The meeting took place at 10:00 A.M. on April 6—the day that the United States formally declared war upon Germany—at Compiègne station in the presidential train. Painlevé led the discussion, in a strained and embarrassed atmosphere. Nivelle was bitter and irritated, feeling that his subordinates had let him down and that the government leaders were interfering in matters not within their province.

He repeated his assurances of a strategic breakthrough but his subordinates were less optimistic. De Castelnau had recently returned from a mission to Russia and pleaded that he had been away and therefore could not offer an opinion, although he must have had one.

D'Espèrey said that the German defenses were very strong and one must not expect too much of the forthcoming offensive. Micheler nervously said that they could penetrate the first and second German positions, and perhaps deeper, but could not achieve a great breakthrough on the scale envisaged by Nivelle.

When it was Pétain's turn to speak he proved to be the strongest critic of Nivelle's plan. The other generals were either awed by the gravity of the moment or were reluctant to criticize Nivelle at an official meeting; their outspoken criticisms of the proposed offensive in private were now greatly toned down. Pétain said that a strategic breakthrough was impossible; the French did not possess the means to effect it. Even if, by some miracle, the French troops did break through the German lines there were not enough reserves available to exploit the victory. If the weather were good and if the attack were carefully planned the French forces might take the first two enemy positions, but the front chosen for the attack was a poor one and the operation, even if a limited success, would be a costly one, at a time when they could not afford unnecessary losses.

Before Pétain could go on Nivelle interrupted him rudely and in an excited tone repeated many of his previous arguments. The commander in chief cited Napoleon's experiences to bolster his arguments and in his excitement confused his historical facts, which Pétain later described with amusement to his chief of staff. Rising from his seat Nivelle at last played the card which perhaps he should have used days before when the government began to question his decisions: he offered to resign. Painlevé and Poincaré hastened to calm him and to refuse his resignation, assuring him that they had confidence in his judgment.

The government officials were in a difficult position. They were not military technicians and if they had halted the offensive which the commander in chief had declared firmly would be a great victory, they would have left themselves open to severe criticism in the future, perhaps for having lost an opportunity to end the war; and a desperate desire to end the war was a deep and overriding consideration.

Nivelle's army group commanders were not a great help to the government, nor could they have been in their subordinate positions. The decision and the responsibility were Nivelle's and the government leaders had either to accept his resignation or his plans, and they chose the latter. They cannot be blamed for their decision even though in retrospect the other alternative seems the better judgment. To accept Nivelle's resignation was to accept the Pétain thesis of a long, drawn out war and it must have seemed desirable to give Nivelle his chance, particularly in view of the latter's confidence in a quick victory. The temptation of Nivelle's promises was too great, and Pétain's alternative too grim.

Nivelle did promise that if the operation were not successful in achieving a breakthrough within three or four days it would be halted, a promise that was not kept when the time came but which served to appease the government leaders for the moment. Pétain objected that such a halt would not be in time to cut their losses and that an operation in full swing could not be halted that quickly; there would be too many other factors to consider. The events proved him to be right.

The meeting ended with everyone unhappy and dissatisfied. Poincaré invited everyone to lunch in his train but even a presidential meal was not enough to ease the strained atmosphere. Since it was Good Friday a double lunch was served: fish for the practicing Catholics and meat for those who were not. For the ministers fish on Friday, in company with generals, could be an embarrassing incident to explain in some future political debate. It is not recorded which lunch Pétain chose.

In the days that followed Pétain saw nothing in the preparations for the offensive which allayed his fears; quite the contrary. He felt that the whole conduct of the war, military and civil, left much to be desired. In a long conversation with the writer Henry Bordeaux, at his headquarters at Châlons on April 10th, Pétain expressed his fears regarding Nivelle's plans. He expected a small, limited success—one which could not be justified by its cost in casualties. The offensive planned by Joffre would have been all right, given the concurrence of the Russians and the Italians, but now all this was changed. With the Americans in the war the French should mark time and give the United States time to send strong support.

He told Bordeaux that the French government wanted to end the war quickly, and for that reason was relying on Nivelle; he felt that this kind of thinking, which sought the easy way out, was the result of France's electoral system and the easy promises of politicians. From a military point of view France should avoid costly operations and should conserve her effectives. When the treaty ending the war was signed France must have a strong army and a numerous population to make French influence felt. "A victory which would leave us weakened to the point of not being able to exploit it would become useless," he declared.[9]

Pétain had the usual prejudices of the French professional officer

---

[9] Henry Bordeaux, *Histoire d'une vie* (Paris, 1959), VI, 57–59,

against the wartime government. He told Bordeaux that France had too many people governing her, too many parliamentarians, too many ministers, too many committees. He said that France should have a three-man government, a sort of triumvirate. In the light of these statements, as well as of similar ones for which he was well known, it is difficult to see how he had the reputation, in post-war years, of being a "republican" general.

On April 11 the French artillery bombardment on the Chemin des Dames front began and on April 16 the attack took place. The Germans were thoroughly prepared. They knew the time and place of the attack, through observation of preparations which were not at all concealed and through captured documents. The weather was rainy and cold, bringing misery to the French troops exposed for weeks in the open, and hampering French artillery and aviation. The attack was a dismal and costly failure from the start..

Pétain's subsidiary attack east of Rheims on the 17th, with Anthoine's Fourth Army, on the Moronvilliers front, was successful in taking all its initial objectives. The enemy apparently did not expect the extension of the offensive to the east of Rheims. But the Fifth Army on his left, as part of the main assault, had not taken its objectives, particularly the heights of Brimont, and his flank was not secured for his further advance. Pétain then planned to halt and consolidate the captured terrain; a new advance would require a methodical preparation. Nivelle, however, ordered him to continue his advance.

Nivelle had by the 18th seen his plans for a quick breakthrough fail and in the days to follow he modified his plans. In order to profit by Pétain's success he ordered the Fifth Army, unable to break through northward, to change its axis of attack to the northeast of Rheims, while the Fourth Army would attack toward the northwest; the converging actions thus disengaging Rheims, which was dominated by German guns. But the initiative was lost; the Germans had by now assembled strong forces in the area and even a limited and modified offensive had little chance of important success.[10]

The government had been following events closely and anxiously and by April 23 there was serious alarm in Paris at Nivelle's conduct of the operation. The full extent of the disaster was not yet known but it was clear from the information available, magnified by rumor, that the operation was a costly failure. From April 16 to April 23 French losses in the battle were 117,000, including 32,000 dead. Every-

---

[10] See *Les Armées françaises* . . . , Tome V, Vol. I, 689–712; also Serrigny, 122–124.

where the enemy second positions remained intact and at many points the first positions were not taken.[11] The government could not insist that the commander in chief honor his promise to halt his unsuccessful operation because of the effect such an action would have had on their British allies.

The British Arras offensive, launched on April 9, had been at first strikingly successful, with the taking of Vimy Ridge. Haig wanted to follow up his advantage and Lloyd George supported him. On April 21 the British Prime Minister conferred with Ribot, Painlevé and Nivelle and got them to agree to continue the French offensive in order to draw off German reserves from Haig's front.[12] Nivelle's persistance in his attacks, at this point at least, had the concurrence of his government and was strongly desired by the British. But his action now was limited, local, and a supporting one for the British, and the ambitious scheme for a grand and decisive victory was gone.

On the 25th Nivelle learned that Pétain, in the new attacks ordered by the commander in chief, had given objectives to the Fourth Army which were more limited than the two had previously agreed upon. When requested to explain, Pétain told his superior that the changes were the result of a study of the difficulties of the terrain made by himself and General Anthoine. A chastened Nivelle did not insist. The attack in any case failed with heavy losses.[13]

On April 27 a Major Heilbronner from the War Ministry visited Pétain's headquarters to get the latter's opinion, on the operation still in progress. He said that it had been decided in Paris to replace Nivelle but that Poincaré wanted to wait for a local success in order to hide from public opinion the magnitude of the disaster. We have no record of the rest of Heilbronner's conversation with the general but it is likely that he informed Pétain that he would succeed Nivelle as commander of the French armies in France. Painlevé had no need to send an officer to find out what Pétain's opinion was of the offensive; he knew well enough; and it does not appear likely that the emissary would tell Pétain of his commander's dismissal before Nivelle himself were informed unless Pétain were to be his successor.

That afternoon Nivelle came to see Pétain. The strain was beginning to show on Nivelle and he appeared to be overwhelmed by his

---

[11] Henry Bidou et al., La Grande Guerre, Vol. IX of Histoire de France Contemporaine, Ernest Lavisse, ed., 256.

[12] Lord Maurice Hankey, The Supreme Command, 1914–1918 (London, 1961), Vol. II, 624. Later, when British casualties began to mount, Lloyd George began to change his mind.

[13] Les Armées françaises . . . , Tome V, Vol. I, 745–754.

misfortune. He had come to offer Pétain a post close to him as his chief of staff, an offer which the latter promptly refused. The offer in any case illustrated how dramatically the validity of Pétain's military theories had been vindicated by events. Nivelle had dinner with him that evening, apparently still unaware that his dismissal had been decided upon.

Pétain was accompanied most of the next day by the English journalist and military analyst, Colonel Repington. He endeavored to convince the influential *Times* correspondent of the soundness of his views, an important consideration for the General since the British were not favorably inclined toward him because of what they considered his excessive defensive-mindedness. In fact the British General Henry Wilson had already irritated War Minister Painlevé by giving him an unsolicited estimation of Nivelle's high qualities and a correspondingly low one of Pétain. Repington became a firm supporter of Pétain and not only wrote a flattering article on the French General which duly appeared in the *Times* but also wrote to Lloyd George and Sir William Robertson, C.I.G.S. to praise him warmly.[14]

On April 29 Pétain was summoned to Paris where he conferred first with Painlevé, then with Ribot. The latter told him, after requesting that he be discreet about what was said, that he was being made Chief of the Army General Staff, with the promise to succeed Nivelle as commander in chief in the near future. Pétain was to be counselor to the government on the technical value of the plans of the high command; his ascension over Nivelle was therefore already implicit in his functions. The government did not dare relieve Nivelle too quickly for fear of what enemy propaganda would make of it. Such a dismissal would be an admission of how serious the defeat had been.

The British were by no means alone in their objections to the proposed change in the French high command. Painlevé was considerably hampered in his attempt to put France's military effort in Pétain's hands by opposition from cabinet members, members of the parliament, and even from the President of the Republic. The British objections were based on their fear of a slackening in the French offensive effort while French political leaders saw in Pétain a threat to constitutional government.

Pétain had made no secret of his dislike of the politicians and his disapproval of the way France was governed. He had made comments to President Poincaré himself which were highly critical of the government and his authoritarian views were notorious in parliamentary

---

[14] C. à C. Repington, *The First World War* (New York, 1920), I, 540–549.

circles. When Painlevé proposed the nomination of Pétain to the high command at a cabinet meeting he encountered lively opposition from Maginot and Malvy (Interior). Maginot, an ex-sergeant of infantry who had been badly wounded early in the war, threw his crutch on the table to emphasize his protest and Malvy was only a little more restrained in denouncing the peril that Pétain represented to the republic.[15]

Despite the opposition Painlevé had his way; there was really no other logical choice. Nivelle obviously had to go; he no longer had the requisite moral authority in the army even if the political leaders wanted to keep him. And Foch was still under the cloud of his Somme failure. Pétain was popular in the army and his military theories had been proved sound; he was the only leader in whom the army would have confidence at the moment. It was plain enongh to the government leaders that Pétain as commander of the French armies represented less of a danger to French political liberties than did a loss of the war.

The post of chief of the army general staff had been a dormant one for years. Prior to 1911 the government had carefully kept separate the functions of commander in chief of the army and that of the chief of the general staff. The commander in chief-designate (vice-president of the Higher War Council) had charge of high-level planning, maneuvers, staff-journeys, and the like, but had little control over promotions, appointments and other personnel matters. The latter functions were performed by a military man filling the post of chief of the general staff under the direction of the minister of war. In this way the parliament, to whom the minister was responsible, kept control of the organization and personnel of the army.

In 1911 Minister of War Messimy decided that it was desirable to give the commander in chief-designate a direct control of the personnel who would, upon mobilization, come under his orders. This was accomplished by attributing to the commander in chief-designate the functions formerly exercised by the chief of the general staff, with the minister of war still the final authority. The military man who held the post, General Joffre, was considered fairly safe from a "republican" point of view. When the armies took the field in 1914 Joffre automatically became their commander and the post of chief of the general staff ceased to exist until Pétain's appointment in 1917. Its functions then were vague and Pétain immediately moved to define them as strongly as he could.

He arrived in Paris on May 1, 1917 and was installed at 4 *bis,* boule-

---

[15] Abel Ferry, *Les Carnets secrets (1914–1918)* (Paris, 1957), 175–177.

vard des Invalides in the magnificent Empire office that Joffre had occupied before the war. He brought with him a plan for the powers of his new office which he submitted to Painlevé on May 3. The War Minister must have been astounded when he read it because Pétain planned that the Chief of the General Staff should take general command of the war effort. He would command the allied armies in France and in the Balkans. He would no longer be responsible to the Minister of War but would answer directly to the War Committee of which he would be a member. His position would be at least on a cabinet level, yet he would not be answerable to the parliament.[16]

It is doubtful whether Pétain expected this remarkable document to be accepted; he probably submitted it as a statement of the kind of wartime organization he thought would be most effective to win the war. In any case Painlevé lost no time in defining Pétain's role as he had explained it on April 29, that of a subordinate of the War Minister and a technical counselor to the government. Far from expecting that the military high command would assume increased powers, the government from this time on maintained a closer control of military operations. Until April 1917 the government had controlled only the "general direction" of the war; that is, political, diplomatic and economic questions, leaving the high command almost independent in military matters. From now on the government took a closer control of the military direction of the war.[17]

Nivelle's troops were still battering at the German positions on the Aisne front. A breakthrough was no longer to be thought of but Nivelle hoped desperately for local successes to redeem himself; and there was still the question of continuing pressure on the Germans in order to assist the British Arras offensive, although the latter had, after its initial success, reduced itself to the usual bitter and useless slugging match. Nivelle planned an offensive by the Fifth Army on May 1, an attack which included among its objectives the heights of Brimont. By now some of Nivelle's subordinate commanders were finding means of complaining privately to the government about these useless and costly attacks. The government leaders were alarmed at Nivelle's plans and Painlevé intervened directly.

On the evening of April 29 (the day of Pétain's appointment) Painlevé telephoned Nivelle and suspended the attack "provisionally," pending an interview between Pétain and Nivelle. Painlevé's letter of

---

[16] See Serrigny, 131, 132.
[17] See General Laure, "Le Commandement en Chef des armées françaises, du 15 mai 1917 à l'armistice," *Revue militaire française*, Vol. 61, 1936 (Paris, 1936), 6, 7.

May 1 to Nivelle clarified his order and made it apparent that Pétain had the authority to decide on the proposed attack. After an interview with Pétain, Nivelle telegraphed on May 1 to Micheler to carry out the attack on May 2 but with very limited objectives and excluding the massif of Brimont. By May 4 the attack had failed with heavy losses; if Brimont had been included in its objectives the losses would have been even heavier. After the war some military critics complained that Painlevé's interference in the Aisne offensive had caused its collapse and they referred principally to his order suspending the Brimont operation. These complaints were quite unjustified; it was Pétain's influence which put the halter on Nivelle on April 29 and his intervention to some extent saved the Fifth Army from yet another useless bloodletting.

On May 4 an important British-French meeting took place in Paris to clarify the joint objectives of the two allies and the methods by which these objectives would be sought. In the morning the military leaders of both countries—Robertson, Haig, Pétain and Nivelle—met. Pétain was aware of the British uneasiness regarding his military theories and he met the issue squarely. In fact he dominated the meeting.

Pétain told the conference that he was not "defensive-minded," that he had a taste for the offensive as much as anyone. He was, however, opposed to ambitious offensives aimed at breakthroughs, with great strategic objectives. This kind of operation had cost them dearly in the past and had never succeeded. The allies must be realistic; in their desire to end the war quickly there was a danger that they might prolong it.

He advocated that the allied armies on the western front should remain on the offensive but should seek tactical victories which would consume the enemy reserves. They should attack with limited objectives, supported by large artillery concentrations; the aim should be to kill Germans, not primarily to conquer terrain. This kind of carefully planned attack would always succeed, with relatively small cost to the attackers, and would gradually wear out the enemy. When the German reserves were exhausted the time would come for the big offensives. The war therefore would not be a short one and they must prepare for a long-term affair. This would not, however, prevent them from utilizing whatever circumstances might arise to shorten its duration.[18]

---

[18] Bordeaux, VI, 79, 80; [David] Lloyd George, "L'Offensive de Nivelle," *La Revue de Paris* (August 1934), 837, 838; Hankey, 626–628; *Les Armées françaises* . . . , Tome V, Vol. I, 787–789.

Pétain must have been persuasive because he won the British generals over. In the afternoon a larger conference took place which included the government leaders, Lloyd George, Ribot and Painlevé. Robertson read a memorandum of what had been decided upon unanimously by the generals in the morning: they were of the opinion that it was essential to continue offensive operations on the western front but they were equally of the opinion that it was no longer a question of breaking through; they must attack relentlessly with limited objectives and with the fullest use of artillery. The plans for a great strategic victory in 1917 were no longer in effect because the situation had changed since they were drawn up.

The Pétain policy had prevailed.

The government leaders accepted the conclusions of their military commanders. Lloyd George was very concerned about the crisis caused to his country by the submarine menace and wanted to be sure that the French were not going to relax into a defensive attitude. He was, however, impressed by Pétain's method, which coincided with his own ideas. Ribot assured the Prime Minister that the French policy remained an offensive one but that his country had to guard against heavy losses to conserve her depleted effectives. What neither he nor Pétain could know was that the mutinies which soon after broke out in the French army would effectively curtail the French offensive effort for many months.

On May 11 Nivelle was called before the War Committee and was asked to resign. Not only did he refuse but in justifying himself he tried to shift the blame to certain of his subordinates. This made a poor impression on those members of the council who heretofore had been sympathetic to him. Nivelle had already sought scapegoats among his subordinates and had dismissed certain of them against whom he was particularly irate, including General Mangin, the Sixth Army commander who had boasted that he would sleep in Laon on the night of D-day, April 16. On May 15, 1917, the government announced that Pétain had replaced Nivelle as commander of the Armies of the North and Northeast. Foch succeeded Pétain as Chief of the General Staff.

The Aisne offensive was grinding to a halt. Before his dismissal Nivelle had succeeded in taking Craonne and part of the Chemin des Dames. These successes came too late and at too high a cost to justify the whole operation, and compared to the original objectives of the offensive they were minuscule.

Pétain wanted to continue pressure on the enemy to retain the German reserves on the Chemin des Dames front and to rectify his front-line positions which had been left in a ragged and precarious condition by the broken-down offensive of his predecessor; but the French army was in no condition for further offensive action. On June 3rd General Maistre, who had succeeded Mangin as commander of the Sixth Army, when ordered to resume the attack on the Chemin des Dames informed Pétain that the Sixth Army would have to "be stabilized on its [present] front for some time. Under present conditions we must have no illusions: we would risk seeing the men [refuse] to leave the trenches [to attack]."[19] Pétain agreed and let Maistre give up all plans for offensive action, and other operations as well were called off in response to the pleas of their commanders. For the next several months the French army was partly immobilized by mutiny, largely weakened by indiscipline, and wholly permeated with depression and war-weariness. That Pétain patched up this broken instrument so that it could fight on through 1918 put his countrymen and their allies greatly in his debt.

---

[19] Lt.-Col. Henri Carré, *Les Grandes Heures du général Pétain* (Paris, 1952), 171; also *Les Armées françaises*, Tome V, Vol. II, 422.

6

Mutiny

At no point in the course of World War I was the military effort of the Allies in greater danger than in the spring of 1917. Even the German sledgehammer blows of 1918, although cause for great anxiety, were not sufficient to bring the Allied cause as close to disaster as did the breakdown in the moral fibre of the French Army in 1917—the army upon which had fallen in large measure the brunt of the war and which was the main "sword" of the Allies. When General Pétain assumed command of the army sections of it were in open revolt with many more to follow; and the whole structure was threatening to collapse in either passive or active mutiny. It was perhaps the greatest feat of Pétain's career that he took command of a beaten army in full contact with the enemy, rejuvenated it, revived its faith in itself and above all in its leaders, and put it back on its feet in time for the tests of 1918.

If the offensive of April 16 was the "worst kept secret of the war" the crisis of morale which followed it was the best kept. It was a matter of strategic life or death that the Germans should not know of the vital weakness besetting their principal enemy and extraordinary measures were taken to prevent leakage of the information. The Germans inevitably learned that some elements of the French army were affected by mutinies but not until after the war did they know the full truth.[1]

The secondary reason for a shrouding of the facts, that of national pride, would persist into the postwar years. It is more difficult to

[1] Erich von Ludendorff, *Ludendorff's Own Story* (New York, 1919), II, 28.

obtain a complete and detailed picture of the situation than perhaps of any other event of the war. The French army was the only army on the western front to mutiny in the field during the war, but it was the army with the most reason to do so. It was perhaps unfortunate for Pétain's fame that one of his greatest services to France should be in connection with an episode which the nation would have preferred to forget.

The immediate cause of the collapse was the Chemin des Dames offensive of April and May 1917, an operation which had been held out to the troops as the culmination of their efforts and the beginning of the end of the war. Its failure led to despair and disillusion, followed by rage and rebellion among the combat troops. But one abortive offensive is not sufficient to break the spirit of a brave army; the principal factor underlying the moral breakdown was simply a general and profound war weariness, resulting from three years of savage conflict marked by a succession of seemingly useless offensives.

By January 1917 the morale of the French soldiers was poor. They were discouraged and despaired of ever winning the war. Then in March and early April their morale improved, judging by their correspondence. Their mail was censored and the high command was able, through the postal control system, to keep fairly well informed on the general state of army morale. The extravagantly optimistic prognostications made by Nivelle's headquarters with regard to the April offensive lifted spirits; "the offensive that is going to win the war" gave the men involved a feeling of elation which had been lacking since the early days of the war, particularly in view of the promises made to them that their victory would not be a costly one. The Nivelle "method" guaranteed a relatively bloodless operation.

The cruel facts of the April 16th fiasco were all the more brutal to the participants because of the contrast with the promises; they seemed to illustrate the futility of their efforts. There would never be a breakthrough; it was impossible to win a military victory, they thought. They had done all that brave men could do and yet could achieve nothing. The war must end.

The new commander in chief, in his reports to the minister of war in June, was inclined to put the blame for the disorders on the civilian home front and the civilian government. This was partly because he believed that this was the truth of the situation and partly because his military pride made it difficult for him to blame the army for what were, in the eyes of a professional officer, disgraceful weaknesses. He blamed socialist agitation and pacifist propaganda in the interior, which he demanded be suppressed. He was particularly indignant against the minister of the interior, Malvy, whom the army leaders believed to be too indulgent toward defeatists and pacifists and perhaps even guilty of treason. Some of the press, Pétain said, was too critical of the war effort and copies of the newspapers which cried out for a negotiated peace, some of which subsequently proved to be subsidized by the German secret service, reached the front where they had a deplorable effect on the combat troops.

Much of what the commander in chief said of the home front was true; soldiers on leave were influenced by the pacifist propaganda, which they brought back to the front with them. Another problem was the news from Russia, where, the soldiers read in the press, the Russian troops were electing their own officers and had otherwise escaped the firm bonds of military discipline. The two Russian brigades serving with the French on the western front were a local source of infection, although they were speedily removed by the authorities. But the root of the problem was not defeatism or pacifism on the home front or in the army; as far as these concerned the army they were symptoms rather than causes. The heart of the problem, as War Minister Painlevé ascertained through independent investigation, was the deep-seated and justified bitterness of the soldiers against the military direction of the war which seemingly demanded endless sacrifices in blood and suffering to no purpose. By April 1917 over a million French soldiers had died, not to mention the many more wounded, and the military situation had not changed appreciably since September 1914.

The troops and combat officers felt a deep bitterness toward a military method "in which the sacrifice of men was out of proportion to the results obtained." They felt that higher headquarters were too distant, both literally and figuratively, from reality and that their offensives were not prepared properly with an on-the-spot study of the terrain or with adequate artillery preparation.[2] They were being hurled at unbroken barbed-wire entanglements, unsilenced machine gun nests, and subjected to inadequately answered artillery bombardments; those who were left could see no end to it and no longer any reason for it. They had taken all that flesh and blood could be expected to endure.

There were other complaints as well, less vital and less lethal but nevertheless valid. The food at the front was poor; for a nation that prides itself on its cuisine the French soldier of 1914–17 was badly fed. The French army still had not adopted the rolling-kitchens which the Germans had used since 1914 to bring hot food to the combat infantry. Even when the *poilus* were out of the line, in what were

---

[2] Paul Painlevé, *Comment j'ai nommé Foch et Pétain* (Paris, 1923), 153–175; also Jean de Pierrefeu, *G.Q.G. Secteur I* (Paris, 1922), II, 15 *et seq.*

supposedly rest areas or training camps, the food was poor and their quarters squalid, cold and insect-ridden. Nivelle, the artilleryman, and Joffre, the engineer, both *Polytechniciens*, did not have the infantry officer's concern for the welfare of his men; this, the first concern of a good infantry officer, had been bred into men like Pétain since Saint-Cyr.

The soldiers also bitterly criticized the furlough system. They did not receive regularly the furloughs which the law allowed them, in order to see their families and get away from the rigors of the front for a time. Prior to the April offensive most leaves were cancelled so as to have as many men as possible available for the attack. The men sometimes did get home leave but not often and not regularly; and this was a prime source of complaint as well as a contributory cause to the low birth rate in France during the war. Twenty years later the lack of effectives available to the French army in the face of the growing Nazi menace would testify to the short-sightedness of the high command and the government.

An important factor in the moral breakdown of the troops, although this was one which the investigators did not advance, was the fact that three years of heavy casualties had skimmed off the cream of the nation's manhood and the new drafts were now scraping the bottom of the manpower barrel. This is not to say that there were no longer many good men left in the army, which would be an unfair statement; but warfare is sometimes the converse of the survival of the fittest, with the better men usually the first to fall, and the armies could not muster the same self-sacrificing zeal in 1917 that they had in the early war years. Much of the best of the nation's manhood was dead or seriously injured; the survivors were veterans but what they had gained in experience they lacked in spirit.

The grievances of the soldiers were so deep-seated that the revolts, having once broken out, spread with great rapidity. Although completely spontaneous the eruptions occurred in so many different sectors as to illustrate a general prevalence of discontent. Various dates are sometimes given for the beginning of the mutinies but the first serious incident took place on April 29 when members of an infantry battalion refused to obey their officers; then on May 4 two regiments of infantry were affected and on May 16, the day after Pétain assumed command of the armies, a battalion of chasseurs rebelled.[3] These were scattered cases, however, and it was not until May 25 that the

---

[3] Ministère de la Guerre, État-major de l'Armée—Service historique, *Les Armées françaises dans la Grande Guerre,* Tome V, Vol. II, 192; also, for Pétain's own account, Sir Edward Spears, *Two Men Who Saved France* (London, 1966), 67–128.

mutiny began in earnest; then for more than two weeks, until June
10, the army ceased to be an effective fighting force as regiments in all
sectors refused to carry out orders. If the Germans had attacked during
that dangerous period they might well have achieved a decisive victory. After June 10 instances of active, collective revolt tended to di-
minish, but the crisis was not over until autumn.

The incidents for the most part took the form of infantry units
refusing to return to the front after a period of rest or, if they eventually agreed to go back into the line, refusing to make any more attacks,
although they often did say that they were willing to hold the trenches
against German attack. What kind of a defense they would have put
up in the event of an enemy offensive remains problematic; there was
an incident late in June when the Germans did attack and scored a
local success near Verdun when two complete battalions of French infantry gave themselves up without a fight. The remainder of the regiment susequently was dissolved by the French high command and its
personnel scattered among other units.[4]

The mutineers for the most part continued respectful to their officers and there were few acts of violence, since the officers with whom
they came into immediate contact usually shared their dangers and in
fact many officers below the regimental level sympathized with them.
There was, however, an incident in which a general was shot and
hospitalized. Curiously enough the mutinies began in units which had
not taken a direct part in the attacks of April 16—in the Tenth Army,
which had been held in reserve to be ready to exploit the breakthrough
that was expected in one or two days after D-day. Since this army was
the army of exploitation for a victory that never occurred perhaps the
disillusionment there was greater than among the actual sufferers of
the first attacks; for the latter were stunned and shocked by their
bloody repulse and could expect to be relieved soon because of their
fatigue and losses, while the former would have to go into the line to
continue a battle that everyone knew was lost. The battered units of
April 16 would become mutinous later, when ordered back into the
line, and the Sixth Army, formerly commanded by General Mangin
and badly mauled in the offensive, became the most seriously affected
by the rebellion.

In one instance a village was taken over by mutineers and fortified;
they set up a "soviet," named a leader and requisitioned supplies from
the local stores. Their delegates demanded higher pay, regular leaves,
and assurances that there would be no more assaults on enemy posi-

---

[4] See Maréchal Fayolle, *Cahiers secrets de la Grande Guerre* (Paris, 1964),
229.

tions before his trenches and barbed wire had been destroyed by careful artillery preparation; this last request is significant not only for its
reasonableness but for its indication that the troops would continue
to fight if properly led.

In another case a regiment withdrew into a wood and refused to
give themselves up. Another crowd of mutineers marched on the
Soissons railroad station with the intention of seizing a train, proceeding to Paris, and then to march on the Chamber of Deputies to
present their demands. They were turned back by a regiment of loyal
cuirassiers who trained machine guns on them—the cavalry because of
its traditions, its high proportion of career soldiers and officers and,
above all, its relatively low casualties due to a lack of cavalry action in
a trench war, remained, for the most part, loyal and trustworthy (although one regiment of dragoons did mutiny) and were used extensively to repress disorder in the mutinous infantry. Infantry units
would not have fired on other infantry; as the Swiss mercenary pike-
men of the sixteenth century would say, "Dog doesn't eat dog."

A serious incident concerned the near-lynching by mutineers of
three gendarmes whom they beat half to death and hanged by the
legs from a tree after the policemen had tried to rescue a medical
officer who was being attacked. Fortunately ugly incidents of this
nature were rare. Other units presented letters signed by all their
members demanding that an honorable peace be concluded at once
and throughout the army there were innumerable incidents, involving
stone throwing, window breaking, shouting "Vive la paix" and singing the Internationale.

Conditions were particularly bad on the trains and in railroad sta-
tions, where men going and returning on leave—and there were many
of these after Pétain instituted a liberal furlough system—assaulted
railroad personnel and military police, broke windows, and even de-
railed a locomotive, thus extending disorders into the interior as far
as Nantes and Bordeaux. On June 6 the President of the Republic
was warned against a proposed trip to a ceremony at Rheims, for
fear that he would be stoned by soldiers. He did make the trip, however, unstoned.[5]

If the war were to continue and if France were not to be defeated;
if the invader were to be forced to evacuate French territory, the armies
had to be rejuvenated and the principal concern of the government
and the high command was how best to accomplish this. Draconian

[5] Raymond Poincaré, *Au Service de la France* (Paris, 1932), IX, 144–188;
Les Armées françaises . . ., Tome V, Vol. II, 193, 194; Lt.-Col. Henri Carré,
Les Grandes heures du général Pétain (Paris, 1952), 101 *et seq.*

measures were not the answer, the government concluded, and General Pétain was in agreement. Before the mutinies were over twenty-one chasseur battalions were affected by it and if the élite of the French infantry were unwilling to continue to fight under present conditions obviously something was very wrong. Many commanders demanded instant and rigorous application of the death penalty, universally applicable to troops who mutiny in the face of the enemy and particularly applicable in this case when the security and future of the nation were involved; immediate and severe repressive measures seemed to many officers to be required. But Pétain thought otherwise and the government would not have permitted drastic steps in any case.

Admirers of Pétain after the war made much of his clemency and forebearance but the fact was that Painlevé and Poincaré were in constant and close touch with the situation and made it quite clear to the high command that the men in revolt were not only soldiers but were Frenchmen and were to be treated accordingly. The War Committee was convinced that the crisis was a result of military blunders, not governmental mistakes; and in this case, at least, they were right. France owes much to the commander in chief who nursed the broken army back to health but all praise too should go to Minister of War Painlevé, the worried little mathematician who found himself in a position of political responsibility at a crucial moment in French history, a man who rose above himself, anquished and hesitating but in whom crisis brought out character and a measure of wisdom.

Pétain probably was the only general in the French army who could have restored order. He was respected and admired throughout the army as a man whose tactical views had proven sound; and he was known for his concern for the lives of his troops—in contrast to many other generals like Mangin and Nivelle whose high rank was reputed to have been bought at the price of countless lives—and as a man who had risen in the army through merit and without favor. He had watched, since 1915, the progressive deterioration of morale under conditions of faulty military doctrine and techniques against which he had been counseling since prewar days, and although his advice too often had been ignored there was now still a chance of rectifying the situation by the application of his own carefully developed ideas. Nevertheless he was not a gentle man—his whole life had been one of discipline—and if drastic repressive measures proved to be necessary he would be the one to apply them, within the latitude allowed him by the anxious civilian cabinet.

In his report to the War Minister listing the causes, as he saw them, of the mutinies, he had complained about the restrictions placed

Pétain was born in this house on April 24, 1856.

Colonel Pétain reviews troops at Arras in 1914.

Pétain as General, about 1918.

Pétain conducts an inspection at the fortified section of Verdun.

The General exchanges salutes with the British high command.

After the war Pétain was made a Marshal of France. Here he is seen as the Commander-in-Chief of the Army.

The Commander-in-Chief rides down the Champs-Elysées on November 11, 1919.

Pétain with President Alexandre Millerand.

Pétain as Chief of State of Vichy France.
Meeting with Hitler at Montoire.

The 90-year-old Marshal remains silent at his trial while his lawyer, M. Isorni, pleads his case.

Pétain's tomb at the Isle of Yeu.

upon the action of military courts-martial which lessened their severity and weakened their deterrent effect. He demanded that ring-leaders be subjected to summary courts-martial, whose sentences would be executed without delay, to serve as an example to the other soldiers and would-be mutineers. In view of the gravity of the situation the government realized that extraordinary measures would be required but they were reluctant to put this power in the hands of the high command, even if they knew that Pétain would use the power spar-ingly.

Ever since the Dreyfus case the government had insisted upon the strictest procedural rules in military trials. It had reinforced the pro-tection afforded the accused by the law of April 27, 1916, supple-mented by the decree of June 8, 1916, which gave all prisoners con-demned by military courts the right of appeal, for a review of their case and a pardon, to the President of the Republic. The commander in chief requested that this law be revoked; its application was time consuming and much of the effect of the sentences pronounced by the *Conseils de guerre* would be lost if the mutineers knew that they could delay or avoid the penalty.

In spite of Pétain's arguments the law remained in effect but to partially meet his demands the government, by a law of June 9, 1917, removed the right of appeal for a review of their cases from prisoners convicted under articles 204 and 217 of the Code of Military Justice. These articles covered the instigation of rebellion in the army and armed rebellion itself, in face of the enemy, and therefore were ap-plicable to the mutinies in progress. The idea was to shorten the time between the crime and the execution of the penalty and thereby con-tribute to the maintenance of discipline at the front. In the middle of July 1917 the instances of collective mutiny fell off sharply, thanks to Pétain's superb handling of the situation, and the government asked him to return the right of appeal and pardon to the President of the Republic, which was done.

In view of the serious nature of the crisis the number of mutineers actually put to death was remarkably low and was confined to some of the worst offenders and ringleaders. From May to November 1917 there were 412 death sentences in the armies under Pétain's com-mand. Of these the Commander in Chief commuted 219 and the chief of state—outside of the period in which Pétain was the sole authority—commuted 137. The men thus reprieved were sent to the penal colonies outside of metropolitan France, although their former comrades thought that they were shot. Of the remaining 56 prisoners one escaped and never was recaptured and 55 were shot. But the 55 unfortunates were not all mutineers: 8 were guilty of crimes of a civil nature, such as rape and murder; 25 were guilty of flagrant "collective" mutiny; and 22 were convicted of various military crimes of which a certain number were mutineers. There were, therefore, at the most, between 30 and 40 death penalties actually executed in connection with the mutinies, a small number considering the proportions of the outbreaks.[6]

These figures refer only to death penalties; there were thousands of lesser punishments of penal servitude meted out. In May the *Conseils de guerre* condemned 2,477 men, 21 of them to death, and in June, the critical month, the figure rose to 4,406, of whom 203 were condemned to death. Most of the death penalties were commuted by Pétain. In July the figures decreased and there were 59 death penalties pronounced by the military courts, most of which were commuted.

The above figures are sound and have never been seriously disputed. An event as dramatic as a modern army in revolt has given rise to many stories and rumors, such as regiments having every twentieth, tenth or even fifth man taken out of the ranks and shot. These accounts must remain "stories" as they cannot be substantiated and are undoubtedly the result of imagination and rumor. Neither the government nor the high command ever thought seriously of such drastic procedures and no execution of a death penalty took place in the army without the concurrence of the Commander in Chief.

There is even a story, with no basis in fact, that a group of 250 men were taken out into No Man's Land, left there, and subjected to artillery fire by French guns until they were dead. This story has gained fairly wide currency but it is not only untrue, it is incredible. If the high command wanted to kill 250 men there are more effective and efficient ways of doing it than by shooting at them from a distance with artillery pieces. Men who have lived through artillery bombardments of high explosives can attest to the amazement they have sometimes felt, when the fire lifts, that so many men have survived the pounding. If soldiers have taken cover it would be almost impossible for artillerymen to guarantee to kill every man, even if none of them moved; and in the case of 250 mutineers we can be assured that they would have scattered in every direction, even seeking shelter in the German lines. It is very likely that many would have escaped death.

A possible basis for this rumor might lie in one of Pétain's disciplinary measures, instituted in the French army of 1917–18, which con-

---

[6] See *Les Armées françaises* . . . , Tome V, Vol. II, 206. Also Painlevé, 144–146; Carré, 115. Pétain claimed that 30 mutineers were executed; see Spears, 103.

sisted of the formation of disciplinary companies, one for each division, to which men who otherwise would have been condemned to death or to terms of penal servitude were assigned. These companies, led by specially selected officers who were rewarded with quick promotions, were given the most difficult and dangerous missions—and if the men survived they were happy to get back to their old units.[7] General Pétain was preoccupied with a shortage of effectives and it was far from his practical nature to waste men who could be employed at the front. These companies also met the problem, common enough in a long war, of dealing with soldiers who commit crimes and deliberately seek imprisonment in order to avoid combat duty.

The sanctions and repressive measures were only the beginning of a solution to the problem of a rehabilitation of the shaken army. In former days a commander could address his troops personally and influence them by the force of his personality; Julius Caesar could persuade a mutinous legion to plead for reinstatement simply by addressing them as "citizens" instead of the customary "soldiers." But a modern commander is remote from the troops under his command and it was that remoteness which had contributed to some extent to the troubles.

Pétain could not address the whole French army but he undertook to visit personally as many units as he could, and managed to see the men of ninety divisions, which comprised the bulk of the army and even included many divisions not openly involved in the disorders. During these visits he spoke to gatherings of the officers and non-commissioned officers, and one "good" man selected by his comrades from each company. Thus in every billet and in most companies there was someone who personally had been interviewed by the Commander in Chief, an attempt, at least, to establish personal contact with all the troops.

For weeks he traveled by train and automobile, up and down the front, alternately scolding and listening to grievances, distributing decorations where deserved and discussing local problems. This was something new to the soldiers, most of whom had never seen a general above the brigade level and rarely then. They noted and the news spread, as it was supposed to, that the new Commander in Chief was taking a personal interest in the welfare of front-line soldiers, making himself personally responsible for the amelioration of conditions. Men who had looked upon themselves as forgotten cannon fodder began to regain their military pride and some measure of patriotic self-sacrifice. Actually General Pétain was merely applying

---

[7] See Brig. Gen. E. L. Spears, *Liaison, 1914* (London, 1930), 473.

to an army the same principles of concern and care for his men that he had done as a matter of course to a platoon of chasseurs when he was a second lieutenant, but it is remarkable how other generals had forgotten those elementary obligations.

As had been remarked earlier in this book the French officers, even the professional career officers, were for the most part of bourgeois or lower-class origin but had adopted the aristocratic attitudes of the old officer class, affecting a contempt for politicians, for the republic, and for the masses. Since the officers in the French army were badly paid— Pétain in 1914 as a colonel after thirty-six years service was drawing monthly the equivalent of what would be today about $450—perhaps much of their peacetime political and social frustration can be attributed to the fact that they had upper-class pretensions on *petit bourgeois* incomes, an anomaly and almost an impossibility. In wartime their contempt for the masses was easily converted into an indifference to the sufferings of the soldiers; they had not adopted the aristocratic *noblesse oblige* which would have required a real sympathy and concern for the men in their charge. They were still at heart bourgeois, nineteenth-century bourgeois, who could be as indifferent to the sufferings of the soldiers as their brothers who had gone into industry were indifferent to those of the wage earners.

The German officer, even the nonaristocratic one, manifested greater affection and concern for his men than did his French counterpart; the aristocratic traditions of the German officer class called for this concern and the German soldier as a result was treated better than the French soldier. The deprivations which the German soldier endured were due more to the British blockade than to the indifference of his leaders and he usually was not herded into battle with the unconcern for losses that French leaders seemed to have prior to Pétain's appointment to supreme command.

In interviewing the soldiers and attempting to establish a personal relationship with them, Pétain did not become overly familiar or otherwise step down from his dignity as a leader. It would have been out of character for him to do so and the veteran *poilus* would have quickly discerned the superficiality of a hearty, ear-pulling familiarity. He was as cold and distant as always, often stern and severe, although he could cajole and praise when circumstances warranted it.

Henry Bordeaux, an eyewitness of one meeting in June 1917 between the commander and a mutinous regiment, has left this account: the general walked slowly toward the troops, alone, with a dignified and even majestic attitude. He talked to them, not familiarly and not with showmanship but as man to man, and said that they had of

course reasons to complain: the war had lasted too long and it was
almost too much to endure. But it had been imposed upon France by
Germany and it had to be won. They must be patient; he was looking
to their welfare and would improve conditions, particularly regarding
food, wine, furloughs and reliefs. He guaranteed that he would not
throw them into battle without good artillery support and that he
held their lives as dearly as his own. Then he appealed, with elo-
quence, to their emotions: behind them were their wives, their children, the old people, the nation and the land. Without the soldiers
all would be lost to Germany; they must be patient and resolute and
they must believe in France and be strong as some drew their strength
from a belief in God. The witness records that the men were greatly
affected and some even moved to tears.[8]

Pétain gave orders to the army that in the future combat officers
were to be encouraged to submit their views to higher headquarters
regarding the execution of orders for combat operations. This directive was designed to meet the persistent complaint that too often headquarters far in the rear with no knowledge of local conditions insisted
on carrying out plans or movements over the protests of the executants, who could see the danger or uselessness of the orders. Thenceforth combat officers would have a hearing for their ideas, derived from
their local intelligence reports and personal knowledge of the enemy
and the terrain on their front.

Measures were taken to ease conditions of service for the soldiers:
a furlough system was established and the accumulated leaves of the
past several months, which had been cancelled to keep the maximum
number of men in the trenches for the April offensive, were reinstated.
The rationing system was reorganized with better food the object;
rolling kitchens were developed to bring hot food to the forward
units. The liquor ration was closely regulated and the sale of wine
to the troops by vendors in the Army Zone was restricted. It had been
shown that most of the serious outbreaks of rebellion had occurred
among soldiers who had been drinking too much in the rear areas,
which may be one reason why the mutinies usually took place when
the troops were out of the trenches. Behind the lines the men had
too much money in their pockets—their accumulated pay augmented
by a combat bonus—but there was little for them to do except to drink.
There had been too many civilian dispensers of cheap wine to take
advantage of their idleness and temporary affluence. Pétain arranged
a system of enforced savings for the soldiers so that some of their
accumulated pay would not be available until they went home on

---

[8] Quoted in J.-R. Tournoux, *Pétain et de Gaulle* (Paris, 1964), 58.

leave. He organized rest camps behind the lines, with clean quarters and pleasant surroundings and facilities for recreation, and units in the future would receive regular and more frequent reliefs from the trenches.

No facet of the problem went unexplored. On Pétain's staff were literary men and scholars, notably Captain Henry Bordeaux and Lieutenant Madelin, who were delegated to do intensive research to find historical precedents and the remedial measures taken in the past under similar circumstances. Madelin, in particular, was assigned to study instances of mutiny in the armies of the Revolution and the Empire.

The commander in chief believed that all the measures taken at the front to calm the unrest in the armies would be of little value unless something was done to stop the contagion spreading from the interior. He took a firm line with the government and demanded that the defeatist propaganda emanating from the Socialists, the pacifists and the strikers in the interior, whose influence reached soldiers at the front through the newspapers and soldiers returning from leave, be halted. On May 31, in reporting to the War Committee on the mutinies which were then reaching serious proportions, he firmly advised against permitting French Socialists to participate in the forthcoming international meeting at Stockholm. He said that such a participation would be construed by the army as "the equivalent of an armistice." It would not be possible to revive and maintain the fighting spirit of the army if the French Socialists were allowed by the government to go.

He linked the leaders of the mutinies to activity on the part of trade unions, particularly the well-organized and powerful General Confederation of Labor. He further warned that he would not exercise the command requested of him if they did not take the necessary measures against pacifist propaganda.

In his reports to civilian authorities Pétain always painted as black a picture as possible but in this case his alarm had some justification. The Ribot government, partly as a result of Pétain's strong representations, did refuse passports to the Socialists, much to the wrath of the Socialist deputies in the parliament. If France became committed to peace negotiations, however informal, as a result of the Stockholm conference, it probably would have been tantamount to a negotiated peace on unfavorable terms, so weary and despondent were the majority of Frenchmen, soldiers and civilians, in that bleak spring of 1917.[9]

---

[9] Poincaré, IX, 154; Jere Clemens King, *Generals and Politicians* (Los Angeles, 1951), 179, 267 (footnote 47).

The Socialists in the Chamber of Deputies were no longer imbued with the "Sacred Union" concept, born of a burst of patriotic emotion in 1914 but fallen to disillusionment in 1917. In a secret session on June 29 they challenged the government for its lenient treatment of the authors of the Chemin des Dames disaster—a military court of inquiry composed of Generals Foch, Brugère and Gouraud later in the year let their fellow generals off leniently, as might have been expected—while enlisted men were being shot for mutiny. The French Socialists were highly suspicious of Pétain, whom they believed to be politically reactionary. One Socialist deputy, Pierre Laval, whose destiny would bring him close to Pétain many years and one war later, expressed deep sympathy for the mutineers and denounced the government for depriving the workers and the soldiers of hope and confidence by denying the delegates permission to attend the Stockholm conference.

Meanwhile the unrest in the armies, particularly the violent aspects of it, were diminishing, thanks in good measure to Pétain's firm and intelligent handling of the situation. To give an indication of the extent and duration of the mutinies, and mentioning only the incidents termed "collective acts" of violent rebellion, there were 10 cases reported between April 29 and May 25, 80 cases between May 25 and June 10, then a drop to 20 serious outbreaks from June 11 to July 24, only 5 from July 2 to July 24, 3 in August and 1 in September.

The climax apparently was reached on June 2 when in one day there were 17 units of regimental size in active revolt. Between May and September there were 119 acts of "collective" mutiny—when whole units openly defied authority—which does not take into account individual acts or the passive resistance of other disaffected units. Fifty-four divisions, comprising more than half of the French army, were openly mutinous and at one time it was feared that there were only two loyal divisions between Paris and Soissons.

These were the serious cases recorded in the statistics, but the gravest fact facing the high command was that the army as a whole had lost its will to fight. Pétain could bring the troops back to a sense of duty and could carry on with the war but he had no illusions as to the quality of his army. There was little spirit left, merely a mechanical acceptance of the inevitable; nevertheless the army was a smooth-running machine of veterans, cynical and cautious but efficient, who would keep the war alive until reinforcements from across the sea could arrive to force the decision.

Pétain felt that the form future operations would take would be determined by the relative strength of the opposing forces on the western front and not by the will of the commander. His own strategic ideas, as well as his tactical plans, could now become the rule for the armies since he was in a position to put them into effect. It was obvious that an army riddled with mutiny could not go on the offensive; the government and other generals including General Foch, who had succeeded him as Chief of the General Staff, were agreed on that point. During its period of convalescence the army could only adopt a defensive attitude.

The British were planning a great offensive in Flanders, designed to take the Belgian coastal ports from which German submarines were operating with devastating effect against allied shipping; and Pétain had agreed in May, while he was still Chief of Staff, that the French would support this attack with offensive operations of their own. But when the mutinies paralyzed his forces he had to inform Field Marshal Haig's headquarters, in early June, that he would have to go back on his promise, that the British could expect no major French operations that summer. The British went ahead with their offensive, which dragged on, costly and futile, throughout the summer and early autumn of 1917, in a series of attacks which Pétain admitted gave the French army time to recuperate but which he said, with reason, had ruined the British army. To those who questioned his plans for the future he had a simple answer: "I am waiting for the Americans and the tanks," and neither of those two elements, American soldiers or tanks, would be available in quantity until June 1918. France therefore had to gird herself for a long war and the government, in the summer of 1917, was in agreement that nothing decisive could be accomplished before June of the following year—as was the future Premier Clemenceau, who was then president of the Army Committee in the Senate.[10]

In a speech before the Chamber on July 7, 1917, War Minister Painlevé outlined the plans agreed upon between the War Committee and the high command. He told the critical deputies, still seething over the April offensive and greatly upset by the mutinies, that no longer was the army being directed by theorists who, in affecting a Napoleonic touch, had put into operation bold and ambitious plans whose grand appearance hid their emptiness and lack of preparation. These theorists had foolishly thought that they could in several days break and disperse great armies which were, in effect, nations in arms. From now on the armies would be in the hands of a commander who had long been the advocate of a strategy which would conserve French

---

[10] Paul Painlevé, "La Politique de guerre de 1917. Réponse au général Mangin," *La Revue de Paris,* March 15, 1922 (Paris, 1922), Vol. II, 303.

strength until such time as the allies could go on the offensive with
superior forces, and when that time came the French army must still
be powerful enough to play a decisive role. General Pétain's method,
one that he had adhered to when it was unpopular and against the
trend of military thought, would economize on lives and preserve the
army for the "supreme battles," when the time was right. Painlevé
then described briefly the essence of Pétain's "method," the tactics
which would be put into practice and would maintain the French
army at a high combat potential while preserving its effectives.[11]

The new commander in chief's "method" was a tactical system
which had been maturing for years, during the period when he was
professor at the War College and brought to a high development since
1914. The war had brought few surprises to Pétain and he was usually
one step ahead of tactical developments. After he became installed
as Chief of the General Staff in Paris during April and early May
1917 he drew up a synthesis of his tactical system which he intended
to apply to the armies. Normally he did little writing himself: letters,
reports, directives and other written documents emanating from his
headquarters were drawn up by his staff officers who submitted them
to their chief. He went over them carefully, however, and made many
changes, both in content and in style. Therefore his chief of staff,
Colonel Serrigny, was surprised on May 10, 1917 when his chief
handed him a three- page document, written in his own hand, which
described the form that the war would take from that time on. Apparently Pétain did not care to trust to others the translation of his
thoughts upon so important a matter, one to which he had given
considerable thought.

The study ended with these words, which are worth repeating:

> The objectives of the war cannot be attained without having
> first destroyed or at least reduced the enemy reserves; it is to weaken
> those [reserves] that we must devote all our forces. To achieve this
> we should not launch great attacks in depth, with distant objectives.
> These attacks are long in preparation, costly in effectives—for the
> attacker generally suffers more than the defender—and they do not
> benefit from surprise. Moreover they tend to dilute the artillery
> preparation in depth over the whole of the enemy positions whereas
> if all the projectiles were concentrated on the first position they
> would produce a greatly superior effect. The method of wearing
> down the enemy while suffering a minimum of losses oneself con-
> sists of increasing the number of limited attacks, conducted with
> a great reliance upon artillery; of striking continually against the

---

[11] Paul Painlevé, *Paroles et écrits* (Paris, 1936), 171–182.

arch of the German structure until it collapses. If the structure is not rebuilt, then, but only then, we can proceed to the pursuit.[12]

Serrigny remarked that the document resembled a professor's lecture more than it did a commander's order and Pétain laughingly agreed and told his subordinate to touch it up as he wished. This paper was the origin of Directive No. 1, submitted within a few days to the War Committee and then sent on May 14 to General Nivelle. Nivelle—who was, however, relieved the next day—was requested to pass it on for action to his army commanders and to formulate future plans of operation in conformance with it—plans which would have to be submitted in advance to the Chief of the General Staff for his approval.

After Pétain's assumption of command on May 16 he issued the Directive No. 1 to the armies under his own name. This directive to army group and army commanders stated that the "equilibrium of the opposing forces in presence on the north and northeastern fronts does not permit us to envisage, for the moment, a breakthrough of the front followed by a strategic exploitation," but that they should, nevertheless, keep pressure on the enemy aimed at wearing him down with a minimum loss to themselves. The attacks would be limited in depth and would take place all along the front at points where small but real tactical victories seemed possible.[13]

In these attacks, on narrow fronts, the infantry would be spared as much as possible while artillery and other means of destruction should be used to the fullest extent. The idea was to use up the enemy reserves, not to effect a great breakthrough.

This strategy, and these tactics, were not adhered to by the British commander, Field Marshal Haig, who employed methods in his 1917 offensive which the French military and civil leadership thought had been discredited in the Somme battles of 1916. Ypres and Cambrai cost the British, from June to December 1917, 450,000 men,[14] in the effort which Pétain said had "ruined" the British army. Haig and his supporters claimed that these operations cost the Germans dearly, which they did, and contributed to the victory of 1918, which they probably did in an indirect way. But they did not achieve their original objectives, which Haig had stated to be principally the elimination of the submarine bases along the Belgian coast; and the men who

[12] Général Serrigny, *Trente Ans avec Pétain* (Paris, 1959), 135, 136.
[13] Général Laure, "Le Commandement en chef des armées françaises, du 15 mai 1917 à l'armistice," *Revue militaire française* (Paris, 1936), Vol. 61, 18, 19.
[14] Henry Bidou, *et al., La Grande Guerre,* vol. IX of *Histoire de France Contemporaine,* Ernest Lavisse, ed., 265.

were killed and maimed, the finest of their generation, were lost for the great battles of 1918.

Even assuming that Haig's 1917 offensives did ultimately shorten the war, which cannot be proven one way or the other, the war would have been won anyway in 1919 principally by the Americans and the additional men from the British dominions across the sea, and Haig, at the most, merely substituted casualties from the United Kingdom for those of an ally who could better afford them demographically. In assessing the damage done to the people of Europe by the World War I bloodlettings an important point to consider is the appalling dearth of competent leadership in European countries in the late 1930's. The trenches had taken their toll of potential leaders and statesmen; the only survivor of the infantry and the trenches in a position of leadership was the half mad Adolf Hitler.

Haig's theories were not shared by Robertson, Chief of the Imperial General Staff, who in June 1917 subscribed fully to Pétain's doctrine of limited offensives conducted in accordance with the principles expressed in Pétain's Directive No. 1 (although he did not acknowledge Pétain as the originator of those principles),[15] nor by Prime Minister Lloyd George, who had no faith in Haig or his methods and who believed in Pétain's strategy of small attacks, limited in time and objectives.[16]

Haig's operations in the summer of 1917 did help the French during the period of the mutinies; this Pétain readily admitted. He had thought since early 1916 that the British should undertake large-scale operations to relieve the hard-pressed French armies of the burden of the war which they had been carrying since 1914, but he thought that the methods employed by the British high command in Flanders were unsound.

The limited and circumspect strategy which the French armies adopted after May 1917 was in fact all that they were capable of at the time. Even the kind of limited attacks specified in the Directive No. 1 were out of the question in June and July, the months of the worst mutinies. Merely to hold the line was difficult enough and in those months the Germans attacked the positions on the Chemin des Dames which Nivelle had taken in May and succeeded in recovering part of the ground that they had lost. In August, however, Pétain felt that he had the situation well enough in hand to undertake a small

---

[15] Victor Bonham-Carter, *The Strategy of Victory, 1914–1918* (New York, 1964), 251.
[16] Lord Maurice Hankey, *The Supreme Command, 1914–1918* (London, 1961), vol. II, 598.

offensive in the Verdun area, to gain a small success in order to hearten the troops and the country, to keep the enemy off balance, and to give some sign to the British that the French armies would remain active.

The attack took place north of Verdun on August 20, on both sides of the Meuse. The affair, very carefully prepared, was a moderate success, capturing several thousand prisoners and a sizable strip of territory. After the initial surprise was gone and after a penetration had been made beyond the range of the original artillery preparation, stiff resistance was encountered and when the Germans concentrated their reserves at the point of the attack Pétain halted the operation, in conformance with his strategy. The moment that an offensive reached a point of diminishing returns—that is, when the advantages gained would not be commensurate with the losses incurred, it was to be halted, and a new operation was to be undertaken elsewhere, as meticulously prepared.

In October a larger attack, the battle of Malmaison, took place and was a substantial victory. General Maistre's Sixth Army made the attack on an eighteen-mile front north of Soissons, against the plateau which supported the right flank of the German positions along the Chemin des Dames. The point selected for the operation was of tactical importance, but as it was in the area of Nivelle's April offensive it enjoyed an unhealthy reputation among the troops and the French public. A new failure there could have had serious effects on the morale of the army and the public, as Pétain warned his subordinate, Franchet d'Espèrey, commander of the Northern Army Group. Nevertheless the attack was a great success; with the plateau taken the German positions on the Chemin des Dames were outflanked and they had to evacuate their whole line on the plateau to retire behind the Ailette.

After the enemy retreat Pétain halted the operation, on November 1, like a cautious gambler who leaves the game when he is ahead. In eight days he had forced the enemy out of the positions which had stopped Nivelle's offensive the previous April; by concentrating all his forces on one vital point he had won the whole. French losses in killed, wounded and missing were 14,700 men while the enemy lost about 40,000 men including 11,500 prisoners, as well as 200 artillery pieces, 720 machine guns and 222 mortars. To give an idea of what Pétain meant by an artillery preparation, from October 16 to 26 the French gunners fired two million 75 millimeter shells and 850,000 heavy artillery shells, concentrated on a relatively restricted target area, with a proportion of one gun to every six meters of front.

Despite the careful preparation there was considerable nervousness at Sixth Army headquarters before the attack. It was the first large-scale operation since the mutinies and was, to some extent, a test of the therapeutic measures taken by the high command to restore the morale of the army. To make matters worse, on the day before the attack a monitored enemy radio communication indicated that the Germans had learned the hour and the day that the infantry assault would take place—the intense artillery assault which was already pulverizing their forward positions had warned them that a major operation was in progress—and General Maistre's headquarters, considerably upset, asked if the attack should go forward as planned.

Both the army group commander and the Commander in Chief authorized them to go ahead, but the attack was advanced one-half hour—the only change that could be made at that late date to avoid some of the German counter-preparation artillery fire, which would fall on the forward trenches packed with assault troops at zero hour. But the operation, with that minor change, proceeded as planned; when the infantry moved forward, supported by tanks, the French artillery fire, rising to a crescendo of violence, lifted to cover the German batteries which had begun to fire on the French attacking waves and against the German rear positions and communications to interdict the movement of the enemy reserves.

Some French writers later talked of the great joy, almost delirious, of the French troops who had won such a significant gain at such a relatively small cost. It is difficult to believe that the exhausted survivors of the assault waves, relieved to be still alive, cold, muddy, lousy and hungry, thought of much more than a quiet, dry place to lie down. There was nothing that could make a *poilu* delirious with joy in November 1917 except the news that he could go home to stay. But the French infantrymen, as connoisseurs of good and bad attacks, were satisfied that the promises of their commander regarding the material preparation for future operations and the careful management of effectives were not only sincere but feasible. They saw that French generals could plan a successful operation as well as could the commanders of the German soldiers who opposed them; and it also was gratifying to see, for once, a conquered battleground with more German dead bodies on it than French.

An interested observer of the Malmaison offensive was the commander of the American Expeditionary Force, General John Pershing, with his chief of staff and other aides. General Franchet d'Espèrey was his host and guide. After the battle was seen to be progressing nicely and Pershing was about to return to French G.Q.G., d'Espèrey asked the American to tell Pétain how things were going. The army group commander's simple request was merely a courteous gesture to please his guest and important ally but the French Commander in Chief apparently was a little cross that the new arrival from across the sea should presume to explain to him the movements of one of his own armies. At any rate when Pershing started to give Pétain the details of the battle the latter cut him off by remarking that he received information by telephone every quarter of an hour.[17]

Actually the relationship between Pétain and Pershing was and remained cordial. There was little friction apparent between the two and any problems that Pershing had with French leaders, military or civil, were not caused or exacerbated by Pétain, who could be charming and cooperative when he wanted to be. He did not attempt to conceal from his new allies how badly they were needed and how critical his situation would be without them. In their first meeting, on June 16, 1917, at Compiègne, he had disturbed the American General by his remark that he was pleased that the Americans were coming but "hoped that they were not too late."[18] The mutinies on that date had the French armies all but paralyzed and if Pétain could spur his American colleague to hasten his preparations and expedite the arrival of his fresh troops by alarming him as to the French ability to hold on, he would not hesitate to do so.

Pershing's impressions of the low state of French morale in June 1917 were not all derived solely from his contacts with Pétain. Pessimism and even defeatism were evident to him from many of his contacts with French officials, both formal and informal. For example, at a lunch on June 22 President of the Council Ribot and Mme. Ribot both emphasized, to Pershing, the depression of the French people. On the previous evening Pétain had carried on this theme, with the object of persuading Pershing to "use his influence to strengthen the resolution" of the French civilian government and to persuade President Wilson to do likewise. Pershing did what he could, in press releases and in reports to his government; for a man who affected a disdain for politicians Pétain could do some artful behind-the-scenes maneuvering when he thought it desirable.[19]

Unwittingly Pétain was reinforcing Pershing's determination to keep the American troops, as they arrived, organized in their own units under their own officers and independent of the French armies,

---

[17] Général Paul Azan, *Franchet d'Espèrey* (Paris, 1949), 161–163.
[18] James G. Harbord, *The American Army in France, 1917–1918* (Boston, 1936), 85.
[19] See John J. Pershing, *My Experiences in the World War* (New York, 1931), I, 74–76, 96–99.

except insofar as some association would be necessary for training purposes. The French desire, shared by Pétain, to incorporate American
infantrymen into the depleted French ranks was a ridiculous proposal
anyway, and not only for reasons of national pride. Pershing expected
the war to be terminated sometime in 1919, after large-scale operations
conducted for the most part by large American armies, and he had
no intention of indoctrinating his troops with the static trench mentality of his allies nor did he want his men contaminated by the low
state of morale and depression infecting the French troops, which the
French commander made no attempt to hide from him.

As the year 1917 drew to a close General Pétain had reason to be
satisfied, if not elated. The collapse of the French armies had been
averted; the troops were as content as could be expected, mollified by
better living conditions in the field and in the rear, by the new
furlough system, and above all by the new military method which
gave each of them some hope of surviving the war. The Malmaison
victory had heartened the whole army. Therefore in October 1917 the
commander in chief of the French army could head a report to his
government with these words: "In general the morale of the army is
good."[20]

Morale probably is a relative matter; in 1918 French civilians and
soldiers were so startled when they heard American soldiers singing
as army trucks carried them to the front that they still talked of it
years later. Frenchmen were more accustomed to hearing their own
men bleating like sheep when they passed through villages, as they
did during the Verdun battle and again during the time of the
mutinies. French troops, with too many of their voices stilled, had
stopped singing by late 1915.

---

[20] *Les Armées françaises* . . . , Tome V, Vol. II, 1273, 1274.

7

1918 — The Siege Is Lifted

Throughout the war, since September 1914, the major problem facing the French high command and government was the German occupation of northern France. The military efforts of France for three years —excepting the minor efforts made at Gallipoli and Salonika, both operations undertaken upon the urgings of the British and over the objections of the French high command—had been directed toward the one goal: that of expelling the enemy from French soil. The "On to Berlin" slogans of 1914 had soon changed to "the Germans are at Noyon" cry of Clemenceau's journal, a cry which expressed the principal fact governing the conduct of the war and the attitude of the French people, civilians and soldiers. Without the German occupation of French territory France would have made peace in 1917; neither the country nor the army would have kept up the struggle for more ambitious objectives, not even for the recovery of Alsace-Lorraine.

The defensive strategy of Pétain was therefore suited to the limited objectives of the government in 1917 and in fact was the only practical policy open to a nation whose army was not strong enough to defeat the enemy and whose major ally, Great Britain, was herself exhausted and stricken by the bloody sacrifices of 1916 and 1917—sacrifices which had helped France but had done little to further British interests. One of the thoughts uppermost in Pétain's mind, even before the Bolshevik seizure of power in Petrograd, was the slackening of the Russian war effort, and its complete cessation after November 1917 confirmed his fears. With Russia out of the war the German high command could shift sixty or more divisions from the east to the western front and

144

the Germans could be expected to utilize their preponderance of power in the west in major offensives in the spring of 1918. In 1917 it was not expected that American troop strength could reach decisive proportions before late 1918 or perhaps even 1919.

Until the American forces could arrive in overwhelming strength and until the French army could be equipped with great quantities of the modern instruments of war, particularly heavy artillery and tanks, Pétain could see no sensible alternative to a defensive strategy on the western front. The French army, recovered from the mutinies but still in no condition to undertake large-scale offensive operations and suffering from a shortage of manpower, must, he thought, maintain its positions with a minimum of casualties. Already he had, since assuming command of the armies, reduced the average monthly casualty figure from 80,000 to 36,000 men, an economy which was vitally necessary if France were to meet the demands of the great battles which he expected in 1918.

Even with a careful husbanding of the remaining manpower the French forces on the western front were reduced, in 1917, from 109 infantry divisions to the equivalent of 97. Actually Pétain managed, for the time being, to keep the number of infantry divisions at the figure of 108 but in order to do this he reduced the number of battalions in a division from twelve to nine. French infantry divisions which had, in 1914, numbered between 15,000 and 16,000 men were reduced by the end of 1917 to approximately 9,000 men each. It was not merely an erosion of morale that plagued the commander in chief but also an erosion of effectives; all the measures taken, the calling up of older classes, the lowering of physical standards for recruits, and the hasty recall of wounded men from their convalescence, were not adequate to keep the army up to strength. Numerically and qualitatively the French army was undergoing a crisis of effectives.

We have seen that Pétain's tactics for offensive operations, as ordered in his Directive No. 1 and exemplified in the Malmaison attack in October, were designed to economize French manpower while using up the enemy's reserves of manpower, a necessary precondition, in his strategy, for the final offensives which would one day end the war. With powerful German offensives expected in the spring of 1918 the French Commander in Chief decided to put into operation new defensive tactics which had been maturing in his mind throughout the war but which were so radically different from the methods normally in use in the French army that he knew that he would encounter stiff opposition from unit commanders.

The "Instruction for the defensive action of large units [units of divisional size or larger] in battle" of December 20, 1917 was a radical change from the accepted defensive method which prescribed the holding of every foot of terrain, no matter what its value or the cost. This method, which put so much value on the forward positions, meant that the first line was to be held by great numbers of men, because that would be where the main battle would be conducted, with the second and third positions relatively thinly held. The enemy artillery bombardment, preliminary to an attack, therefore fell on the densely manned forward positions and inflicted heavy losses on the defenders before the attacking infantry reached those positions. Not only was this costly in manpower but it left the second line, which often soon became the first line in an attack, relatively lightly held, and it also meant that there were fewer reserves available for the counterattack.

Pétain's instructions were meant to change this method; the advanced positions would be thinly held by strong points and advance guards; the bulk of the defenders would be concentrated in strong positions in the second line, out of range of the enemy's trench mortars and much of his artillery. Losses in the preliminary artillery bombardment would be reduced; the German assaulting waves would encounter resistance on the first line but would be effectively stopped on the main line of resistance and then the French reserves would counterattack and recover the lost ground. Defensively Pétain was returning to a modified war of movement, with the forward line constituting his advance guard and the second line his main body; but the overriding strategic thought was that the war on the western front was a war of siege; terrain meant little except insofar as it aided or hindered the siege operations, and attrition was the guiding principle behind all operations. An offensive like Malmaison was a *coup de main* against the enemy's siege works.

These new tactics caused considerable uneasiness and even opposition among subordinate commanders, thoroughly imbued with a defensive *à outrance* outlook. Commanders asked: Were positions often so dearly won to be given up so easily? Pétain went to great pains to explain that he envisaged giving up nothing; that his method would reduce casualties and inflict greater ones on the enemy, and that territory would not be lost. But the unrest continued and throughout the spring of 1918 one of his greatest problems was enforcing this tactical system upon unwilling commanders who considered it a point of honor to hold all ground and to recover immediately at any cost ground momentarily lost.

General Ludendorff, the only other ex-infantry officer to command his nation's armies on the western front—Haig was a cavalryman, as was Sir William Robertson; Joffre was an engineer and Nivelle and Foch artillerymen—was applying a tactical system to his armies which was similar to Pétain's—an elastic, or mobile, defense in depth, which permitted front-line positions to be temporarily abandoned and which maintained a strong force of trained counterattack units in rear positions. German commanders would wait out a French attack—much of the French artillery fire would fall on empty space, and picked troops would hold the forward positions with large numbers of machine guns as long as they could. The counterattack would then recover the lost ground from the disorganized attackers. Ludendorff's position in Germany was such, militarily and politically, that he could enforce his directives upon unwilling subordinate commanders—and he had his die-hard, hold-the-line opponents too—but Pétain had much greater difficulty and never did entirely succeed in having his ideas carried out to the letter. Perhaps the difference lay in the fact that it was easier for Germans to relinquish French soil than it was for Frenchmen.

Pétain's Directive No. 4 of December 22, 1917 to army and army group commanders outlined his conceptions of the form future operations would take. He said that with Russia out of the war the Allies were faced with a German army which would be considerably reinforced by its armies from the eastern front. The Directive stated: "The Entente will not recover its superiority in combat effectives until the American army is capable of putting in line a certain number of large units; until then we must, under the penalty of an irremediable wastage [of our forces], conserve an expectant attitude, with the well-founded idea of resuming, as soon as we can, the offensive which alone will give us final victory."[1]

In this directive the Commander in Chief elaborated upon his new defensive tactics, from a higher-command point of view, advising army commanders to hold the bulk of their forces in the secondary positions with the primary positions containing only enough troops to slow the enemy advance; in the secondary positions should be the general reserves which would be used to counterattack or to execute counteroffensives on the flanks of the zone (or pocket) of penetration or on a part of the front adjacent to that zone. The commanders were enjoined to assure, on their respective fronts, the immediate organization of the secondary positions, destined to become the true theater of battle, and at the same time to prepare their forces for offensive actions so that the high command could undertake rapid counter-

[1] Général Laure, "Le Commandement en chef des armées françaises, du 15 mai à l'armistice," Revue militaire française (Paris, 1936), Vol. 61, 169.

offensives. Above all they were to keep up the physical and moral well-being of the troops under their command and supervise the training of units on the division and army corps level.

This idea, which apparently meant maneuvering in retreat, with a willingness to abandon front-line positions under attack, aroused so much opposition from some army commanders that Pétain had to go around personally to the higher commands to clarify his orders. He explained that maneuvering in retreat was not the essence of his method and that the front line should be held until a higher command ordered a retreat, but experience had amply shown that the front line could always be taken by a determined attack, no matter how strongly defended—the preliminary artillery bombardment assured that—and one should attempt to minimize losses by not concentrating too many men in the forward positions. Since the first lines are doomed to capture anyway in a determined attack one should hold them with only enough strength to slow and dislocate the progression of the enemy and to give warning and time to prepare counter measures to the second line. Counterattacks should not be partial efforts made by the local commanders but should be well-organized operations conducted methodically by a higher command on a larger front, employing flanking and encircling maneuvers.[2]

The extent to which there was vagueness and ambiguity in these orders, which some commanders found difficult to comprehend or accept, was due to the difficulty or unwisdom of laying down an exact line of procedure to fit any and all circumstances. A good military leader should be a virtuoso who plays by ear, adapting his general method to each particular situation as it arises, and Pétain knew that the conduct of each operation would depend upon many factors peculiar to itself: the nature, extent and timing of the attack; the terrain over which it was conducted; the forces in being on that front; the availability of reserves; the relative importance of the sector involved; and any other circumstances which might arise. He could only lay down a general line of conduct hoping that the initiative, intelligence and imagination of the subordinate commanders could fill in the rest. This demanded more of the French officers than did the old and simple formula of automatically fighting for every piece of ground at any cost, of commanders ordering an attack or a counterattack to meet any emergency; and it is no wonder that many were disturbed. Three years of trench warfare had established a fixed-line

---

[2] See Ministère de la guerre, État-major de l'armée—Service historique, *Les Armées françaises dans la Grande guerre*, Tome VI, Vol. II, 41–46.

mentality which could not be easily changed, particularly in an officer corps which was not, even in peacetime, noted for an independence or originality of thought.

Opposition to his methods was not confined to the Commander in Chief's military subordinates, some of whom had important political contacts in the parliament or the cabinet. Governmental leaders were alerted to Pétain's radical departure from the established system; for example General Micheler, reduced from an army group to an army command after April 1917, was close to Antonin Dubost, president of the Senate, and his criticisms of the defensive policy of his superior led to cabinet-level attacks on Pétain, a situation which Ludendorff did not face in Germany.

Micheler did not hesitate to approach the President of the Republic, on December 9, with his complaints of what he termed the "inertia" of the high command; he advocated that the French armies go on the offensive so as not to leave the initiative to the Germans.[3] Since Pétain had not been particularly reticent about criticising the high command to political leaders who questioned him when he was a subordinate commander, he now could hardly complain when his own subordinates did the same. All the same, Micheler would not survive the war as an army commander.

During the autumn of 1917 the Commander in Chief had to defend his policy at lively meetings of the War Committee—which included the President of the Republic, the president of the council of ministers, the ministers of war, navy and munitions, and sometimes, by invitation, other leading personalities. Senator Paul Doumer, the president of the Economic Council (and former president of the Senate) , Senator Antonin Dubost, and Paul Deschanel, president of the Chamber of Deputies, all were opponents of Pétain's apparent lack of activity and sharply criticized his refusal to engage in large-scale offensive operations. His "I am waiting for the Americans and the tanks" formula piqued their patriotic pride; after three years of savage conflict was the war to be prolonged so that a new and disinterested ally should win the glory of the victory? Surely Frenchmen could defeat the Germans. Doumer had four sons killed in the war and he was not at all inclined to permit the Frenchmen who remained to curtail their sacrifices now after so many precious and beloved young men had died. Generals Foch and Weygand, the latter recently appointed French military representative on the allied Supreme War Council, supported Pétain's thesis that offensives on the French front

---

[3] Raymond Poincaré, *Au Service de la France* (Paris, 1933) , IX, 406–413.

were impossible at that time; the armies had not yet fully recovered from the April disaster or the mutinies and were not capable of large-scale offensive operations.

It is a curious commentary on the complexity of the situation that leading civilian officials were demanding offensive action and the leading military figures were counselling prudence. Critics of the French high command since the War have often failed to note the civilian contribution to the many faults committed. Fortunately both Painlevé, when he was President of the Council, and Clemenceau, who succeeded him in November, supported Pétain, as did President Poincaré.

So bitter were the attacks of Dubost and Deschanel, who represented a substantial current of opinion in the parliament, that Pétain felt his competence was being questioned. The military policy which he was following was imposed upon France by force of circumstances and by factors beyond his control; no other policy was possible, and his patience finally snapped at the War Committee meeting of December 13, when he retorted that if anyone believed that he had a better method than his to conduct the war then he, Pétain, was ready to step down as commander. He had once told Colonel Repington that if the politicians did not like the truth they could get someone else to lie to them; and this was his attitude on that December day.

Premier Clemenceau hastily came to the General's support; there could be no question of Pétain's resignation. The French army must hold and last; they could not gamble on an all-out offensive now. Clemenceau supported the policy of his Commander in Chief completely, and President Poincaré added his support although he was disturbed by complaints which Prime Minister Lloyd George had made to him personally about the apparent French military inactivity. The spring of 1918 was therefore the first spring of the war for which no major offensives were planned by the allies.

Pétain's plans for 1918 did not by any means envisage inactivity, but his attacks would be limited ones—in conformance with the strategy and tactics outlined in his Directive No. 1. He had explained to the War Committee in early October that he planned to be always attacking in two or three sectors simultaneously on the French front and hoped to have the British always attacking on two sectors on the British front. The enemy would have difficulty holding against this strategy because they could not counter two points of friction at once. But for this strategy, or for a defensive strategy if the Germans should launch a major offensive, he needed to increase his reserves; and in order to acquire those reserves he requested that the British take over

more of the French front, relieving two French armies on the left of
the French front and extending the British line to Soissons. He also
requested that as American contingents arrived they be incorporated
into French divisions to fill out the depleted French formations rather
than taking over part of the line as an independent army.

He had some success with the British. Haig extended his line, although only as far as the Oise, thus relieving substantial French forces;
but it meant that the British Fifth Army front was stretched thin and
it was on this new British front, recently taken over from the French,
that the massive German attack of March 21, 1918, fell with so much
success for the enemy. Pétain's quarrel with the British on this subject was the perennial one between the two nations during World
War I: French armies held a far greater proportion of the front than
did the British; but the British argued, with justice, that the French
line included large sectors—such as those in the Vosges Mountains—
which were inactive and easily defensible, thus requiring fewer troops
to manage, while their own front was an active, sensitive and dangerous theater of operations.

Pétain argued his point without heat. It was his duty as the French
Commander to further French military interests, and Haig defended
the British point of view with equal force but with a corresponding
willingness to compromise; the two commanders therefore worked
in an atmosphere of mutual respect. As Haig put it when questioned
by President Poincaré regarding his relations with Pétain: "Together
we speak neither French nor English but the language of military
men."

Pétain had less success with the Americans in his attempts to relieve his manpower problems. General Pershing stoutly refused to
emasculate his forces by using them to fill out French divisions. Even
in the British army the Dominion troops—Canadian, Australian and
New Zealand—fought as separate units, and this in an army where
there was no language barrier. The practical difficulties of the French
plan were manifold, not to mention the indignity of the proposal.
Pershing was not going to use his fresh young Americans to prop up
a sagging French war machine. If the war was going to be won by the
Americans it would be under their own flag and under their own
officers; the American high command did not have as much faith in
French military skill as French officers had themselves, although
Pershing could not say so.

Premier Clemenceau appealed over Pershing's head to President
Wilson, but Wilson supported his military commander. Pétain, after
the attempt, accepted this decision with good grace, which as a matter

of common sense he probably expected anyway, and he got on well with the Americans; but Clemenceau and Foch kept up the attack on Pershing and it required much tact and determination on the part of the latter to maintain his plan to organize independent American armies in France. As for Pétain, as American forces in France grew larger in 1918 and a certain amount of friction developed as Americans sometimes were the object of a French attitude of condescension or patronage, he issued instructions to his officers that the susceptibilities of their new allies should be respected and suggested that the *amour-propre* of a sensitive and intelligent people required a modicum of tact. As events proved, Pershing lent his troops, in small and large detachments, to serve under his French and British allies in far greater measure than they ever were willing to do for each other.

In January and February Pétain came under a certain amount of pressure from Clemenceau regarding his Directive No. 4, which General Foch had led the French Premier to believe was too defensive in its apparent willingness to abandon terrain. Clemenceau feared that excessive withdrawals would have a bad effect on the morale of the country and he also feared that if the idea were taken up by the British high command they would be, not unnaturally, too inclined to abandon territory not their own national soil. There was logic behind the French leader's apprehension but Pétain by no means planned large-scale withdrawals; his instructions were tactical innovations only, designed to relax the rigid linear warfare mentality which was so costly in manpower. Clemenceau need not have feared the British adoption of a planned withdrawal policy either—which never was a Pétain idea anyway; his allies were as bound by public opinion regarding the fixity of fronts as were the French, and also the British high command was only too well aware of the lack of depth behind their lines to the Channel.

General Foch also began to complain privately that the French Commander in Chief should not remain on the defensive but should plan offensives to forestall the expected German spring offensive. His argument was that one offensive can counteract another, as the allied Somme offensive in 1916 had relieved the pressure on Verdun. This advice worried Clemenceau, who communicated this concern to Pétain. The latter informed the Premier, quite succinctly, that he was conducting the operations of the French army in conformance with the means available to him; they must be realists and realize that the great battles of 1918 would be decided by the forces in presence and not by the will of the high command.

Clemenceau did not press the issue, but relied on the good sense of his military commander, whom he described to President Poincaré as the "best of our leaders"—although he regretted that Pétain sometimes talked too pessimistically.[4] In any case Foch, in his official pronouncements, was more cautious than in his private ones. His report of January 1, 1918, to the military representatives of the allied Supreme War Council at Versailles—organized at the Rapallo conference of November 7, 1917—expressed views on the military situation and suggestions for future operations which were no whit different from those of Pétain. The report recommended that in the event the enemy did not attack in the spring the allies launch attacks against limited objectives, to wear down the enemy reserves; then, when those reserves were used up, they were to proceed to large-scale operations with more ambitious objectives.[5] Pétain had been recommending that strategy since 1915.

General Foch was anxious that the allies adopt a really unified military command under one general—a logical and necessary step which Pétain had wholeheartedly endorsed both at meetings of the French War Council and of the allied Supreme War Council. The principal opponent among the allies to this project were the British, since the generalissimo so appointed would logically be a French officer—and Foch saw himself as the best candidate for the position. That energetic and capable officer, who had lost his only son and his son-in-law in the first battles of 1914, had already proved his ability to organize and coordinate allied forces in the early years of the war, in the battles of the Yser and of Ypres in 1914 and in Artois in 1915. His operations in 1915, however, had been fruitless and very costly and his lack of success on the Somme in 1916 had placed him in a temporary eclipse. In early 1918 his star was again ascending and his only real rival for the supreme command, should it ever materialize, was his former subordinate at the War College, Philippe Pétain. Naturally ambitious and convinced, with a certain amount of justice, that he was the best man for the important post, Foch was not above undercutting his apparent rival at every opportunity.

Foch criticized Pétain's defensive and offensive doctrines to government leaders and hoped to have the commander of the French armies removed and superseded by General Fayolle,[6] who would be, he expected, more complaisant and less of a threat than was Pétain, whose realism and dry, sardonic appraisals of the military situation

---

[4] Poincaré, IX, 367.
[5] Marshal Foch, *The Memoirs of Marshal Foch* (New York, 1931), 236.
[6] Maréchal Fayolle, *Cahiers secrets de la Grande Guerre* (Paris, 1964), 251–257.

and military policy in general were the antithesis of Foch's "will to victory." Foch had a blind faith that the driving spirit of the Commander should sweep away all obstacles by its intensity and its refusal to recognize that obstacles existed.

Perhaps Pétain's religious scepticism kept him from sharing Foch's sublime conviction that victory would be won if only they had faith enough. Foch was very religious; prayer and devotion were part of his daily life and his spiritual convictions no doubt gave him the strength and confidence lacking in Pétain. General Fayolle, also a devout Catholic—who, many years before, in the peacetime army, often had been shocked by his comrade Pétain's penchant for off-color jokes and spicy stories—was distressed by Pétain's pessimism with regard to the war but he himself at times was so discouraged that he was led to comment, privately in his diary, that it would take the direct intervention of God for France to win the war.

Pétain, by temperament a sceptic, could not lean on the hope of divine aid and could only hope for a more worldly intervention. His *deus ex machina* was the American army; but the German high command was convinced that the war could be won by the Central Powers before the United States could create a great war machine from almost nothing and Pétain was not so sure that the Germans were not correct. Foch's relative lack of sensitivity to combat casualities might also be a reflection of his otherworldly outlook. He probably was more inclined to think of the lost young Frenchmen as souls gone to the heavenly reward due their sacrifice while Pétain could only think of them simply as putrescent bodies hanging on the wire in no man's land.

The question of the allied unified command was not settled until the German breakthrough on the Somme in March 1918 forced the issue. In the meantime the allied heads of government, through the Supreme War Council, decided, in lieu of a unified command, to constitute an allied reserve force of divisions from each army, under the leadership of Foch, which would be used to counter any enemy breakthrough which might occur. Pétain was not happy about giving up some of his reserves to a general reserve force but he agreed to furnish ten divisions (thirteen had been requested of him); Haig, however, refused to contribute any divisions from his western front forces and the plan fell through. After Haig's refusal to participate Pétain no longer was obliged to comply with the plan; he and Haig worked out an agreement by which each guaranteed to come to the other's aid in the event of a serious offensive against one of them. Foch, who had hoped that his control of the large general reserve of thirty divisions would lead to his automatic assumption of control of the allied armies in France—whoever controlled the reserves would be in virtual control of operations—dropped the plan in disgust.

Pétain may or may not have been pleased that Foch was blocked in his attempts to use the general reserve force to win control of the allied armies. It is certain, however, that he was willing to serve under Foch as allied Commander in Chief if British objections to the subordination of their armies to a foreigner could be overcome. In early November 1917, when Painlevé was still Premier, he and Lloyd George summoned Pétain to London to get his reaction to a plan to make Foch the real military director of the allied armies in France. Painlevé and the Prime Minister had talked of creating a post of Chief of the Inter-Allied General Staff, with Foch filling it. Foch would have commanded the Anglo-French reserves in the rear until such time as British public opinion would permit his acceptance as Commander in Chief of the two armies. Lloyd George raised the question of Pétain's willingness to accept this subordination of his command and Pétain told the two cabinet leaders that he would be glad to serve under Foch, whom he warmly praised.[7]

At the meeting of the Supreme War Council, from January 30 to February 1, 1918, when the plan to organize the general allied reserve was adopted, Pétain objected vigorously to the proposal, as did the British commanders Haig and Robertson, arguing that it was not good policy to put the front under one command and the reserves under another; but he did say that he was in favor of a single, unified command and that he would serve under anyone whom they appointed.[8] He might often have been pessimistic but he was in many ways a bigger man than most of his detractors.

Of detractors he had a formidable list. The ousted but still influential Marshal Joffre was very hostile to the Commander in Chief, whose policies he found too defensive. He resented above all the fact that Pétain had replaced all of his former associates—the "Young Turks"—in the Operations Bureau of the General Headquarters, an obvious repudiation of the former commander's methods and policies. Other offensive-minded generals were likewise hostile; Mangin, for example, who was relieved of his command after the April 1917 affair but who was permitted again to command French troops, and who in 1918 commanded an army, nursed an animosity that bordered on hatred. General Micheler not only found Pétain too defensive minded

---

[7] Paul Painlevé, "Le Maréchal Pétain au Maroc," *Les Annales Politiques et Littéraires* (Paris, July–December 1925), Tome 85, page 21.
[8] Laure, 176–178.

but even the "Trinity of Versailles," as he termed the Supreme War Council, earned his contempt for what he thought was excessive caution.

Pétain had always been a man of few friends but the jealousy and rancor attendant upon his accession to high station and the acceptance by the country of his once scorned ideas, with a concomitant rejection of the *offensive à outrance* theorists who had almost ruined France, bred a special kind of resentment. However, the ordinary soldiers in the army understood and knew what was happening; their bodies and their lives were at stake, and they were the manhood of France who would return home one day as civilians. Without seeking favor Pétain had found it, among the people of his country.

Foch's agreement in December 1917 that the French forces were unable to undertake large-scale offensive operations against the Germans, who were now able to concentrate all their forces on the western front, did not survive the month of January 1918. The British for months, officially and unofficially, had been expressing their unhappiness with the French waiting attitude. Foch was willing to ingratiate himself with the British, hoping eventually to win their approval of his appointment to supreme command; and since he was not responsible for the conduct of the French army he began to talk of allied offensives on the western front. He could not have his way and he must have known that Pétain would not permit him to have his way; he was therefore able to pose as a man of action, in contrast to Pétain's caution, without it costing him or the French army anything. If his proposals for a spring offensive, or counteroffensive as he preferred to call it, had been carried out they would have crippled the allied armies and Germany might well have won the war in the spring or summer of 1918.

On January 24, 1918, a conference of allied commanders, with their chiefs of staff and including Foch and Robertson, was held at Pétain's headquarters at Compiègne. At this meeting Foch advised that the best method to halt a powerful German offensive was for the allies to launch a powerful counteroffensive; he cited the experience of 1916 when the Somme offensive disengaged the German Verdun offensive. Pétain disagreed; he pointed out that the situation in 1918 was very different. Now the Germans had enough strength, with their forces from the eastern front, to launch more than one offensive. They must be careful and guard their precious and dwindling reserves to meet the German attacks.

The French commander said that he now had ninety-seven infantry divisions with an infantry strength of from 5,000 to 6,000 men each (these were the new "triangular" divisions, consisting of about 9,000 men of all arms, of three infantry regiments each, as compared to the former four-infantry regiment "square" divisions. The British and Germans had similarly reduced the size of their infantry divisions.) and eight cavalry divisions, two of which were dismounted. By the end of 1918 Pétain would have to break up many of these divisions, perhaps as many as twenty, as replacements for the others. The wastage of an offensive now could ruin the French army. Pétain said that he agreed with Foch in principle as to the desirability of making plans now for future offensives—but, he asked, where were the necessary reserves to come from? He just did not have the manpower.

Robertson and Haig also agreed in principle that offensive action was necessary but they, like the French Commander, could not see where the reserves would come from. The British army was exhausted and depleted by the great exertions of 1917. What they did not mention was that Prime Minister Lloyd George was withholding replacements from the British army in France by keeping the new drafts in England; this was his means of keeping Haig from embarking upon new offensives which threatened to destroy the manpower of the nation, a laudable intention but hardly consistent with his prodding the French to active offensive operations. Haig and Robertson said that they looked to the Americans for the reserves which would be necessary for future operations.

General Pershing then described the problems which he was encountering on the formation of an American army, among them shipping problems, delays at French ports, shortage of railroad transport and lack of munitions and equipment. All present expressed surprise at the American difficulties, including Foch, who as Chief of the General Staff in Paris should have been familiar with them. Foch said that none of these questions had been referred to him, and at this Pétain, who was smarting from Foch's interference in the conduct of his armies, snapped that one should not wait for these things to be brought to one's attention but should look around and find them. His attitude was that Foch, who was free with recommendations for offensives which would require large masses of reserve manpower, would perhaps be better employed in organizing the war effort in the interior, which apparently was in need of attention, in order to expedite the formation of those reserves. When the meeting ended the general agreement seemed to be that no offensives could be undertaken without the Americans.[9]

[9] See John J. Pershing, *My Experiences in the World War* (New York, 1931), I, 299–313.

On March 21, in the early dawn, the long-anticipated German offensive broke upon the British Fifth Army front on the Somme, at its point of juncture with the French army. Ludendorff's intention was to split the allied forces and to roll the British army back to the Channel coast. His strong, brilliantly planned attack broke the British defenses completely and within a few days the Fifth Army virtually ceased to exist, with 80,000 of its men in German prison camps. The German high command had perfected new techniques which recovered for them the element of surprise, a factor which had been lost in World War I due to the necessity for protracted preliminary artillery preparations which often lasted for weeks and which gave ample warning to the defenders that an attack was underway. At Malmaison Pétain had reduced the artillery preparation to two days, which was short for allied offensives; but the Germans on March 21 limited their preliminary bombardment to five hours, employing a heavy proportion of gas shells. It was a powerful artillery assault, nevertheless; the guns had been carefully concealed, as were all the preparations, and they were zeroed in mathematically rather than by registering actual shell bursts on the intended targets.

Specially picked and trained assault formations—brought into the line in the final days and hours and under cover of darkness—infiltrated and bypassed strongpoints, breaking through to a great depth, followed by the regular line infantry. The British defenders had never really recovered, in numbers and spirit, from the crushing battles of 1917 and in addition were spread too thin on the front recently taken over from the French. Their reserves were too distant since the British high command, judging by its own experience, did not believe that rapid and deep breakthroughs were possible. The British forward positions were thinly held, somewhat in the manner prescribed in Pétain's defensive method, but there was no strong second line, the main line of resistance—or at least none adequately prepared. The Germans also benefited from a dense fog that, augmented by smoke and gas shells, blinded the defenders and concealed the attackers.

Under the terms of the January 1918 mutual assistance agreement, it was decided that six French divisions must be ready to intervene in less than four days on the British front, at the first signal from Haig. Throughout the first day of the attack the gravity of the initial breakthrough was unknown at the French G.Q.G.—as indeed it was unknown at the British G.H.Q. News came out of the sector under attack very slowly because the collapse was so great as to result in a breakdown of communications. Nevertheless Pétain was uneasy and at 10:00 P.M., without yet having heard from Haig, he alerted General Pellé's force consisting of three divisions, a battalion of chasseurs and a regiment of heavy artillery for possible transfer to the point of the attack. At noon on March 22, at the request of Haig, Pétain sent this force; and elements of it were engaged, as they arrived, on the next day. By March 25 twenty French divisions were engaged against the German breakthrough, between the Somme and the Oise, in far greater measure than Haig had asked or than the allied agreement had called for—a noteworthy feat of French arms particularly in view of the fact that in the same period few British reinforcements reached the beleaguered Fifth Army.

More than a third of the French army was in movement toward the north between March 22 and 26, in reaction to the German drive. Even the French troops in Italy were started back to France and the totality of the French reserves were committed in the direction of the breakthrough. Before the German penetration was halted thirty-four French infantry and six cavalry divisions were sent to the threatened point, being engaged piecemeal as they arrived, often without their artillery and sometimes even without their machine guns—logistically an important undertaking.

Pétain's intervention would perhaps have been faster had he not been worried that the Germans were preparing another offensive which would fall, his staff and intelligence reports told him, on his Champagne front. As late as the 25th a French parliamentarian found, on an inspection tour of the French forces in Champagne, that all the generals of the army in that sector, from the army commander to the divisional generals, still thought that an offensive was imminent on their front, an impression which the enemy had cleverly given them by making preparations in the area and by planting false information for French Intelligence. Actually General Duchêne and his subordinates were not mistaken in expecting an attack but they were off in the timing. Ludendorff utilized his preparations on the French Sixth Army front for an attack a month later, on May 27.[10]

10 Abel Ferry, Les Carnets secrets (1914–1918) (Paris, 1957), 226; Henri Bidou, "L'Offensive allemande de 1918 (21 mars–16 avril)," Revue des deux mondes (Paris, 1918), Tome 45, 417– 445; X [probably Louis Madelin, of Pétain's staff], "La Bataille de France de 1918," Revue des deux mondes (Paris, 1918), Tome 46, 241–302; Paul Painlevé, Comment j'ai nommé Foch et Pétain (Paris, 1923), 294–298; Laure, 192–194; Jean de Pierrefeu, G.Q.G. Secteur I (Paris, 1922), 128 et seq.; see also Historical Section, The Committee of Imperial Defense, History of the Great War, Military Operations, France and Belgium, 1918, comp. Brig. Gen. Sir James E. Edmonds (London, 1935), I, 101, 102, 296, 330–337, 392, 393, 399, 427, 448–450.

On the evening of the 24th Clemenceau paid a visit to Pétain's headquarters and had dinner with the Commander in Chief there. Pétain, in his report on the situation to the Premier, gave the news in his usual somber fashion—and there was much to be somber about. The Germans had crossed the Somme, which should have been an important obstacle. To make matters worse, the British in their retreat were tending to withdraw toward their bases on the coast, and with Pétain concerned about covering Paris a gap was developing between the two armies. No sooner would the French forces, flung hastily into the battle, as they arrived extend the French line to reach out to the British, then the British would withdraw their right. He asked Clemenceau to bring pressure to bear on the British to get them to support themselves on the French army and not to force him to extend his forces indefinitely to reach them.[11]

It was apparent that the commanders of the two allied armies were each concerned, quite properly, with the vital interests of his own country: Haig had to keep his line of retreat open to his coastal bases in order to safeguard his army, and Pétain had to protect the vital heart of France. This question was an inevitable one between the two allies whenever they were seriously threatened by an enemy advance—the situation arose again in 1940 when the British evacuated their army through the port of Dunkirk instead of fighting to rejoin the main French forces in the south as Weygand directed—and one that was not new in the war. Early in the war, in August 1915, the British commander, Sir John French, inquired in writing of Joffre if, in the event of a German breakthrough which might threaten to split the French and British armies, the British should cover the coast at the risk of breaking contact with the French, or if they should uncover the coast and retire to the south to assure the liaison with their allies. Joffre replied that if the enemy should ever break through and approach the sea, menacing the communications of the two armies, the British should cover at all cost the Channel ports—Dunkirk, Calais and Boulogne—which were of the utmost importance to the allies, while during this time the French would concentrate around Amiens and would attack the enemy in his southern flank.[12]

The question arose again in June 1918, after Foch had assumed the supreme command, when the Germans again threatened the allies

---

[11] Georges Wormser, "Foch doit à Clemenceau le commandement suprême," *Revue de defense nationale* (January–June 1949), New Series, Vol. VIII, 754–775.
[12] *Les Armées françaises* . . . , Tome III, 296.

with successful penetrations on a large scale; Clemenceau and Pétain agreed in advance that if it came to a choice the French armies should cover Paris in preference to Calais.[13] Unified allied command or no, the vital interests of the nation would come first in a crisis; individuals might sacrifice themselves for the good of their fellows but nations do not.

Yet if Pétain were really concerned solely with covering Paris and had decided to abandon his ally he would not have been scattering his forces by stretching his line northwestward toward the Somme or by unstintingly throwing men into a gaping hole in the line where they were often caught up and engulfed by the flood before they could establish a line. He would have been concentrating his forces instead and withdrawing his left flank to secure it and his army. His problem was to do his best to stop the German advance and to reestablish contact with his ally whose right flank had been withdrawn from him with the virtual disappearance of the unfortunate Gough's Fifth Army, and at the same time plan ahead for the possibility that the enemy might succeed in separating the two armies and force each to fight individually. Planning for the worst is not the same as accepting it.

On the same day as Clemenceau's visit Pétain ordered General Fayolle, commander of the reserve group of armies entrusted with the operation between the Oise and the Somme, to keep the French army intact and not to let his army group get cut off from the main body. He further ordered that if it were possible Fayolle should maintain liaison with the British forces. The security of the French army and the fate of the country were to be his first consideration but if it were at all possible—and he gave Fayolle two armies comprising ten army corps of forty divisions, the totality of the French reserves, with enormous quantities of heavy and light artillery, to make it possible—the two allies should remain in contact and the front broken by the British defeat should be reestablished. This was a sensible and proper order under the circumstances and one which would cover his subordinate should the need arise. It is interesting to compare the explicit directions which Pétain gave to his subordinate commanders in moments of crisis with the vague and noncommittal directives in which Joffre sometimes took refuge in 1914, notably to Lanrezac and to Sarrail, when the French armies were in full retreat. On the other hand they were not quite so explicit as those of General Foch who in moments of crisis simply ordered an attack.

---

[13] Poincaré, X, 237.

A conference of allied leaders took place at Doullens on March 26, out of which came the unified command which the French had long sought and the British had long opposed. Haig's desperate need for French reserves and the enormity of the disaster on the Somme had convinced him of the necessity for a supreme commander. The wily French Premier, Clemenceau, exploited the situation to the full in getting his nominee, Foch, appointed generalissimo.

On the journey to Doullens Clemenceau confided to a companion that he was going to seize the occasion of the British defeat to impose upon them the unity of command which he considered essential to the successful prosecution of the war. The "Tiger" was in good humor, for the news from the front the night before indicated that the Germans might be held before Amiens and that they apparently were unable to exploit their breakthrough.[14]

At the conference Pétain distressed the allied civilian leaders, as he usually did, with a bleak portrayal of the situation. He told them of the great numbers of divisions which he was hurrying into the line but which were coming slowly and were often not fresh. He made no optimistic promises for the future but merely outlined the realities of the situation and the realities were not pleasant. He probably overdid his realism—there is always hope no matter how dark the picture seems to be—but Pétain's temperament, at this stage of the war, allowed him no bursts of happy optimism.

Foch, on the other hand, was as ebullient and aggressive as Pétain was gloomy; his listeners were heartened by his lively expressions of enthusiasm and encouragement. It took very little persuasion at this point for the British to accept Foch as supreme commander; in fact Haig suggested it. And so Clemenceau had achieved one of the neatest political coups of the war: France now had an ideal command situation; her own armies remained under the immediate command of Pétain, whose known prudence would ensure that French blood would be expended parsimoniously, while all the allied armies, including the new armies of great numbers of fresh Americans, would be under the overall command of a French officer whose known propensity for offensive action without an inhibiting concern for losses ensured a dynamic prosecution of the war effort.

Foch's eager and optimistic approach to the problem and Pétain's coldly discouraging view were not mere manifestations of their respective temperaments, however. The second battle of the Somme in March 1918 was a test, in a way, of two divergent military philosophies,

---

[14] Général Mordacq, "Le Commandement unique," *Revue des deux mondes* (Paris, March–April, 1929), Vol. 50, 834–858.

upon which each of the protagonists had staked his reputation—and indeed the lives of his countrymen and the fortune of his country. Pétain had thought and taught that with the forces on the western front generally in equilibrium, with a small preponderance on the German side in the spring of 1918 to be sure, a breakthrough on a large scale was not likely by either side and certainly an exploitation of a breakthrough was not possible.

He believed, and his whole organization of the French military defenses was based on that belief, that an attacker could not progress beyond the second positions of the defender, for the latter would have brought up his reserves to counter the breakthrough and the attacker would have to halt his advance to "prepare" the new opposing line with artillery fire, a new and time-consuming operation. Hence his emphasis upon limited attacks to take the adversary's first positions only, to use up his reserves, then, at some future date, to take the offensive when the enemy's reserves were gone.

Foch on the other hand, like Haig, Joffre, Nivelle, Mangin, and many other general officers, had a distinctly offensive viewpoint and had believed, and many men had died in a test of that belief, that a breakthrough and a strategic exploitation of the breakthrough was possible and attainable. The German offensive of March 21 was a great success, it seemed, and Foch at Doullens saw his point of view vindicated; the civilian heads of government, including Lloyd George who was not present, who had come to Pétain's way of thinking and who had conceived a profound distrust of the Haigs and the Fochs, now found that perhaps the latter two had been partially right after all. At any rate it was obvious that there was no simple solution to the problem.

Pétain saw his theories apparently disproved; even though the Germans would be stopped in this particular offensive they had scored an amazingly successful victory and who could tell how many more of these operations would be forthcoming? Basically his ideas were sound, as the future proved, but at the moment his nerve was shaken.

As for the immediate battle situation the German drive was losing its impetus and was grinding to a halt. Already on the evening of the 28th, the day after the Doullens conference, General Humbert, Third Army commander, reported to G.Q.G. that the enemy was being held on the front Lassigny-Noyons, on the southern flank of the penetration. While this was not in the main direction of the German drive it was on the "shoulder" of the bulge created by their advance and the successful defense there was a good sign. On the 29th there was further evidence of a slackening in the progress of the enemy and by the 30th it was apparent that the situation, while still dangerous, was under control. The massive efforts of the French army enabled it to take hold on its new fifty-mile front and the British resistance also stiffened.

The German attackers were exhausted by their efforts and had outrun their supplies and artillery. They had advanced thirty-six miles, the largest advance by far of any army on the western front since 1914, but it was apparent that given the technical limitations of transport and equipment in World War I it was not possible to crush the opposing armies while they still had reserves to rush into the breach. The great number of casualties which the Germans were losing in this and subsequent efforts to end the war in the spring of 1918 was using up their own reserves, a wastage which would, in effect, shorten the war by six or nine months. They were held before Amiens as the allied line stiffened; the German artillery so brilliantly organized on the 21st was now left far behind and by the 29th the French artillery, which had taken longer than the infantry to get into position, was thundering out a murderous barrage of fire.

On April 3, 1918, the Beauvais agreement between the allied powers further defined Foch's position as strategic director of the allied armies, with their respective national commanders retaining the right to exercise "in its plenitude the tactical conduct of their armies." Thus Pétain was still responsible, at least in theory, for the methods used by the French armies, offensively and defensively. The French army in the north, however, with the British in Flanders, came directly under Foch's command and the latter gave orders to them to defend their ground foot by foot; there would be no relinquishing of terrain, no maneuver in retreat.

Not only were the French troops directly under Foch's command given orders to hold every foot of ground but the supreme commander sought to forestall the expected German offensive, or at least to keep the enemy off balance, by himself going over to the offensive, in operations so conducted as to cause Pétain considerable uneasiness. The latter reported to President Poincaré that the troops in the north, no longer under his command, were being thrown into poorly prepared attacks reminiscent of the former disheartening offensives and their morale, which he had so carefully restored after the mutinies and so jealously guarded, was beginning to decline. General Fayolle, commander of the Reserve Army Group, also was disturbed and he complained to Poincaré that this type of operation had already cost them dearly in manpower during the war, with little to show for it.[15]

---

15 Poincaré, X, 169.

French troops, however, by 1918 had learned how to defend themselves, not only from the enemy but from their own high command.
Attacks were not pressed home with vigor; when stiff opposition was
encountered the attacking units would be likely to halt their advance
and their officers would report to higher headquarters that the attack
had been stopped by strong enemy resistance. If they then received the
order to press the attack "at all cost" that meant that they should keep
trying. In the defense French troops had learned not to hold untenable, or even difficult, positions under determined attack. The report
of such a withdrawal would be something like: "Unable to hold when
our lines were overwhelmed."

In fairness to Foch and to other commanders who were accustomed
to ordering units to "hold at all cost" or to "retake the positions at
all cost" or to undertake a "mission of sacrifice," we should note that
such phrases had a semantic value which was not at all literal. In
order to ensure that the soldiers, and the combat officers too, would
offer a determined resistance in a defensive operation or would attack
with a certain amount of vigor, commanders had become accustomed
to issuing orders which in many cases were rhetorically handsome but
not meant to be taken literally, as both the issuer and the recipients
of the order understood.

In the first weeks of the war in 1914 an order to hold a particular
position in the path of the enemy "to the death or at least until twelve
o'clock noon" which was given, quite seriously, to a small unit in the
I Army Corps, could cause a certain amount of amusement but by
1918 such military phraseology in the French army was commonplace.
The French soldiers understood each other but outsiders were sometimes confused when faced with these semantics. For example, American troops in June 1918, thrown into the line to stop a victorious
German advance, were amused by the orders of a French army commander that they "must hold the line at all hazards" and then a second message telling them to dig trenches several hundred yards in
the rear in case they had to fall back.[16]

Pétain's concern for a decline in morale of the French soldiers was
not confined to the armies in the north. The troops under his own
command were also weary and dejected. The German spring offensives
were so powerful and so tactically successful that many Frenchmen
had lost hope. Abel Ferry and two other deputies, on a mission to the
front in April 1918 for the Chamber of Deputies, were appalled at the
attitude of the soldiers whom they saw, dejected, dispirited and hostile

---

[16] S. L. A. Marshall, *The American Heritage History of World War I* (American Heritage Publishing Co., Inc., 1964), 280.

to their leaders to a degree that alarmed the parliamentarians who had vivid memories of the mutiny nightmare of 1917.

At one point the deputies were surrounded by about a hundred soldiers who demanded that a peace be made with the enemy; the angry men complained of the interminable and costly war and of their allies who were not, the *poilus* thought, doing their fair share.[17] Ferry's discerning and informed comments on the poor morale of the worn-out soldiers and war-weary civilians in France carry special weight because that gallant soldier and statesman was killed on the field of battle in 1918 and his observations had been written while the incidents were fresh in his mind. Not published until 1957 they have an immediacy and candor which many postwar accounts and memoirs lack. After the war a certain amount of patriotic or martial pride in France tended to romanticize or gloss over that which made an unpleasant memory, but close observers like Ferry in 1918 feared that France would suffer a military collapse like that of Russia. However France, with the aid of her allies, managed to finish the war intact and emerged victorious; her collapse was delayed until 1940.

A further difference between the French high command and the Supreme Command lay in their respective opinions as to the probable area of the next German attack. Foch was convinced that the region north of the Somme offered the most advantageous conditions to the enemy and he concentrated the greater part of the strategic reserves in Flanders and close to Amiens, over Pétain's protests. The latter correctly estimated that the Germans would attack in Champagne. This difference of opinion had serious repercussions, for when in fact the German blow fell on the French front in the Chemin des Dames sector on May 27, Foch clung to his belief that the main attack would be made in the north, thus withholding the reserves desperately needed by Pétain.

The enemy could not have made a better choice in their point of assault than the Chemin des Dames, for that "calm" front was held by shattered British and French divisions sent there for rest after the March battle—divisions which were given to Pétain to replace fresh divisions withdrawn to the north.

General Duchêne, commander of the Sixth Army on the front of attack, had planned his defense in direct contradiction to Pétain's method as outlined in his Directive No. 4 but in conformance with Foch's directives: the bulk of his forces was concentrated in the first line with the second line weakly held; he planned to conduct the battle on the first line with no thought of withdrawal. He justified these

---

[17] Ferry, 229, 230.

dispositions to Pétain and Franchet d'Espèrey, Northern Army Group commander, both of whom were very concerned, by pointing out that this front was too close to Paris to consider giving up any ground, that his first line had good defensive terrain features, and that a withdrawal in this region—of the April 1917 offensive—would be bad for public opinion and troop morale. Pétain said afterward that he had given in because it was obvious that to enforce compliance Duchêne would have had to be removed from his command and also because he felt that his method, not yet tested and confirmed by success on a large scale, was still subject to further study and to a consideration of divergent ideas. In any case he felt that it was too late to make major changes in the dispositions taken by Duchêne.

Duchêne actually was complying with Foch's note of May 5, 1918, which virtually countermanded Pétain's Directive No. 4. Foch wanted the front line positions to be held at all cost; units must fight for every foot, with no thought of a maneuver in retreat; he specified that the second line should be lightly held, therefore the bulk of the forces should be in the front line. So Duchêne's troops were concentrated in the forward positions where they were a compact target within easy range of the heavy bombardment which the Germans delivered upon them, a blow which cracked the Sixth Army in a few hours.

The German attack on May 27, preceded by a short but extremely violent artillery preparation, succeeded completely in breaking through the first and second lines in one bound and swept on towards Paris, covering thirteen miles in one day and crossing three rivers, until they were finally held early in June in a battle on the Marne in which the Americans played an important role. The shaken French forces braced themselves for a renewed assault, for both sides recognized that the Germans must achieve victory now or never, as the American weight had begun to make itself felt.

French public opinion was so alarmed at the German success that there was an outcry for sanctions against the commanders responsible and a demand for the removal of Foch and Pétain by some members of the parliament; but Clemenceau defended his two commanders. Before the German breakthrough at the Chemin des Dames Pétain had protested the withdrawal of troops by Foch from his front to meet an offensive in the north, an offensive which did not materialize. It would seem that Pétain was right and Foch was at fault; but the latter had in fact divined Ludendorff's initial intentions correctly, for the German Commander in Chief intended his attack against the French front to be diversionary, to attract allied reserves to the south, and then he planned to make his main effort in the north. However, when the diversion proved to be so great a success Ludendorff decided to make it his main effort and to push towards Paris.[18] Foch had guessed correctly but had failed to follow his opponent's change of strategy despite Pétain's remonstrances—a change brought about by the German tactical success on the Aisne.

The controversy did settle one matter: the Beauvais agreement of April 3 had, upon the insistence of the British, reserved to the commander of each national army the right to appeal to his government if he thought his army were endangered by Foch's instructions. When Pétain attempted to avail himself of this outlet, during his conflict with Foch regarding the taking of reserves from his front, which he regarded as thinning it beyond the bounds of prudence, and also regarding his demands that the British undertake to hold a larger share of the front, President of the Council and Minister of War Clemenceau made it clear to Pétain that the right to appeal did not apply to him. Therefore Foch exercised a control over the French army which he could not apply to the British or American armies in France and Pétain was subordinate to him in a way that Haig and Pershing were not.

However, with Pétain his differences with Foch were not a personal matter but were matters of principle. On the day after the grave defeat at the Chemin des Dames he told an associate that he expected to be relieved of his command for the disaster. The officer with whom he was speaking, General Serrigny, then a divisional commander, objected that the defeat was not Pétain's fault but was Foch's if anyone's, since the latter had taken all the French reserves toward the north to support the British army for fear of an attack there. Pétain replied that this was true but that he would not protest or defend himself because Foch was necessary for the victory and he would do nothing to sap his authority.[19]

Pétain was less worried about the enemy breakthrough on May 27 than was the government and the country. He told his staff officers that the German attack would be contained and that the worst was now over. He felt that if they could hold until the end of June they would be in an excellent situation and in July they would go over to the offensive; after that "the victory will be ours."[20] Not only was this an accurate appraisal of the situation—Pétain could see the wastage of the German reserves behind the apparent victories and he also

---

[18] Erich von Ludendorff, *Ludendorff's Own Story* (New York, 1919), Vol. II.
[19] See Serrigny's testimony at Pétain's trial in 1945, Maréchal Pétain, *Le Procès du Maréchal Pétain* (Paris, 1945), I, 480, 481.
[20] See Pierrefeu, 199, who was present when this was said.

saw the buildup of the American forces—but, more remarkably, he had said in the spring of 1917 that June 1918 would mark the turning point in the war, when American troops and the tanks and other equipment would turn the tide.

His remarks to his staff, made at a time when it seemed that the enemy was sweeping everything before him, illustrate a curious facet of Pétain's personality: usually glum in the presence of politicians and his military superiors or peers, he displayed another side of his personality to his subordinates. Perhaps he was a pessimist by nature but at least some of it was a calculated attempt to impress those responsible for decision making with the gravity of the situation—partly to impress them with his difficulties or to spur them to accepting his point of view and partly to gratify what seems to have been a perverse pleasure in shocking or alarming people.

The enemy had struck two heavy blows at the British in March and April; his May 27 assault across the Aisne which reached the Marne was his third effort; a fourth and fifth were yet to come in June and July. On June 9 an attack fell upon the French Third Army on the Oise and although it was stopped within a few days it succeeded in breaking through the first two positions, inflicting heavy casualties upon the defenders. General Humbert, commanding the Third Army, had organized his resistance in the first line; he did not believe in Pétain's method for defensive operations and he was supported by Foch, who was a frequent visitor to his headquarters.

In early June he had been ordered by Pétain and Fayolle, his army group commander, to conform to Pétain's directives. Humbert made a partial reorganization of his defense system but it was not sufficient and Fayolle again, on the eve of the attack, prodded him to complete the preparations as instructed. But too much time had been lost and the subordinate commanders and troops were not completely oriented on their new role nor were the secondary positions properly prepared. Due to the opposition of the subordinate commanders to the new defense system, in which they too felt themselves supported by the attitude of the government and the Supreme Allied Command, there were still too many troops in the first line when the attack took place, resulting in another German breakthrough, which was stopped by French and American counterattacks.[21]

The half-measures taken to comply with Pétain's method had mitigated to some degree the extent of the penetration but stubborn attachment to old principles had enabled the Germans to achieve sub-

---

[21] *Les Armées françaises* . . . , Tome VI, Vol. II, 276–291.

stantial gains. There was lively scene between Pétain and Humbert
in which the exasperated Commander in Chief, in the presence of
other general officers, subjected his subordinate to a tongue-lashing,
a proceeding foreign to his normally reserved temperament. Humbert
was fortunate, however; Duchêne had been removed from his command after the May affair.

The final enemy blow fell on July 15, with the enemy's strength
concentrated for one last desperate effort. This time the scene of the
attack was the Fifth and Fourth Army fronts on both sides of the
Rheims salient. The battle situation was saved by the action of the
Fourth Army east of Rheims, commanded by General Gouraud. During the month of June the latter organized his front in complete accordance with Pétain's Directive No. 4. His front line was lightly held,
with the main line of resistance organized on the secondary positions,
some three kilometers in the rear, out of range of the bulk of the German artillery and trench-mortars. The front line was really a series of
advanced posts, arranged in a checkered pattern of small strongpoints
so that their machine gun fire crossed.

The German artillery barrage fell on nearly empty space and the
attacks were completely defeated on the second positions. The first
line had to some extent broken up the enemy attack before the light
forces there fell back—or were overrun—canalizing and delaying the
advance. The German schedule was disrupted by the new technique;
the advancing waves of infantry lost touch with their rolling barrage.
After the attack broke on the French second line Gouraud took the
offensive against the disorganized Germans and threw them back.
This action brought Gouraud personal fame, resulted in the breakdown of the final German offensive effort, and proved the value of
Pétain's defensive method.[22]

For the first time a major German assault—twenty-five divisions on
a twenty-eight mile front—was thrown back with heavy losses and
without having taken prisoners or cannon. One of Pétain's staff officers summed up Pétain's plan, demonstrated by the July 15th battle,
as one to let the enemy take the initiative of the attack and then to
act against him in a counteroffensive; in short, the "counter-punch."

West of Rheims the Fifth Army under General Berthelot fared less
well. This army was hurled back in disorder and the German drive
was stopped only by a determined American resistance on the Marne

---

[22] Général Gouraud, "La Bataille du 15 juillet 1918," *Revue des deux mondes,*
XLVI (July–August 1928), 667–672; *Les Armées françaises . . . ,* Tome VI,
Vol. II, 454–468, 485–494.

and by French reserves which were available to Pétain because of
Gouraud's successful defensive operation. Berthelot, a 250-pounder,
formerly staff officer to Marshal Joffre when the latter was commander
in chief, had been recently appointed by Foch to command the Fifth
Army and it was obvious that he had no intention of conforming to
Pétain's elastic defense method. Foch was shuffling the command of
the French armies to give their direction the offensive-mindedness
that he thought had been lacking since Pétain took charge in 1917.
For example, Mangin, of April 1917 notoriety and since then a general
without employment, was given command of the Tenth Army, and
General Anthoine, Pétain's chief of staff, was removed and the post
given to General Buat, formerly commander of the Fifth Army and
an officer in tune with Foch's ideas.

Foch's efforts to give an aggressive, offensive-minded attitude to the
French forces was, after July 1918, a sensible approach, for the allies
were entering a phase of the war when they would be able to pursue,
with superior resources in men and equipment, a series of offensives
against the weaker German army. It is a little sad, nevertheless, that
some of the generals who had been mistaken in their methods for four
years should lead the victorious survivors in the final stages of the war.

Throughout these defensive battles from May through July Pétain
and Foch were at odds over the basic principles to be employed. To
Pétain the German breakthroughs meant a return to conditions of
open warfare; to Foch they meant a renewed insistence upon holding
every foot of ground. The same lack of imagination which had produced the offensive *à outrance* theory also underlay the concept
of *résistance à outrance*. Both ideas displayed a fixity of thought
which left no room for freedom of action or maneuver and both were
productive of heavy losses with little other profitable result. It is
curious that whenever the conditions of open warfare which the allies
had sought so eagerly in their offensives throughout the war were
thrust upon them by the action of their adversary, they immediately
and frantically attempted to reestablish the familiar continuous front.

Although the Germans had been unable to achieve the decisive
defeat of the allies before the Americans could arrive in great numbers, the recent battles had driven the French to the very limit of
their resources. By the end of July Pétain was giving more and more
of his front to the fresh American divisions, replacing his own depleted
formations. On July 31 he sent a memorandum to Foch giving an eval-
uation of the remaining French effectives. He reported that he had no
more fresh reserves and his deficit on that day exceeded 120,000 men;

his immediately available replacements numbered 19,000 men with an expectation of only 29,000 more within the next two or three months. He advised that his troops were in good morale but were fatigued to an extreme. His report concluded with these words, "We are at the end of our effort."[23]

Joffre had been right when he said that victory would go to the side with the final battalions but the final battalions would be American. Almost a million and a half dead young Frenchmen would not be present for the Pyrrhic conclusion.

Pétain had said in 1917 that he was waiting for the Americans and the tanks. Both of these were reaching the front in large numbers in the summer of 1918 and the French Commander in Chief was responsible in large measure for the development and employment of the armored, tracked vehicle which would help break the entrenched stalemate on the western front.

The primary tactical problem facing the commanders on the western front during World War I was the fact that automatic weapons had rendered fronts inviolable to attack unless the attacker could crush the opposing positions with his artillery. The problem was not solved even after the armies received sufficient artillery pieces and ammunition to effectively silence the enemy's machine guns, break gaps in the barbed wire and demolish his shelters and strongpoints, because the attackers could then only operate effectively within the range of their own guns; beyond that they could not penetrate.

The attacker could break through the first positions, given sufficient artillery penetration; but he would be stopped on the enemy's secondary positions, relatively unaffected by the preliminary bombardment. The attacking force would then have to halt to bring up artillery to "prepare" the enemy's secondary positions, but the artillery of that era, largely horsedrawn, could not move forward quickly enough, over terrain torn up by its own fire, to support the attacking infantry before the enemy's reserves could arrive at the threatened point.

Generals who had spent their lives studying classical military theory, designed for wars of movement, found themselves frustrated by a siege war which they had not foreseen and which many of them never understood. The tank was an answer to the problem and Pétain was one of the earliest commanders to see its value.

He first came into contact with the idea of the new weapon during the battle of Verdun when Paul Painlevé, then Minister of Inventions,

23 *Les Armées françaises* . . . , Tome VII, Vol. I, 132.

came to Verdun to see the shell-pocked terrain, which the designers of the tanks, actually a British invention, had to take into consideration in developing the tracked vehicles.

Pétain normally was distant and even uncooperative with visiting politicians but in this instance he was so intrigued by the new idea, which promised an answer to tactical problems which had plagued him since 1914, that he and Painlevé became friends and thereafter worked closely together. When he was promoted to an army group command his command became the testing ground for the development of the French tanks.

In the abortive Chemin des Dames offensive of April 1917 the French tanks made their debut on a relatively large scale and they were not at all successful. Most of them were put out of action and destroyed on the plain of Juvincourt by enemy artillery fire, and the majority of their crews, so enthusiastic and proud of their revolutionary weapon before the battle, died in the flaming hulls. The tanks would suffer from engine failure, which rendered them immobile and an easy target for enemy guns; or they would become stuck in the difficult and muddy terrain, or they would be destroyed by enemy fire as they maneuvered, slowly and clumsily, in massed formation in open terrain.

So great was the failure of the tanks in their first venture on the French front that there was some question at G.Q.G. as to whether their production would be continued. To manufacture them in quantity so that their employment would be useful it would be necessary to devote considerable industrial productive capacity as well as raw materials to their manufacture, but all these already were being taxed to the utmost to supply the armies and any new effort would be at the expense of artillery production. Yet the production of cannon, the most powerful weapon that the army had, was a vital consideration and to create a new instrument, one that had already failed on the battlefield, at the expense of artillery production, took courage or at least imagination on the part of the high command.

Many staff officers at G.Q.G. in the summer of 1917 advised Pétain to forego the production of tanks; their need for artillery was greater and the tank appeared ridiculous or at least a gamble to some of them. But the Commander in Chief decided to go ahead with a large-scale manufacture of the new weapon and he initiated a program for the manufacture of 2,500 light tanks, scheduled to be ready by July 1, 1918, following this with an order for 500 more. His plan was to go on the offensive in July 1918 when he anticipated the presence of

3,000 light tanks and 1,000,000 American soldiers in France. His "I am waiting for the Americans and the tanks" formula of 1917 was not mere rhetoric.[24]

The Germans at that time chose not to produce large numbers of tanks, partly through military conservatism and partly because of a shortage of steel, and the few tanks that they had in 1918 were mostly captured ones.

In the Malmaison offensive of October 1917 Pétain used tanks with great success. French soldiers had found in the Chemin des Dames battle that the tanks performed poorly when used independently in massed formation. They were clumsy, prone to engine failure, and easily stopped by obstacles; the best method for their employment was found to be in small groups in close conjunction with the infantry. These tactics worked well and during the 1918 battles, as at Malmaison, the tanks worked in close support of the infantry rather than attempting to work alone.

Even if tanks in massed formation could break through the enemy positions, the model 1917 Renault—with a maximum speed of less than five miles per hour—could not exploit its victory because of its very limited range of action, its frequent engine failure and its light armament. The tanks needed the support of the infantry as much as the infantry needed them.

The difficulty was compounded by Pétain's decision to concentrate on the production of light, rather than heavy, tanks. In this way he was able to get more machines for his armies with the material, time and labor available than if he had opted for heavy tanks; but the seven-ton Renault was greatly inferior, for example, to the contemporary British Mark V of twenty-seven tons. The Renault could not cross a wide trench; the infantry had to fill in or bridge trenches and ditches for the tanks and the latter as often followed the infantry as preceded it.

One can see in this tactical development the germ of the French concepts on armored warfare which were outmoded by 1940. The tank progressed greatly in twenty-two years from a technical point of view but French military men were still thinking in terms of the lessons learned in 1917 and 1918 and their tactical methods did not keep pace with technological developments.

---

[24] Painlevé, *Comment j'ai nommé Foch et Pétain*, 208; Général Velpry, "Tactique d'hier et de demain," *Revue militaire générale* (Paris, January–June, 1938), II, 158, 159. Velpry in 1916 and 1917, as a staff officer in the Operations Bureau at G.Q.G., worked on the development and employment of tanks and in 1918 he commanded the first regiment of tanks in the French army.

All is not mud and blood in war; there are pleasant moments and often romantic ones, even for the privates. Generals of course fare much better and it would have been out of character for Pétain to have given up his propensity for amorous adventures simply because his military responsibilities had increased. As a famous and popular general, and handsome despite his years, he naturally had many opportunities for flirtations, some of which might have gotten him into trouble had he been a general in an army not French.

Colonel Serrigny, Pétain's *chef de cabinet* until November 1917, has related in his posthumous memoirs various incidents concerning Pétain's flirtations, some of which he was able to cut short by pointing out to his superior the dangers of adverse publicity. However, one incident in 1917, if it is true, went beyond the frivolous stage and could have been a serious security problem. French Intelligence intercepted a communication from the German ambassador in Madrid to his government containing the information that a mistress had been found for the French Commander in Chief whose pay was to be 12,000 pesetas a month.

When confronted with a copy of the message by Serrigny and asked if he suspected the identity of the woman involved, Pétain, after some hesitation, admitted that he did. From that time on the Commander in Chief exercised more caution in his relations with women and fewer of them gained access to him.[25]

Pétain's personal life assumed a more tranquil aspect after 1916 when he found his old sweetheart, Eugénie Hardon, who was a nurse in a hospital at Châlons-sur-Marne—although the episode with the lady from Spain came a year later according to Serrigny's account. Mme. Hardon had a son but was divorced since 1914 from her first husband—whose release from a German prison camp Pétain arranged —and she had rented a small house for herself and son where she was often visited by her old friend. This relationship continued throughout the remainder of the war and provided the relaxation and family life that Pétain had never had.

After the German offensives had subsided in July the allies went over to the offensive. Pétain perplexed the enemy by employing a different method of attack on each front. In most cases he went without a lengthy preliminary artillery bombardment, which obtained an element of surprise. His Tenth Army followed behind a rolling barrage, not stopping for strong points of resistance but encircling them and reducing them with tanks which accompanied the assaulting

---

[25] Général Bernard Serrigny, *Trente Ans avec Pétain* (Paris, 1959), 142.

troops. His Fourth Army did not attack with the others but opened up a violent artillery bombardment on its front so that the enemy could not be sure where the main blow would fall. The Sixth Army took the enemy first line by surprise, as it was lightly held in the "elastic defense" method, but did not immediately proceed to the principal line of resistance; instead it halted, brought up artillery and subjected the secondary line to a rigorous pounding before proceeding with the attack.

The enemy's reserves had been depleted; those of the allies were augmented by the accretion of the American troops, and it was time for the long-planned general offensive, which took place throughout the remainder of the summer and the autumn.

Throughout the period of offensive action against Germany during the closing stages of the war Pétain had to manage his reserves very carefully to keep up the tempo of operations with his meager forces. Not only were his forces barely sufficient numerically but the quality was no longer of the best, and had not been since the mutinies. The Germans could divide their divisions into two categories: "shock" divisions, still of high quality (although greatly diminished after the spring offensives) and used for difficult assignments, and divisions of poorer quality, used only defensively, to hold sections of the front. The French could make no such distinctions, as a matter of policy, with their troops.

Pétain adopted a "noria" system of employing his forces—not because he wanted to but, as he said, through force of circumstances — in which divisions were carefully withdrawn from combat before they had suffered too greatly, thus husbanding their strength and their morale. It meant a constant shifting of roops from front to rear, and from battle to battle, in a perpetual movement, a system which the Germans never had to employ, nor had any other army for that matter.[26]

After July the Americans took over more and more of the battle from the French, permitting the latter the luxury of their "noria" system. American divisions numbered approximately 28,000 men each, three times the size of French or British divisions; they were each the equivalent of an allied army corps. The purpose of this large size was, according to General Harbord, partly to better utilize the few American officers who had staff experience or who had commanded large units, but largely so that American divisions could remain indefinitely

---

[26] See Général H. Fournier, "Les Armées françaises dans les opérations offensives de 1918—la 'noria' des réserves," *Revue militaire française,* LVI (1935), 159–161, 185–187.

in combat, without relief or substantial reinforcement, living off their own effectives.[27]

Four years of warfare had not only greatly weakened the French but the British and Germans also had reached the point of exhaustion. In the allied offensive from July to November 1918 the main allied drives were made by the British armies on the left and the Americans on the right. Since the old armies were no longer of high combat value the British on the left used fresh Australians and Canadians, with two American divisions, as shock troops, while on the right of the giant pincer movement the French used the Americans. The French armies in the center advanced over territory which fell to them as a result of the successful offensives made by the allies on their flanks.

The Germans had few shock troops left and were compelled to submit. The war went to the side with the last battalions but the last battalions of value were non-European. This was a whisper of the future, as yet too intangible to be recognized, a distant preview of 1945 when the armies of the United States and of the Soviet Union met on the Elbe, across a prostrate Europe.

With the British driving the Germans back in the north, forming the left arm of the pincer movement, the Americans were stubbornly driving toward Sedan and Mézières as the right arm of the movement. Pershing had been persuaded to give up his plan for an offensive farther east, toward Metz and the Briey iron region, which would have been less costly and more productive of strategic results, to fall in with Foch and Haig's request that he attack in a northerly direction to converge with the British drive. This meant that the Americans had to attack through the Argonne forest and along the west bank of the Meuse, probably the most difficult country on the western front outside of the Vosges mountains.

In this drive the American forces were liberally and generously supplied with artillery, tanks, aircraft and any other material aid that Pétain could give them. His own troops were able to move slowly forward as the Germans retreated and in early October the French Commander ordered his armies over to the all-out offensive. At this stage they were to pursue the attack with all energy, with unlimited objectives and allowing no respite to the enemy. To some extent these commands were simply rhetorical formulas designed to ensure that the French forces would continue to apply at least a modicum of pressure to the Germans facing them; after four years of savage con-

[27] James G. Harbord, *The American Army in France, 1917–1919* (Boston, 1936), 103, 104.

flict in which French armies had borne the heaviest burden they were now content to let their allies bloody themselves on the German defenses.

The American drive toward Sedan and Mézières thoroughly alarmed the Germans and threatened to cut off their armies in the north, which were retreating before the British forces. The new German Commander in Chief, Wilhelm Groener, who had replaced Ludendorff, said in his memoirs that ". . . the American breakthrough north of Verdun had brought the [German] army into a catastrophic position."[28]

If the Americans were to cut the important lateral railway line which ran through Carignan and Sedan the enemy would have difficulty in supplying his armies in northern France and Belgium and also would have difficulty in evacuating them through the relatively narrow gap between Liège and the Ardennes—in a sort of reverse Schlieffen Plan. Hence the fierce German resistance to the American Meuse-Argonne offensive, to counter which the German high command committed forty-three different divisions, totalling 470,000 men,[29] and their alarm when the Americans broke through.

Pétain also was planning a large-scale offensive through Lorraine toward the area southeast of Metz, in which the Americans would have had the predominant role. This offensive was planned for November 14 but was cancelled by the Armistice, a fact which Pétain never ceased to regret. It would have posed a serious threat to the Germans—flanking the Metz-Thionville fortifications, penetrating German territory beyond the Sarre, and cutting off the retreat of the German armies in the north.

Marshal Foch called a meeting of the allied commanders, Pétain, Haig and Pershing, at Senlis on October 25, to obtain their opinions on the terms of a possible armistice with the enemy. The purpose of the meeting was to determine what terms would render the German armies incapable of resuming effective military operations should the peace negotiations break down. Pétain felt that the most effective way to put the German armies out of action was to deprive them of their heavy materiel and the best way to ensure this was to require their withdrawal to the east of the Rhine at such a rapid pace that the enemy could not remove the bulk of his equipment, guns and ammu-

---

[28] Quoted in Gordon A. Craig, *Politics of the Prussian Army, 1640–1945* (Oxford, 1955), 345, 346 and footnote. See also Helmut Haeussler, *General William Groener and The Imperial German Army* (Madison, 1962), 150, footnote 15.
[29] Pershing, II, 388.

nition. He brought with him to the conference a map, which he spread out; it showed the territory between the allied positions and the Rhine and he had red arrows showing the stages of the proposed enemy withdrawal with a time-table. He would give them fifteen days to complete the movement.

Pétain also specified that allied bridgeheads should be established across the Rhine at Mainz, Coblenz and Cologne. In addition the Germans would have to hand over to the allies 5,000 locomotives and 100,000 railway cars in perfect condition.

It was finally decided at the meeting that the enemy should surrender 5,000 cannon, 30,000 machine guns (later reduced to 25,000 at the request of the Germans so that they could maintain internal order in their own country) and 3,000 trench mortars. They would have to retire to the east of the Rhine leaving a neutral zone on the east bank.

These and other provisions of the military armistice, including the maintenance of the allied blockade of Germany, Pétain considered so severe that the Germans would reject them; in fact it was his hope that they would reject them.

According to Mme. Hardon, who became his wife, he was very disappointed when he realized that the negotiations with the Germans would prevent his launching the offensive he had planned in Lorraine. He was deeply moved, more emotional than she was accustomed to seeing him, and was almost in tears, something his staff officers, who were usually petrified by his freezing formality, would have found difficult to believe.[30]

"Is it possible that they will deny me that?" he said, referring to his planned invasion of the Rhineland. He felt that it was a mistake to permit the Germans to march home in good order; after four years of occupation of French soil he wanted to drive them into Germany, to make them feel defeat.

On a December morning in 1918, on the Esplanade in the city of Metz, President Poincaré and President of the Council Clemenceau jointly presented Pétain with his marshal's baton, before a guard of honor composed of the commanders in chief of the allied armies. The presentation was made under the statue of Marshal Ney, perhaps symbolic and significant, as Ney also was a military hero and also was subsequently dishonored and condemned by a politically inspired court.

---

[30] Pierre Bourget, *Témoignages inédits sur le Maréchal Pétain* (Paris, 1960), 44.

8

The Rif Campaign

With the signing of the peace treaty with Germany the French army high command reverted to a peacetime footing, which meant that the title of Commander in Chief ceased to exist. Marshal Pétain continued on active service and continued to be commander of the army by virtue of his new position of Vice-President of the Higher War Council, to which he was appointed in 1920. In 1922 he also received the title of Inspector General of the Army.

In September 1920 the sixty-four year old marshal married his sweetheart, Annie Hardon. General Fayolle, his old comrade in arms, who soon also would be promoted to a marshalcy, was his best man. Fayolle doubtless was satisfied to see his friend, whose footloose bachelorhood he sometimes had found disconcerting, safely confined by the bonds of matrimony, although the civil marriage to a divorced woman in the office of the mayor of the 7th *arrondissement* in Paris, without subsequent benefit of clergy, perhaps was not as he would have preferred it.

The Marshal had purchased, in 1919, a villa at Villeneuve-Loubet in the Alpes-Maritimes department, the Mediterranean region where the newly wedded couple first had met so many years before. The purchase of the villa, called the "Ermitage," was made possible by Pétain's salary as a marshal; he had no other income and his wife was without means.

Gone was his prewar intention of settling near Saint Omer in the Pas de Calais. Not only did the climate of Pétain's native region suffer by comparison with that of the Midi but the place had ceased to attract the old soldier for other reasons. The agricultural country of his birth had long since been changed by the march of progress into a region of coal mines and industries, a land where the peasants had become, since the late nineteenth century, a small minority in a working class population. Since 1919 the people of Cauchy-à-la-Tour, where Pétain was born, have voted communist or socialist. And of course the Pas de Calais had no attraction at all for Mme. Pétain.

The lure of the soil was strong enough, however, to cause the Marshal, like Cincinnatus to whom he jokingly compared himself, to think of seriously cultivating his land. He grew grapes for wine, raised chickens and kept bees, and had two or three cows for milk. He hoped to make his estate self-sufficient in produce but this hope dimmed during the 1920's. In January 1934 he wryly admitted, in a letter to a nephew, that the produce of his land cost him more than if he bought his wine, eggs, honey and milk in the market.

Pétain's problem with the Ermitage was that he could not spend enough time supervising the work at the villa but had to leave it in the hands of employees, whose wages absorbed the profits and who, he suspected, were not giving him fair value for the wages that he paid them. His first farm manager, a retired noncommissioned officer, had to be dismissed for lack of interest and lack of competence; but even the local workers whom he hired either could not or would not make his land self-sufficient.

Still, there was the climate and the sun, and the Pétains spent as much time as they could, particularly during the winter months, at the Ermitage. But the retirement from public affairs was delayed again and again, and the Marshal and his wife found their visits to the south becoming increasingly infrequent and short. Pétain tried to sell his property at Villeneuve-Loubet but was unable to find a buyer who would pay what the place had cost him. In 1945 the Ermitage was confiscated by the state, as was all the rest of the condemned Marshal's property, and is today used by the department of the Alpes-Maritimes as a place for family vacations as part of the state social welfare program.

With Europe temporarily at peace it might have been expected that Marshal Pétain would no longer be called upon to lead French armies to war, but this was not the case. In 1925 a situation developed in the French North African territory of Morocco which threatened France with the loss of that valuable possession and a diminution of prestige in the Arab world which would have had serious repercussions in her other North African territories and might have resulted in a weakening of France's strategic position in the Mediterranean basin.

Dissident tribesmen in Spanish Morocco and northern French Morocco rose against the French in an action which had long been smoldering, and was more of a war than a revolt, since the affected area had never been conquered by either France or Spain. The Rif was a mountainous and virtually inaccessible region lying largely in Spanish Morocco but extending south into the French zone. Neither Spain nor France had ever succeeded in occupying or administering the area.

The Spaniards had already suffered defeat at the hands of these hardy mountaineers and the Riffs, flushed with victory and unawed by European armies, looked southward for new conquests. Their extension in that direction brought them into open conflict with the French colonial troops in French Morocco and ultimately with the full power of the French army, directed by Marshal Pétain.

Some years before the Riff tribes had been united under the hand of Abd-el-Krim and with these Berber tribesmen, traditionally avid for loot and conquest, he descended upon the Spanish forces who were attempting to pacify the country. In July, 1921, he inflicted a crushing defeat on the Spanish General Silvestre at Anoual, wiping out a Spanish army of 20,000 men. This victory gave the Berber chieftain complete control of the Rif, for the Spanish fell back upon the coast and abandoned their forward positions in the hills.

Abd-el-Krim's prestige was enhanced by this achievement, which assured his position as sovereign of the Rif, but more concretely his victory netted him 120 Spanish artillery pieces, thousands of modern rifles as well as machine guns and automatic rifles, and millions of rounds of amunition. With the millions of pesetas which accrued to him from the ransom of Spanish prisoners he was able to buy the services of European officers and, with a number of deserters from the Foreign Legion as instructors and artillerymen, his forces presented a professional appearance which gave a new and, to France, a disturbing tone to African colonial warfare.[1]

The hard core of the Riff forces consisted of 20–30,000 regulars and added to this were perhaps 100,000 irregular warriors. To guard

---

[1] Vice-Admiral C. V. Usborne, *The Conquest of Morocco* (London, 1936), 244–260; André Maurois, *Marshal Lyautey,* trans., Hamish Miles (London, 1931), 264–269; Anon., "Vues d'ensemble sur les affairs Nord-Morocains en 1925," *Revue des Deux Mondes* (January, 1926), a semi-official account, 72 *et seq.*

against this menace the French Moroccan resident-general, Marshal Lyautey, had some 25,000 men in 1924 when the complete inactivity of the Spanish army in Spanish Morocco exposed the French frontier to the increasing pressure of the encroaching Riffs.

In March of that year Lyautey moved some of his troops across the Ouergha River to establish small posts on the heights beyond, in the traditional fashion of colonial warfare. The valley of the Ouergha runs from east to west through the Rif mountains and was roughly twenty-five kilometers south of the demarcation line between the French and Spanish zones. The area north of the Ouergha, that is, the region between the river and the Franco-Spanish frontier, had heretofore been unoccupied by the French. Lyautey now moved in, in response to the appeals for help from the buffer tribes who lived in the fertile Ouergha valley and who were suffering from the inroads of the Riffs.

Lyautey had in mind another consideration which made his move a military necessity: the security of the city of Fez which lay some fifty kilometers south of the Ouergha, with no natural obstacles between it and the river to slow the advance of marauding tribesmen. The city of Taza, east of Fez, and the Fez-Taza railway, the principal communication with Algeria, were also menaced and had to be covered by the curtain of troops north of the river.[2]

In the spring of 1925 at the start of the campaigning season the Riffs unleashed a full-scale offensive on the French outposts north of the Ouergha, and upon the neutral tribes lying within the buffer area, forcing most of the latter to join with them against the French and greatly increasing thereby their strength in effectives. The small French forces were rapidly overrun despite their professional caliber —they were largely Foreign Legion, French colonial regulars, and colonial native troops; the Ouergha River barrier, itself no serious obstacle, was breached in several important places and the city of Taza appeared to be in imminent danger of capture. The fall of Taza would cut the Moroccan–Algerian communications, splitting the French forces, forcing them on the one side to retire to the east to protect the Algerian frontier and the forces in the west to fall back on Fez, which city would be partially encircled and seriously jeopardized.

The gravity of the situation penetrated into the parliamentary halls of the government in Paris, on a day which Paul Painlevé, President

[2] Paul Painlevé, *Paroles et Écrits* (Paris, 1936), 345–351.

of the Council and Minister of War, later described as the "feverish" day in July when the "fall" of Taza was announced in Paris.[3] Lyautey had been sending warnings of the impending attack to the government and had been complaining of the insufficiency of his forces but his warnings and appeals for reinforcements had not received much response. France's postwar army, relying upon an eighteen-month conscription system imposed upon a population tired of war, was stretched thin by her other colonial commitments and by her occupation army in Germany, particularly the large forces which had been dispatched into the Ruhr to enforce reparation payments.

The Premier–Minister of War hastened to Morocco to get a first-hand impression of events there. Although the threat to Taza had been averted, largely through the efforts of Lieutenant-Colonel Giraud, the overall picture was still grim and it was clear that a major effort would be required of France to restore the situation.

Large reinforcements of men and material were already on the way, and with the probability that even larger segments of the French military power would have to be drawn from Algeria and Tunisia, from metropolitan France, and from the occupying Army of the Rhine, the larger question of French strategic requirements became involved. The problem then became one for the high command, concerned with the twin problems of the frontier covering force (couverture) and mobilization; and Marshal Pétain as virtual Commander in Chief of the French army became directly involved.

Pétain, despite his pleading of advanced age and lack of colonial experience, was persuaded by Painlevé to proceed to Morocco in his role of Inspector-General with powers to examine the situation and to recommend to the government the proper steps for future action. At the same time Painlevé hastened the evacuation of the Ruhr which fortunately had been planned for July, 1925, and sent the troops thus obtained directly to the scene of the conflict, the Moroccan Division being the first to go in early July.

The threat to French interests in Morocco, and the French government's reaction to it, was complicated by the composition of the Chamber of Deputies elected in May, 1924. A coalition of Socialists and Radical-Socialists dominated the Chamber and there was a strong left-wing opposition to anything smacking either of colonialism or militarism. It is significant that the announcement of Pétain's assignment was made on July 7, four days after the 1925 session of the Chamber

---

[3] Journal officiel de la République française, Chamber of Deputies, Section 2, session of December, 1925, p. 4858.

had adjourned, when the government's action could not be challenged by the hostile deputies in open session.

Marshal Lyautey had suggested that General Weygand, Marshal Foch's former chief of staff, be appointed to take over the direction of military operations in northern Morocco—Lyautey's administrative duties as resident-general made it desirable that the military command should be made a separate function—but political hostility from the Left precluded the designation of a general with Weygand's pronounced conservative views. Lyautey himself, who once had been a Royalist, was an object of suspicion.

Pétain's popularity and prestige, both in the army and among the veterans of the War, insulated him to some degree from political acrimony. It is curious how the Marshal's military successes, and above all his defensive military doctrine and his concern for the lives of the soldiers under his command, had gained him the support of the liberal elements of French political leadership. He was not a "liberal" in the sense that he had great loyalty or devotion to republican institutions; but in his philosophy he was above all else realistic in his acceptance of that which he could not change, and he developed a tolerance, and probably even a liking, for the republic which had bestowed so much honor upon him.

When first consulted by the government Pétain advised that the Moroccan affair be considered in the context of the North African question as a whole and that measures be taken to secure the cooperation of Spain, with a view to undertaking and coordinating large-scale operations by both countries. He pointed out that the heartland of the Rif lay largely in Spanish territory and that French military action in the northern area of her own zone could not be decisive by itself. Unless the hard core of Riff resistance were wiped out there would remain a permanent source of unrest, a focal point of dissidence, and a constant drain upon French manpower and finances.

After inspecting the forces in Morocco and examining the situation on the spot, Pétain sent his aide, General Georges, back to Paris to request the immediate expedition of reinforcements equivalent to three divisions, emphasizing that a large proportion of them should be white Frenchmen. He felt that too great a reliance upon native troops made an unfortunate impression on the natives of North Africa. Then he proceeded to Tetuan in Spanish Morocco where he consulted with General Primo de Rivera, the Spanish dictator, on July 28, with a view toward persuading the Spanish to make a determined effort against the common enemy and to ensure that their combined action be closely coordinated to obtain the maximum results. He then continued on to Paris to make his report.

Pétain's recommendations for future operations which he presented to Painlevé and cabinet members Briand and Caillaux were designed to utilize to the fullest the resources of the French army and in conjunction with the Spanish to encase the Rif in a massive, converging ring of steel—an operation which had more in common with the methods employed on the western front in the recent war than with the traditional colonial flying-column à la Bugeaud, of nineteenth-century colonial warfare fame. He planned to maintain a firm defensive position on the western and central portions of the French front, from Ouezzan on the left to the region north of Fez in the center, while making his main offensive action in the east. The offensive would push northward from the Taza area and westward from the direction of Algeria.

This plan had the advantage of avoiding costly commitment in the west and central mountains, extremely difficult terrain, while operating mainly in the relatively easier eastern region. At the same time the Spaniards would push south from Mellila, on the Mediterranean coast, join hands with the French in the valley of the Kert, and together they would drive westward against the center of Riff control. It was in the east that the best opportunity offered itself for cooperation with the Spaniards, an aspect which Pétain considered essential to the whole operation. With steady pressure also being exerted along the whole French front, and from the Spanish front at Tetuan in the northwest, the Riffs would be hemmed in and slowly squeezed into submission by overpowering forces.[4]

The government approved the recommendations and requested that Pétain assume direct command of military operations in Morocco to carry them out, leaving Lyautey as resident-general in control of the civil administration. Since Pétain was senior in rank to Lyautey the new appointment automatically relegated the resident-general to a subordinate status, a fact which could not fail to wound the latter—whose great achievements and reputation were largely bound up in Morocco—no matter how delicately or diplomatically the situation were handled.

While on his way back to North Africa Pétain received the news that Lyautey and the local military commander, General Naulin, had

---

[4] Pétain's note on the subject in Lieutenant-Colonel Auguste Laure, *La Victoire franco-espagnole dans le Rif* (Paris, 1927), 49, 50. Laure was a member of Pétain's staff during the campaign, served as liaison with de Rivera, and had access to important orders, papers, and communications.

conceived their own plan and were in the process of executing it. The details of their projected operation, which seemed so well along in the planning and preparation that a change would be impractical, were directly contrary to the ideas which Pétain had developed and intended to carry out.

The plans of the soldiers in Morocco were wholly in the tradition of colonial warfare as developed by the French during almost a century of successful North African campaigning; the mobile column idea that had been first employed by General Bugeaud in Algeria in 1840 and that had become the basic tactic for the French army on active service against hostile irregular tribesmen, was now to be utilized in conformance with proven techniques. Lyautey and Naulin planned two parallel thrusts, in the center of the French front north of Fez—where Pétain had planned to go on the defensive—which would drive straight into the most difficult mountain country, aiming at surrounding a large buffer tribe which had gone over to Abd-el-Krim and forcing it to renew its allegiance to France. This was to be the first of several similar operations.

The primary objective of the projected operation was therefore of a political nature, to recover political control of disaffected tribal units, with the military decision a secondary aim. The plan had its merits and was of a type which had certainly been used with success in the past, but the colonial officers were not considering the larger picture and also were ignoring important new factors which had entered into and changed traditional colonial warfare.

The old tactics were designed for use against unorganized irregulars, armed with the crudest of firearms, and to be carried out by professional career soldiers and Foreign Legionnaires. Krim's forces—equipped with artillery, modern rifles and automatic weapons, with a plentiful supply of ammunition, and with an excellent organization and communications including telephone and telegraph—were a far cry from the enemy of former days. Conversely the French conscripts doing their short-term service and rudely transported into the bleak mountains, exposed to a severe climate and confronted with a cunning and fanatical enemy who in his own habitat was an excellent fighter, were not the troops for the dashing forays of old.

With these thoughts in mind Pétain continued his way back to Morocco, stopping off at Algeciras in Spain to confer again with de Rivera, to solidify the entente and to confirm the arrangements previously tentatively decided upon. It was agreed that in the ensuing campaign the French troops might temporarily cross the demarcation line into Spanish territory, a provision necessary if the French were to be able to pursue to its close the planned elimination of the Riff center of revolt. The Spaniards agreed, in conjunction with the combined operations, to land a force in the Bay of Alhucemas, on the northern coast of Spanish Morocco, and to proceed from there against the city of Ajdir, the capital of Abd-el-Krim.

Pétain's conference with de Rivera was held, perhaps symbolically, in the Hotel Maria Christina where the Algeciras conference of 1906 took place, when the primacy of French and Spanish interests in Morocco was recognized by the other great powers. At a banquet on the evening of August 21, as reported by the correspondent of the *New York Times* in Madrid, Pétain was reputed to have made a curious toast to the military dictator, head of the Spanish Directorate, as follows: "I toast Primo de Rivera who through his intelligence and patriotism was able to reestablish discipline and order in Spain. Perhaps circumstances may make it necessary to do in France as was done in Spain."[5]

It was fortunate for the Marshal's case during his trial in 1945 that this reported statement was not unearthed to be used against him, to show that his alleged conspiratorial intent vis à vis the French republic was of long duration. The prosecution at that time used less likely evidence with which to charge the old man with malice toward the Third Republic.

After his conference with the Spaniards Pétain proceeded to Morocco where he advised Lyautey of his own plan, so different from that of the local commanders. Lyautey agreed to the new proposal; he might have planned something of a similar nature if he had had the authority and the large forces which were now committed by the French government to the pacification of the Rif. Nevertheless he could not help but think that his authority and position in Morocco had been undermined by Pétain's assumption of control and in September he resigned his post as resident-general and retired to France. A certain amount of coolness between him and Pétain resulted but it was not of long duration; in time they were reconciled and when Lyautey died in 1934 Pétain pronounced the eulogy at his funeral.

The new commander proceeded to Rabat where he held conferences with Naulin and other local commanders. Here he had more difficulty gaining agreement with his plans. The officers involved, most with long colonial experience and conscious that Pétain had none, were imbued with confidence in the value of their plan and were reluctant to modify it even to adopt a plan of larger scope. The situation was

---

[5] *New York Times,* September 10, 1925.

not unlike that during the World War, when Pétain's theories were
not considered by some officers to be dashing enough for French soldiers; the loss of some four and one-half million casualties just a few
short years before was apparently not a sufficiently chastening experience. However, Pétain had the authority and the full backing of the
government and his views prevailed.

In order not to waste the preparations and planning that had gone
into the proposed attack of General Naulin, Pétain permitted it to
take place as scheduled but on a reduced basis with limited objectives,
and incorporated it into his own larger plan. He issued a memorandum[6] which outlined the disadvantages of the old plan, including the
arguments that its objective was political and not decisively military,
and pointed out its limited scope. The advantages of his own proposed line of action were explained, with references to the more favorable terrain features in the east, with better communications and
closer proximity to the Algerian supply lines, and to the chances of a
more far-reaching success by converging attacks from both French and
Spanish bases.

The French had by this time amassed a large army, liberally supplied with heavy artillery, including 155 millimeter guns (heretofore
not used in Africa), airplanes, and even tanks and armored cars, although the terrain was so difficult that the troops got more service out
of their mules than they did from the armored vehicles. The Riffs had,
by increasing their military power, promoted themselves to a level of
European warfare and they were to find themselves the bewildered
recipients of a hail of bombs, strafing aircraft, heavy artillery bombardments, and the probing attention of tanks and armored cars where
terrain permitted. French officers of the colonial school grudgingly admitted that the Pétain method worked well but they complained that
it was not "glorious."[7]

In 1917 when Pétain had assumed command of the French armies
in France, the average monthly rate of casualties fell markedly, partly
in response to his particular techniques but also because the French
army went on the defensive. To some extent this pattern repeated itself in Morocco although there he went on the offensive. During the
months April through July, 1925, before he took command in Mo-

---

6 Reproduced in Laure, 69–72.

7 See Captain Hubert-Jacques, *L'Aventure riffaine, et ses dessous politiques*
(Paris, 1927), for an exposition of the point of view of those who deplored
the application of Western Front techniques to colonial campaigns and who
regretted the passing of the "good old days."

rocco, French combat forces, operating on the defensive, averaged 8 per cent casualties per month. After Pétain's advent to command, and his going over to the offensive, losses fell in August and September to 4 per cent per month among the combat troops and in October to .6 per cent.[8]

As Pétain explained in a letter to Painlevé, his main concern was to avoid large losses while at the same time achieving a maximum of results. He claimed that the concentration of large forces permitted a methodical and rapid execution of operations with a minimum of casualties; he pointed out that in dealing with the natives the mere manifestation of powerful armies often led to success with little expenditure of blood on either side.[9] This of course was in 1925 when a certain condescension with regard to the military potential of the "natives" was a normal European reaction. As World War II proved, if it needed proving, the threat of powerful armies was enough to cow many small European nations in the path of a superior war machine, notably Denmark, Holland, Belgium and even France itself, which was not so small.

Nevertheless the Marshal was right in 1925 in calculating that the demonstration of a powerful army would impress not only the Berber tribesmen of Morocco but other North African natives as well. "Glorious" or not, his plan proceeded as scheduled. The Spanish landed a force of 20,000 men in the Bay of Alhucemas on September 8; on October 2 de Rivera took Ajdir, the former capital of Abd-el-Krim. Operations of the French north of Taza and the Spaniards south from Mellila effected a junction of forces and the combined armies attacked toward the center of Riff power, maneuvering on the Taza-Ajdir axis. Before the rainy season put a halt to the offensive, all the ground lost in the previous spring was recovered and a firm base was secured for the stabilization of a winter front, pending future operations. The Rif was now firmly hemmed in from all sides; it remained only for the spring weather to permit a resumption of hostilities, when the converging armies of Spain and France would crush the opposition and for the first time since the occupation of Morocco by Europeans be enabled to penetrate and administer the hardy Berber tribes of the mountainous interior.

After the situation had been thus secured and stabilized for the winter months Pétain returned to France, arriving on November 7. Normally reserved in the presence of the press, he made an unusual statement to the newsmen awaiting him at Marseille: "Abd-el-Krim

---

[8] Anon., *Revue des Deux Mondes* (January, 1926), 85.
[9] Laure, 90–93.

is encircled. He is no longer to be feared. Military actions are ended. I hand over the situation to the politicians."[10]

Inasmuch as a large French army was still tied up in Morocco and heavy fighting would develop in the spring before the Riffs were finally conquered, some people took exception to what they thought was an unduly optimistic appraisal of the situation. At least Pétain, usually condemned for his pessimism, had achieved a reversal of the customary criticism.

---

[10] *New York Times,* November 8, 1925.

9

The Organization of the High Command in the Inter-war Period — The Unified Command Concept

One of the most obvious lessons of World War I was in connection with the total mobilization of all a nation's resources for the prosecution of modern war and the need for a centralized command of all the various forces necessary to achieve victory. It was commonly accepted that the lack of a single commander over the allied forces in France for the first three and one-half years of the war was a weakening factor for the allied side and that the appointment of Ferdinand Foch as Commander in Chief of all allied armies in France in March 1918 was a determining factor in the allied victory.

It also seemed apparent that the degree of hierarchical unity attained by the Germany army, and the extent to which it was independent of civil control, was one of the reasons for its great strength and the source of much of its power during World War I. Military men argued that once war has been undertaken by the civil government—other, ordinary, measures of pursuing the political objectives of the nation having failed—the technical conduct of hostilities should be left to the technicians. That the Germans carried this concept to extreme and that the German military leaders of World War I finished by pursuing objectives which properly belonged within the realm of the civilian politicians did not disprove the fact, they said, that within the purely technical sphere it is best to leave the actual military operations to the technicians concerned.

Within the armed forces themselves it became apparent in a highly complex civilization that the various arms of the service could no longer retain autonomy and that modern war demanded a high degree of centralization. Yet it is only since World War II that the United States, for example, has instituted a unified command of the armed forces and only the realization that with modern weapons a potential aggressor is at their doorstep induced Americans to adopt this concept. France, however, has always had a potential aggressor at her doorstep and after World War I the most able of her military leaders saw the necessity for abolishing the old inter-service rivalry and the particularism of each arm, and the need to institute for their country a unification of the armed forces command structure.

Marshal Pétain, who thought that France had won the war in spite of her political organization and not because of it, was the foremost and the most prominent of the advocates of this concept, for which he worked vigorously from 1919 until 1939. The French government slowly and hesitantly evolved toward a realization of the centralized command recommended by him, and by 1939 had achieved some of the organizational reforms which he recommended; but they still retained too much of what he thought was an imperfect system and they went to war with a divided command and organizational structure. The completeness of the French defeat in 1940 was due in part to weaknesses in the organization of the high command.

The principles defining the respective spheres of the military and the government in time of war, with which France entered World War I, were set forth in the regulations of 1913. The civil government retained control of the higher conduct of war but it was recognized that the conduct of operations was the prerogative of the military. This definition of roles might have sufficed had the theater of war remained sufficiently remote for the two spheres not to conflict; but the greater part of the hostilities took place on French soil, with the nation living periously under its immediate shadow, and the degree of authority which the military leaders and the civilian ministers exercised varied according to the pressure of events and to the personalities of the leaders involved, with the intervention of the parliament exerting a third influence.

In 1914 General Joffre had been given complete independence in the conduct of operations by Premier Viviani and Minister of War Messimy. His position was further strengthened by his victory on the Marne, which enhanced his prestige (his failure in the battle of the frontiers nothwithstanding), and by a lowering of governmental prestige as a result of the departure of the government for Bordeaux under the threat of the initial German offensive. Subsequent ministers either defended Joffre against all attacks (e.g., Millerand) or were unable to exert their authority over him (e.g., Gallieni) until revulsion against heavy losses with few apparent results led to Joffre's resignation in December 1916. His successor, General Nivelle, did not enjoy the confidence of War Minister Painlevé, a distrust proved justified by the failure of the April 1917 offensive and the subsequent mutiny of the French army.

Since the immediate dismissal of Nivelle was not practical—for morale reasons vis à vis the French nation, the army, the British and the enemy—Painlevé recreated the post of Chief of the Army General Staff, the holder of which would be "technical counsellor" to the government, would answer directly to the minister of war, and would function independently of the army high command. General Pétain held this post for two weeks, then replaced Nivelle as Commander in Chief of the French army. General Foch followed Pétain in the new post which he held until his appointment as generalissimo of the allied armies. He then abandoned the title of Chief of the Army General Staff and no successor was appointed.

Of the many ministers of war which France enjoyed, or endured, during the war, only Millerand confined himself to administrative matters, leaving military matters to the high command. Ministers Galliéni, Lyautey, and Roques interfered in operational matters, and the Painlevé war ministry—acting on the advice of General Pétain—stepped directly into the conduct of operations by suspending Nivelle's offensive against the heights of Brimont, an intervention perfectly justified in this case.

The Clemenceau ministry—Clemenceau held the portfolios of Premier and war minister simultaneously—completed the reversal of the non-interference policy of 1914. This forceful statesman did not hesitate to intrude frequently in the domain of the high command, sometimes unwisely. He at times gave Pétain tactical advice, and once even technical—on the fixing of barbed-wire entanglements, an intrusion that Pétain merely ignored.[1] Clemenceau's nagging at Foch with regard to his control over the American army and his uninformed judgments on the conduct of the American army's operations in the Argonne are good examples of the less desirable aspects of civilian interference in warfare.

Shortly after World War I the reorganization of the high command

---

[1] Maréchal Franchet d'Espèrey, "Note sur la conduite supérieure de la guerre," *Revue militaire générale,* 2nd Series, II (January–June, 1938), 137–152.

to adapt it to the necessities of postwar politics, domestic and international, became of pressing importance. In the summer of 1919 Pétain's General Headquarters submitted a plan to the Clemenceau ministry, expressing ideas which indicated the frame of mind of the military regarding the degree of organizational unity which they thought desirable. The dispatch with which the ministry rejected these proposals in turn reflected the civilian politicians' distrust of the professionals, who had just concluded a war and were now groping for status in an environment where their peculiar talents were not likely to be considered of paramount importance to the state.[2]

The plan submitted by Pétain seems innocuous and logical enough from the standpoint of military efficiency in any country, but France had particular need of it because of her traditional ministerial instability. The minister of war was a transitory figure on the political scene, in wartime as well as in peace, and the disadvantages of having the Army General Staff serving directly under a ministerial "bird of passage" was a source of irritation to French military leaders.

In January, 1920, the Higher War Council (Conseil supérieur de la Guerre) and the Army General Staff were reconstituted. The Council, created in 1872 and since 1888 the chief organ for preparing France for war, was placed under the vice-presidency of Marshal Pétain. The president of the Council was the Minister of War, and Pétain, the next ranking member would be the Commander in Chief of the French army if war again broke out. The holder of the post was therefore in peacetime the highest ranking soldier and in effect was the army commander. The naming of Pétain to the post meant merely the conversion of his wartime role of Commander in Chief of the French armies to its logical peacetime equivalent.

Serving with him on the Council were the two other Marshals of France, Joffre and Foch—the rank of marshal automatically conferred membership and later Franchet d'Espèrey and Fayolle were similarly invested—and it was decided that nine generals would be chosen to act on the Council. The latter were generals-of-division by rank and were appointed with a view to their eventually, in time of war, commanding army groups or armies.

The Higher War Council was responsible for planning the mobilization and the concentration of the armies for the outbreak of hostilities, for studying and modifying, as the situation required, the general strategic orientation of the army and its general organization and training, as well as the adoption of new armament. It was, in short,

2 Général Mordacq, *Le Ministère Clemenceau* (Paris, 1931), IV, 40, 48–62, 95, 96.

the final military authority, subject to civilian control through its subordination to the Minister of War and through him to the Premier and ultimately, of course, to the parliament.

In January, 1922 the Poincaré ministry took office with Maginot as Minister of War. The hostility which those two statesmen had had for Pétain in 1917 had long since given way, in the general satisfaction with the victory over Germany, to a feeling of confidence. In military matters they promptly moved to give Pétain, and the high command generally, a stronger and more rational position, in that the activities of the Chief of Staff of the Army would be subject to Pétain's scrutiny and approval, although nominally the office would still remain under the authority of the Minister of War. A new high post was created and Pétain was named to it, that of Inspector-General of the Army, and he was to be technical advisor to the Minister of War, while retaining his position as Commander in Chief (designate) of the army.

Although this decree merely regularized a position which Pétain already in effect held, it made official a lessening of the independence of the Chief of Staff of the Army, to the benefit of Pétain as army commander and Inspector-General, and seemed to be a downgrading of the Minister of War, to the advantage of the same high military authority. In fact it seemed to give Pétain a position in the War Ministry itself, an invasion by the military of a civilian cabinet office, responsible to the parliament, that good "republican" politicians could not accept.[3]

The apparent weakening of the war minister's prerogatives was sufficient to arouse the ire of the Socialist and other left-wing elements in the parliament. The government encountered such determined resistance to the project in the Chamber of Deputies that the section of the decree giving the vice-president of the Higher War Council the equal right with the War Minister to countersign measures proposed by the Army Chief of Staff—Article Five—was not pressed, although Pétain did retain the post of Inspector-General.[4]

Pétain's popularity with the country and with all shades of political opinion was not in question during this episode and the deputies in the Chamber, even when most bitterly combating the measure, were emphatic in declaring that Pétain personally was not the object of their attack. What they feared, they declared, was an encroachment of the power of the military in general; even the most extreme left-wing members were enthusiastic in their approval of Pétain as the

---

[3] New York Times, January 17, 19 and 22, 1922.
[4] Journal officiel de la République française, 1871–1940, Parliamentary debates, Chamber of Deputies, Section 2, I (January 19, 1922), 57–68.

leader of the French army. The point is emphasized here because it is important for an understanding of Pétain's role in France to know that his prestige, carried almost to adulation, cut across political lines and that Frenchmen of all parties were one in accepting him as a great and sympathetic figure.

The popular admiration of the Marshal, justly earned during World War I and maintained through the years as the behind-the-scenes events of the war became more fully known to the public, continued right up to 1940 and was an important factor in the political events of that year and of those that followed. It might seem incongruous now to know that Pétain was thought of as a "republican" general in those days, but he was so thought; and the complex chain of events that led from that pinnacle of popularity of post-World War I to the unhappy denouement in 1945 is not one that can be dismissed with the facile explanations of some of the French politicians of post-World War II.

Either Pétain had been a remarkable actor for twenty years or there is an element of insincerity in those Frenchmen whose adulation turned to reprobation. Pétain's family background was conservative peasant, his education conservative Catholic and his career conservative army; to look to him to be a staunch supporter of the Third Republic in the early 1940's, when that institution had failed politically and militarily, would have been the height of naïveté.

In any case, the controversial Article Five of the decree of January, 1922, which had been drawn up by Pétain and Maginot working together, did not survive its exposure to parliamentary debate, and the Army Chief of Staff remained entirely subordinate to the Minister of War and under civilian control, and not subject to the Inspector-General—commander in Chief-designate as the proponents of the measure had hoped. The attitude of the parliament was perhaps not surprising in view of the example given them in Germany of the unfortunate consequences of allowing a general staff to assume such powers that it escaped civilian control entirely and usurped policy-making prerogatives not within its competence.

In France during the 1920's, however, the desired unity of action, and the direction of the Army General Staff by the commander who would lead the armies in time of war, was achieved without actually being laid down by law, through the personal ascendancy of the commander. Pétain reserved an office near the Army Chief of Staff, General Buat (appointed in 1920) and he conferred with him almost daily. Both Buat and General Debeney, who succeeded him in 1923, had served under Pétain during the war and he had influence over them and in effect remained their leader. Therefore from 1920 to 1930, when Debeney retired, Pétain was the director and the most important single military authority in France, exerting an influence and continuity of policy which was particularly important because of the transitory nature of the War Ministry on the shifting political scene. The accretion of power to one individual aroused no antagonism from the politicians because the position was a personal one, not sanctioned by law, and the incumbent was trusted.

In 1930 General Weygand was named to succeed General Debeney as Chief of Staff of the Army. He had been chief of staff to Foch during the war and was not of the Pétain following. Although he submitted important questions to Pétain for his examination, the close harmony and agreement between the Army Chief of Staff and the commander in chief-designate no longer existed.[5] This temporary situation was resolved in 1931 when Pétain, having reached the age of seventy-five, retired from active service and was replaced as vice-president of the Higher War Council by Weygand, who in turn was replaced as Chief of Staff by General Gamelin.

The question of the relationship between the Chief of Staff and the vice-president of the War Council was finally resolved in 1935 when Weygand retired and Gamelin succeeded him while still retaining the post of Chief of the Army Staff. The two posts therefore were combined, ending the dual structure of the French high command which had existed since 1920. From then on the Chief of the Army Staff also filled the post of vice-president of the Higher War Council and served directly under the war minister for all important questions involving the composition of the army, its effectives, its armament and its mobilization.

The divided and weak organization of the high command prior to 1935 was not an accident. The all-powerful legislature in France resisted any effort to centralize, and thus strengthen, the directing authorities of the armed forces. In 1930 Maginot, again Minister of War, wanted to combine the posts of Chief of the Army Staff and vice-president of the Higher War Council, as was later done in 1935, and he planned to give General Weygand, as next ranking military figure after Pétain, the position. Weygand was too well known for his right-wing political sympathies and the proposal ran into the inevitable political opposition. Threatened with an interpellation on the matter by the opposition, the government dropped the project.[6]

---

[5] General Laure, *Pétain* (Paris, 1941), 246.

[6] General Gamelin, *Servir* (Paris, 1946), II, xxvi, xxvii; also the *Journal officiel* . . . , Chamber debates (January 21, 1930), 81–85.

The fusion of the two posts was effected in 1935 because Gamelin was acceptable to the left-wing deputies. His nomination was, however, opposed by many of the military, prominent among whom was Marshal Pétain, and their lack of enthusiasm for Gamelin as commander in chief of the French armies was proven justified in 1940.

On May 9, 1940, on the eve of the German offensive through the Low Countries, Premier Reynaud, at a meeting of the cabinet, decided to remove Gamelin from his command for demonstrated incompetence. Only one cabinet member's voice was raised in Gamelin's defense, that of Daladier, who could hardly have done otherwise since Gamelin was his appointee. The German attack the next day forestalled the dismissal.

Gamelin was reputed to be a good "republican" and was the protégé of Édouard Daladier, a leader of the Radical-Socialist party, and was therefore approved by left-wing politicians—or at least was considered safe by them. So the French nation had a high command reflective of its politics and the weakness of the high-level military planning of the 1930's was, to a certain extent, a result of French political instability.

Pétain's retirement from active command of the army did not mean the end of his participation in military affairs. He was named to a new post, Inspector-General of Air Defense; he continued, as a Marshal of France, as member of the Higher War Council; and during 1934 he served as Minister of War in the Doumergue government. In these capacities he campaigned for the organization of the nation's air defenses, for a reorganization of the army high command, for a powerful bombardment air force, for increased effectives for the army to meet the resurgent German threat and to fill the gaps in the nation's trained manpower during the "hollow years," and above all for a unified command to integrate under one authority the three services of land, air and sea, as well as the industrial mobilization of the country.

As we have seen, the Higher War Council was designed to be the final military authority acting as consulting body to the Minister of War, and the advice and opinions of this body were supposed to govern the general military preparation of the country. In January, 1935 a decree further defined its functions: the Council should be consulted on all matters relating to the organization of the army and the preparation for war. Articles Five and Six of the decree specified that the government was obliged to seek the advice of the Council on the dispositions taken for the mobilization and the concentration of the armies; on the adoption of new armaments; on the fortifications of the frontiers; and in general on any military questions that the Minister wanted to submit to it.[7]

But from 1936 to the outbreak of the war the role of the Council, composed of the most eminent military men in France, became more and more modest. It was not called upon to discuss the important military questions that should have been examined by its members and its recommendations were not sought. Its meetings became more and more infrequent and Daladier, who was Minister of War from June 1937 until the war and who was considered unfriendly to the War Council, never consulted it for important questions and rarely for matters of detail.

The growing coolness between the government and what should have been its principal advisory commission on military matters had its origin in France's political troubles. Government leaders were aware that the Higher War Council was largely right-wing in its political sympathy, and that it was distressed by the left-wing orientation of French politics, by the Popular Front, by the interruptions in the manufacture of war materials because of strikes and occupations of the factories by the workers at a time when Germany was rapidly rearming, by the alleged dissemination of Communist propaganda in the army, by the intrusion of politics into the reserve officers' associations—the reserve cadres were of paramount importance in the French "nation in arms" system—and by the perennial ministerial instability. Some members of the Higher War Council criticized the political system bitterly and agitated for political reform, and this helped widen the gulf between them and the politicians.

Daladier suspected, perhaps with reason, that members of the Higher War Council had connections with clandestine right-wing organizations like the Cagoule; nevertheless his reluctance to consider the advice of his highest ranking army commanders was symptomatic of a serious and dangerous rift between the government and its army.

Only Gamelin, politically acceptable and on close terms with Daladier, maintained contact with the government, although even he complained that often during critical periods he could not approach the Minister. And he was vice-president of the War Council and Chief of the Army Staff, the man who would be expected to lead France's armies if war should come. In this way did the foremost body of

---

[7] *Commission chargée d'enquêter sur les événements survenus en France de 1933 à 1945* (Paris, 195?), III, 637–639, testimony of General Georges.

military experts in France progressively suffer eclipse during a most
critical period.

The question of a unified command for any nation's armed forces
should begin with the problem of the relationship of the government
to the military high command. Once it is admitted that the higher
conduct of a war is a government affair—and in France this question
was not in doubt—then the organization of the governmental machinery, or bureaus, for the purpose of studying the needs of the country, its objectives and its line of policy, and then transmitting its
directives to the armed forces, is of primary importance.

The attempt to resolve the question of control began as far back as
1906 when a decree creating a bureau for the preparation of war was
passed. It consisted of the civilian cabinet ministers concerned—War,
Navy, Foreign Affairs, or others—who were the deciding voices. Called
in as the need arose, for consultation only, were the military leaders;
they had no voice in deciding overall policy. This council, called the
Higher Council for National Defense *(Conseil supérieur de la Défense
nationale,* and not to be confused with the Higher War Council composed of soldiers and described above) was presided over by the Premier or by the President of the Republic.

This organism never assumed a serious role and during World War
I it played no part. It continued to exist in a nebulous fashion during
the 1920's until 1929 when a decree enlarged its membership to include all members of the Council of Ministers, joined by the military
leaders, the latter still on a consultative basis. It was therefore the
Council of Ministers itself, called together as usual as France's governing body but this time for the purpose of studying a specific problem of a politico-military character. The military were called in but
only for technical consultation; they had no vote in the decisions
made. As General Weygand later pointed out, the Higher Council
for National Defense was in theory the organ that would give expert
consideration to important matters relating to national defense and
then advise the government as to its proper line of conduct, but
since the Council for National Defense consisted of the whole Council
of Ministers, who were also the "government," and since the military
were only consulted for details of a technical nature, the result was
that the Council of Ministers called itself together in special session to
give itself advice.[8] Allowing for the General's professional bitterness

---

[8] *Commission chargée d'enquêter* . . . , Supplement, I, 242, General Weygand's testimony.

at the exclusion of the military from government deliberations, one can see that the institution was a cumbersome and illogical one and was not well calculated to meet the exigencies of modern warfare.

In 1930 and 1931 the Higher Council for National Defense was further enlarged, with the addition of Marshal Pétain in his capacity as Inspector-General for Air Defense, and also by adding other public functionaries, the intention being to centralize the mobilization of the nation's entire resources for modern "total war." But this organism was again simply the ordinary governing body enlarged for a specific purpose when it ought to have been streamlined for the purpose; in any case the Higher Council for National Defense, as such, never met after 1933.

Throughout the 1920's Pétain had agitated for a unified command of the armed forces, on an operational level, and for a unification of the governmental departments charged with the national defense. With the advent of the 1930's, a period marked by an enlargement of the scope and nature of warfare due to the increasing power of aerial armament and with the menace of a renascent German militarism becoming more apparent, he increased his efforts.

Formerly the division of responsibility between the War and Navy departments had been a relatively simple one, with the respective spheres of each usually easy to define. When undertaking combined operations, involving the close cooperation of the army and the navy, a commander could be designated from either of the services to direct that particular operation. But in 1928 the French government organized a separate air force, formerly a branch of the army, and created an Air Ministry to function on an equal basis with the War and Navy departments. The coordination of the three ministries in a modern war promised to be unnecessarily complex, wasteful, and inefficient; and Pétain bent every effort to centralize the direction of these three functions in one agency.

In December, 1931 he expressed his views and his recommendations in a letter to the Premier, advocating the creation of a Ministry for National Defense which would coordinate and have full authority over the three rival departments of air, land and sea.[9] Three months later André Tardieu, the new Premier, took an important step in the direction desired by Pétain by creating a Minister of National Defense but his reform was not completely in accord with the Marshal's conceptions. Pétain was pleased that the step had been taken but he thought that the new organization was a faulty one in many respects and he was not satisfied with it.

---

[9] Laure, 340, 341.

Pétain was in favor of retaining the War, Navy and Air Ministries but would have created a sort of super-ministry, a minister of national defense having authority over the three departments.[10] He further planned that a general staff for national defense be organized and that its chief of staff would, in time of war, be the overall commander of the combined armed forces. The Tardieu government, however, abolished the Ministers of War, Navy and Air and instituted a single Minister for National Defense, a post filled by François Piétri. The office was a political rather than military one, but even so it came under the fire of parliamentarians who were ever wary of a centralization, and thus the strengthening, of the armed forces high command.

Not only were the politicians of the Left hostile to the measure but the unification of the services was strongly opposed by the navy and the air force. Both feared that the army, or the former War Ministry, would be the dominant member in the new Defense Ministry, which would lead to their relegation to a secondary status; and the navy in particular thought that a centralized department to allocate the funds budgeted for national defense by the parliament would work to its disadvantage. The Navy and Air Committees in the Chamber and in the Senate reflected these fears and worked against the new institution.

In suppressing the three former ministries, instead of keeping them but uniting them under a higher authority, Tardieu perhaps attempted too much. Worse still, Pétain thought, the new ministry was not provided with an organ for technical studies—a general staff composed of army, navy and air force specialists—and political opposition to a concentration of military authority prevented the appointment of a chief of staff for national defense. Also, to assist the Minister for National Defense in the complex task of administering three departments, Tardieu gave him two under-secretaries of state, one for general administration and the other for armaments. However capable the new minister might be, he and his two under-secretaries could not exercise the proper direction over the administrative and technical functions and functionaries of the three departments of war, air and sea, and in 1932 the system fell with the Tardieu ministry which had created it. The old ministries of War, Navy and Air were reconstituted. The failure of the experiment served to delay the adoption of Pétain's proposals for several years.[11]

---

[10] Phillipe Pétain, "Défense nationale et commandement unique," *Revue des deux mondes,* XXXV (May–June, 1936), 13.
[11] General Duchêne, "Avons-nous un Ministre de la Défense nationale?" *Revue des deux mondes,* XLIV (March–April, 1938), 45, 49; also George London, ed., *Le Procès Pétain* (Lyon, 1945), 384, 385.

Before the collapse of the brief attempt to consolidate the three military ministries, the Minister of National Defense did effect one potentially worthwhile reform. In March, 1932 Piétri created a High Military Committee (*Haut Comité militaire*) presided over by himself as Minister and comprising the three vice-presidents of the Higher Councils for War, Navy and Air (we have already discussed the Higher War Council; the Navy and Air Councils were similar organizations, in their particular spheres) and the three chiefs of staff of the army, navy and air force. Piétri intended that this Committee should establish a close contact and a certain amount of harmony between the commanders of the three services.[12] This was the closest that he came to establishing a unified command on an operational level. Pétain was not consulted on the creation of this Committee and his views were ignored. Apparently his desire for a general staff for national defense and a single, unified command was too strong for him to accept this watered-down version. In any case the idea suffered partial eclipse after the fall of the ministry which had conceived it.

In June of the same year the High Military Committee was reorganized, this time comprising the three ministers of War, Navy and Air—these offices having been recreated after the failure of the Tardieu plan—the respective chiefs of staff of the three armed forces, and Marshal Pétain. The vice-presidents of the Higher War, Navy and Air Councils were no longer members of this important organization: this meant that Weygand, politically unpopular, no longer took part in it—although he was commander in chief-designate of the army— while Gamelin, as Chief of the Army Staff, did take part. Pétain accepted membership even though he continued to deplore the lack of a permanent staff or, as he always put it in recommending his thesis, "a permanent organ for studies." Most of the military and other advocates of a unified command structure used this euphemism during the 1930's; the words "general staff" and "chief of the general staff" smacked too strongly, to sensitive political ears, of a powerful command on the German model.

The virulent political divisions in France which prevented any further rationalization of the national defense structure at that time were only one aspect of an unhealthy situation that weakened the national life as a whole. Matters came to a head in late 1933 and early 1934 with the Stavisky scandals, riots or near revolution in the streets

---

[12] Commandant Jean Vial, "Le Défense nationale: son organization entre les deux guerres," *Revue d'histoire de la deuxième Guerre mondiale*, No. 18, 5th Year (April, 1955), 16.

of Paris and the dreary picture of one cabinet after another admitting its impotence and giving way to another, equally powerless coalition. The French State seemed to be sinking into a quagmire of governmental instability and political anarchy; particular interests of party or class, social and economic affiliations or predilections, political passions fed by emotion rather than by reason all combined to weaken the nation. Advocates of reform became more demanding in calling for a strong, stable government—one that could achieve some measure of national unity over particular interests.

In February, 1934 the Doumergue government was formed, with Pétain as Minister of War. When he was first approached to enter the cabinet he thought he saw an opportunity to put his pet project into operation: that a ministry might be created to unify all aspects of national defense. He requested that he be given a minister of state portfolio with powers to coordinate the three departments of War, Navy and Air.

But Doumergue apparently thought that his task of leading a disturbed nation would be delicate enough without trying too soon to effect major innovations in the government. At any rate Pétain's proposals were turned down and he had to be content with entering the cabinet as Minister of War, a position from which he could work for the adoption of his ideas.

In June 1934 Pétain addressed the Senate in an appeal for a unification of the armed forces. He pointed out the inadequacy of the present High Military Committee for the task of coordinating the nation's military efforts on an operational level. Under the present system, he said, the Premier presided over the Higher Council for National Defense—merely the Council of Ministers convoked for a special purpose —which body was provided with a general-secretariat, headed by an army general officer, to organize the industrial mobilization of the nation in time of war. Pétain wanted a similar organ for the combined military forces, to direct the overall military operations. He carefully avoided mentioning a "generalissimo" or a "general staff for national defense" and a "chief" thereof but tried to show that his proposed organization merely duplicated on the military side, for the conduct of operations, what had already been done for the direction of the civilian and industrial preparation for war. He pointed out that the Premier, responsible for both the general-secretariat and the High Military Committee—that is, for the industrial and economic war effort as well as the actual overall military conduct of a war—had too formidable a task for one man. He left unsaid the fact that the instability of ministries led to lack of continuity in the higher direction of the country's war effort.[13]

Pétain assured the Senators that no startling innovations were necessary to carry out his proposals. He pointed out that all the essential organs already existed: the Higher Council for National Defense, the High Military Committee, and the military commanders responsible for operations. All that was needed was an organization to form a liaison between the various functions, to study the nation's defense needs and plan its policy, and to prepare and carry out the decisions of the government. He advised that a well-informed military man be placed at the head of the new "organ" and that this official be a sort of war-counsellor to the Premier.

It seems apparent that Pétain had himself in mind for the post; he was considered the foremost military personality in France and, despite his age, he would have been the logical choice for the position. His popularity with people of most shades of political thought ensured little opposition to his appointment if the post were created. Nevertheless his efforts toward unification of the nation's military forces were disinterested enough; he continued to fight for his idea long after there was any possibility of his benefiting personally by the reform.

Pétain's recommendations for a unified command of the armed forces were backed by Doumergue, who also argued Pétain's thesis in a speech before the Senate; but they could not overcome the hostility of the parliament. The proposals formed part of a larger plan for a reform of French political institutions, for the strengthening of the government at the expense of the omnipotent and sometimes irresponsible Chamber of Deputies, and when this plan failed (reform had to wait until the political revolution of 1958, when de Gaulle and the Fifth Republic assumed power) the Doumergue ministry fell, on November 7, 1934, and Pétain's position as War Minister ended with it.

Premier Flandin succeeded Doumergue—the Radical-Socialist party agreed to accept Flandin after he promised to abandon any project for a revision of the Constitution—and asked Pétain to remain as Minister of War; but the Marshal had had his fill of politics and refused to enter the new government. He had associated himself with the Doumergue ministry during a time of crisis and for the purpose of reforming French political and military institutions, and when the government of which he formed a part fell from power on the very

---

[13] *Journal officiel* . . . , Senate Debates, June 19, 1934, 697, 698.

issues which were its *raison d'être,* he was not enough of a politician
to continue in office just for the sake of being in office.

With his War Department portfolio gone he was no longer a member of the Higher Council for National Defense or the High Military
Committee. But a week later a presidential decree reinstated Pétain
as a permanent member of the Council—which, as we have seen, never
met as such after 1933 anyway. The decree stated: "The interests of
the country and of the army in the present circumstances demand that
Marshal Pétain should retain the opportunity of making his counsels
heard upon all questions involving national defense."[14] He was also
reinstalled in the High Military Committee.

In June, 1935 it seemed as if Pétain might succeed with his plans
for a unification of the nation's armed forces, with himself at the head
of the new organization. On May 31 the Flandin government resigned
and the president of the Chamber of Deputies, Buisson, attempted to
form a new ministry. His cabinet included Marshal Pétain who was
to fill a new post of Minister of National Defense and who would head
the combined forces of the land, sea and air. But the Buisson ministry
did not survive its first day of parliamentary debate and went the way
of other ministries, this time on the issue of full powers for the government to meet the economic crisis that afflicted the country. What
interests us here is the brief attempt made to implement the Marshal's
recommendations. He planned to take with him General Georges—
his old chief of staff in Morocco and the general who would command
the French armies in the northeast in 1940—as a sort of chief of staff
for national defense but who would not have had the title. Aside from
the political difficulties which such an official appointment would
have encountered, it would have been indelicate to subordinate General Gamelin, now Army Chief of Staff and vice-president of the
Higher War Council, to Georges, his junior in rank.

This experiment was too short-lived to give us an indication of
what Pétain might have achieved, but as to what he might have attempted we are better informed. The Marshal published an outline
of his ideas on national defense unification in an article in May 1936
in the *Revue des Deux Mondes.*[15] This article had an impact on
French military thinking and was quoted widely, in and out of parliament, by the partisans of the unified command concept and had
some influence on subsequent attempts by successive governments to
centralize the armed forces high command.

---

[14] *New York Times,* November 13, 1934.
[15] "Défense nationale et commandement unique," (May–June, 1936), 5–17.

Pétain argued for a permanent organization in time of peace, strongly centralized, which would assure a unity of direction in everything pertaining to the military preparation of the nation. This central organ would serve as arbitrator between the three commands of the land, air and sea. No existing organizations would be disbanded —he had in mind the unfortunate Tardieu experiment of 1932—and he would continue the three existing ministries of War, Navy and Air. They would, however, be subordinated to a Ministry of State for National Defense which would have the power to coordinate everything pertaining to national defense.

His strongest argument for a unified command was based on the potentialities of modern air warfare. He described the possibilities of air power and pointed out that the priority of missions in modern war could not be left to any one of the services to decide, and that only a central authority could have sufficient knowledge of overall strategic requirements and could be objective enough to employ the available aircraft in a manner best suited to the nation's interests and objectives. He thought that only a high command independent of the Army and the Air Force could logically employ its air strength, strategically and tactically, to best advantage; in war both the Air Force and the Army would have their own ideas as to how best to use air power to meet particular situations as well as to attain long range objectives, and a single commander would be necessary to make the decisions.

He pointed out the necessity for a single command to orient the national defense doctrine to keep abreast of technological developments, and for arbitration between divergent theses; he showed the need for a central authority to divide the defense budget among the services, with a view to overall efficiency and economy. He also felt the need to have one authority distribute the nation's manpower effectives where they would be needed most: in the 1930's France was in serious difficulties in regard to military manpower, as well as in finances, and economies in both could best be achieved by a single command. He stressed the need for harmonizing the armament programs to avoid unnecessary duplication and of directing technical research with the common needs of all three services in mind.

The new super-command would be responsible for establishing a defense policy for the State and plans of campaign comprising all the armed forces, corresponding to different hypotheses. This would necessitate the creation of a General Staff serving under the Minister, recruited from highly qualified officers of the army, navy and air force (he also recommended that a war college for the combined services be created, so that these staff officers would be properly trained) and at the head of this staff would be a Chief of General Staff for National Defense.

Two organs already existing, the General-Secretariat of the Higher Council for National Defense and the High Military Committee would, Pétain planned, serve under the Minister for National Defense: the General-Secretariat to prepare the civilian aspects of modern war (industrial mobilization, stockpiling of raw materials, civil air defense, and the like) and the High Military Committee to occupy itself with military operations. The Minister of National Defense would preside over the High Military Committee and the new General Staff for National Defense would be its planning instrument.

Pétain obviously hoped that the minister of state who would be the Minister of National Defense would not be a politician and would enjoy a longevity of tenure not given to the usual French cabinet member: between 1919 and 1939 France had forty-three changes in government, an average of less than six months per ministry. The benefits accruing from the new organization presupposed a continuity of policy and effort that would be largely lost if the ministerial post concerned were continually vacated and filled by different individuals, subject to the vagaries of national politics. His hope was academic; he must have known that the Chamber of Deputies would not countenance any individual of ministerial rank who was not subject to their peremptory recall. In any case he thought that the institution of a Chief of Staff for National Defense would insure a tolerable measure of continuity and stability to the new high command.

We have indicated that the military in general were supporters of Pétain's unified command proposals but it should be noted that the commander who would be most affected by them, General Gamelin, was not at all enthusiastic. Asked for his opinion in March 1936 by the Premier, Gamelin replied that the "single military commander" concept was primarily a matter of personal prestige; that is, in time of need a leader with great prestige, if there were one, would naturally assume the overall direction of operations. The General followed this odd statement—odd because it obviously is not sound military practice to defer the organization of one's forces until the stress of circumstances during hostilities does it for you—by declaring that instead of having a single commander, the War Committee—the High Military Committee would in wartime change its name to the "War Committee"—should be the coordinator of the armed forces. He said that the "facilities for contact" between the services would provide sufficient unification and that these facilities already existed in the War Com-

mittee. He further recommended that a supreme arbitrator, in the
person of Marshal Pétain, render decisions in the name of the War
Committee.[16]

While this might be flattering to the Marshal personally, Gamelin
was no help in getting Pétain's ideas accepted by the civilian government, whose reluctance to proceed with a unification was strengthened
by the unfavorable report of the man who would command the army
in time of war.

In June 1936 the Popular Front government of Léon Blum acceded
to some extent to the pressure for centralization of the nation's military defenses by again creating the cabinet post of Minister for National Defense, with Daladier as the incumbent. It did not make the
mistake of abolishing the existing Ministries of War, Navy and Air,
as the 1932 Tardieu government had done, but it weakened the position by having the Minister for National Defense serve at the same
time as War Minister. In effect this merely extended the prerogatives
of the War Minister so that he had some vague function of coordination vis à vis his Navy and Air Minister colleagues: coordination only
—he had no authority over them.

The same decrees reconstituted the High Military Committee, giv-
ing it a new name: the Permanent Committee for National Defense.
It was presided over by the new Minister for National Defense and
War, Édouard Daladier; it comprised the Ministers of Navy and Air,
Marshal Pétain as France's foremost military representative, and the
three Chiefs of Staff of the Army, Navy and Air Force.

These measures taken by the Blum government were in response
to mounting pressure for a command unification, spurred by the
knowledge that the totalitarian countries had already achieved a
single, centralized command and that it behooved France to follow
suit in self-defense. This whole question is a good illustration of some
of the disadvantages under which a democracy labors when in com-
petition, or conflict, with nations which have authoritarian governments. The French parliament was faced with the problem of preparing a military organization which could best protect the national
interests while at the same time guarding against a usurpation of
power by a right-wing military element. National security and republican liberties sometimes seemed conflicting values.

The reform made by the Blum ministry intended that the Minister
of National Defense and War should coordinate the action of the
three armed forces regarding armament programs, industrial mobilization, and expenditures for national defense. But "coordination," as

---

[16] Vial, 22.

specified in Article Five of the decree, was not enough; what was needed, Pétain thought, was a central authority, not a coordinator. The whole system rested upon Daladier's powers of persuasion and personal prestige, for the French Constitution specified that the Ministers of Navy and Air were responsible only to the legislature and no one minister could give orders to another. Daladier not only had no real power to impose his will but he did not even have much moral power, due to his dual role as Minister of War and Minister of National Defense, because this duality of function made him on occasion both judge of and party to inter-ministerial disputes.[17]

Pétain reacted strongly against this attenuated version of his plans; what he wanted was a Minister of National Defense who would have authority over the three services, a minister who could command, not cajole. But he was opposed in this by the minister in question himself, Daladier, who insisted that each ministry retain complete autonomy, under the direction of the Premier.

The French during this period, having once decided to institute an official position that was repugnant to Gallic republican ideals, had a curious propensity for installing in that reluctantly instituted office a man who was not a partisan of, or was actually an opponent of, the granting of powers that he himself would hold. Examples of this include the one just cited: giving Daladier, an opponent of a centralized authority in the military preparation of the country, the portfolio of Minister for National Defense and War. Other examples are (later, in 1938) making Gamelin the Chief of General Staff for National Defense, the one high ranking military man who was, or professed to be, lukewarm to the unified command idea. An earlier example was that of Piétri, installed in 1932 in the short-lived post of Minister of National Defense, who was an avowed opponent of the unified command idea.[18] This somewhat naive insurance against usurpation of power had the effect of emasculating in advance the authority which it was the intention to create.

Not only was Daladier averse to an extension of the powers of the Minister for National Defense but he opposed the institution of a unified command on the operational level, a generalissimo over the nation's armed forces. At a meeting of the Permanent Committee for National Defense in December 1936 he reiterated his opposition to

[17] General Debeney, "Le Problème de la couverture," *Revue des deux mondes*, XXXVI (November–December, 1936), 292, 293; also the *Journal Officiel* . . . , Chamber Debates, I (January 28, 1937), 208.
[18] *Journal officiel* . . . , Chamber, I (January 29, 1937), 250–252; Piétri argued strongly against a unified command.

the creation of such a post in time of peace; it was his opinion that a time of war would be soon enough to take such a risk with democratic liberties, and the appointment of a supreme commander could wait until the moment he was needed. He was seconded in his argument by Pierre Cot, the Minister of Air, who also was hostile to an authoritative Minister for National Defense, basing his opinion on the belief that the proposal would permit the departments of War, Navy and Air to elude their responsibility to the parliament.

Pétain spoke out strongly against the theses of Daladier and Cot and pointed out that the plan to postpone the appointment of a supreme military commander until hostilities had actually broken out could only result in dangerous improvisation; it was necessary to prepare in peacetime the organization with which France would go to war. He also argued that the plan to substitute as much as possible the War Committee for a unified command was a poor one; the constant intrusion of this Committee into operations in wartime could only lead to feebleness and confusion. But the Marshal encountered the united resistance of the rest of the Committee members; they were all opposed to his position, the opposition of the Chief of Naval Staff being particularly strong.

Pétain was accustomed to the Committee's opposition toward his plans for military reorganization. Only a few months previously, at a meeting in October 1936, he had circulated a memorandum which reiterated his demands for reform and which requested the members to reflect that perhaps they would not have much longer, in peace, the time to effect a remodeling of the nation's military structure. His memorandum met with no response.

From 1936 on, at almost every meeting of the Permanent Committee for National Defense—which usually met each month—he pressed for adoption of his plans for unification but he could get little satisfaction. In 1936 the only concession made to Pétain's proposals was the creation of a College of Higher Studies for National Defense, an institution for the training of officers for the modern direction of combined operations of land, sea and air. He had urged the creation of this institution earlier in the year.

In 1937 the unified command question was hotly debated in the Chamber of Deputies, the partisans of the reform leaning heavily on Pétain's recommendations and prestige. The Popular Front government fought against the idea and Daladier, as Minister for National Defense and War, was its spokesman. The government thesis was that the sea and air forces should not be subordinated to an army commander; that the latter would not be able to handle so many functions at once. This of course begged the question; Pétain did not want the army commander also to command the sea and air forces; he wanted a commander who would be above all three services, an impartial judge with a general staff that would be appropriate to the great task.

The government argued that what was needed was simply a coordination of the three Chiefs of Staff for ground, air and sea forces and that the Permanent Committee for National Defense was well qualified to perform this essential function. The backers of the unification idea were distinctly in the minority in the Chamber and the deputies voted overwhelmingly in support of the government.[19]

At a meeting of the Permanent Committee for National Defense in December 1937 the issue came up again when Daladier—still Minister of National Defense and War although the Blum government had fallen in June—brought up the question of organizing the high command so as to provide for the inclusion of North Africa in case of war. Pétain replied that the question would not arise at all if the nation had a unified command. Even if they could not get such a combined services high command, he said, they could at least have a special staff that would act for the Permanent Committee, or for General Gamelin, and could provide solutions for problems before they arose—in other words to prepare plans to meet various hypotheses, thus preparing for contingencies before they occurred.[20]

Daladier replied that the Committee had the legal authority to appoint a single commander if need for one should arise during a war. As for a staff, he said that one already existed: the General Secretariat of the Higher Council for National Defense (we have already seen that this organ was concerned primarily with the civilian and domestic aspects of mobilization). Pétain retorted that a secretariat was not a staff but the other members of the Committee, including Gamelin, Admiral Darlan and Pierre Cot, backed Daladier. Darlan in particular, as Chief of Naval Staff, opposed Pétain and declared that meetings of the respective Chiefs of Staff of the three services would suffice to regulate the combined forces in action and that only when a particular operation had been studied should a commander be appointed. The meeting ended with the old Marshal in opposition to the whole Committee.

---

[19] *Journal officiel* . . . , Chamber, I (January 26, 28, 29 and February 2, 1937), 166–168, 200, 250–252, 292.
[20] *Commission chargée d'enquêter* . . . , Documents, II, 254, the minutes of the meeting of the Permanent Committee for National Defense on December 8, 1937.

In January, 1938 a series of important decrees altered the nation's military structure, bringing it closer to the type of organization demanded by Pétain; closer, but not close enough to suit the Marshal. The section of the decree which dealt with the Ministry of National Defense and War gave that post—still held by Daladier—some increase in power. Instead of "coordinating" the functioning of the three ministries concerned with military preparations the Minister now would approve "as the final authority" the action of all the armed forces, as well as the direction of armament programs, industrial mobilization, and expenditures for national defense.

The reform was a hesitant one. The Minister for National Defense remained as head of the War Ministry and therefore was not the final impartial arbiter that he should have been.

The new decrees created an important post, one which Pétain had been demanding for years, that of a Chief of Staff for National Defense. Gamelin was named to fill the office. But here too weaknesses in the system existed. For one thing, the Chief of Staff for National Defense was not provided with a staff; that is, without a staff for the combined services, a General Staff for National Defense. Another weakness lay in the fact that Gamelin retained his position as Chief of Staff of the Army, thus giving him the awkward role of filling two posts, on two different levels, in the same military hierarchy. This ambiguity of functions had a disastrous effect on the military operations in 1940. Gamelin was supposed to command the Army and at the same time exercise overall command of the armed forces. This could not be done well by one man, particularly with the inadequate staff arrangements that were devised to serve the command arrangement.

During the year 1938, with the international situation worsening and the danger of war becoming greater, well informed military men in France clamored for a Minister of National Defense with a full and unambiguous authority over defense preparations, and for a real commander of the armed forces, properly provided with a general staff.

On February 4, 1938, the Germans had officially instituted a unified command system which had been in the making since 1935. The *Führer* exercised personal command of all the armed forces through the Supreme Command (*Oberkommando der Wehrmacht*) , with General Keitel as Chief of Staff of this department as well as Minister of War. This unity of command undeniably helped the German military preparation. In addition German industry was integrated into the military effort.

The French Senate then took up the cry, in February 1938, demanding through its Army Committee the immediate creation of a general staff for a supreme command, detached from the individual services and above them all. In April Daladier, the Premier as well as Minister for National Defense and War—a rather considerable assignment for one office-holder—replied to this demand by a report to the President of the Republic in which he reiterated the old idea that when war broke out the War Committee could delegate General Gamelin to "coordinate" the land and air forces. The War Committee would retain overall direction and would issue "instructions" to the Commander in Chief, thus neatly confusing the higher direction of the war with the conduct of operations.

Daladier seemed obsessed with the "Aulic Council" idea, perhaps finding safety in numbers. One cannot, perhaps, blame him too strongly since General Gamelin himself had espoused the same idea since 1936; it was one welcome to good republican, parliamentary ears. But in the Senate, more conservative than the Chamber, the Army Committee continued its demand and in February 1939, in a secret meeting Daladier promised the Committee that he would undertake a complete reform of the organization for national defense. This promise was not kept, not even after war broke out.[21]

Vainly Marshal Pétain, who by now was something of a venerated relic rather than an influential military adviser, criticized the government policy. He protested that in modern warfare events moved too rapidly and military operations were subject to unforeseen variations requiring instantaneous decisions; the leadership of a "council" would be inadequate. He said that they would need the quick thinking of a single commander who should be assisted by a staff working at the combined services level.[22] These words were not heeded by the policy makers and France went to war equipped with a military apparatus whose command was weakened by a democratic diffusion of authority and responsibility, against a totalitarian adversary possessing a war machine with an efficient functioning due in part to a relatively well organized, and centralized, higher direction.

After the disastrous events of 1940 General Gamelin was as quick to point out the anomalies of his office as he had been unprotesting while there was yet time. According to him his function was only to "coordinate" the three services and he protested that he was no "generalissimo." He had delegated General Georges to command on the

21 Jean Febry, *J'ai Connu . . . 1934–1945* (Paris, 1952), 139.
22 See Pétain's preface to General Chauvineau, *Une Invasion est-elle encore possible?* (Paris, 1939), xx.

northeast front—that is, the armies facing the German and Belgian frontiers—with full powers there; and therefore Georges, according to Gamelin, was in the same position of authority over the armies in action against Germany as Joffre had been in 1914, while Gamelin occupied himself with the higher direction of the war in all theaters.[23]

This attempt at passing the buck for the defeat in 1940 to his subordinate does not merit serious attention. The global aspects of the war were of secondary importance when the German armies were massed only 150 miles from Paris.

What Pétain had warned against occurred; there was no single, overall authority. The division of responsibilities between Gamelin and Georges was never clearly defined and the command of the army suffered from it. General Weygand later said at the Riom trials that troop training and discipline also suffered from it although the general may have been groping for reasons to explain the poor performance of French soldiers in 1940.

The staff and headquarters arrangements worked out to serve the high command were a product of the inefficient organization and were inadequate for the task. General Gamelin had his office at Vincennes but had no staff there. General Georges, in command of the armies in the northeast—the bulk of the French Army and the decisive theater—had an incomplete staff headquarters at Ferté-sous-Jouarre. The real General Headquarters for the French Army was at Montry, somewhere between Gamelin and Georges and was supposed to serve them both. Here were the central—and essential—Staff organs of the Army: G–2, G–3, G–4, the centers for railroad and communications networks, and the like. Thus there was on one hand the general who commanded the armies and on the other a leader with a more general authority embracing the whole war effort, with little settled as to the responsibilities of each and neither one of them possessing a General Staff. The Staff headquarters was located between the two and shared by both.[24]

Georges protested repeatedly to Gamelin during the winter of 1939–1940 that as commander of the forces which would decide the main issue of the war he should have a greater control of the General Headquarters' working and command organs. Gamelin, backed by Daladier, refused, basing his refusal on the fact that he himself had

---

[23] Gamelin, I, 18, 79; also *Commission chargée d'enquêter* . . . , II, 368, 399, 400–403, for Gamelin's testimony. Also see his letter of December 26, 1947 to the *Commission chargée d'enquêter* . . . , III, 577.

[24] *Commission chargée d'enquêter* . . . , VI, 1605, General Weygand's testimony; also Vial, 29.

greater need of the Headquarters since he was concerned with the combined functioning of all theaters of operations: the northeast, the Alps, North Africa and the Near East.[25] Pétain's proposals to establish a separate General Staff for National Defense, if carried out, probably could not have done much to change the outcome of the war but they would at least have prevented most of this confusion.

Pétain was still in contact with his old friend, Georges, and wrote to him in early 1940 telling him that he was aware of the unfortunate situation resulting from the "bad" organization of the armies. He deplored the misunderstandings between the leaders and the confused responsibilities in the high command, and the unfortunate effect the knowledge of these differences and weaknesses had on morale. He encouraged Georges to stick it out and to keep confidence in the future.

When the Germans struck in 1940 the speed and efficiency of their attack played havoc with French command arrangements. General Gamelin found himself presented with a series of *faits accomplis* and never was able to catch up with the situation.[26] The divided high command organization was not equal to the exigencies of modern warfare and only when Gamelin was removed and replaced by General Weygand did France have a military commander who grasped all the threads of the command, who assumed direction of the operations himself, aided by a staff and headquarters immediately under his control, and who gave a firm and responsible leadership to the shaken Georges and his armies. But military organizations are not improvised in the face of "lightning warfare." France finally had a unified command, and a single commander, but too late.

---

[25] Pierre-Etienne Flandin, *Politique française, 1919–1940* (Paris, 1947), 370, 371; also *Commission chargée d'enquêter* . . . , III, 675–679, testimony of General Georges.
[26] See Gamelin's own testimony, *Commission chargée d'enquêter* . . . , III, 577, (copy of his letter to the Committee).

10

The Manpower Question, 1919–1940

At the conclusion of the war in 1918 exhausted France looked to a quick demobilization of her armies. The cry to "get the boys home" after more than four terrible years of war was strong enough so that the government demobilized the army faster than the high command liked.

Marshal Pétain hoped to keep a fairly large force under arms, so that France's interests vis à vis Germany, as well as elsewhere, would be adequately protected. He hoped that the maintaining of this force could be justified by using the army as a working force to restore the devastated regions of northern France. In this way the soldiers would pay for the cost of their upkeep and at the same time would accomplish an important public service. But his idea to use the victorious French soldiers as labor battalions got the reception from the government which might have been expected. The war-weary people of France demanded a rapid demobilization, and got it, after the "war to end wars."

It is usually difficult for any general to watch, unprotesting, the reduction of military manpower in the forces which he commands, and sometimes the protests are justified, in the light of his responsibilities and the mission which has been assigned to him. But in 1919 France's position seemed secure enough to allow her to relax. Germany was still the principal potential adversary but she had been reduced to impotence militarily; an allied Army of Occupation stood guard on her territory.

The Treaty of Versailles reduced the German Army to 100,000

long-service soldiers and provided for the occupation of the Rhineland
for fifteen years by allied troops. The Rhineland was demilitarized,
without time limit, as was the east bank of the river to a depth of
fifty kilometers. Also, the United States and Great Britain had promised to come to France's aid if she were attacked, although this agreement was not subsequently ratified by their respective legislatures.

The situation, then, permitted a reduction in the term of service
for French conscripts and by the law of December 17, 1921, the term
was reduced from three years, which it had been since 1913, to two
years. The effective strength of the army was reduced to 826,000 men.[1]

But a two-year compulsory service still seemed too much to those
who would have to serve and already in 1920 and 1921 there was
agitation in the Chamber of Deputies for a term of service of only
eighteen months. Marshal Pétain, as Commander in Chief-designate
of the army, opposed any reduction unless other measures were taken
to strengthen the army, such as recruiting a larger regular force of
professionals. Although the conditions which he demanded were not
met, the legal term of compulsory service for all Frenchmen was
reduced, on April 1, 1923, to eighteen months.

The question of the size of an army is not an academic one but
is directly related to the mission which is assigned to it. For the
organization of the French army in peacetime Pétain and other military leaders agreed that its principal mission was to assure to the
country, upon the outbreak of hostilities, a powerful frontier covering
force (*couverture*). The covering force would be provided by the active
army—the standing army including regulars and the class of conscripts
currently undergoing its period of training and duty. This protective
covering force would have to be strongly reinforced almost immediately by the rapid mobilization of the younger reservists who had
most recently completed their term of service. Behind this protection,
and covered by it, the nation should have time to mobilize its resources
in order to wage the kind of total war that would probably be necessary, judging by the experience of World War I.

The assurance of this defensive organization—the high command
was not "defensive-minded," considering the existence of the Army of
the Rhine occupation force, offensive in concept, poised to strike into
the heart of Germany, but the French strategic orientation as a whole,
politically and psychologically, was defensive—was dependent upon
the number of effectives in manpower which the laws of the country

---

[1] Anon., "L'Effort militaire français durant 21 années d'armistice," *Revue
des questions de défense nationale,* IV (May–June, 1940), 172.

provided for it, and Pétain was occupied throughout the remainder of his military career with the vital question of military manpower.

The eighteen-month law did not provide from France's small population, with its declining birth rate, enough manpower to serve the army properly, at least under its old organization. After successive reductions in the number of active divisions in the early 1920's Pétain had refused to lower the number of remaining divisions below thirty-two, despite pressure to do so from the Army Committee of the Chamber. He insisted that thirty-two divisions were necessary and possible, assuming that 100,000 career soldiers would be maintained, along with 200,000 native colonial troops, the larger part of the latter being stationed in France. He also had expected 30,000 new civilian employees for the army and strict observance of Article Two of the eighteen-month law which prohibited exemptions from military service.[2]

But these calculations had not worked out. Exemptions granted by the Chamber of Deputies had resulted in an annual loss of 30,000 men to the army. The figure of 100,000 regulars had not even been approached and funds were never made available to hire the 30,000 civilian employees. The war with the Riffs which broke out in 1925 meant that twenty-two regiments of native troops planned for France were occupied in North Africa. The thirty-two division army could not subsist on the recruitment law of 1923; units were skeletonized and a feeling of unease and frustration prevailed throughout the army.

The question of military manpower inevitably became a political one, with the left-wing majority in the legislature after the 1924 elections insisting on a shorter term of compulsory service and a military organization based on a militia concept, a "nation in arms." The eighteen-month service law seemed too long to them and they demanded its reduction to one year. The Higher War Council, headed by Pétain, unanimously opposed the one-year service idea, which was being studied in the Chamber of Deputies in 1925, contending that such a short term would so weaken the army that it could no longer adequately fulfill its mission.[3]

Political proponents of a one-year service—led, in the Chamber, by Daladier and Renaudel, spokesmen for the Radical-Socialists and the

---

[2] *Journal officiel de la République française,* 1871–1940, Chamber of Deputies, Extraordinary session (December 19, 1925), p. 4478; also Jean Fabry, "Ou va notre armée?" *Revue des deux mondes,* V (September–October, 1925), 251–253.

[3] Lieut.-Col. Reboul, "Le Projet de service d'un an," *Revue des deux mondes,* XXVII (May–June, 1925), 33, 34.

Socialists respectively—argued that since France had no imperialist or aggressive aims she had no need for an offensive army and could get by with a small defensive force capable of halting an enemy on the frontiers long enough for the nation's mass of reserves to arm and assemble. One year of training for conscripts seemed more than enough to them; their proposition was based, in part, on the assumption that it takes only four months to train a soldier.

Pétain realized that the one-year law was inevitable given the temper of the parliament, which reflected public opinion. With the German army confined within the limits of the Versailles Treaty and the German economy in a state of collapse, no external danger seemed to threaten the security of France, and he knew also that a majority in the Chamber of Deputies had been elected in 1924 on platforms which included promises to the electorate of an alleviation of personal military charges in the form of a one-year term of service. But if the eighteen-month law of 1923 did not provide enough manpower to maintain the army, the proposed one-year law certainly would be inadequate.

The conditions which Pétain had posed as prerequisites to the eighteen-month law had been promised by the lawmakers but had been disregarded. The one year law was inevitable but this time he would insist that the necessary conditions which would make a one-year law adequate to maintain the army be made law before the reduction in service was made.

The Higher War Council laid down these prerequisites to a one-year law: the recruitment of a larger number of career soldiers, which would give the army a good nucleus of trained regulars and a force ready for action; the authorization and funds to engage civilian employees to fill service functions formerly done by soldiers and to maintain the mobilization centers, in order to ensure that the conscripts, as well as the regulars who trained them, would utilize to the fullest the reduced training period. For the maintenance of internal order in France the high command proposed the creation of a force of gendarmes which would be on a semi-military basis and which would leave the army free for strictly military duties.

They proposed the development and maintenance of instruction camps for the maneuvers and training of the conscripts as well as for the large numbers of reservists who would, under the new system, play so large a role in the nation's military preparedness. They also demanded the creation of mobilization centers to provide for the rapid mobilization of the reserves when needed, a function formerly filled by the regular units themselves to which the reservists were assigned.

Without the fulfillment of these conditions the high command could not agree to a further reduction in the length of service.[4]

The one-year service would require a reorganization of the French army because its organization, dating back to 1873, was based on an army composed of conscripts serving for several years after having been trained, with a strong nucleus of regulars. This reorganization would have been necessary in any case since the law of April 1, 1923, providing for eighteen months of service, had proved itself inadequate and had already caused the army considerable difficulty. The old army organization could not work well with the fewer effectives allowed it under the law.

Since the one-year law would make imperative a drastic change in the structure and nature of the army the high command had been working on plans for a new army organization. At a meeting of the Higher War Council in January 1926 the final draft was approved, to be submitted by the Minister of War, Paul Painlevé, to the parliament. The plan constituted a complete reform of French military institutions and was designed to prepare the way for the application of a one-year term of military service.

The most important consideration in the plan was, as always, the frontier covering force. Pétain had advised the government that a minimum of forty divisions was needed to ensure this. But an annual class of conscripts amounted to only 240,000 men and, allowing six months for training, this meant that the army would have only half a class, 120,000 soldiers, available for operations at any given time. (The class would be called up one half at a time, every six months, so that a demi-contingent would be training while the preceding demi-contingent would be serving in the active units.)

The forty divisions would, however, not all be active in peacetime. The peacetime active units would consist of twenty divisions only, but would be automatically doubled at the outbreak of hostilities by the calling up and incorporation of the three most recently discharged classes. Immediately upon mobilization, cadres of regulars from the first twenty divisions, the active divisions, would leave their units and form a framework for the second twenty divisions. They would be replaced in the original twenty divisions by reservists and the second twenty divisions also would be composed largely of reservists. These forty divisions would constitute the frontier covering force, the combat army, behind which the bulk of the nation's forces would be mobilized.

---

[4] *Journal officiel* . . . , Chamber, Extraordinary session, December 19, 1925, pp. 4480, 4481.

The first forty divisions would therefore be composed mostly of reservists; and the bulk of the army, to follow shortly after, would be formation divisions, wholly reserve divisions with hardly a regular army officer or man in them. The militia system, the "nation in arms" long advocated by the socialists, had come into being. Not that all the antimilitarist critics were yet satisfied: Edouard Daladier opposed the measure and proposed a peacetime force of fourteen divisions instead of twenty.[5]

The government project in its final form, as proposed to the legislature, counted on 240,000 men of the annual class for its implementation, and it demanded the recruitment of 106,000 career soldiers as a prerequisite. It also insisted on the employment of 45,000 civilian functionaries to serve the army and release soldiers for military duties, as well as the creation of a gendarmerie of 15,000 men—Mobile Guards —to free the army from duties involving the maintenance of internal civil order.

The Poincaré ministry made the voting of this law a matter of confidence and despite left-wing opposition the project was made law in June 1927, with every article of the government's plan accepted.

France now had an entirely new military system. Formerly the active army, containing regulars and recently trained conscripts still in service, was *the* army, which changed from a peacetime to a war footing merely by the absorption of the reserves, which it incorporated into its own ranks. From now on the regular army, although it continued as the main agent for the frontier covering force, existed mainly in peacetime as an instrument of instruction, a vast military school in which the annual classes were trained and then returned to civilian life where they remained as a ready reserve. The French army was for all practical purposes a reserve army, a potential force rather than an actual one. The reserve units, comprising the bulk of the army, enjoyed an organization of their own, an existence apart from the regular army. The socialist aversion to a professional standing-army had in effect achieved an old aim: national defense by means of a militia, a "nation in arms."

The fact that France could no longer meet or make a show of military force, could no longer respond to external events, without a large-scale mobilization—it goes without saying that any move she did make would be a response or reaction to outside pressure; she certainly constituted no aggressive threat to anyone except, perhaps, the Riffs and the Druses—had important repercussions during the 1930's on the international diplomatic scene.

[5] *Journal officiel* . . . , Chamber, II (June 16, 1927) , 1915.

The Army Organization Law of 1927 set the stage for the One-Year Law, which was passed by the legislature in January, 1928. The high command had planned their case well and the conditions which they judged to be "preliminary and indispensable" were written into both laws. Article 49 of the 1927 law on the organization of the army provided for the conditions mentioned above: 106,000 career soldiers, 45,000 civilian employees for the army, and the recruitment of a Mobile Guards unit. Then in the 1928 recruitment law, providing for a one-year service, Article 102 reiterated the same conditions and made the application of the present law contingent upon the realization of those conditions.

It was freely admitted that the experience of the 1923 eighteen-month law, in which the prerequisite conditions demanded by Pétain were promised but not carried out, had taught the high command a lesson; and now no law reducing the term of service would be acceptable unless the necessary conditions were realized before its application.

The opposition to the Law, in the Chamber, was of course not because the term of service was being reduced but because of the conditions that went with it. The left-wing deputies wanted passage of the bill without the Article 102 mentioned above. As Daladier had earlier pointed out, in proposing a smaller military establishment, the Locarno Treaty guaranteed the demilitarization of the Rhineland, and many French politicians at this time believed that universal disarmament was attainable and perhaps imminent—a belief which culminated in the euphoria of the Geneva disarmament talks in the early 1930's.

Proponents of the 1927 and 1928 Laws frequently used Marshal Pétain's name and prestige to override opposition to particular portions of the bills under consideration in the parliament, quoting his words of approval or disapproval in regard to measures under discussion. They used this technique particularly to get passage of the prerequisite conditions. In all the political attacks made upon the army and the military in general during the debates it is remarkable how no one, no matter how extreme his politics, ventured to assail, however mildly, the Marshal.

Pétain was the military leader most liked by the *poilu* of World War I and the one most easily accepted by the political left after the war. Yet there was nothing in his background to make him even remotely politically ultraliberal. In a way he was caught in a situation not of his own making; his reputation as a careful manager of men's lives during the war endeared him to the common people, the veterans, and to the liberals and the left-wing, yet his own political convictions were not at all left-wing.

He went along with this current because it was the easiest and the most popular way, and became known as a "republican" general. But Pétain was not merely playing a part; he actually did his best to work with the republic, much to the disgust of right-wing officers like Weygand, and came to think of himself as a general who could manage, if anyone could, the politicians. It was fortunate for the army, in that period when a virulent antimilitarism was so strong a factor in national politics, that it had a leader who was acceptable to all shades of political opinion and who could bridge the gap between the high command and the legislature.

Pétain, whom Léon Blum in 1938 called "the noblest of our military chiefs," changed his political coat, or rather donned one, after the defeat in 1940, when he was almost in his dotage. The manner in which the politicians of the 1930's appeared to him to have mismanaged France's preparation for the war with Hitler angered him and his latent distrust of the left-wing, never very far from the surface, led him to turn on the politicians of the left when events brought him to power.

In 1928 Pétain was not at all overjoyed with the new army but he was too much of a realist to try to stop something that was obviously the will of the majority of Frenchmen, and with the inclusion of the prerequisite conditions he felt that they could make do with the new system, for the time being, in the light of the 1928 international situation. As he later put it, the allied control in Germany had only just ended and the Reichswehr was still contained, "in appearance, at least," within the Versailles Treaty limits of 100,000 men, and the French army still occupied Mainz on the Rhine.[6]

He thought that the active forces still left to France by the "nation in arms" advocates would just suffice, for the time being, to hold the Germany army until the mass of the nation's forces could be mobilized, should war occur. The army in France was reduced to 100,000 men of the conscript contingent, even though the annual class averaged 240,-000 men, because after the air force, the colonial army, and the auxiliary services got their share there remained only 200,000 men, one half of whom would still be in training while the other half, after training, would be serving in the combat army. To these latter 100,-000 add 50,000 regulars serving with them—the rest of the professionals would be tied up with instruction and other duties—and Pétain had

---

[6] Marshal Pétain, "La Securité de la France au cours des années creuses," *Revue des deux mondes*, XXVI (March–April, 1935), p. I.

an army of 150,000 to face the German army numbering, officially, 100,000 men.

The French military leaders did not expect much from the reserve formation divisions, as a force capable of combat very soon after hostilities had commenced but they supposed, "perhaps too easily" as the Marshal put it, that an adversary's preparations for war would be detected in time and the period of diplomatic tension preceding hostilities would give them ample warning so that the reserves could be called up and committed at discretion.

Pétain's appraisal of the mediocre value of reserve formations, as opposed to a trained, long-service army, contrasted strongly with the contemporary political insistence upon a mass of reserve soldiers, civilians called up in an emergency, and the prevalent scorn for long-service professionals. He complained that by an "unfortunate paradox" the French were evolving toward a militia military system just at a time when the technology of war was becoming more and more complex, requiring higher standards of training.[7]

The prominent political leaders in government in 1927 and 1928 gave their entire support to the new French military system, except for those who, as we have noted, thought that the reduction in the military establishment did not go far enough. In the ministry men of all parties—Poincaré, Barthou, Briand, Painlevé, Herriot, Tardieu, Sarraut and Marin—were behind the measure, as were leaders in both houses of the legislature, including Albert Lebrun, president of the Senate Army Committee. One note of protest was raised in the Senate when a senator, General Hirschauer, formally expressed his regret at the disappearance of the horse cavalry.[8]

The one-year service was put into practice with the demi-contingent called up in October 1929. It was a twenty-one-year-old class, for one of the provisions of the law specified that the age of induction be raised from twenty to twenty-one years of age. It was hoped that a sort of reservoir of manpower would be formed in this manner, to be used to make up the deficit of manpower during the "hollow years" of 1936–1940. The plan was to reduce the draft age to twenty years again, in stages spread over the "hollow years."

The so-called "hollow years" were a result of World War I. As a result of a 50 per cent drop in the French birth rate during World War I the classes born in 1915 through 1919, coming of military age in 1936–1940, were reduced by one-half; the normal complement of an annual class decreased from an average of 240,000 men to 120,000. The

---

[7] *Ibid.*, pp. II–VIII.
[8] Paul Reynaud, *Mémoires* (Paris, 1963), I, 240–244.

high command and the government hoped in 1928 largely to provide for this future deficit by raising, temporarily, the age of induction to twenty-one, a hope which was to prove illusory. France just did not have the population to meet its military charges during the 1930's without sacrifice and serious effort, without a longer term of military service for all Frenchmen.

The population crisis provided a troubled background against which French military leaders strove to maintain a military force adequate for the nation's commitments and security. The declining birthrate was an old phenomenon but it reached serious proportions in the twentieth century, particularly during and after World War I. The terrible casualties of the war, affecting the youngest and best men of the country, greatly aggravated the problem; and from the end of the war the high command was preoccupied with a manpower problem which influenced much of their planning. For example the idea of the Maginot Line, the completion of which was scheduled for 1935 at the beginning of the "hollow years" period, was based to a large extent upon manpower considerations. Neighboring countries, Germany, Austria and Italy, also suffered heavy losses in the war but they had larger reserves of young people and a higher postwar birthrate. France was in a position of demographic inferiority vis à vis her neighbors; Germany alone had a population twice that of France.

In 1931 Pétain retired from active service but continued, as a member of the Higher War Council, his preoccupation with the question of military effectives. The War Council was engaged, during the early 1930's, in a running battle with parliamentarians who wanted to reduce further the army establishment. This was the era of economic depression, pacificism, left-wing opposition to all things military, and the Geneva disarmament talks. The proposals emanating from Geneva would have further reduced the French military system to a militia status and the Higher War Council bitterly opposed these proposals, pointing out that France not only had her own security to maintain but she also had military commitments to assist Belgium, Poland, Czechoslovakia, Yugoslavia and Rumania in the event those countries were attacked. France needed these allies as much as they needed her.

The parliament used indirect methods to reduce the strength of the army and to circumvent the Laws of 1927–28 which had guaranteed a certain number of effectives to the high command. The One-Year Law had strictly limited the system of leaves and furloughs, to ensure that the army would be kept up to a minimum strength, but the parliament took liberties with this limitation so that conscripts were getting thirty-five days leave during their year of service. In addition, the dates of the induction and release of the biannual contingents were tampered with, so that one demi-contingent was released early and the next one called up late, thus creating an interval of about a month between the contingents. In this way the service of one year was reduced to about ten months.[9] This nibbling away at the military effectives had at first an adverse effect on the training of the citizen-soldiers and then began, the generals complained, to weaken the structure of the army itself.

The Chamber of Deputies aimed another blow at the army by an attack on its officer complement in early 1933. Without consulting the high command or making a combined study of the effects such a move would have—they knew full well that the army would never agree— they ordered the retirement of 5,000 officers of the active army, to take place over a period of five years. This measure, which would have deprived the army of one-sixth of its regular officers, was in violation of Article Four of the law of March 28, 1928, relative to the constitution of cadres and effectives, and if fully carried out would have had a unfortunate effect on the army, materially and morally. The results in 1939 would have been even more serious. The high command hedged on its application and through the year 1933 they only let go about 1,800 officers, mostly old captains of less than the best quality. In 1934 Marshal Pétain became Minister of War and stopped all further application of the law.

Pétain's accession to the War Ministry was opportune in other respects, for the military situation had reached a crisis stage. The parliamentary nibbling at army effectives, becoming more and more serious throughout 1933 and early 1934, was brought to a halt by the Marshal, as well as were other deteriorations in the French military establishment. There was great relief in military circles, and a bitter post-World War II critic of Pétain, General Gamelin, admitted that the appointment of the Marshal as War Minister in February, 1934 dissipated the "nightmare" that hung over the high command.[10]

Note has been taken of the plan gradually to reduce the draft age from twenty-one to twenty years over the "hollow years" to meet the manpower deficit through 1936–1940. In the early 1930's another, supplementary, plan was put into effect, called the "Bernier Plan" for the deputy who conceived it. This expedient too was of little value —you cannot make something out of nothing and the French man-

---

[9] *Commission chargée d'enquêter sur les événements survenus en France de 1933 à 1945* (Paris, 195?), Dépositions, I, 97, 98, 112, 113; also General Gamelin, *Servir* (Paris, 1946), I, 147.

[10] Gamelin, II, 108; also General Debeney, "Encore l'armée de métier," *Revue des deux mondes*, XXVIII (July–August, 1935), 289, 290.

power crisis could only be met by an increased length of service—but it was an interesting experiment and indicated the intense desire to retain a service of one year and yet be strong enough to meet national security needs and commitments.

The Bernier Plan proposed to economize on manpower by not calling up one month's "births" each year, from 1932 to 1935, and then using this "saving" during the crucial 1937–1940 period. By raising the draft age one month each year they would only take from the annual classes eleven months' "births," thus decreasing the annual contingent from 1932 to 1935 to about 220,000 men but saving about 20,000 men per year to be used later to meet the "hollow years" manpower crisis.

The Plan had been tried in 1932 and the loss of 20,000 men from the already insufficient contingent was more than General Weygand could stand. When the Chamber proposed to make the project a law in December 1933, the exasperated commander in chief-designate of the French army called the Higher War Council into session to forestall it. He felt that the unanimous disapproval of the Council would force the parliament to halt its project and he knew that he could count upon the support of Marshal Pétain.

The meeting of the War Council took place on December 18, 1933, presided over by Minister of War Daladier—who was a partisan of the Bernier measure—and after a lively discussion a vote was taken. Eleven of the members, including Pétain, sided against the Minister and three of them, including Gamelin, approved the measure, thus destroying the unanimity Weygand had hoped for. After the meeting the parliament went ahead with the Plan, voting it into law despite the expressed disapproval of the Higher War Council.[11]

The Bernier Plan, impractical as it was, did not last; for Marshal Pétain, as Minister of War in 1934, in trying to stay within the framework of the One-Year Law while at the same time hoping to have the strength to counter the German rearmament, used up one-half of the manpower economies accumulated to date under the Plan. The rest were used under subsequent ministries and the annual "saving" of one month's "births" was discontinued.

During the stormy year of 1933 Pétain had no illusions about the necessity for France to raise its terms of military service to two years, but political opposition to such a measure was too intense. He felt that it would be useless to attempt to get it in the prevailing political climate and that instead an effort should be made to get an augmenta-

---

[11] Gamelin, II, 105–107; also, for Weygand's account of the episode, *Commission chargée d'enquêter* . . . , VI, 1594.

tion in the number of career soldiers. He did, however, ask André Tardieu to suggest the idea of a two-year service in the Chamber, which the latter did on December 19, 1933, during the heated debate on the passage of the Bernier Law, and the proposal ran into the expected bitter opposition.

When Pétain became War Minister in February 1934 his most pressing problems were that of military manpower and the nation's reluctance to support a longer term of personal military service. He knew that the German army had slipped the chains of the Versailles Treaty, for the German high command had begun the expansion of their army immediately after the withdrawal of Germany from the Disarmament Conference in October, 1933, and French Intelligence was reporting accurately on this development.

In February and March 1934 Pétain, as Minister of War, met with the Army Committees of the Chamber and the Senate and advised them that although the two-year service was necessary they could not bring the matter up now because the public would not accept it. He said that they should instead step up recruiting for the regular army, thus enlarging the army by voluntary enlistment and strengthening the frontier protective covering force.

Pétain's policy of trying to get by with what was available and proceeding cautiously in the matter of prolonging personal military service won him little favor with his erstwhile military comrades. General Weygand called together, on his own responsibility, members of the Higher War Council—the Council could only be convened officially by the War Minister—and addressed reports to Pétain complaining of the weakness of the army and demanding a two-year service, as well as demanding that the Higher War Council be officially convoked to express its opinions on the state of the army.

But Pétain would not call a meeting of the War Council, which never met officially during his term as War Minister. Weygand attributed this refusal to the fact that the Marshal had for so long commanded the French army that he felt that he himself could determine what was best militarily.[12] Pétain probably thought it unwise to excite further political opposition by convoking a military body whose conservative tendencies were well known and already discounted. The experience of the December 18, 1933, meeting, in which the Council had pronounced against the Bernier Plan, a pronouncement which had absolutely no effect on the decision of the lawmakers the next day, had demonstrated the impotence of the War Council in important matters of a politico-military nature. In the debate Daladier had re-

---

[12] Commission chargée d'enquêter . . . , VI, 1597.

ferred to the Council's opinion as normal for generals and said that he would have been surprised if they had acted otherwise.[13] This may illustrate the eclipse of the influence of the Higher War Council which persisted until World War II, and it is difficult to see what effect the convocation of that body by Pétain would have had, other than to inflame issues already warm to the touch.

Whenever General Weygand talked to Pétain personally about the duration of the military service, the Minister of War replied that he was of Weygand's opinion regarding the necessity for an increased length of service but the time was not yet ripe for proposing it. Pétain told him that he would raise it gradually, by stages. As the Marshal later explained, when he was Minister of War his concern was to recruit as many men for the army as possible but since it was out of the question for him to begin with a large number he planned to achieve his objective by degrees, gradually to build up to the required figure by small steps that would not excite too much opposition. But the opposition was too strong and the failure of his measured attempt is evidence that France would not have accepted a two-year service in 1934.[14] One of the reasons why the two-year service finally did come into effect in January 1936 was the awkward *volte-face* executed in the Chamber by the French Communist deputies who swallowed the measure, on orders from Moscow, since France and the Soviet Union, who viewed the rising Nazi power as a threat, were then negotiating a military alliance.

In 1934 Lieutenant-Colonel Charles de Gaulle's book, *Vers l'armée de métier,* appeared; in it he recommended the establishment, in France, of a 100,000-man army, mechanized and motorized, composed of professional soldiers. De Gaulle's idea was that this army would be in readiness at all times, like the navy and the air force, and would not be dependent upon the annual conscript contingent for its effectives. Since the success of the German victory in 1940 was due in part to that nation's intelligent employment of tanks and the corresponding French failure to do the same, his recommendation for a small, shock army of armored divisions manned by career soldiers has since received a certain amount of attention as evidence of de Gaulle's far-sightedness.

---

[13] *Journal officiel* . . . , Chamber, December 19, 1933, 4688–4708; the opinion of the Higher War Council on the matter under discussion was almost completely ignored during the debate.
[14] The aged Pétain's testimony to members of the *Commission chargée d'enquêter* . . . , Supplement, I, 168, 169.

In the 1930's the ideas expressed in the book were not accepted by French leaders, military or civilian, except for a few men like Paul Reynaud, and in fact they could not have been accepted. The last thing that left-wing politicians would have permitted to happen in France would have been the creation of a small, professional élite force, a potential praetorian guard, which enemies of the republic could employ in a possible coup d'état. Léon Blum's attitude was typical enough when he said that such a force would have been a disaster for France had it existed in February 1934 during the anti-government riots, and Daladier's opposition was no less sharp.

The military reaction to de Gaulle's proposals was as unfavorable as was that of the parliamentary leaders. There is the simple reason that the aged members of the French high command, relics of another war, were conservative and slow to accept new ideas, but there were also sound reasons for their rejection of the 100,000-man professional army concept. In the first place France did not have enough men of military age to staff such a force and at the same time to properly maintain her other army forces. They had difficulty enough recruiting career soldiers for the army as it was and if the army establishment had to compete with a new élite force which would probably attract many of the best men, the rest of the army, the bulk of the nation's armed forces, would have suffered in quality.

Pétain had no use for de Gaulle's idea. In the first place he did not like the young officer personally; he considered him a self-seeking ingrate. During the 1920's Pétain had befriended de Gaulle, whose attitude and relations with the army hierarchy somewhat resembled his own early experience, and had helped his career considerably. Without Pétain's patronage de Gaulle would not have done well in the army and in fact at one point he might have been put on the inactive list if it had not been for Pétain's protection. The two men had been close and for a time de Gaulle was on the Marshal's staff. It is not true, however, that Pétain was the godfather of de Gaulle's son Philippe, although de Gaulle was not reluctant to let people think that he was.

De Gaulle and Pétain had a falling out regarding the authorship of the book *France and Her Army,* a history of the French soldier. The book was Pétain's idea but de Gaulle wrote it, the first five chapters when he was a member of Pétain's staff. This situation was customary enough in French military circles: the chief was surrounded with a staff of young officers who did his writing for him. Joffre's memoirs were written in this way, for example. In point of fact, Pétain never wrote anything himself and for some of the prefaces of books which appeared under his name he never even read the book. But he did carefully go over all the articles that appeared over his signature and his style and ideas were impressed upon them. When he was paid for an article, as by the *Revue des deux mondes* for example, he divided the amount received equally between himself and the officer who wrote the article.

In the case of de Gaulle's book the latter wanted to receive the credit due him for his authorship, despite the custom and tradition of anonymity which he had accepted implictly when he joined Pétain's staff and began work on the book. Staff officers were expected to accept their role—*les nègres* they were called—as part of their training and terms of service; they were compensated by a relatively easy staff life and the patronage of a high ranking general. But de Gaulle was of a different stamp. If there was one thing that was alien to de Gaulle's temperament—"the turkey" Pétain used to call him—it was anonymity and the Marshal's intention to publish under his own name the work of a subordinate, a work beyond the normal scope of a staff headquarters, was more worthy of a Pas de Calais peasant than of a marshal of France.

Pétain's objections to the de Gaulle thesis were, however, based on sound reasoning. For one thing de Gaulle in his book *Vers l'armée de métier* did not take proper cognizance of the role of airpower in modern war and Marshal Pétain had strong opinions as to the efficacy and potential power of aircraft in operations—opinions which do his military sense credit and were by no means defensive-minded or old-fashioned, a fact which critics of the Marshal often have ignored. He reasoned that if he had a superiority in aircraft he could nail his adversary to the ground, no matter how mobile or armored the opposing forces were; conversely, he argued, if his own forces were well equipped with armored vehicles but lacked aircraft, the enemy could demolish his armored formations because tanks cannot operate against airplanes but airplanes can destroy tanks.[15]

In other words, to Pétain airpower was the key, not armor; but in de Gaulle's book the only mention of the value of aircraft as tactical ground support was that they could lay down smokescreens to conceal the movements of his tanks. It was only in the subsequent editions of the book *Vers l'armée de métier,* published after World War II, that the role of tactical airpower, operating in support of the ground troops and in conjunction with armored divisions, was developed.

In any case Pétain was still at heart a foot-soldier, the *fantassin*

---

[15] George London, editor, *Le Procès Pétain* (Lyon, 1945), 386, 387; General Vauthier's testimony.

classique. Tanks to him were merely adjuncts to his precious infantry; they were tools of the infantry and they existed only to protect and facilitate the movement of the infantry. After his experiences, before and during World War I, it would have been truly remarkable if, in his late seventies, he suddenly should have become a daring advocate of armored warfare, a conception not held by any military leaders anywhere but only by a few innovators like de Gaulle, Guderian and J. F. C. Fuller.

Furthermore, de Gaulle's proposed striking force was an offensive instrument and the French military establishment was basically defensive. Its defensive attitude was written into the 1927 law on the organization of the army, which specified that the sole purpose of the army was to defend her national soil and her overseas territories—a limitation which should have given pause to France's small allies. The civilian government leaders were not only aware of its defensive character but it was they who demanded and planned it that way. Pétain had always been an advocate of the strength of the defensive—a fact which endeared him to left-wing politicians—and de Gaulle's thesis therefore failed on that count.

This episode has been described here because the struggle of Pétain and other military leaders to maintain the strength of the army at a level commensurate with the security of France and with her commitments was a bitter and often frustrating task and de Gaulle's proposals for a 100,000-man professional army, at the expense of the regular establishment even if in addition to it, were impractical and unrealistic in the 1930's when they appeared. Neither the army nor the government could seriously consider them, nor did they.

On April 17, 1934, France formally rejected, in a note to the British government, Hitler's proposal, which Britain's Anthony Eden supported, that Germany be granted parity in the matter of armaments and effectives. The German proposal, first made directly to France in November 1933, was that France and Germany should limit their respective armies to 300,000 men each. The Germans refused to include their Brown Shirt and other para-military formations, which represented a considerable force, in the 300,000 figure, but Louis Barthou, French Foreign Minister in the Doumergue cabinet, wanted to accept the German proposal, which would have included Italy, and had actually drawn up a reply to the British government indicating that acceptance in principle. However, in a last minute cabinet meeting a majority of the cabinet members voted—the taking of a formal vote was rare in French cabinet decisions—to reject the plan. Pétain as War Minister painted a somber picture of the German rearmament efforts already taking place in violation of the Versailles Treaty and Ministers of State Tardieu and Herriot were equally opposed to trusting Hitler in a military agreement.

The French high command believed that they had a considerable lead over the Germans in armaments and that Germany, so recently weakened by the severe economic depression, had not the financial means to catch up militarily. In this they reckoned without the great capacity of German industry and the efficiency of a totalitarian economy, but the French miscalculation did not change matters appreciably inasmuch as Hitler's word was worthless in any case.

With Germany openly rearming—the German budget published on April 9 disclosed a considerable augmentation in military expenditures—Pétain worried about the lack of French response to the threat. He thought first in terms of increased manpower but parliamentary opposition to an augmentation of the military service blocked any immediate enlargement of the army. He realized that he would have to proceed by degrees and wait for a change in the climate of public opinion.

Several weeks after the note of April 17 was drawn up Pétain obtained approval from Premier Doumergue for an attempt to get a short prolongation of the term of military service. He planned only to raise the term from one year to fifteen months, a small enough increase and one which fitted in with his plan to get the desired army strength in small steps. He presented his proposal privately to members of the Chamber Army Committee but Léon Blum, Socialist leader in the Chamber, got wind of it and immediately organized opposition to the measure, and it never came up for debate in the Chamber.[16]

The one bright spot in the 1934 picture for the military leaders was the protection afforded by the large segments of the Maginot Line then nearing completion. They had planned to complete the major frontier fortifications by 1935, the start of the "hollow years" crisis in effectives; and in 1934, thanks to the progress already made, a larger part of the French forces could be shifted to the Nord, the department facing the Belgian frontier.

But the economies in manpower that the French army was able to effect as a result of the frontier fortifications were already discounted by the politicians and the latter linked the voting of funds for the completion and improvement of the Maginot Line to the continuance of the one-year term of military service. Their idea was that the sup-

16 New York Times, May 4, 1934.

posedly impregnable line of fortifications would permit France to maintain a smaller army. This presented a problem for the War Minister who needed both the fortifications *and* a larger army. The military planned to use the Maginot Line to bolster France's sagging military manpower, not to replace it.

In June 1934 a bill for further military funds came up before the Chamber of Deputies and the debate that ensued clearly defined this issue. Édouard Daladier, speaking in the name of the Radical-Socialist party, declared that they would vote the necessary funds for the frontier fortifications but only if it were clearly understood that these works were to take the place of large numbers of soldiers. He emphatically declared that if it were shown that an extension of the term of military service were necessary, he and his party would refuse to vote the funds earmarked for the Maginot Line. His point was that the vote should put an end to all talk of increasing the terms of compulsory military service and a "vital point" in his reasoning regarding the necessity for the funds in question was that a fortified belt protecting France's frontiers would permit the acceptance of a new "structure" for the army.[17]

By a new "structure" for the army Daladier meant that cement and steel from now on would take the place of men. He spoke of a revolution in the military art consisting of an inviolable and unbreachable *couverture,* a system of forts manned by a relatively small number of specialists. He hinted strongly that "certain high military authorities" were not in favor of the fortifications for that reason.

Despite Daladier's protestations to the contrary, the vote for funds to complete the frontier fortifications in June 1934 was a species of political blackmail in that the funds were directly linked to the one-year service. Pétain had to accept one to get the other. At a meeting of the Chamber Committee on Finances he was asked bluntly if the sums to be voted for the fortifications would assure the Chamber that there would be no prolongation of the term of military service. The War Minister tried to hedge, saying that such a prolongation would not be necessary "now." The Committee pressed him for a definite answer and Pétain told them that "the question [of a longer service] does not arise now" but "I don't say that it will not arise."[18]

At a meeting of the Army Committee of the Chamber on July 3, 1934, Pétain told the members that he intended to try to stay within the limits of the One-Year Law unless unforeseen events necessitated exceptional security measures. But, he told them, in order to fill the

[17] *Journal officiel* . . . , Chamber, June 15, 1934, 1532, 1533.
[18] *Journal officiel* . . . , Chamber, June 15, 1934, 1537.

gaps in the army ranks he would have to call up the full conscript contingent in October 1934, thus disregarding the Bernier Law and also using up the small reserves of manpower which had been accumulated under that law. He also intended to intensify enlistments and reenlistments in the regular army and hoped to recruit large numbers of army specialists. The Committee approved the War Minister's projects although it eventually meant that the 1934 budget for the maintenance of army personnel was exceeded by 192 millions.

A few weeks later the Chamber passed a decree legalizing the new policy of accepting an unlimited number of recruits for the regular army. This abrogated a law of 1932 which had limited such enlistments at a time when economic conditions were forcing young men to join the army in larger numbers than the parliament desired.

But, as it turned out, Pétain's recruitment efforts for more professional soldiers were unsuccessful as a measure to meet the manpower crisis. Not only did the declining birth rate and the population problem affect the numbers of young men available for recruitment but the continuing economic depression had, paradoxically, an opposite effect than it had had in 1932. Now fewer men would join the army when they were unemployed because of the unemployment relief measures which had been taken by the government. An unemployed worker received ten francs daily in benefits from the state, a sum much greater than that which he would receive as a soldier and one that cost him less effort.

Pétain bowed to parliamentary demands and strong public opinion pressures on the one-year service question because he was realistic enough to recognize that France would not accept a greater personal military burden at that time, and he needed the support of the Chamber of Deputies to get funds for the frontier fortifications. But the linking of the military budget to the one-year service could be worked both ways and in the autumn of 1934, when the War Minister was faced with a reduction in his 1935 budget for armaments, he used the same device to get his funds that the opponents of a longer military service had used against him.

In an attempt to balance the budget the Minister of Finances refused to allow a large augmentation of expenditures planned by Pétain for the motorization of the army and the modernization of its equipment. Pétain's chief argument to gain his point—and his funds—was to show that the increased efficiency accruing to the army as a result of the measures he proposed was in line with his attempts to ensure the continuance of the One-Year Law. He pointed out that the army must have the best matériel if it was to function well with the reduced number of men allowed it by the present compulsory service law. While the Finance Minister refused to allow the increased expenditure in the regular budget, a special law was voted by the parliament providing the funds that the Marshal wanted.[19]

When the Doumergue government fell in November 1934 Pétain left the War Ministry but he remained concerned with the question of military manpower. Upon his recommendation General Maurin succeeded him as War Minister and Maurin took the post, he said, only because Pétain asked him to.

Pétain and the new minister were in agreement that the one-year service had to be discontinued; France could no longer afford the luxury in the face of the coming "hollow years" and German rearmament. Maurin had the question restudied by the Army General Staff and they reported that a two-year term of service was a vital necessity. Pétain, no longer holding an official position, decided to speak out and take his case to the country.

On March 1, 1935 a feature article, over the Marshal's signature, appeared in the *Revue des deux mondes*. In it Pétain reviewed the present French military system from its creation in 1927–1928. He pointed out that this system was put into effect when the German army was limited by the terms of the Versailles Treaty, and the small French army resulting from the One-Year Law seemed adequate enough for its defensive role. But present circumstances were far different; Germany had rearmed and the French system no longer corresponded to the military needs of the nation.[20]

Pétain said that the militia system under which the bulk of the French army, the reserve or formation divisions, became ready for active service after a relatively long period of time would not be able to meet the demands of a modern war. He stressed the danger of a "lightning war," a sudden attack by an enemy employing armored vehicles and air power. To meet this type of warfare, for which Germany was preparing, he demanded an army of trained soldiers, not an army of hastily mobilized civilian militia.

He explained that during the previous year, 1934, desiring to spare the country an increase in its burdens, he had tried every means possible to make the one-year service yield enough men to assure the nation's security. He had hoped that he might barely succeed. But now he knew that it could not be made to work, due to the failure to

---

[19] *Journal officiel*, Chamber, November 23, 1934, 2574.
[20] Marshal Pétain, "La Securité de la France au cours des années creuses," *Revue des deux mondes*, XXVI (March–April, 1935), pp. I, II.

recruit enough career soldiers and also due to the acceleration of German rearmament.

He concluded his article by warning France that she could only have peace by being strong, so strong that a potential adversary would hesitate to attack her. If France were feeble, war would be only a question of time. The advice that you must prepare for war to preserve the peace, the Roman *"Si vis pacem para bellum,"* culminated his plea for a two-year term of compulsory military service as the only means of giving the army the trained manpower it needed to assure a minimum of security vis à vis a resurgent and inimical Germany. His was a plea to Frenchmen to prepare themselves for war to ensure peace.

Two weeks after Pétain's article appeared and had prepared public opinion with the weight of the Marshal's prestige, the Flandin government, through Minister of War Maurin, introduced a measure in the parliament which proposed to prolong the term of military service in a manner which would give them the two-year service without actually changing the present recruitment law. This could be done by applying Article Forty of the law of 1928 which permitted the government, in exceptional circumstances, to retain the classes in service beyond the one-year period. In this manner the two-year service was not yet actually voted by the parliament but the high command in effect got the two-year extension on a temporary basis, presumably to last only through the "hollow years."

In arguing his cause Maurin drew heavily on Marshal Pétain's authority to sway the deputies—it seems likely that the publication of the Marshal's views and the government project were concerted actions—and in the Senate the president of the Senate Army Committee also invoked the opinions of Pétain, "our greatest military leader" he called him, to get the support of that body.[21]

The inevitable Socialist opposition, lead by Léon Blum who made an impassioned debate against any prolongation of the term of military service, failed to halt the project and the government carried its measure. The next day, March 16, 1935, Hitler announced the repudiation of the military clauses of the Versailles Treaty and the reintroduction in Germany of compulsory military service; he proposed to raise a peacetime army of twelve army corps or thirty-six divisions.

On April 16, 1935, the High Military Committee met and unanimously approved a delay of three months in the release of the class

[21] *Journal officiel . . . ,* Chamber, March 15, 1935, p. 1045; Senate, March 15, 1935, p. 301.

due to be released in April. There was no adverse reaction from the people or the troops. The contingent called up in April would serve eighteen months and the contingent of October, and subsequent ones, would serve two years. From then on the system of the demi-contingents, so disliked by Pétain and the high command, would be stopped and the annual class would be called up in its entirety, to serve for two years. This temporary arrangement was legalized by a vote in the Chamber of Deputies in January 1936, over the noisy protests of the Socialists but with the strained approval of the Communists, now strangely patriotic, cynics thought, who fell in line with Moscow's desire to strengthen France against Germany.

As far as Pétain and the French high command were concerned the decision to raise the military service to two years was not an answer to Germany's rearmament, although Hitler's action made the longer term more palatable to the French public. It was, rather, a measure deemed vital in any case to offset the halving of effectives during the "hollow years." The two-year service would not double French effectives; it merely permitted an army establishment approximately equal to the one-year service of normal years, the years prior to 1936. Therefore France was actually no better off than she had been before; she was merely keeping her army at a level while Germany was proceeding with an armament effort which would put her far ahead in peacetime army strength.

Pétain's excursion into politics in 1934 had not diminished his prestige with the French public. A curious poll was taken by a French newspaper in January 1935, in which Frenchmen were asked to vote for the man whom they would prefer to have as a dictator, if France had to have a dictator. Pétain polled the most votes, with Pierre Laval coming in second. Next in order of the largest number of votes received were Doumergue, "Marianne," Herriot and Flandin.[22]

This incident may or may not be significant but it is fairly certain that the Marshal had little desire for political power. He was conscious of his great age and by 1938 he was complaining to a parliamentarian, Deputy Jacquinot, that he could work only three or four hours each day because of his advanced years.[23]

Publicists like Gustave Hervé, who in his "C'est Pétain qu'il nous faut" suggested that the Marshal assume political leadership in France, angered or irritated him; and he had no association with the clandestine right-wing organizations like the Cagoule, although he was

[22] New York Times, January 11, 1935.
[23] J.-R. Tournoux, Pétain et De Gaulle (Paris, 1964), 163–166.

aware of their existence. One of his staff officers, Georges Loustaunau-Lacau, during the days of the Popular Front organized the "Corvignolles," a network of army officers whose purpose was to maintain an undercover surveillance in the army to counter suspected Communist subversion. The Marshal undoubtedly approved of this activity but he was not directly connected with it and in any case the Corvignolles were not a threat to the French state. If there had been more Loustaunau-Lacaus in France in 1940 the war might have taken a different turn, panzer divisions notwithstanding.[24]

Pétain seems to have had a feeling that he would be needed and that he should keep himself free of any political faction. He sensed that France, divided politically and increasingly insecure militarily, would have need in the future of his ability to restore morale, as he had done in 1917, although he did not foresee the enormity of the disaster which would come in 1940.

In March 1936, when Germany remilitarized the Rhineland in violation of the Versailles Treaty and the Locarno Pact, the inadequacy of the French "nation in arms" system resulting from the laws of 1927–1928 on the reorganization and recruitment of the army was revealed in a dramatic manner. Pétain had accepted the laws which made the French army virtually a militia because political pressure and a war-weary public opinion made it necessary and then only because the relative weakness of Germany and the international situation as a whole seemed to permit, in the late 1920's, the relative relaxation of French military preparedness.

But he stated publicly in 1935 that the French system, which relied too heavily on reserve formations hastily mobilized in a moment of danger, could not cope with the "lightning war" tactics of which modern, mechanized armies with their air forces were capable. At that time he urged France to organize a larger peacetime army, which his countrymen began to do; but the adoption of a two-year service was not sufficient to counter the type of aggression which occurred in March 1936 unless the country had the will to use its army.

Inasmuch as Pétain had practically retired from official functions in 1936 the events of March enter this account only insofar as they demonstrate the effects of a military system which was formed when Pétain was actively involved. In the decisions made by the government

24 Commandant Loustaunau-Lacau served with distinction in both World Wars, was a member of the Resistance during the German occupation, and was turned over to the Gestapo and a German concentration camp by Pétain's Vichy government.

during the March crisis the Marshal had no part; he was not consulted by the Premier nor by any minister, nor by the army commander, General Gamelin. The High Military Committee, of which he was a member, was not convoked until March 11 and then, strangely enough, the Rhineland problem was not discussed because the Minister of Foreign Affairs was in London. It was not until March 13 that General Gamelin made a courtesy call to the old Marshal and informed him of the decisions already taken.[25]

Pétain's warning of 1935 regarding the weakness of the French military organization was not an isolated one. General Weygand had made similar protests to the government in 1932 and again in 1934, warning them that even operating at peak efficiency the active army was incapable of fulfilling its primary mission of a frontier covering force without calling up the reserves. But the parliamentary faith in reserve units was unshaken; the old theory, so dear to the socialists and some liberals, of a national defense by calling all the citizens to arms in an emergency, a "mass levying," still could count on support from a large segment of the French people, understandably reluctant to bear a constant peacetime military burden.

The French government was aware prior to March 1936 that the Germans were preparing a coup in the demilitarized area of the Rhineland. When the government consulted the military authorities, in the person of the Minister of War, Maurin, with a view toward preparing counter-measures to the German move, they were told that the active army was just capable, with its own resources, of defending French territory alone, and that for any offensive into German territory they would have to mobilize the reserves, a general mobilization, with all the concomitant complications from a diplomatic as well as a domestic public opinion point of view. Some politicians were later to pretend great surprise and dismay at the "discovery" that France did not have an army adequate to sustain its foreign policy, or sufficient to carry out its obligations to its allies; but that fact had already been written into the laws of 1927–1928 and they had had repeated warnings since then.

On Saturday, March 7, 1936, German troops occupied the demilitarized zone in the Rhineland. France made noisy protests but did little else and her weakness was revealed for all the world to see. She could hardly make a military move without a general mobilization, a long and complicated process that would partially suspend all other national activity. And that the country would not stand for; neither the parliament nor the government would force the issue; they could not even if they wanted to, with general elections only seven weeks

---

[25] Alfred Conquet, *Lumières sur l'histoire* (Paris, 1963), 137, 157.

away. The French people were not willing to fight another major war just to keep German soldiers off German soil and the French government did not dare to engage the nation in a military adventure when neither France nor her allies had been directly attacked.

It will be remembered that the military organization resulting from the 1927–1928 laws provided France with just enough trained men for a twenty-division active army. But the plan was that upon mobilization the active divisions would transfer the greater part of their cadres to reserve divisions and these cadres would be replaced, in the original active divisions, by reservists. The French army would be in a state of flux and disorder just at the moment when it should have been most ready. Alternatively, if the high command kept its active units intact and used them for a limited thrust into the Rhineland, without detaching the regular cadres, the formation of the reserve divisions, vitally necessary if large-scale operations developed, would be seriously compromised. And large-scale operations seemed a very likely possibility if France moved against the Germans in the Rhineland.

The military could not guarantee that a military action, even of limited scope, would not evolve into a major war and were therefore reluctant to compromise the eventual general mobilization by using the units of the standing-army already constituted. But a general or even a partial mobilization was attended by diplomatic dangers which the government was not willing to incur, to say nothing of the strong public sentiment against any military move at all.

France had three choices: a mobilization, with all the attendant diplomatic and political risks; a limited operation designed merely to force the Germans to evacuate the Rhineland but incurring the risk of setting off a major war and finding the careful mobilization plans for organizing the reserve formations, vital to the army, thrown out of kilter; or simply accepting the German *fait accompli*. The latter course was chosen. From that time on the relative military strength of France vis à vis Germany was on the decline. France's allies and friends were shaken and troubled; six months later her closest ally, Belgium, broke the military alliance that bound them. The nation-in-arms concept was a failure.

The steps which France took to remedy this situation between 1936 and 1939 have no place here as Pétain was not directly involved. The desperate unwillingness in France to accept the risk of a war, with the tragic memories of World War I still alive, led that nation down a series of steps to the war that was inevitable and the defeat which, in retrospect, also seems inevitable. When France went to war in 1939 her large army of reservists was able, thanks to the Maginot Line and

Germany's preoccupation in Poland, to take its place and methodically prepare itself. Although the commander, General Gamelin, was later to complain that the defeat of May, 1940 was due in part to a lack of effectives,[26] other postwar analyses have shown that in sheer numbers France and her allies were not inferior to the German forces which swamped them.

---

[26] *Commission chargée d'enquêter* . . . , Supplement, II, 406, 407, Gamelin's testimony.

11

Pétain and the Frontier Fortifications

One of the most interesting, and often the least understood, aspects of France's military preparation in the inter-war period is that concerning the conception and construction of the system of fortified works on her northeastern frontier which came to be popularly known as the Maginot Line. Marshal Pétain was prominent in the conception and the planning of the system.

The Maginot Line commonly evokes the stereotyped image of a line of elaborate forts created by an old-fashioned or inept military leadership with concrete on the brain, an amusing picture of an imposing "Wall of France" that the French neglected to extend far enough and behind which they foolishly waited until a nimble invader simply went around the "Wall," thus rendering the whole expensive creation useless and even ridiculous. Its place in history, therefore, needs clarification and amplification unless we are to believe that the French high command and government leaders were stupid men, which they were not.

Before 1914 the trend of French military thinking had been to look down upon fortified positions as being too defensive in concept and probably of little use in modern war. The fortified defenses planned and built by Séré de Rivières in the late nineteenth century therefore were allowed to fall into neglect and some were even dismantled and destroyed. Fort Douaumont at Verdun was abandoned to the Germans without a fight and later had to be won back by bitter and costly attacks. General Pétain found, when he assumed the command at Verdun, that most of the heavy guns had been removed from the forts

245

for use by the field armies and the fortified positions were not even included or utilized in the defensive organization of the high command.

The battle of Verdun demonstrated the value of concrete and steel fortifications and the war as a whole was a lesson in the power of the defense when it was solidly ensconced in or behind well-prepared and well-built fortified positions. Marshal Pétain was not alone in his appreciation of this factor; a whole generation of officers and Frenchmen, or the survivors thereof, had learned in a grim school that the attackers of prepared positions usually had to accept heavy casualties to take them, casualties which mounted in direct proportion to the amount of care that had gone into the construction of the defenses.

It followed that if in peacetime a nation constructed elaborate fortified defenses directly in the path of a potential aggressor, that enemy would have to accept great losses to gain his way and perhaps would hesitate to make the sacrifice at all. At any rate he would be held up long enough for the defender to organize himself behind the cover which his forts offered, without too much cost to the defenders.

French strategic planners came to the conclusion that it would be wise to prepare the frontiers in peacetime so that they would be semi-impregnable in war, "semi-impregnable" only, because no competent military man thought that any fort could not be taken if the attacker were determined enough and willing to accept the sacrifice that his effort called for.

An important lesson of World War I was that a nation like France must preserve every part of her national soil because she would have need of all her resources, natural and human, in a modern total war. She could not employ the classic maneuver-in-retreat strategy, the trading of space for time, that a country like Russia could afford. The question was particularly crucial for France because much of her industries and natural resources was concentrated in the north and northeast, close to the frontier. For example, the great mines of the Briey basin lay in some places as close as five hundred yards from the border.

In 1914 France lost valuable industrial and coal and iron mining areas in northern France, as well as the populations there, and was condemned to fight the entire war on her own soil, accepting the devastations that this entailed. After the war French planners determined that in future wars their frontier covering force, the *couverture*, would hold the enemy right at the frontiers while the nation hastily armed herself completely in the rear of this advance guard.

But a covering force for a frontier measuring many hundreds of miles from Dunkirk to Nice meant large numbers of men and in postwar France the tendency was for a smaller army and a lighter military burden for the war-exhausted population, a population which even at best was at a disadvantage demographically in relation to France's more populous neighbors. The high command therefore had to consider other, artificial, methods of providing this covering force and they thought in terms of well prepared fortifications, the efficacy of which they had learned by actual combat experience.

Immediately after World War I Pétain occupied himself with the question of the defensive organization of the nation's frontiers, a problem requiring the particular attention of the Commander in Chief because of the changes in the technical aspects of warfare and also because the return of the provinces of Alsace and Lorraine to France necessitated a completely different defensive plan of operations than in the pre-1914 period. He therefore, in 1921, addressed a "Memorandum on the Defensive Organization of the Territory" to other members of the Higher War Council for their opinions and suggestions. This memorandum contained the gist of the Marshal's ideas on the subject of frontier defenses and stressed the need for protecting the national territory at its political limits, so as to protect all the nation's resources.[1]

Instead of returning to the old isolated forts characteristic of the pre-1914 period, he advised that in modern war one should prepare in depth, and he advanced the idea that defences should be nothing less than battlefields prepared in advance, in peacetime; battlefields that were so organized that the defender held all the advantages. This was not a new idea, that of entrenching oneself before a battle in carefully selected positions and waiting in place where the enemy had to attack, but what was new was the Marshal's idea that the fortified line should be a continuous one, on a vast scale, with few or no intervals for an enemy to infiltrate or encircle the defenders. It is reminiscent of the Italian Wars of the early sixteenth century when the advent on an important scale of gunpowder and firearms led the best commanders to entrench their forces solidly in prepared positions, flanked by natural *points d'appui,* where the enemy had to attack them and where they shattered the attacking enemy's formations with small loss to themselves. Pétain, impressed by the firepower of the twentieth century, was doing the same thing but on a much grander scale, in keeping with twentieth-century national mobilization and total war concepts.

---

[1] General Laure, *Pétain* (Paris, 1941), 277.

He was supported in the War Council by General Buat, Army Chief of Staff, but was vehemently opposed by others, including Marshal Joffre and General Guillaumat, who held that the defensive system should be a discontinuous line of fortified regions, each covering a certain area and separated from the rest by an interval. Vainly Pétain argued his case, urging that the line be backed up by a defense in depth, a succession of positions; and he based his argument on the experiences of the late war where continuous fronts such as the German *Hindenburg* and *Hunding* Lines had had great value. Neither side in the controversy doubted the efficacy of fortifications; the question was one of application.

In any case the financial situation in France at the time prevented any serious consideration of an expensive program of fortifications and the question remained unsettled, although a commission was set up under the presidency of Joffre to continue the study. The international situation was still in France's favor: Germany was still definitely beaten; France and her allies occupied German territory; and France's real *couverture* was her Army of the Rhine, a strong occupation force established on the left bank of the Rhine and ready to carry a war immediately across the river into the vulnerable heart of Germany.

The official doctrine of the high command in 1924 was built around an army of thirty-two divisions, well trained and ready for action—the effects of reduced terms of compulsory military service had not yet made the existing army organization impossible—and able to carry the war into Germany while the bulk of the nation mobilized, and also able to ensure that any fighting which did take place would be on German soil. But troubles in Morocco and Syria requiring a serious military effort by France, a growth in the strength and capabilities of Germany, and a reduced French army establishment resulting from the One-Year Law, combined to force a revision of Pétain's and the high command's strategic orientation. France's military attitude vis à vis Germany was changed from an offensive one to a defensive one and the knowledge that the occupation of the Rhineland was a temporary one—in fact it was prematurely ended in 1930—and the specter of the approaching "hollow years" crisis in effectives, led to raising once again the question of a protective fortified system on the frontiers.

The reduction of the term of military service, making the French army virtually a militia, was against the unanimous advice of the Higher War Council headed by Pétain. The parliament based its action on the idea that France had no need for an armed force capable of offensive action but needed only a defensive military organization, since she had no intention of attacking anyone but would only defend herself if attacked. Deprived of a strong combat instrument by the legislature—an army with a weak offensive capability is hardly an army at all—the military had to place their reliance on a system of fortifications even if they did not want to. The defensive orientation of French strategy which persisted until the outbreak of World War II was to a great extent the work of the civilian parliament, representing the will of the people, and not necessarily the product of an innate defensive-mindedness in the army high command.

The commission set up under Marshal Joffre in 1922 to study the fortification question had not arrived at any definite solution and in December 1925 a new commission was created, called the Commission for Frontier Defense, under the direction of General Guillaumat. The Higher War Council directed the commission to begin the studies with the new frontiers of Alsace-Lorraine, where the problem was the most urgent.

On the east the Rhine offered a natural defense line of some value to Alsace but on the northern frontier of Alsace-Lorraine there were no natural defenses and the "hole" of Lorraine was a natural invasion route. The occupation of German territory between Lorraine and the Rhine by French troops for the time being assured this frontier, as the Rhine is the important natural barrier in that area, but the eventual withdrawal of the French occupation forces from the Rhineland would leave that part of the frontier uncovered. The industrial centers in the region were of great value and the relative strategic proximity of Paris also gave the defense of Lorraine and northern Alsace a high priority.

In late 1926 and early 1927 the Commission presented its report proposing three fortified regions: one in the vicinity of Metz extending along the Lorraine plateau and covering the valley of the Moselle; another in the region of the Lauter, from the Rhine and the Haguenau forest to the lower Vosges west of Bitche; and the third in south Alsace facing eastward and closing the "hole" between the Vosges and Jura mountains and covering the Belfort gap. The latter fortified system covering Belfort was never built because limitation of funds required that some works considered even of primary importance be cancelled. The first two projects when finally constructed became the backbone and principal bastions of the Maginot Line system.[2]

---

[2] General Debeney, "Nos fortifications du nord-est," *Revue des deux mondes,* XXIII (September–October, 1934), 249, 250; General Gamelin, *Servir* (Paris, 1946), I, 238, 303; General Prételat, *Le Destin tragique de la Ligne Maginot* (Paris, 1940), map on pp. 24, 25.

With regard to the frontier in the department of the Nord, covering the classic invasion route across the Belgian plains, it should be noted that during the 1920's and early 1930's France and Belgium had a firm military alliance which envisaged the rapid transportation of French forces into Belgium at the first sign of danger, a defense taking place on the Belgian rivers, principally the Meuse, or better still an offensive with the combined armies moving into an important and vulnerable area of Germany. In the late 1920's the selection of the northeast frontiers by the high command as of primary urgency for fortification was a perfectly rational one.

It was vital that the work get underway as soon as possible because shortly after the Commission made its report France revamped her military organization in the laws of 1927–1928 which provided a protective frontier covering force—always France's foremost military preoccupation—of twenty active divisions, a force which, it was hoped, could be rapidly mobilized and transported to the frontiers. This army was expected to provide time and protection for the bulk of the French forces to mobilize but would be too small to do much more than that, particularly if part of it were operating in Belgium as well; and in any case there would be several days' delay in getting the covering force in place. During the delay period there had to be manned frontier fortifications to form the primary *couverture* function.

The planned frontier fortifications were therefore intended by the military to form a part of their *couverture* plans and were not to be a Gallic version of the Chinese Wall. That conception was to come later and was not that of the men who planned and built the defense line.[3]

The Commission also presented another report summing up its studies concerning the technical form of the fortifications themselves. It proposed large, powerful works, which we might call "forts" although they hardly resembled forts in the old sense of the word, containing artillery pieces of heavy caliber protected by a carapace of cement impervious to the heaviest artillery shells and also protected against poison gas. The huge forts would contain observation facilities and would be laid out so that the artillery and infantry weapon fire from each would flank the other, providing a crossfire. Deep below the

---

[3] For War Minister Maginot's ideas see the *Journal officiel* . . . , Chamber, December 10, 1929, pp. 4235, 4236 and Pierre Belperron, *Maginot of the Line,* trans., H. J. Stenning (London, 1940), 87. Also, for the army's point of view, General Debeney, *Sur la sécurité militaire de la France* (Paris, 1930), 40–42.

forts would be quarters for the garrisons and outside them would be deep anti-tank ditches. Between the large forts, to connect the system and provide a continuity of fire, would be smaller works of the same type and isolated casemates, in line with Pétain's insistence upon a continuous line.

The lessons of World War I went into the planning of the forts, particularly those derived from the battle of Verdun where fortifications had proved of value to the defenders. After the Verdun battle the French army engineers had made a detailed study of the effects of bombardment on the forts there and were impressed by the manner in which the fortifications had withstood artillery fire—far exceeding the expectation of their builders. Some turrets were impervious to the heaviest guns known, up to 420 millimeters; and aside from the extreme discomfort sometimes suffered by the men inside from concussion, fumes, or lack of supplies, the heavy fortifications proved to be excellent defensive works. The experiences at Verdun convinced the French high command of the efficacy of fortifications and had an important influence on their conception and design of the Maginot Line system. As Pétain put it, concrete alone could not stop an enemy but it multiplied the resisting power of soldiers who were smart enough to use it properly, and his views were shared by his contemporaries, competent military men.[4]

During the inter-war period French military thinkers became enthusiastic about the strategic and tactical possibilities offered to an army by a well-planned system of frontier fortifications. Books and articles appeared pointing out the advantages of fortified defenses prepared well in advance. Historical studies of French fortifications were written which went back to the work of Vauban, citing Napoleon's opinions on forts when used properly, and studying the system of forts constructed by Séré de Rivières during the nineteenth century which were so poorly employed in World War I. In 1925 Captain Charles de Gaulle published a study of French forts from Vauban to World War I and strongly advocated the construction of fortifications on France's frontiers, and de Gaulle was only one among many officers who shared that conviction.[5]

The publication of German documents, archives, and the World War I memoirs of German commanders revealed the influence that

---

[4] Henri-Philippe Pétain, *La Bataille de Verdun* (Paris, 1929), 144–154; also Col. Benoit, "Les Forts de Verdun dans la bataille," *Revue militaire française,* LIX (1936), 44–49.

[5] Captain de Gaulle, "Role historique des places françaises," *Revue militaire française,* XVIII (December, 1925), 356–382.

the existence of the forts in the east of France, outdated and scorned by the French leaders though they were, had upon German planning for the war and the actual operations. The Schlieffen Plan was in large measure determined by the fact that France's eastern frontier presented such a formidable barrier to an attack from that quarter that the only sensible thing left for the Germans to do, they thought, was to go through Belgium and break into the French "fortress" from that direction. Schlieffen's memorandum of December 1905 compared France to a big fortified place, of which the exterior *enciente* of the Tour-Verdun and Epinal-Belfort sectors was almost impregnable. He concluded from this that the German armies must attack through northern France, north of the line Sambre-Meuse, which they did. These facts made a great impression upon the French military thinkers of the 1920's.

The eastern wall of fortified natural terrain features could, of course, have been breached by the Germans in 1914 if they had been willing to pay the price in men and time, but while the men were expendable enough, the time was not, as the German plan called for a rapid knockout of France before the ponderous Russian armies could concentrate. Von Moltke expressed this idea in 1912 in a memorandum which stated that the Germans must avoid an attack on the "French fortified curtain of the east" which would cost them time and deprive the German army of "the élan and initiative of which it has the greatest need."[6]

It is here that we have in its simplest form the best reason for building fortifications: they force the invader to spend time and effort at a place of one's choosing, deprive him of the initiative, and, in fact, force him before the event to modify his plans and choose a less desirable alternative plan to avoid the forts; thus his attack is canalized into a route which will give the defender enough time and space to recover the initiative.

The French military men of this period could show how the German troops that had to be left behind in 1914 to besiege fortified places like Maubeuge and Antwerp deprived the German armies of important effectives needed to complete the Schlieffen Plan; how the fortified city of Paris helped swerve von Kluck's army into a position which made the first battle, and victory, of the Marne possible for the French; and how the Verdun fortifications also made that victory possible. So great was the desire of the Germans to avoid the French eastern frontier, which offered a slower means to the end they desired,

---

[6] Quoted in Lieut.-Col. Morin, "De l'Utilité de la fortification permanente," *Revue militaire française*, XXXVI (May, 1930), 193.

that they preferred to add two unnecessary enemies to their list, Belgium and Great Britain, in order to maneuver in an area relatively more accessible. If such a result could be achieved without even consciously attempting it, reasoned the French high command, how much more could be gained by carefully planning the same thing?

In the early 1930's there was a certain current of opinion among France's allies, or hoped-for allies, that accused the French high command of deliberately building the fortifications in the northeast with the aim of forcing the Germans to attack through Belgium and thereby forcing Belgium and Britain again to side with France whether they liked it or not—for Britain could not remain aloof with Belgium falling into the hands of a great European power—and the former Chief of Staff of the French army, General Debeney, felt obliged to disclaim the idea publicly.[7] Such a purpose was not the primary motive that prompted the building of the Maginot Line in the northeast—there were enough other good ones—but the result was the same; and the additional advantage that ensured France would not fight alone as she did in 1870, with the rest of Europe interested but idle bystanders, was probably not lost on French thinking.

The French military writers of this period all advanced many reasons why France should construct elaborate frontier defenses: the need to protect the industries and resources located at or near the borders; the necessity for a barrier to delay an invasion while the French nation-in-arms mobilized; the need for well-prepared defenses which could be held by a relatively smaller number of men in a given area, because France was outnumbered two to one in population by Germany; the value of a fortified barrier in deflecting an invasion into an area of France's choice—that is, the canalizing of the enemy's attack, thus depriving it of some of its élan and initiative. These writings take on added significance when one considers that in France articles written by army officers could not be printed in military journals without the prior approval of the office of the Army Chief of Staff.

There was no thought among the military that the fortifications would replace the traditional armies and absolve France of all other defense preparation; rather, they were intended as an important supplement. The idea was that the frontier defenses would permit the *couverture* to hold with relatively fewer effectives, thus leaving the bulk and the best part of the French army free to mass itself in a powerful *masse de manoeuvre* to strike at a time and place of its own

---

[7] General Debeney, *Revue des deux mondes,* XXIII (September–October, 1934), 258.

choosing. The latter plan, to regain some of the initiative inevitably lost by a nation who will not attack first, a nation which, because of its political and social ethos, must remain on the defensive and wait to be attacked, was not the least important idea that went into the planning of the fortified system.

To put it in simple terms, the Maginot Line was to be a shield for France, the warrior, and her army was to be her sword. While the shield protected the vital parts of her body, the sword could be drawn and wielded in a manner best suited to the conditions of the moment and to the opportunities that presented themselves. The enemy could of course break through sections of the Line but the shock of his attack would be broken and his invasion limited in depth; the surprise element would be lost to him. As Marshal Pétain put it, in an interview with a journalist, the Maginot Line could be broken through at a cost and he prayed that the German army would try it, because the elements which did get through would be a perfect setup for the French counteroffensive, and he added, "I'd like to be in command of the allied army then."[8]

To return to the building of the defenses, the report in 1927 of the Commission for Frontier Defense on the type of forts that should be constructed gave rise to differences of opinion in the Higher War Council. Marshal Pétain cut short these discussions, which were leading nowhere, and in the summer of 1927 he personally went on an extensive tour of the frontier regions which would be fortified. He traveled through Lorraine, surveyed the lower Vosges, the banks of the Rhine, the regions of Belfort and the northern Jura. Each day of his journey he left the city in which he was staying at the moment—Metz, Bitche, Strasbourg or Belfort—early in the morning and toured the countryside until nightfall, getting out of his car every five or ten kilometers and examining the topography.[9]

At the end of his journey Pétain's plans were made. He accepted in general the recommendations of the Commission although he made certain important modifications which gave increased depth to the fortified regions and also provided a centralized stronghold within each region to increase the possibilities for a lengthy resistance.

Next the actual structure of the fortifications engaged his attention. The Commission's recommendations for concentrated fortifications, large works in the classical manner as opposed to many small dispersed defenses, ran into considerable opposition in the War Council. Pétain backed the idea of the large works in preference to the small ones.

---

[8] Philip Guedalla, *The Two Marshals: Bazaine, Pétain* (London, 1943), 342.
[9] Laure, 282, 283.

He said that the dispersed defenses, based in concept on the field fortifications that troops actually erect on active service, would require too many effectives to man them and would thus defeat one of the basic purposes for building the defenses: the economy of manpower. Also, large forts with a concentration of power would be better suited, for morale purposes, to the type of soldiers who would serve under the militia system—mostly reserves or young recruits who would, generally speaking, not be of the quality necessary to hold out well in small isolated forts. Larger forts also gave more opportunity for the utilization of modern technological devices: communications, anti-gas precautions by means of controlling the air pressure in the works, heavy guns of large caliber, elaborate observation techniques, and a better provision for the comfort and safety of the garrison.

Pétain's conclusions were adopted by the Higher War Council and at the end of 1927 the Council presented a report to War Minister Painlevé, putting in the category of primary urgency the fortifications in the regions mentioned above and also indicating a succession of works of secondary and tertiary urgency. Due to financial limitations only certain of these could be realized, even among those considered of primary importance. The funds requested by the Minister in the parliament in 1928, for the 1929 program, concerned construction at three essential points in the northeast: Rochonvillier and Hackenbek in Lorraine and Hochwald in Alsace. These three forts, underlined as of vital importance, had to be completely in place before any other construction could be started elsewhere.[10]

At the end of 1928 the Higher War Council, led by Pétain, formulated certain conditions for the defensive organization of the national territory which were translated into government directives by the War Ministry in January 1929. They concerned the general preparation of the territory, particularly that nearest the frontier, in terms of road and rail communications, transmission networks, facilities for the unloading of troops and supplies and for the evacuation of the civil population, and the furnishing of electric power. Bitter experiences like that of Verdun in 1916 had taught the army the value of not having to improvise such things in times of emergency.

The directives also included the recommendations of the War Council with regard to the fortifications of the frontiers along the lines described above. Each fortified region would be adapted to its own particular terrain features and other local conditions, instead of being built in conformity to an overall uniform plan of construction. The

---

[10] Paul Painlevé, *Paroles et écrits* (Paris, 1936), 390–392.

frontiers which were not included in the plan for the large fortifications would be, nevertheless, provided with lesser defenses, each conforming to local terrain and other local considerations.

At the end of 1929 André Maginot became Minister of War and the task of securing the necessary funds from the parliament was his. So well did he do his part in this connection that the fortifications, the actual construction of which was started during his administration, came to be associated with him and his name was attached to them in popular parlance. During the preceding years he had followed the development in the planning of the frontier defenses in his capacity as president of the Army Committee of the Chamber and the project therefore was by no means new to him.

Perhaps Maginot's most important contribution was his insistence that the funds for the construction of the fortifications be in a lump sum, that the building of the works be treated as a single program, as was the procedure in naval construction. Normally the army budget had to be voted each year, giving the parliament a chance, which it well utilized, to discuss and debate military items in the annual budget and to modify those expenditures which it thought were not appropriate. Maginot succeeded in modifying this jealously guarded prerogative of the Chamber and secured an appropriation of 2,900,000,000 francs for a program of construction extending over the years 1930–1934. In 1934, when the question of further funds for the completion of the forts arose, Marshal Pétain was Minister of War and the legislature approved the government's budget partly because the Socialists and the Radical-Socialists thought that they saw in the Maginot Line a means of replacing, or at least deemphasizing, the traditional army.

Pétain followed closely the constructions on the frontiers, and the plans for the important works begun in 1930 all passed under his eyes for his approval and sometimes modification. Pétain, General Debeney, and General Belhague, Inspector-General of the Engineers, formed a sort of triumvirate which handled all questions relative to the constructions; the feeling was that if too many opinions were solicited the work would not quickly get under way or be completed. While this secret and authoritarian procedure did not please some of the military, notably General Gamelin and the local commanders in whose regions the forts were being constructed, it did facilitate the speedy realization of the defenses, and that was what Pétain wanted.

During the year 1930 it was decided to extend the Metz fortified region, originally planned to stop at Thionville in the west, northwestward to the Longwy-Longuyon region, facing the Luxembourg frontier and protecting the important Briey basin. Maginot obtained the additional funds from the parliament and Pétain spent the summer of that year studying the area and planning the defenses as he had done in the east. The new Chief of Army Staff, General Weygand, and the Vice-Chief, Gamelin, wanted to establish the French front right at the frontier on the heights which dominate the plateau of the grand duchy. Pétain opposed this, believing that the heights on the border had a "dead angle" in front of them; that is, guns placed directly on the heights could not cover the lower forward slopes and the attackers could move up through that close zone without the defenders' artillery coming to bear effectively on them.[11]

The Marshal instead preferred—and his preferences were accepted since he was still Commander in Chief—to establish the defenses farther to the rear, on the plateau or on the reverse slope of the heights, thus giving himself a greater extension and a better field-of-fire. Gamelin later admitted that tactically the Marshal's decision was sound but he complained that strategically it was not because it left a small portion of French territory uncovered.

The fortifications were of an entirely new character, probably the most powerful defenses ever built. The experiences of the battle of Verdun during World War I had considerable technical influence on their construction. For one thing, the disappearing turrets of the Verdun forts had proven themselves practically invulnerable. In normal position, when not firing, the roof only of the turret was exposed. This consisted of a thick dome of steel resting upon a base also of steel; the whole was covered by, and enclosed in, a great mass of special reinforced concrete covering an area of several hundred yards. In this position nothing could come out of the turret but nothing could go in.

Direct hits from the heaviest guns, up to 420 millimeters, could inflict no damage. When in its most vulnerable position, in position to fire, the turret only emerged a foot and a half and then only for a few seconds. Observation was of course constant; the target was observed, the range plotted and hits observed while the turret was in its closed position.

On the other hand the light works, those of less than, roughly, two hundred yards in extent, could be destroyed by hostile fire or so damaged as to be unusable. There the value of large works as opposed to small dispersed ones, was demonstrated. Also, it was learned that the fortifications had to be provided with a strong ventilation system to disperse fumes from the explosives or from poison gas. There had

---

[11] Gamelin, II, 23, 24; *Commission chargée d'enquêter sur les événements survenus en France de 1933 à 1945,* Supplement (Paris, 195?), II, 405, 406.

to be deep shelters for the combatants so that they could rest, sheltered from the noise and the demoralizing vibration of the concrete when being fired upon and under attack for prolonged periods. These lessons all went into the construction of the Maginot Line.[12]

Verdun had taught that small lookout turrets, separated from the main fort or not, which projected and presented a frontal embrasure, could be rendered unusable by small-arms fire. It was also learned that the enemy heavy artillery fire soon dug large craters in the area around the forts; and that if the defenders lacked short-range weapons with lofty trajectories that could fire in a high curve into the shell holes utilized by the attacking infantry, close defense was rendered very difficult.

The value of a continuous line of fortifications consisting of forts, trenches, casemates and the like was verified by experience and it was learned that isolated forts could not hold out for long. This was one of the reasons why Pétain insisted upon a continuous line, for the system was greatly strengthened when the forts were mutually supporting. In 1940 the only Maginot Line fort taken by the Germans by direct assault was that of La Ferté near Sedan, the last work in the line of heavy forts and therefore deprived of lateral support. Attacks elsewhere on the continuous, connected defense line were beaten off with relative ease.

When Pétain was supervising the construction of the defense system his basic idea was to choose the best terrain features for the positioning of his artillery, then to build fortified works to protect the guns and then link up the fortifications where he could by underground galleries. To withstand the punishment they would have to take from modern armament they would have to be well shielded and the line had to be able to withstand artillery and aerial bombardment from all angles, even from the rear. Also—not falling into the same trap as did the British at Singapore, where the guns all pointed one way, out to sea, so that the Japanese could come from the rear through Malaya with relative impunity—the Maginot Line gun turrets were built so that they could revolve and dominate the terrain in a complete circle. If an enemy broke through one section of the line his troubles were by no means over but were, in fact, just beginning.

The main pillars of the line were the great works or fortresses, each possessing several disappearing turrets of the type described above, armed with cannon, and mortars and machine guns, and also having several casemates. These combat positions were connected by deep

12 André Schorp, "Doit-on réarmer la ligne Maginot?" Revue de défense nationale, N.S., XIV (January–June, 1952), 189–194.

shafts to a network of subterranean galleries—to barracks and maga-
zines deep underground which were connected with the surface by
tunnels that went back to entrances several miles in the rear and which
contained railway tracks to facilitate the underground transport of
supplies, munitions and personnel. These shelters were proof against
any bomb or shell then known and in fact, according to some postwar
opinion, they would still be proof against an atomic bomb of the
Hiroshima type.

In some instances where the lessons of the Verdun forts were ignored
the functioning of the line was weakened. For example, the idea of
having short-range weapons like small mortars or grenade-launchers,
to use in close defense against enemy infantry infiltrating by means
of the deep craters caused by heavy artillery fire, was not taken seriously enough. The loss of La Ferté in 1940 was partly due to that
factor. Also, after 1935—when Pétain was no longer directly concerned with the fortifications—the line was extended farther westward
and to economize in money and time smaller forts were built with
fixed turrets—not the disappearing turrets of the main Maginot Line
positions—into which it was possible to fire from the outside at an
angle of forty-five degrees, which the Germans did at La Ferté, again
contributing to the fall of that place.

When the frontier defenses were in the initial stages of construction
the question of who was going to man the forts became a troublesome
one for the high command. The forts were supposed to ease the manpower problem, not add to it. At first it was found necessary to break
up some of the active army units to provide trained personnel for the
complex task of serving the forts, but this was an awkward arrangement. The active army was so limited in numbers by the Army Reorganization Law of 1927 that the high command found that in order
to assure the *couverture* the army had to be deployed almost in its
entirety along the frontiers, as a cover in an emergency. This left the
subsequent maneuvering operations—that is, attack, counterattack and
counter-offensive—to be performed by the troops least qualified to
carry them out: the reserves who then formed the bulk of the French
army.

In the early 1930's a special corps of fortress regiments was formed.
Perhaps 25 per cent of the men in these units were the *frontaliers,*
reserves who lived in the frontier regions and who could get to the
nearest forts quickly in an emergency. About 50 per cent were reservists who came from the populous areas of the Nord department and
Paris. This corps had a nucleus of regular officers and men but was
composed mostly of reservists from the older classes—the younger men

were kept for the field armies—who were specially trained to man the Maginot Line and who had a somewhat separate organization from the rest of the army. They were called up for training, and mobilized in emergencies, on a separate basis.

In 1940 the forts proved their worth. For the most part they were not attacked, a fact that should not invite the thought that they were of no use. By being so strong that they were considered too dangerous to attack they well served the function for which they were built. We are interested, however, in determining how well the elaborate defenses worked under actual attack and we have two instances to guide us. The first was at La Ferté near Sedan, where the Germans succeeded, as already noted, in capturing the positions, the only Maginot Line fortress to be taken by direct assault.

La Ferté was at the extreme western end of the Maginot Line and was consequently deprived of the lateral support which was an integral part of the working of the system. Also, the artillerymen of the two 75 millimeter gun casemates which protected the main fort had retreated, in line with the general *sauve qui peut* of May 1940. Yet the fort, manned by a young lieutenant and fifteen men, held off a large German force, heavily reinforced by artillery units, for three days.[13]

The main fort of La Ferté was one of the newer and weaker types erected after 1936, with a fixed turret and open embrasures. The Germans succeeded in putting an 88 millimeter shell right into the turret, knocking out one section of the fort. Then German infantry and combat engineers approached the fort, using the deep shell craters caused by their own heavy artillery fire for cover—since the fort was isolated there could be no lateral support from neighboring forts which would have coped with this situation—and they finished the operation with flamethrowers and explosives directed and thrown into the embrasures of the fort.

The inferior construction of the fort and its relative isolation were diametrically opposed to the ideas of Marshal Pétain; this type of construction was not part of his plan. For an idea of how his type of fort, the main Maginot Line defense works, stood up under determined attack we may look at that of Hochwald in northern Alsace in the Haguenau sector.

Here the Germans began their attack on May 14, 1940, using the most powerful explosives known at the time: artillery of 420 millimeters and aerial bombs from 1000 to 4,400 pounds. The bombing was done by Stuka dive-bombers which, in the absence of anti-aircraft

13 Lieut.-Col. E. J. Debau, "La Fortification a-t-elle vécu?" *Revue de défense nationale*, N.S., XII (January–June, 1951), 623–637.

defense—this was withdrawn along with the field troops who were sent to the west to meet the German breakthrough there—were assured of the time and freedom to place their bombs at leisure and from a low altitude, just as if on the practice range; but aside from minor damage the casemates, turrets and guns continued to function.

The enemy attacked on the ground with two infantry divisions reinforced by a regiment of heavy fortress artillery. These attacks were beaten off with heavy losses by the well-placed fire of the guns of the forts, whose coordinated fire arrangements had been prepared long in advance and whose excellent observation never ceased to function. Each fort could fire upon the other if enemy infantry got so close that the defenders could not reach them from the interior and could fire on each other's fronts to cover areas that could not be covered by the fort under attack, thus providing mutual support.

The German breakthrough and advance in Belgium and northern France outflanked the Maginot Line and swept around it in the west and in the closing stages of the campaign approached it from the south. Also, the French field troops had been removed from the intervals between the forts to reinforce the crumbling front in the north and west, so that after June 14 enemy troops were able to infiltrate into the fortified area. The Hochwald forts were therefore encircled from the south and attacked from both sides but still the Germans could not make any impression on them. Several days after the armistice the defenders gave up their forts to the enemy who were surprised to find that the incessant pounding had not caused any serious damage. A front of nineteen miles had been held by 9,500 men in the fortifications, under constant bombardment from May 14 until after the armistice, against forces four times their number, and had only given up because of the armistice. This indicated the value of the Maginot Line forts and justified the confidence of the builders.

Not only did the Hochwald forts make a determined resistance but the rest of the Maginot Line defenders could not understand why they should lay down their arms in June 1940, when they had not been defeated, although they were encircled. They continued to resist after the armistice had been agreed upon and after the rest of France had ceased fighting, until the exasperated Germans informed the French government that if this resistance continued they would bombard the city of Lyon. The French General Headquarters then sent three officers to General Georges, commander of the armies in the field, with the mission to contact the commanders of the works of the Maginot Line and order them to surrender. He gave them directions to follow so that they could effect liaison with the commanders of the forts, an operation not easily done because everything that showed itself within range of the forts was swept with fire. Upon a promise by the Germans that they would be accorded the full honors of war—a promise that was broken—the defenders gave up.[14] Thus these mighty fortifications remained inviolable within the limits of the mission which had been assigned to them.

Tactically the forts were a complete success. But what about strategically? Did they do all that was expected of them and did they justify the enormous sums spent on them? And why was the north of France on the Belgian frontier not also fortified, thus, presumably, sealing off the whole border from invaders?

The problem that Pétain and other French military planners in the 1920's faced with regard to the building of frontier fortifications was: where would be the best places to build? Which were the most vulnerable points on the frontiers? The tremendous cost of the project precluded the building of a complete line of defenses along every portion of the frontier, even if they had wanted to. We have seen that the planners first turned to northern Lorraine and Alsace as the opening that had to be closed first. This was a natural invasion route from Germany into France, the route which the German armies of von Moltke in 1870 had successfully traveled, before France lost the provinces, and the route that they probably would have followed again in 1940 had the Maginot Line not existed. With Alsace and Lorraine again part of France's national territory, Pétain insisted, it was essential to fortify them first.

France had 530 miles of frontiers to worry about, not counting her Pyrenean border with Spain; 219 of these were on the Italian border and could be defended easily because of the mountains. From Maubeuge on the Belgian border to the Swiss border the frontier is about 300 miles long, without any natural obstacles, except for eastern Alsace where the Rhine offered an appreciable defense line.

The initial defense works inaugurated by Pétain when he was Commander in Chief closed the principal gaps in this expanse, and the best invasion route for the Germans was thus barred. At that time the route through Belgium was of secondary value to the Germans because it would take time, both in traversing the country and also in subduing the Belgian army with the limited military resources left to Germany by the Versailles Treaty—time which the French high command would have used to advantage.

An attack by Germany on Belgium would have brought the immediate assistance of the French armies to the Belgians. Since 1921 those

---

[14] *Commission chargée d'enquêter* . . . , III, 752, General Georges' testimony.

two countries had been united in a firm military alliance aimed directly at Germany, which called for the movement of French armies into Belgium at the first sign of trouble, to take their places beside the Belgians on the German frontier. The development of the "Belgian maneuver," which culminated in Gamelin's abortive movement in May 1940 that cost him the war, will be considered later. It will suffice to say here that the defense of Belgium and France was considered a single problem; the erection of fortifications on their common border would have posed diplomatic and political problems, not to mention strategic ones. It is not practical to make a military agreement with a country and then build defensive fortifications along the common border, which seem to rule out the application of the agreement.

We have explained that Pétain's idea of frontier fortifications were based upon a sound utilization of existing terrain features. Along the frontier of the Nord, the French department bordering on Belgium, there were no natural defense features. Belgium and France form a strategic whole and France's natural frontiers in that area are on the Belgian rivers, preferably on the Meuse, right at the German frontier— if not on the Rhine itself, in German territory, as the French military leadership would have liked in 1919. The building of fortifications on the Belgian frontier therefore posed problems of a technical nature even if the psychological ones arising from the idea of fortifying oneself on an ally's border did not already exist.

In meetings of the Higher War Council in 1926 and 1927 Pétain formally took a position on this and was unanimously supported by other members of the Council. He asserted that it was not possible to fortify directly the frontier of the Nord because the line of the frontier there offers no natural defense advantages. Also, and very important, the industrial complexes in that region are immense and are located right at the frontier, making their defense impossible without going out in advance of them, into Belgium, to make the defense there. He said that the industries of the region were so close to the border that if he could not defend them in advance of them, in Belgium, he would have to build his defense line in the rear of them.[15]

In order to construct a line of fortifications at the frontier Pétain would have had to build them right through the factories and mines of one of the heaviest concentrations of industry in Europe, thus partially destroying them in peacetime and making a battlefield out of

---

[15] Lieut.-Col. Tissier, *The Riom Trial* (London, 1942), 40; Gamelin, II, 68; Paul Reynaud, *In The Thick of The Fight,* trans., James D. Lambert (London, 1955), 85, 86 and footnote.

them in time of war. Alternatively he could have built them in the rear of the industrial region, seeking a more rational defense line and leaving the industries and population centers to their fate if an invader should come through Belgium. Both these alternatives would have led to outraged protests from the burghers of such places as Lille, Roubaix, and Valenciennes in the Nord—not to mention the Belgian high command and government which would not have understood their ally's action. The Marshal concluded that the only true defense of northern France lay in Belgium and he therefore planned a rapid movement forward of the French armies into Belgium at the first sign of danger.

It would be difficult to overemphasize the importance of these facts in studying the planning of Pétain and the French high command during the inter-war period: the absence of any natural frontier at the political boundaries of France and Belgium and the problem arising from the economic structure of the area; for France and Belgium not only form a strategic whole but also an economic unit, bound together by interdependence of centuries' standing. On the French side of the border the industrial grouping is very extensive: the textile group of Lille-Roubaix-Tourcoing; the metallurgical group of the Sambre River, from Aulnoye to Jeumont; the group of coal beds from Condé-sur-Escaut to Isbergues combined with rich iron ore workings; and the innumerable machine industries as well as many chemical industries which are derived, in general, from coal.

These industrial centers extend right to the Belgian frontier where they have reached out to be near the Belgian population centers just across the border, from whence they get most of their labor. These Belgian localities in turn are situated directly on the frontier to be near the industries to which the Belgian workers go daily, crossing the border to do so. The Belgian laborers are attracted by the relatively high wages offered by the French industries but they prefer to remain in their own country to live because of the cost-of-living advantages there as well as a natural reluctance to uproot themselves when there is no reason to do so, since the boundary is a political one only and is artificial in other respects.

This phenomenon is true in the three important salients extending into Belgium from France, those of Lille, Valenciennes and Maubeuge, where the industries have formed great agglomerations, densest near the frontier in order to approach the reservoir of Belgian labor. The daily migration across the border, amounting to some 60,000 to 70,000 Belgian workers, created an additional effect with military implications, in that the transportation problem led to the construction of a large network of roads and railway lines running perpendicular to the frontier and connecting Belgium and France as if they were one country. Thus not only do geographic factors work to give easy access to an invader from the north but modern communications also facilitate the swift movement of large bodies of troops into France, and vice versa. A war of movement in this country was almost mandatory even if the building of fortifications along the frontier was not precluded by the dense concentration of industry and population.[16]

It was for these reasons that Marshal Pétain held to his idea that Maginot Line fortresses in that area were not practical and that northern France must be defended in Belgium. The experiences of two world wars seem to bear out his theory; a defensive organization in depth assuring the protection of France's northern front involves Belgium and France together and should be based on the Meuse if not on the Rhine itself. It will be remembered that until 1936 the German army was confined to the east bank of the Rhine.

Pétain's program of 1927 was the one under which the Maginot Line got started and for which Maginot as War Minister in 1930 obtained the funds from the parliament. It was understood that on the northern frontier ("against which an aggression would run into delays," as Maginot put it—referring to the fact that the German army had a less easy access to that frontier than it did to Alsace and Lorraine) would be provided with light field works and would be treated as a "battlefield of the moment," that is, war of an open character which would take form as the situation developed. Only two simple lines of casemates were planned for the Nord, one on the edge of the forest of Mormal west of Maubeuge and the other on the edge of the Raismes forest south of the Escaut from Condé to Maulde.

Maginot explained the ideas of the high command to the Chamber of Deputies in telling them that they could not have permanent defenses everywhere, not only because the cost would be prohibitive but also because it did not make sense to erect, along the whole length of the national frontier, a kind of "Wall of France." The fighting in the north, if war did come, would be in the conventional manner.[17]

A certain amount of opposition to this thesis emerged, particularly in the parliament, and in 1932 it was proposed that the frontiers of the department of the Nord also be fortified in the Maginot Line manner. Much of the impetus for the proposal came from the constituents of the deputies from the unfortified regions who paid the taxes that went

---

[16] Jean Chardonnet, "La Frontière française du Nord," Revue de défense nationale, N.S., XII (January–June, 1951), 16, 17.

[17] Journal officiel . . . , Chamber, December 10, 1929, pp. 4235, 4236.

into the defenses erected elsewhere and who demanded that they too be protected by forts. This was a constant problem that hampered the high command throughout the history of the frontier fortifications: the problem of reconciling the civilian demands for a concrete protection—in both senses of the word—with the dictates of what the military leadership considered to be a sound strategy.

In 1932, when supplementary funds amounting to 250 million francs were voted for the frontier defenses, the Higher War Council met to consider the best way to apportion the spending thereof. Pétain did not attend the meeting because he had retired by then and although he was still a member of the War Council he did not want to inhibit the action of the new Commander in Chief, Weygand, or detract from his authority. He did, however, put his conclusions into writing and submitted them to the Council, thus influencing the members' decision.

Pétain reiterated his reasons of 1927 for not fortifying the Nord frontier and declared that conditions had not changed. He said that his idea was to prepare a mobile force equipped with mobile matériel —mechanized artillery, movable cupolas, some tanks and other new equipment which would be used to set up a defense line—to move quickly into Belgium and fight there instead of on French soil. He was against any idea of preparing a barrage on the border. The enormous expense of the forts plagued him and he pointed out that France could not afford to build elaborate defenses there and at the same time prepare the equipment necessary for a war of a mobile character. The war of movement which the Marshal envisaged in 1932 did not include armored divisions. France did not have any, nor in fact did any other country.

Pétain also deplored the defensive psychology that was behind the plan for it meant that the valuable support of the Belgian army would be lost to the French—to say nothing of the advantages of using Belgian territory for an arena rather than French—as he felt that fortifications in the north would mean an abandonment of the Belgian army to its own resources at the beginning of a conflict, leaving it nothing but the prospect, if it were beaten, of being received as the remnants of a defeated force at the French frontier. A valuable opportunity to use the combined Franco-Belgian strength would thus be lost. General Weygand agreed with the Marshal and the War Council voted against prolonging the Maginot Line.

It is interesting to note that Pétain, in the same note, recommended that the funds proposed for the Belgian project be used instead to build a powerful, for that period, offensive air armament which would,

by its retaliatory
There was little "

The Belgians vie
with some misgivin
mand were not quit
man front of contac
mand made this feelir
line was prolonged w
the Luxembourg fror
Gamelin's reply that
would still act as a dete
be reluctant to invade I
permanent defenses exist
Belgians against an attac
gesture from the French s

Pétain's objection to the
department on the ground
early 1930's when France,
through a period of econom ..., the budget
for defense purposes was one ... sufferers from this condition and the question of for ...ations for the northern frontier was
dropped for the time being, not to be raised again until 1934 when
the Marshal was Minister of War.

Several weeks after he became Minister of War, Marshal Pétain
appeared before the Army Committee of the Chamber and, after re-
viewing the German military situation and describing the extent of
German rearmament, he advised that a more efficient organization of
the fortified sectors of the northern frontier would have to be undertaken. He did not mean that forts of the Maginot Line type would be
constructed there; the same arguments against them still applied. He
meant that as a precaution a system of field fortifications suitable to
the terrain could be built, and also heavy forts in areas where conditions permitted.

In March 1934 the Marshal spoke to a meeting of the Senate Army
Committee and again indicated to anxious Senators from the Nord
that some defense works could and would be envisaged there but they
would not be of a nature to protect the large industrial complexes
which were too close to the frontier and which had to be protected
in Belgium. He pointed out that the frontier was protected west of
Montmédy by the Ardennes forest and hills. This forest was not impenetrable—although in 1934 there was little chance of contemporary

18 *Commission chargée d'enquêter* . . . , Supplement, II, 444, 445.

—but if the enemy did get through,
andled on French soil by the French
area that the main German breakthrough
ubject of the Ardennes will be discussed at
pter 12.

te in the Chamber in June 1934 on further funds
tions, Pétain asked for 1,275 millions, 292 millions of
be for new construction on the northern frontier, from
dy to the department of the Nord. His appearance before the
ber, his first as War Minister, was greeted by loud applause from
e left, center and right—a rare occurrence in the faction-torn parliament.[19]

The next day Daladier, speaking for the Radical Socialists, also recommended construction in the north and gave as his reason—it was probably also Pétain's—the need to satisfy the inhabitants of northern France, who wanted the protective shield of the Maginot Line extended to cover them. He also said that defenses there should please the Belgians because it would discourage the Germans from going through Belgium. With regard to the latter point, one suspects that he had been influenced by his friend General Gamelin.

Despite the allocation of a portion of the funds voted to build works in the Nord, the economic situation prevented any large-scale construction there, even if the War Minister really wanted to. Actually most of the money was used to finish old projects for which the money previously allotted had run out due a rise in costs. To give an idea of the tremendous sums spent on the Maginot Line, a burden doubly onerous during the prevailing acute economic depression, by 1935 a total of almost five billion francs had been spent—prewar and preinflationary francs. Under these circumstances further large constructions could hardly be envisaged when an extensive modernization of the equipment of the army was also taking place.

After 1934 Pétain no longer was responsible, officially or unofficially, for defense planning. Extensive German rearmament in 1935, and the repudiation of the military clauses of the Versailles Treaty, led to some hasty reevaluations of their position by the French high command, but the need for modernization of the army and in particular the reconstitution of the war industries, allowed to fall into disuse since World War I, took a higher priority than expenditures for forts in the north.

Beyond the permanent fortifications built to cover Maubeuge, and

---

[19] *Journal officiel* . . . , Chamber, June 14, 1934, p. 1496.

some lesser constructions, the situation in the north remained the same, with the initial plan to carry the war into Belgium still intact. The Minister of War in 1935 and early 1936, General Maurin, and the Commander in Chief of the army, Gamelin, decided that even in view of the increased German menace it would not be practical to build heavy works of the Maginot Line type in the Nord, except at two small points to cover the immediate approaches to Maubeuge and the Valenciennes gap. In addition there were the casemates along the Mormal and Raismes forests, built under Pétain's program of 1930. Elsewhere in the Nord Gamelin planned a line of anti-tank ditches and a barbed-wire screen with simple gun emplacements.[20]

In 1936 France's strategic position in western Europe was struck a blow which altered her situation considerably. As a result of the French passive acceptance of the German remilitarization of the Rhineland in March, and an apparent shift in the balance of power, Belgium decided to break the military convention that had bound her to France since 1921. She did this in October 1936 and from that date the question of France being able to defend her northern frontier by advancing into Belgium became problematical. Pétain's thinking had been predicated on the assumption that France could rely on a willing ally in the north for a prolongation of the French frontier defense along a more rational and strategically advantageous line; France's northern strategic frontier lay on the Belgian rivers. The defection of Belgium changed everything. But the Marshal's successors, in command from 1936 to 1940, did not orient French planning and preparation to cope with the completely different situation. The fact is that they were not quite so "fortification minded" or "defense minded" as some postwar critics have said.

The geographic and economic factors which had influenced Pétain's decisions, with regard to not fortifying the north, still existed after 1936, so that his successors were faced with the same problems, although the uncovering of that frontier by Belgium's declaration of neutrality, as well as the German remilitarization of the Rhineland, put the situation in a somewhat different light.

The politicians of the prewar era also recognized that it was impractical to fortify the Nord in the same manner as had been done elsewhere by the Maginot Line. In the Chamber of Deputies during the session of January 28, 1937, Deputy Quenette spoke matter-of-factly of the impossibility of fortifying the line west of Maubeuge because in order to do so they would have to raze some of the vast

---

[20] Gamelin, II, 184, 185, 249, 250.

agglomerations of industries that cover the length of the frontier there. He pointed out that it was only in Belgium that the frontier of the Nord could be defended, and his words were accepted calmly by the Chamber, a body that was always quick to challenge or oppose a controversial question.

The best that was done was to dig deep and wide anti-tank ditches, backed by banquettes of earth and reinforced by rails placed perpendicularly, across rural sections of the department of the Nord, probably more to satisfy the local inhabitants that they were being protected than for anything else. Even these measures ran into trouble because the peasants whose fields were cut sometimes complained bitterly that they could not get from one side of the ditches to the other to cultivate their lands. Thus a deputy from the Nord in December 1937, in the same speech in which he complained to the government about the inadequate fortified protection in his region, also complained that the work that was being done was hurting his constituents' lands.[21] Apparently the people there wanted military protection as long as it did not hurt their particular property, and if the meager works which were constructed aroused so much complaint one wonders what would have been the outcry if some of the industries in the Lille-Roubaix-Turcoing complex had been razed in order to construct substantial forts of the Maginot Line type.

In closing this summary of Pétain's involvement with the Maginot Line a few words are in order on the state of mind and the intentions of the builders of the barrier of cement and steel, as well as on the results of the Line from a strategic point of view. The French high command and Pétain have been accused of a "defensive mindedness" that led to the defeat in 1940. To a certain extent this is true; they did feel that in modern war the defense is stronger tactically than the offense, and that an army of reservists was capable only of a war of position. But the unpreparedness went deeper than that, deep into the national psychology of a people who had lost the cream of their manhood, as well as most of the skim, in the first World War, and who lived in morbid fear of another such holocaust.

The military planners of the Maginot Line looked to the forts to enable them to hold vast stretches of the frontier with relatively few effectives so that they could employ the bulk of their forces offensively at places and at moments of their own choosing. In this way they could compensate for the numerical inferiority of France relative to Ger-

---

[21] *Journal officiel* . . . , December 3, 1937, 2644–2652.

many and the declining French birth rate. They also had to compensate for the "hollow years" of 1936–1940 and for the paucity of effectives permitted them under France's recruitment law of the one-year service. From this point of view the fortifications served the purpose for which they were built. But the civilian population came to consider the frontier barrier as a shield behind which they could live in peace and security, safe from the attacks of a strong and inimical neighbor.

The military leaders knew that fortifications are not literally invulnerable; they can only be made nearly so. They expected that their forts would oblige an enemy to hesitate before attacking them, fearful of the losses in men and time that such an attack would involve, so that his hesitation would give them time to prepare and his attack would be canalized into an area of their choosing. In 1940 as in 1914 the Germans invaded through the open Belgian plains, just as the French high command expected that they would.

That the French could not cope with this attack does not lessen the value of the Maginot Line; it served its purpose and without it the French would have been in a worse position. Their defeat was due to other causes, of which the morale factor was the principal.

Before World War II there was such a thing in France as a "Maginot Line complex," so-called since the war; a psychological pillow and an almost mystical belief in the efficacy of the fortified shield. But this was a civilian phenomenon, not a military one. The unfortunate fact was that the army for the most part was composed of civilian reservists under the "nation in arms" militia system and the fears and attitudes of the civilians were reflected in the mentality of their army, for it was literally "their" army.

The myth of the impregnable Maginot Line became almost a religious dogma, an article of faith for most Frenchmen. It enabled them to live in the feeling that they were sheltered from harm and that further effort could be dispensed with. Although fortifications properly employed have considerable value, they do not of themselves constitute a complete military system, but wishful thinking obscured that fact.

In 1937 the former Chief of Staff, General Debeney, who served under Pétain during the planning of the Maginot Line, felt prompted to warn that the public was hypnotized by the idea of cement but that the forts were built with a different purpose in mind. They were intended primarily to permit relatively fewer troops to achieve a firm frontier covering force, to give the nation time to arm, so that the bulk of the country's forces could concentrate and undertake offensive operations.[22]

Although the French high command had to stress continuously the defensive nature of the fortifications in order to secure the funds to build them from the parliament, we have, during a debate in the Chamber in June 1934, a hint of the offensive plans held by Pétain which would be made possible through the economies in effectives and other advantages accruing from the forts. During the debate, which Pétain attended as Minister of War, on the voting of further funds for the fortifications, the chairman of the Army Committee spoke for the high command, and expressed views approved by Pétain, in declaring that although France had renounced all aggressive intentions she nevertheless had not renounced the offensive as a means of warfare.

He said that France had no intention of accepting lightly the situation of World War I in which most of the fighting took place on her own territory. But since France would not begin a war, and had accepted the position of receiving the first blows, she had denied herself the initiative of operations in any conflict that would develop. The fortifications were planned partially to offset this disadvantage; once the nation had mobilized behind the defenses the army could pass through the fortified line to go on the offensive. This, of course, was before the fortification of the Rhineland by the Germans.

The chairman's views were confirmed by Pétain who spoke after him. The increased tempo of German rearmament, cited by the Marshal, meant trouble for France, but her building of the Maginot Line did not mean that she relied solely on the defenses, and offensive operations were still very much part of her planning.[23]

The War Minister, however, had to be careful in these declarations because it was difficult to get funds voted by the parliament for anything that hinted too strongly of offensive operations. It was here as much as anywhere that the military erred: in order to get money for the Maginot Line they tended to emphasize its great defensive power and toned down the offensive opportunities it offered. The parliament, reflecting the fears of their constituents, wanted no talk of military offensives which they thought of as "militaristic adventures."

The civilian attitude toward the Maginot Line was expressed in the parliament, on the day after the discussion mentioned above, by Édouard Daladier. As far as he was concerned, he explained, the

---

[22] General Debeney, *La Guerre et les hommes* (Paris, 1937), 188, 189, 205, 206.

[23] *Journal officiel . . .* , June 14, 1934, 1495, 1496.

Maginot Line was a revolutionary concept in the military art which would eliminate the need for the traditional army. Now the frontier covering force was the only important thing and he intimated that despite the chagrin of the generals the fortifications would make the old-fashioned army unnecessary.

The political leaders were the true exponents of the frontier fortifications once the idea got underway. The Maginot Line offered them a means to rid themselves and France once and for all of the internal bogey of militarism, and the necessity for maintaining a professional officer corps, of right-wing political orientation, at the taxpayers' expense. Influential and sincere political leaders like Daladier were wholly imbued with a defensive minded strategy and the necessity for France to cover herself, turtle-like, with a protective fortified shell.

The fortifications idea was seized upon by the public as a fetish which permitted them to relax behind their "Chinese Wall." The military oversold the idea in order to get the funds to construct the Line and then they found that they had created a "Maginot Line complex," a monster of public reluctance to undertake great exertion to meet the growing Nazi threat. The average Frenchman felt secure in his possession of an enormous, impregnable shield and was in no humor also to forge and wield a powerful sword as well. He did not want to fight; he only wanted protection.

12

The "Belgian Maneuver," the Ardennes, and French Morale

The dramatic French defeat in 1940 occurred after the French army had executed a maneuver which had been an important part of the high command's armory of plans since World War I. The universal shock at the defeat of what was reputedly the strongest army in the world, in a breathtakingly short time, obscured the actual developments of the brief campaign. But the plans leading to the thrusting forward of the best elements of the allied armies into the Low Countries where they fell into one of the most cleverly executed traps in modern military history is a story which concerns us here, since the plan for the "Belgian maneuver" was Pétain's plan during his tenure as Commander in Chief of the French army in the inter-war period.

Some salient features of the plan, which was put into effect in May 1940, are worth noting. First of all the plan was an audacious, offensive concept, which demonstrates that the initiative and willingness to maneuver of the French high command were not entirely motheaten. Secondly, from the point of view of historical continuity, it is of interest that the plan was markedly different from the notorious Plan XVII—which almost ruined France twenty-six years before her time—and would seem to have been a correction of the errors of 1914 twenty-six years too late. Had the Germans reenacted the Schlieffen maneuver in World War II, the "Belgian maneuver" was admirably suited to counter the move. But the German high command was as uncooperative, from the French point of view, in 1940 as it had been in

274

1914. Thirdly, it would be a mistake to attribute France's defeat in 1940 solely to the strategic errors committed by her military leaders, important as they might have been. She had survived a worse defeat on the frontiers in 1914, because her people and her soldiers had had the high moral resolve to do so; the *poilu* and citizen of 1940 was not the same man as his father.

We have already pointed out that strategically France and Belgium form one system and that the defense of the Rhine is their natural defensive posture against an attack from the east. From 1919 until 1930, when the Rhineland was evacuated, the French army was in a position to take advantage of this fact and on September 7, 1920, General Buat for France and General Maglinse, Chief of the Belgian General Staff, signed a military agreement aimed directly at Germany. It provided that in a period of international political tension Belgium would summon France to her aid and the latter would immediately send an army which would take up positions on Belgium's eastern border.

It was agreed that the French army would relieve the Belgian forces facing Luxembourg and Germany on the general front between Arlon, in Belgian Luxembourg, and Liège, and would also send an army as a reserve to back up the Belgian army holding the line Liège-Albert Canal. If Germany attacked anywhere against France's eastern allies, Poland or Czechoslovakia, France would be in a position to come to their aid by attacking Germany across the Rhenish plains. Throughout this period, the 1920's, when Pétain was Commander in Chief of the French army, the plan in the event of war with Germany was distinctly offensive in nature—a concept made possible by the holding of German territory on the Rhine by French and Belgian occupation forces and by the relative weakness of the German Versailles Treaty army.

In meetings of the Higher War Council in 1926 and 1927 Pétain formally took a position on this, that the "Belgian maneuver" was a vital part of French planning. Not only could they better protect their own frontier of the Nord department by advancing into Belgium, but it was unthinkable that they should stand idle while their small but important ally was beaten; for Belgium alone could not assure the defense of her frontiers against Germany. In 1914 the French high command had deliberately allowed the Belgian army to be neutralized, thinking that the war would be decided in Lorraine; and it was there that the French directed their armies without regard for the Belgians and the decisive theater which the latter defended. Pétain would not repeat that error.

It was not a defensive motive that prompted Pétain's insistence upon maintaining the combined Franco-Belgian project, for it was by means of this maneuver that he planned to carry the war into Germany. The agreement with Belgium did not require an invasion of Belgian soil by the Germans to make it operative; any hostile act by Germany in any direction that violated the terms of the Versailles Treaty would set the plan in motion. Thus even if the Germans started a war but scrupulously avoided touching Belgian territory they would still be subject to attack from that dangerous flank. In this manner France's eastern allies were assured that France was in a position to help them.

By the terms of the military agreement the Belgian and French staffs consulted periodically on problems of joint defense. Their occupying armies in the Rhineland worked in close liaison and the decade of the 1920's was a period of relative security for both countries. But in 1930, when the French government decided to evacuate the Rhineland, the situation changed and the arrangement with Belgium suffered accordingly. France would henceforth be defending her own borders in the northeast and no longer had access to the line of the Rhine. The Belgians therefore had less to gain from the alliance and the arrangements for combined action in the event of a German attack became less binding and less precise.[1]

In the same year Marshal Pétain directed staff studies which were to formulate new plans to cover the new situation. From now on the military cooperation of Belgium and France would not take place automatically but would become operative only if Belgium officially summoned aid from her ally, although a definite military alliance still bound them both. The question then became one of time, because to be effective the French armies would have to have time to get to the Belgian-German front of contact. Under the old arrangement the French armies would take up positions there, if possible, during a period of diplomatic tension or when otherwise warned of trouble—perhaps by military preparations in the enemy country—but this was not so after 1930. In any case improved technology in the machinery of war was making modern "lightning war" techniques possible and the question of time became more pressing.

Pétain decided that if the Belgians did not call the French armies in sufficient time for them to occupy, with the Belgians, the Line Arlon-Liège-Albert Canal—as he had previously planned—he would

---

[1] General Gamelin, *Servir* (Paris, 1946), II, 25; see also Général R. van Overstraeten, *Albert I-Léopold III: Vingt ans de politique militaire Belge, 1920-1940* (Brussels, 1946), 47-49.

then hold the line of the Meuse above Namur—that is, between Namur and the French border—and also the front Namur-Antwerp, covering Brussels. From the French border to Namur the Meuse offers a good defense line but the river swings to the east at Namur and the line Namur-Antwerp has to be held on lesser natural defense lines, principally the river Dyle.

By 1930 the publication by the Germans of documents and memoirs revealed some of the considerations which affected their 1914 offensive operation through Belgium and, although Pétain had already figured them out for himself in postwar studies, the German publications confirmed his judgments. One of the feeble points in the Schlieffen Plan, to which its author had given serious thought in 1912, was this—again a question of time: would the German right wing, the all-important marching wing, be able in time to force the passage of the Meuse at Liège so as to be able to reach the Antwerp-Brussels-Namur region before the French, reinforced by the British and Belgians, could beat them to it? Schlieffen need not have worried; the French high command were not clever enough even to try. But the occupation of that area assured the mastery of Belgium and was indispensable to his Plan.

The Germans feared in 1914 a French move into Belgium which would secure the line Antwerp-Namur before the German army could get there, thus rendering their whole enveloping maneuver impossible. From postwar studies the French high command knew that the front Antwerp-Brussels-Namur was the strategic front on which Schlieffen planned to deploy his armies and that he had urged upon the commanders who would carry out the Plan the greatest possible speed, once the Meuse at Liège was crossed, to attain, in his words, "the zone of strategic deployment Antwerp-Namur."[2]

In 1914 Pétain personally had been affected by the French high command's inability to match wits with their Teutonic opposite numbers, for he had been on the left wing with the Fifth Army which was directly endangered by the German envelopment. It was not likely that the lesson would be lost on him and his insistence upon the "Belgian maneuver," to defend France on the Belgian rivers, was a good plan under the existing circumstances. It should be noted that the maneuver envisaged by Pétain was considerably more circumspect and limited in scope than the one eventually executed in May 1940, and was one well within France's capabilities in 1930.

In 1932, after the Marshal had retired from active military service,

---

[2] Colonel L. Loizeau, "Succès stratégique, succès tactique," *Revue militaire française*, XXXVIII (December, 1930), 372–376.

his former major-general-designate General Debeney declared at a meeting of the Higher War Council that the "Belgian maneuver" was so important to France that if the Belgians were hostile to it the French would have to march into Belgium in spite of them.[3] In the same year Pétain's successor as commander in chief, General Weygand, was alarmed at some of the proposals put forward for France at the Geneva disarmament talks, which would have deprived France of the military means to carry out her plan to defend her northern frontier by advancing into Belgium and would have compelled her to give up any plans for an offensive through Belgium. She would have been relegated to a defensive position on the Franco-Belgian border, a border only alive politically but nonexistent strategically.[4]

In December 1933 the Belgian ambassador to France, Baron de Gaiffier, was told by Pétain that the completion of the Maginot Line fortifications from Basle to Longwy would make a German invasion of Belgium inevitable. The fortified frontier could be turned only by an enemy penetration into France through the Nord department, in a maneuver similar to that of 1914, and in order to avert the recurrence of "an experience which had almost cost the existence of France," the French armies would have to enter Belgium even without an invitation from that country. When the startled Ambassador asked, "But if we fight you?" the Marshal replied, "Then we will fight you!"[5]

On March 7, 1934, Pétain as Minister of War met with the Army Committee of the Senate and affirmed, within the limits of military security, that the plan was still to go into Belgium if the Germans should attack there. It was agreed that although France had no aggressive intentions, she should plan to meet the blows of the enemy with appropriate force if hostilities should occur, and should plan to carry the war to his territory.[6]

In that year General Weygand was able, thanks to the Maginot Line, to transfer a much larger number of his forces to the Nord department and the French high command therefore had a much greater proportion of its forces than before facing the Belgian frontier.[7]

But in 1936, after Germany remilitarized the Rhineland, and Bel-

---

[3] Gamelin, II, 71, 72.

[4] *Commission chargée d'enquêter sur les événements survenus en France de 1933 à 1945* (Paris, 195?), Supplement, I, 239.

[5] van Overstraeten, 99, 100.

[6] Gamelin, II, 129.

[7] *Commission chargée d'enquêter . . .* , VI, p. 1674, General Weygand's testimony.

gium renounced her alliance with France and proclaimed her neutrality, the picture was changed. From then on there were no exchanges
of military information, no meetings of staff personnel, and no per-
missions for French officers to inspect Belgian terrain. Pétain was no
longer responsible for French military planning but it is useful to
follow the evolution of the "Belgian maneuver" to its melancholy
denouement, if only because some of the postwar denunciation of
the Marshal attributed the mistakes of 1940, at least in part, to his
influence.

As we have seen, the Marshal was concerned with the time factor
in his planning for the Belgian operation. If he could not get there
"fustest with the mostest" he was not going at all, at least not all the
way. The Belgian declaration of neutrality ruled out the defense of
the Liège-Albert Canal line by French forces unless the French were
called well in advance—and no one expected the Germans to issue
warnings or invitations before they struck. This left the line Meuse-
Namur-Antwerp as the next defense line and even here Pétain had
demanded, before 1936, ample time from the Belgians so that the
French could move their forces in the wide arc through Belgium and
establish themselves in positions to receive the German assault in the
best possible conditions.

The defection of Belgium in 1936 made these plans problematical
and also ruled out possible French offensive action through this
strategically inviting area—across the Rhine into the industrial Ruhr
and through Hanover to Berlin—to help her eastern allies, Czechoslovakia and Poland, if they were attacked by Germany. All military
agreements with Belgium were cancelled and a mutual defense depended upon the King of Belgium who said that he would call France
if and when he needed her, hardly a promising prospect for an army
whose military doctrine emphasized well prepared and methodical
operations.

Without adequate preparation the advanced defense of Liège-Albert
Canal by the French was ruled out and even the Namur-Antwerp line
could be considered only if the Belgians had made special defensive
preparations there. After 1936 General Gamelin realized this and the
plans for the "Belgian maneuver" were as circumspect as Pétain had
envisaged. If the prerequisite conditions for the Namur-Antwerp
front plan, later called the "Dyle Plan," were not carried out by the
Belgians—the creation of a good continuous defense line, the establishment of troops in well-prepared positions, and the advance agreement
upon a concerted defense plan between them and their allies—then
the French armies would take up positions on a line farther to the

rear, although still in Belgium: on the Scheldt from Condé to Ghent.[8]

On March 23, 1936, in the aftermath of the German remilitarization of the Rhineland, a meeting of the chiefs of staff of the army,
navy and air force took place at Gamelin's home. The General
assured his colleagues that the Channel ports, essential to British
cooperation, would be covered by his plan which was to give battle
on the Escaut (the Scheldt in Belgium). There was no question here
of a defense line any deeper in Belgium.[9] Yet only two months later,
on May 15, Gamelin assured the Belgian high command that his plan
continued to be a French deployment in "middle Belgium" (the
Namur-Antwerp line), with a second army on the Arlon-Chiers-Meuse
(his "bottom of the [Ardennes] net").[10] Obviously the French Commander wanted to assure himself of Belgian support, a support which
would not be forthcoming unless the French were willing to commit
their forces into the Belgian interior. However there was still no plan
for anything beyond this, and even this measure was dependent upon
the completion of the Belgian defensive preparations, which were as
yet nonexistent.

But as time went on and Pétain's influence on high-level planning
receded into the background and gave way to the younger commanders' conceptions, the plan for Belgium began to have an increasingly audacious allure, until by May 1940 Gamelin was playing
Napoleon with the same vigor, and the same unfortunate results, as
Joffre had in 1914. There is much to be said for Gamelin's side, however. For one thing, France's principal and indispensable ally, Great
Britain, attached considerable importance to keeping the Germans
as far to the east in Belgium as possible and therefore were strong
proponents of an extensive maneuver there.[11]

If the Germans succeeded in occupying Belgium they would pose
a dangerous air and naval threat to Britain, one that the latter
country would consider of vital importance and might constrain her
to keep most of her forces for home-defense instead of sending them
to augment the French forces on the French front. France could not
afford this diminution of effectives nor could she afford to watch
with equanimity the loss of twenty-two Belgian divisions. Furthermore

---

8 *Commission chargée d'enquêter* . . . , III, 683–686, General Georges' testimony.

9 *Documents diplomatiques français, 1932–1939*. Second series (1936–1939).
Tome I (Jan. 1–Mar. 31, 1936) (Paris, 1963), 643–645.

10 van Overstraeten, 220, 266, 267.

11 *Commission chargée d'enquêter* . . . , II, 408–410, General Gamelin's testimony.

the occupation of the line Meuse-Namur-Antwerp, taking advantage of the valleys of the Dyle and the Nèthe, would shorten the French front from 80 to 100 kilometers, an important consideration.

Another consideration is important: when Pétain was in charge he had to plan on using an army which, in the early stages of a war, would be a ponderous and relatively less maneuverable instrument, due to the product furnished him by the nation-in-arms system. But Gamelin had the unexpected period of the "phony war" from September 1939 to May 1940 in which his armies were in being and he could reasonably expect that they would have achieved a certain amount of cohesion and efficiency, after eight months of training under arms, which would permit a more ambitious approach to operational planning.

But Gamelin began to think of the movement to the line described above, the Dyle Plan, as a fixed plan and he gradually attached less importance to the conditions formerly considered prerequisite to the move. In addition, he enlarged the maneuver in scope so as to include the Netherlands and this was his fatal error—or one of them. Although his subordinate General Georges, Pétain's old associate, disapproved of the way the Plan was getting out of hand, Gamelin proposed to send an army also into the Netherlands—the "Breda Variant" of the Dyle Plan—and the Seventh Army, containing seven excellent divisions, was dispatched beyond Antwerp into the maritime Scheldt region and Dutch Brabant. There it was lost in May 1940—an irretrievable error, for this army should have been used as a strategic reserve behind the Ardennes front (the pivot of the "Belgian maneuver") where the Germans had no difficulty breaking through the too-thinly-held line.

The original Dyle Plan itself was not a fatal mistake in 1940; the French forces planned for that maneuver were not too great a proportion of the total French army so that adequate reserves could have been retained on national soil, perhaps not to change the eventual outcome of the campaign but at least to have given the French a fighting chance. However, not only were important reserves lost to Gamelin by his enlarged maneuver but he also kept too many of his field divisions deployed behind the Maginot Line, fearful of a breakthrough there, thus partially nullifying the economy of force principle which was a raison d'être of the Line and depriving himself of vital reserves at the crucial front in the north.

Gamelin was so bewitched by his hope of a strategic coup that he actually wanted to provoke the Germans into invading the Low Countries and was pleased, at first, when the German offensive began there. One is reminded of Joffre's satisfaction in early August 1914 when the German offensive into Belgium seemed to play into his hands. Once again the Germans were entering a "trap." Gamelin was not alone in his enthusiasm for the "Belgian maneuver." He apparently was closely seconded by the Premier, Paul Reynaud, who had been convinced by Colonel Charles de Gaulle of the efficacy of the operation. On that subject Reynaud, in his postwar writings, seemed to have suffered a lapse of memory.[12]

The details of the campaign in May 1940 may be omitted here; a brief recital of the main points will give an idea of the disaster that resulted from the allied movement deep into the Low Countries. Since the maneuver was considered the vital one, the one that might decide the war, the allied forces allotted to the operation contained the best elements of their respective armies. All their armored and mechanized divisions were committed there and all their highest quality units. The Germans feinted toward the north and then struck the French thinly held middle in the Ardennes region, the pivot of the allied maneuver, cutting off the allied armies in Belgium.

The French and British lost 39 divisions out of a total of 102; these were their best divisions, containing the greater part of their modern equipment. Three-fourths or four-fifths of France's modern armament was lost and practically all of the British equipment. After that disaster there was little hope of any effective resistance to the Germans in metropolitan France.

None of the French hopes were realized by the Belgian maneuver. The Dutch army, whose ten divisions Gamelin had been concerned with conserving, surrendered in five days, a remarkable performance in a negative sense. The Belgians were unable to halt or even slow the German advance to give the French time to get set on the Meuse, and fulfilled few of the expectations that the French high command had of them. (Of course, the French army itself fulfilled few of the expectations that anybody had of *it*.) Most of the allied units in the operation never became fully engaged and the thirty-nine French and British divisions committed in the Low Countries had little influence on the decisive battle which took place south of them.

Pétain was shocked by the developments and declared that if the allied dash into Belgium had not taken place the army would have avoided disaster and could have put up a good fight, although he doubted that they could in the long run have won the war with their own resources. With the best troops and matériel lost in the north

---

[12] *Commission chargée d'enquêter* . . . , IX, pp. 2760–2772; also Yves Bout-hillier, *Le Drame de Vichy* (Paris, 1950), I, 19.

the remnants of the army could not hold out for long and he considered that there was no other course than to request an armistice— and that quickly, since he deemed it inevitable anyway, so as to preserve as much of national territory and resources as possible. This opinion was shared by General Weygand and most other French military authorities.

Thus culminated the "Belgian maneuver" and it is curious to note that the French high command, who have been berated for their defensive-mindedness and inability to move, were in reality victims of their own audacity, at least in this instance. The movement into Belgium offered excellent strategic opportunities under certain cirsumstances but the French high command went too far in May 1940 by denuding themselves of precious strategic reserves to add weight to their marching wing, thus leaving themselves nothing to counter the German surprise breakthroughs at Sedan and Dinant. They did not have the resources for the maneuver and it was unwise to give it the scope that they did.

Pétain's planning for the defense of northern France and Belgium was circumspect in taking account of realities and would have developed as the situation of the moment warranted. He would not gamble everything on one throw and would have kept a reserve for contingencies. Gamelin's version of the plan, which ended in failure on the Belgian plains, was a gamble in that it was based too much on the expectation of a specific German maneuver. He left himself no resources or room for retreat if his initial guess of the enemy's intentions proved wrong. This was not Pétain's way and the adventurous May 1940 operation was a travesty of his planning.

Once again the French high command had guessed wrong: in 1914 they expected the Germans to attack through Belgium on the right bank of the Meuse and in 1940 they expected them to sweep around the left bank in a repetition of the Schlieffen Plan. In both instances the Germans did just the opposite. But the error in evaluating the intentions of the enemy and the failure in the battle of wits need not have been disastrous in either case if the French had made provision for a miscarriage of their plans, to spread their bet instead of putting everything on the one chance.

Audacious in the north, Gamelin was overly cautious in the northeast where he was hypnotized by the only Franco-German front of contact. There he kept thirty field divisions unnecessarily superimposed on the Maginot Line, which was already well-defended by the fortress troops, so that the density of the troops holding the powerful fortified line was greater than that of the troops on the line of the

Meuse, which was hardly fortified at all, and where the Germans made their main assault.[13] This was a travesty of Pétain's intentions with regard to the fortifications. The purpose of the Maginot Line was to permit the northeast front to be held by relatively light forces, releasing the main armies for operations elsewhere. The thin forces holding the Meuse from Sedan to Dinant were inadequate to hold the Ardennes front for very long and it was there that the issue was decided.

The German breakthroughs at Dinant and Sedan, in the Ardennes region, in May 1940, completely surprised the allied commanders and neutralized the British and Belgians, as well as the best part of the French, armies before the campaign could get fairly started. In a few days the issue was decided and the French received a blow from which they could not recover. How much did Pétain have to do with the inter-war planning that resulted in the debacle and what were the circumstances behind his and other military leaders' apparently erroneous conceptions regarding the impassability of the area for enemy forces?

It should be emphasized that neither Pétain nor anyone else considered the Ardennes literally impenetrable for an army. What they did think was that the wooded and hilly terrain, and the barrier of the Meuse, would make the passage through the area militarily difficult and that it was a region where the advantages were with the defenders, permitting them to economize their forces there and giving them a strong *point d'appui* for operations elsewhere. In this assumption they were quite correct, although the knowledge that their views were on the whole tenable probably would give them no more satisfaction today than would the knowledge to the Romans, after the second Punic War, that it would be extremely difficult for some Carthaginian to bring war-elephants across the Alps.

The Ardennes mountains and forests, lying for the most part in Belgium, had long been considered by European military men as an area where it was almost impossible for armies to maneuver. Yet in August 1914 the French high command launched its Fourth Army in an offensive through the Ardennes hoping to take the Germans invading through Belgium in the flank. The region was difficult but not considered absolutely impenetrable. However, the French attack through the area in 1914 was repulsed with heavy losses, due partly

[13] A. Goutard, "Pourquoi 1940?", *La Revue de Paris* (March, 1956), 88–91; also André Schorp, "Doit-on réarmer la ligne Maginot?", *Revue de défense nationale*, N.S., XIV (January–June, 1952), 189–194.

to poor training and a faulty military doctrine but also due to the rough terrain and dense forests where coordinated and directed maneuver was very difficult. This unhappy experience served to strengthen the conviction that the Ardennes could be considered unsuitable for large-scale operations.

This view was held not by just a few, but by all French military men; generations of officers had been exposed to this conviction. The British and Belgians too, prior to World War II, felt that the Ardennes and the Meuse which cuts it were two very strong natural obstacles and that it could be considered a passive sector which could be defended by light forces. In a sense they were not far wrong; as General Weygand pointed out later, even in 1940 a good French bombardment air force could have wreaked havoc upon the German close packed columns threading their way through the few avenues of approach in this region. Even the German high command had grave doubts about the plan when it was suggested by General Manstein and confirmed as feasible by General Guderian.

The forests of the Ardennes are passable for infantry and vehicles, particularly in dry weather. The scarcity of paved roads makes the passage of vehicles in wet weather difficult. It is the central plateau massif which is the principal obstacle, with its steep slopes and spongy soil, and it should be noted that the Germans did not in fact traverse the Ardennes mountains but flanked them on the north and south.

The valley of the Meuse, which runs through the region is an excellent line of defense. The average width of the river is seventy yards and sometimes the slopes of the valley are absolutely perpendicular and absolutely impassable for vehicles; they are always very steep and difficult. A defender could not ask for a better position to hold a line with a minimum of effectives, particularly when one considers that it would have to be infantry who would force the passage, as tanks could not operate effectively there, and in fact did not.

The central plateau massif of Hautes-Fagnes, the principal natural obstacle of the Ardennes, is roughly contained in a rectangle formed by Mezières and Givet on the western corners and Martelange and St. Vith on the eastern corners. South of this mass is a relatively open region, a small corridor from Arlon to Muno, in Belgian Luxembourg, which leads to Sedan. This the Germans used in 1940. North of the rectangle is another area suitable for military movement, north of the line Givet, Rochefort, Marche, leading to Dinant; and this the Germans also used in May 1940.

As these two corridors approach France from east to west they debouch through two areas, the two that the Germans used, one on each side of the Ardennes: in the north an opening that stretches forty to fifty kilometers from Givet, extreme point of the French frontier, to Namur in Belgium; and in the south an opening from Mezières to Sedan, about fifteen kilometers wide. These are "openings" only in the sense that they avoid the main Ardennes; they are blocked by the Meuse, which good troops could be expected to hold, for a time at least. While the forest between these two "openings" is a region very difficult to traverse, because there are few roads running from east to west there, the two corridors themselves have roads running right into France. It is noteworthy that the German attacks in 1940 in the Ardennes proper, notably at Monthermé, were repelled.

During Pétain's meeting with the Senate Army Committee on March 7, 1934, in his capacity as Minister of War, he explained to the Senators that if special provisions were made in the Ardennes region, it could be considered a zone militarily impenetrable, a "destruction zone." This front would have no depth because the avenues of approach were scarce and narrow. The enemy could not engage himself there with impunity; if he did, the Marshal said, his advance would be "pinched off" when he came out of the forests.[14]

This is a reflection of Pétain's views on the military possibilities of the Ardennes and in fact it represents the views of the other military experts of that period. The Ardennes was so formidable a natural obstacle that the front of approach of an enemy army would be greatly limited in depth. When the enemy emerged from the forests his columns would be vulnerable to attacks on both flanks, from the south by forces based on the Maginot Line and from the north by other mobile units. He could not feed his advance quickly enough or broaden his front quickly enough to engage the presumably more powerful French forces operating on their own national territory, with much chance of success.

This theory did not disregard the possible employment of armored units by the Germans, although in 1934 they did not have any. But the terrain was of a nature that precluded the use of armor except on the few roads. The Ardennes was not impenetrable for infantry but it could be easily defended against it. And tanks could only operate in columns on the few roads; not being able to leave the roads to deploy they would not be able to operate under the best conditions for armored warfare, that is, in a mass tank maneuver leading to a rapid breakthrough. When their columns emerged from the forest they could be cut off by French mobile forces, as Pétain planned.

---

[14] Gamelin, II, 128.

The avenues of approach would of course be covered by French blockhouses, containing French infantry and artillery, as Pétain explained to the Senators in 1934. These defenders, holding positions where all the advantages lay with the defense, could be expected to hold the Germans long enough so that French reserves could concentrate to handle any breakthrough that the enemy might achieve. Of course if there were little effective opposition to the enemy penetration; if enemy infantry could cross the Meuse and occupy the defenses on the opposite banks against feeble resistance and rapidly push beyond the river, broadening their front practically at will and providing a bridgehead for the armored units that followed them, a bridgehead from which the armored columns could sweep across the plains of northern France and Belgium, then all these plans were of little value. But the Minister of War in 1934 could not foresee that: his plans were predicated on a firm defense of the Ardennes and the Meuse; nor could he foresee that the Commander in Chief of the French armies would, in 1940, fail to organize adequate strategic reserves behind the French front which could hope to deal with a German breakthrough.

When Gamelin took command of the army he adopted wholeheartedly the theory of the impenetrability of the Ardennes but he went too far in presuming upon the strength of the obstacle and the quality of the troops who would defend it. He also did not revise his planning sufficiently to take into account the new situation arising after 1936 when the Germans remilitarized the Rhineland and when all liaison was broken between the French and Belgian staffs. The latter consideration is particularly important because the Ardennes region lies largely in Belgium and a prearranged plan with close Belgian cooperation was essential for a successful defense of the area.

Prior to 1936 the plan for the Ardennes in the event of a German attack was for the "Army Detachment of the Ardennes" to defend the western pocket of the Ardennes so as to stop the enemy on the right bank of the Meuse, the area which Gamelin later called the "bottom of the net." The idea was that the Germans would commit themselves in force into this "net," would be stopped on the right bank of the Meuse and the fortified positions, then would be counterattacked on the two flanks of the salient that they had created;[15] the left flank attack would come from the Maginot-Line-based strategic reserves and the attack on the German right flank from the French armies which would have with permission penetrated into Belgium.

After 1936, when Belgium declared her neutrality, the pushing for-

---

[15] *Commission chargée d'enquêter . . .* , V, 1367.

ward of the main French forces to the Belgian Meuse was still envisaged but only if "particularly favorable circumstances permitted the execution of this movement in complete security." Since it was highly likely that hostilities would begin with an immediate invasion of the Low Countries by the Germans it was unlikely that the conditions of security would be effected and that a deep penetration of Belgium by the French could take place.

But, as we have seen, Gamelin gradually came to fix upon a great maneuver into the Low Countries without the prerequisite conditions of security being realized. He still considered the Ardennes an unimportant front strategically and he refused the unfortunate General Corap's repeated requests for a strengthening of his Ninth Army which had the mission of securing the Meuse in the Belgian Ardennes. Corap's army had to advance into Belgium on May 10, 1940, and was broken at Dinant before it could get properly organized. The strategic reserves which might have parried the breakthrough were on their way to Holland.

On the other side of the Ardennes, at Sedan, the front was held by reserve divisions of mediocre quality—the battle proved that they were of poor quality—and the strategic reserves which would have coped with the breakthrough there were unnecessarily deployed behind the powerful Maginot Line; the latter procedure is similar to that of the man who wears a belt and suspenders at the same time. The *masse de manoeuvre* which was supposed to be organized as a result of the economy of force permitted by the Maginot Line was nonexistent or poorly employed. The "pinching off" of the enemy's columns envisaged by Pétain could not take place for lack of pincers.

But even if the strategic errors had not been made it is unlikely that the eventual outcome would have been much different. Pétain's plan for the Ardennes envisaged resolute defenders holding the enemy infantry on the line of Meuse long enough to permit the French high command to organize countermeasures. This firm resistance did not take place.

We have indicated that the French high command thought of the Meuse as a huge antitank ditch which, reinforced by the high terrain on its banks and held by defenders installed in positions well in advance, should be a strong obstacle in an enemy's path. Even if some tanks got into the valley they could not operate in mass until the heights on the left bank had been secured by infantry. It had to be an infantry operation and the French infantry, supported by heavy artillery, should have been able to hold, particularly at Sedan where the defenders were installed in prepared positions on French territory.

Yet the Germans passed easily through the Ardennes against little opposition and effected crossings of the Meuse with their infantry, who quickly enlarged bridgeheads on the left bank which permitted the tanks to cross and to begin the rapid conquest of France. At Sedan the crossing was made "easily," as General Guderian put it, by an infantry regiment from his armored units and a regular infantry regiment, supported by artillery and by dive bomber attacks. French resistance was weak and often nonexistent; positions were abandoned without a fight. The German operation proceeded like clockwork, almost as if the troops were on maneuvers, and was over in a matter of hours. The attack started at 4:00 P.M. on May 13; by 6:00 P.M. the German infantry had cleared the south bank and in a few hours one of the infantry regiments was six kilometers south of the Meuse. During the night the tanks started to cross the river by means of a pontoon bridge and on the 14th they assumed the dominant role.[16]

Contrary to the popular conception of a great wave of German tanks submerging French soldiers fighting with outmoded weapons, the facts are that the river was forced by conventional infantry units, and not too many of them, supported by dive bombers, whose effect was largely psychological, and by field artillery. The French infantry at Sedan were in prepared positions and were supported by prepared heavy artillery, greatly superior to that of the Germans, and amply protected by concrete blockhouses and gun emplacements. The question was to a great extent one of morale; the Ardennes was a strong natural barrier but it had little value as a military obstacle unless the troops defending it were prepared to offer serious resistance.

There is little question but that the military breakdown of France in 1940 was due in large measure to poor morale, and in a curious way the career of Philippe Pétain was closely associated with the morale of his countrymen. This subject was a matter of continual concern to him and the "pessimism" or "defeatism" with which he is often charged was due partly to his instinctive sensing of the mood of the army and the people. If he too often feared the worst in the way of a morale collapse, too often his fears were justified by the events.

In 1917 he had been responsible for the restoration of the mutinous soldiers' morale, as he had done in a smaller way for the Sixth Division in 1914, and the event made a great impression upon him. The Marshal often said, before 1940, that he considered his success in the mutiny crisis of 1917 to be his greatest service to France. During

---

[16] General Heinz Guderian, *Panzer Leader* (New York, 1952), 101–104.

the inter-war period he had not had many illusions about the state of psychological preparedness of Frenchmen to defend themselves against aggression, and the collapse in May and June 1940 came as no surprise to him.

Although the French armies were numbered among the allied victors of World War I, thanks in part to Pétain's patching their shattered fighting spirit together in 1917 so that they could continue the war, France had in some respects the psychology of a defeated nation. In fact she had been physically beaten and only because of her allies did she emerge as one of the victors. The war on the western front took place almost entirely on her territory, causing such damage as to fill Frenchmen with dread at the thought of another such smashing of their national life. Her casualties were very high, almost 1.5 million military dead and a total of 5 million casualties out of a population of only 40 million; this not only caused the loss of a whole generation and more of her best men, but also seriously damaged her demographic future. Frenchmen lived in horror at the thought of another struggle like that one and were in no psychological condition to meet the threat of a resurgent Germany.

It was during Pétain's tenure as Commander in Chief of the army, in the 1920's, that the military establishment was progressively reduced so that by the Laws of 1927–1928 the army became little better than a militia. The military "defensive mindedness" of the French was not a fault of the military leaders, despite the latter's failure to fully modernize their tactics, but was a reflection of the spirit of the nation. The military organization, especially after 1928, was based by the government upon defensive assumptions and reflected a civilian state of mind which, distrusting the army and the "military mind," was concerned with preventing the launching of "adventurous" military offensives—although the existence of treaties with France's small eastern allies presupposed a French capability for offensive military action—and which sought only security against attack.

The political situation in France would admit of no other military posture and the militia-like "nation in arms" concept was a result of the bitter opposition of parliamentarians of the left to all things military. It was this militia which was defeated in the 1940 campaign.

The era of the Geneva disarmament talks and the euphoria produced by the unrealistic hopes attached to the League of Nations reflected the fears of the people of France who wanted to keep what they had without fighting for it and who feared war because they had nothing to gain by it. They failed to realize that democracy and liberty are not birthrights but must be defended and fought for, and the statesmen who might have inspired and led them had perished or spent their youthful strength in the "Great War." In the early 1930's the French high command, which later was stigmatized for having lost a war, fought their own political leaders to keep France from being disarmed in the interests of international amity and were labeled "militaristic" and "imperialistic" for their pains.

France was poorly served by political leaders like Daladier, who encouraged a defensive-minded, passive attitude toward the impending conflict with Nazi Germany; like Léon Blum, who denounced military preparedness and gave the French worker a forty-hour work week—which the worker paid for by a higher cost of living—while Hitler was leading his people, with demonic energy, in an all-out armament production; like Paul Reynaud, who talked bravely in June 1940 of carrying on the fight but whose only action was to submit a pusillanimous resignation; and finally, if one likes, by an octogenarian military hero like Pétain, a relic of another era, into whose fumbling hands a bewildered and crushed people finally placed their destiny.

The pacifism characteristic of the 1930's had distressed Pétain, who foresaw a new conflict, one in which democratic France would be attacked by the totalitarian powers who would be at an advantage militarily because of the preparation which they could enforce upon their citizens. He deplored the pacifism rampant among the youth of the nation, who would have to bear the brunt of the battle, and he began to speak out for a pre-military indoctrination of French youth so that physically and morally they could meet the challenge of France's neighbors.[17]

As Minister of War he was faced with the problem of augmenting the term of compulsory military service, to raise France's military strength to the safety level, but encountered bitter opposition from left-wing politicians, as we have seen—politicians who reflected the wishes of the electorate. He continued to press for a pre-military training for the young men so that months of training would be saved when they were called up for their period of service.[18] Not only were the young men his concern but he also urged that a "higher degree of moral and patriotic education" be given to all citizens because a modern war demands the participation of everybody.[19] He must have known that it was impossible, in a democratic country of that era, to put his suggestions into practice; but he continued to press

[17] *New York Times*, March 25, 1934.
[18] *New York Times*, July 23, 1934.
[19] *New York Times*, December 9, 1934.

for some kind of moral preparation for the war that he saw coming. He felt strongly that democratic liberties were not of much value if powerful undemocratic neighbors could develop a superior force to take them away.

In 1934 as Minister of War the Marshal sometimes was as much concerned about the moral preparation for war as he was for its material preparation. The pacifist and anti-patriotic propaganda which emanated from academic and literary circles disturbed him and he addressed the Minister of National Education, in a speech, as follows: "We are proceeding to a dissociation of French strength at the same time that the central government in Germany is rallying to itself, with enthusiasm, both the leading elements and the masses of the nation. . . . It is a matter of life or death."[20] To this the Communist journal L'Humanité of June 15, 1934 replied: "To oppose this awakening of the military spirit which is attempted in speeches like those of the Marshal Pétain, the workers adopt the spirit of the mutineers of 1917."

Pétain emphasized that the "statist education," as he put it, of Germany, Italy and Russia was not what he advocated for France; but he did feel that schools should teach patriotism and a sense of duty. He thought that the modern education idea, which developed the individual as an end in himself, tended to weaken the society as a whole. He wanted no "mystique of intolerance or of pride" on the fascist model for France; but she had to assure her security and to defend herself and she could not do this without a citizenry imbued with the conviction that France was worth fighting for. Pétain feared the kind of moral collapse that occurred in 1940.[21]

The March 1936 crisis, a prelude in some respects to Munich, when the Germans violated the Versailles Treaty and the Locarno Pact by marching their troops into the demilitarized area of the Rhineland, demonstrated the apparent unwillingness of France to meet her responsibilities. In point of fact one could hardly expect that a peaceful people would fight a major war in order to keep German soldiers off German soil, but the unwillingness of Frenchmen to meet force with force and to submit to a trial of strength in matters affecting national security was obvious enough to everyone, including France's allies and potential enemies. The government let the army high

---

[20] Alfred Conquet, Lumières sur l'histoire (Paris, 1963), 62–66.
[21] Marshal Pétain, speech given on December 3, 1934, at the annual dinner of the Revue des deux mondes. Printed as a supplement to the Revue des deux mondes of December 15, 1934, vol. XXIV, pp. 5–8 (supplementary).

command know that neither the parliament nor the people would accept the eventuality of war if the army should propose a firm military response to the German action and the tone of the press and the utterances of political leaders during the crisis bore out this analysis of public opinion.[22]

This display, and the accession to power of the socialist Popular Front government in the same year, made Pétain despair of his countrymen and their will to meet the Nazi challenge. In the summer of 1936 he exclaimed bitterly to an Englishman that "we have a rotten government and I want to tell you that the French people won't fight," an unhappy comment for a proud French soldier.[23]

It was obvious to him that the unwillingness of the French to accept war if necessary to defend themselves was an open invitation to aggressor nations to risk greater attacks upon French security. In October 1936 he warned his countrymen of this danger; the lassitude of Frenchmen in the face of the declared hostility of Germany and Italy was a surer path to war than a firm front.[24]

At the same time he again urged some kind of military education for French youth, to take place prior to their induction for regular military service. He cited the example of Germany, Italy, Russia and Japan in the pre-military training of youth in para-military organizations and argued that France had to consent to a moral, intellectual and physical discipline; her citizens had to be imbued with a sense of duty. He said that it was not enough simply to provide the material things that would defend France; she had also to be prepared morally.

In March 1938, at a meeting of the Permanent Committee for National Defense to discuss the possibility of military action in the event of war between Germany and Czechoslovakia, and also to discuss the possibility of intervention in Spain, the Marshal warned the Committee that in the question of undertaking a war they would have to consider the state of morale of the nation as well as military considerations; and he said that the French must intensify industrial production by "harnessing themselves to a day and night labor"—the Popular Front shorter work-week at a time when Germany and Italy were working night and day to prepare for war haunted him. He pointed out to the Committee that German production of aircraft was

---

[22] Gamelin, II, 199–212; Pierre-Etienne Flandin, *Politique française, 1919–1940* (Paris, 1947), 198–200; Paul Reynaud, *Mémoires* (Paris, 1963), II, 238.

[23] Pertinax, *The Gravediggers of France* (New York, 1944), 342.

[24] Maréchal Pétain, "La Préparation militaire," *La Revue de Paris*, V (September–October, 1936), 731, 732.

at a rate of 250 airplanes per month compared with the French production of 40, soon to rise to only 60.[25]

Pétain's public statements in 1938 show that he was obviously disturbed by the moral weaknesses and internal divisions of the French. He felt that a spiritual strength, or a sense of duty, was lacking. He warned of serious consequences if the French did not unite and with a sense of duty and discipline conduct themselves as a nation of Frenchmen and not as a group divided. His greatest fear was that the internal political strife would wreck the country.[26] In the same year he presented a new book to the Academy of Moral and Political Sciences, whose author expounded the thesis that the vanquished of 1918 were the victors of 1938—France had lost the fruits of her victory. Pétain said that only by a wise internal policy and a freely accepted national discipline could a people merit their victory and preserve it intact.[27]

In 1938, in spite of Pétain's repeated advice that France must have a strong, offensive bombardment aviation, the high command decided to concentrate on the production of fighter-aircraft, to the detriment of the bomber strength. They felt that they could not have everything they wanted in the way of an air force, given a certain limitation in industrial productive capacity, and they chose to give priority to fighter-plane production, relegating bombardment aviation to a secondary status.[28]

This curtailing of bombardment aviation even before the war started was an astonishing example of a defensive air orientation that stemmed almost entirely from an intense desire to spare the civilian population the horrors of war. By providing the fighter aircraft that could ward off enemy bombing attacks they had to curtail production of the means of bringing the war to the enemy, the only way the war could be won.

When the Germans in 1944 concentrated on the production of fighter planes and let their bomber production go, it was the beginning of the end for them, tacit recognition that they were on the defensive and could only try to ward off the enemy blows. But France, in response to the people's imperious demands for protection, de-

[25] Gamelin, II, 321–331; complete minutes of the meeting of the Committee on March 16, 1938.

[26] Maréchal Pétain, *Parolles aux français; messages et écrits, 1934–1941* (Lyon, 1941), particularly pp. 14–20.

[27] *Revue militaire générale,* 2nd Series, II (7–12, 1938), 139, 140, review of a book by André Fribourg, *La Victoire des vaincus* (Paris, 1938).

[28] *Commission chargée d'enquêter* . . . , Supplement, II, 372, 373, General Gamelin's testimony.

prived herself before the war even began of the offensive instrument that might have helped her, an example of the low state of morale of the French people and the unfortunate effects it had on their leaders, who were responsible to them.

In February 1939 Pétain again publicly called upon the country to prepare itself from a morale as well as from a material point of view. He urged the nation to unite in the face of the fascist peril, to put aside doctrines which divided Frenchmen, and to guard against the forces of disorder. With the war obviously coming he feared the political differences which were dividing and weakening France. She could not face the enemy with a firm front if she were divided within.[29]

The question of French morale plagued Pétain even when he was serving as ambassador to Spain in 1939. The war had broken out and the aged Marshal wondered how he could best serve his country. He explained in a personal letter to a friend his intention to keep out of politics—this was after he had refused an invitation from political friends to enter the government—but asked himself what he could do to render some service. His conclusion was that his age and physical condition precluded his taking a government post but that he still might be able to serve the army in a moral capacity; his position as a member of the Committee for National Defense gave him sufficient authority to make proposals. "Weaknesses could again occur, either at the front or in the rear, as in 1917; the measures taken in that period for a recovery would perhaps again be of some use."[30] Several months later the shattered French army was beyond hope of recovery by anybody.

We have noted that strategic errors and errors in organization contributed to the French collapse in May–June 1940, but that the important cause of the defeat was the low state of French morale. Errors in strategy and organization could be overcome by the will of good soldiers, as they were in 1914; but without morale they did not have a chance against the enthusiastic young Germans whose high morale, based on good organization and effective psychological preparation, fed on victory and increased with experience.

The full extent of the French military weakness in this connection cannot be fully known to us because only the French soldiers involved really know how bad it was and few Frenchmen would, in

[29] Maréchal Pétain, "Le Devoir des élites dans la défense nationale," *Revue des questions de défense nationale,* I (May–August, 1939), 18.
[30] *Le Procès du Maréchal Pétain,* Compte rendu sténographique (Paris, 1945), II, 966, 967.

this generation, write a completely honest recital of the events of the 1940 campaign. Nevertheless there is enough information available to give some idea of the extent of the morale breakdown that occurred. One can observe this in the breakthroughs at Dinant and Sedan which set the whole French military organization tottering, although it should be remembered that any such analysis is always unfair to those soldiers who do their duty well and are struck down or engulfed by superior forces because others in the ranks give way.

We have seen that the French forces at Sedan, in excellent and well-organized defensive positions, were thrown back with ease by two German infantry regiments. The nature of the defense line there was such that the French high command had estimated that it would take the Germans three weeks to a month to break through if they tried—note that the sector was never considered literally "impenetrable"—which would give them ample time to bring up reserves to cope with the situation. Actually the Germans crossed the Meuse at Sedan and drove the French defenders off the opposite bank, or captured them by the thousands, in two hours. Granted that the French high command failed in its responsibility to evaluate correctly the potential strength of the adversary, in armament and tactics; nevertheless there is a great difference between two hours and three weeks.

The French troops holding the position fled in complete disorder, terrified by the German dive bombers; the German infantry, supported by field artillery, had no difficulty in making a bridgehead for the armored divisions which followed. French officers later sadly recounted how their troops ran away without fighting and fresh troops dispatched to the front were often engulfed by the terror-stricken fugitives before they could reach their assigned positions.

Cavalry officers who fell back before the German advance on the right bank of the Meuse, in the Ardennes, noted with consternation that some French blockhouses on the left bank were already evacuated before the Germans got there. General Huntziger, commander of the Second Army in the Sedan sector, watching from the heights above the Meuse, saw his men down in the valley below coming out of their strongholds with their arms over their heads to surrender and he sadly gave the order to his artillery to fire on the positions. Other officers could only report that their troops had disbanded right at the beginning of the action.[31]

Some postwar analysts have excused the collapse at Sedan by pointing out that the divisions in line there were reserve divisions—

---

[31] Gamelin, I, 348–359; also *Commission chargée d'enquêter* . . . , IV, 980.

practically the whole French army were "reserve" divisions for that matter—but at Dinant this rationalization is denied them for there the Germans dispersed a unit of supposedly high quality under the same circumstances as at Sedan and with relatively little difficulty. The Eighteenth Infantry Division, a Series A division with regular army cadres almost equal in numbers to those of the active divisions, which was supposed to hold the Meuse, broke and fled. The initial crossing there by relatively weak German advance infantry elements broke through the French 129th infantry regiment, an active army unit.[32] In the same sector the Fifth and Twenty-second Divisions, one an active army and the other a Series A division, were broken and dissolved by relatively inferior enemy forces.

There is no point in dwelling on this unpleasant subject, but it is important to demonstrate how impossible it is for any military leaders to conduct a campaign if the instrument in their hands bends and breaks whenever it is subject to strain—and to put some of the blame for the 1940 defeat where it belongs: on the French people. In a democracy the people usually get the government that they deserve and in this case they also got the army that they deserved.

Both Gamelin and Weygand who succeeded him tried to stem the rout by ordering the officers to use force to constrain their men to stand and fight, in other words to shoot them if necessary; but this was merely the recognition of a sick condition rather than a remedy. The best strategy in the world would have been of little value in the face of this deluge of disorder.

French government leaders were astounded to learn that 50,000 soldiers who were supposed to be in the Ninth Army which fought— using the term loosely—at Dinant were milling in the vicinity of Compiègne, more than 100 miles from the scene of the conflict and only several days after it. Their rapidity of flight would seem to disprove the theory of the French army's lack of mobility.

The roads leading from the front were thronged with hundreds of thousands of fleeing soldiers, disorganized and out of control, most of whom had thrown away their weapons. One of the strangest sights was that of the soldiers, even in the early days of the campaign, who, weaponless, appeared on the highways carrying valises or duffel bags. Many of them simply went home. German military commanders, as they drove through France, were satisfied with the docility and the cooperation of the civilian population and the retreating French soldiers; the latter, when overtaken by the German

---

[32] *Commission chargée d'enquêter* . . . , III, 628, 716, 745, General Georges' testimony.

columns, simply dropped their weapons and marched off toward the east and the prison camps.

So great was the morale breakdown that the commander of a group of armies, roughly one-third of the French forces in the field at the time of the armistice, ordered that all soldiers still in possession of their rifles when the armistice ended the tragedy should receive the Croix de Guerre. After the armistice many such absurd awards had to be rescinded.

One of the chief reasons that Pétain and others wanted to end the hostilities by an armistice was the prevalent belief that the army was suffering great casualties. This was not true, as was found out later, unless prisoners and stragglers were counted as casualties; but most people thought that losses were heavy and they could see no point in prolonging the struggle and getting men killed all the way back to the Pyrenees when the game was obviously lost and had been since the armies encircled in the north failed to break out.

We may accept, with some reservations, General Gamelin's opinion that the main cause of the defeat in 1940 was the superior German moral and psychological readiness for war and a French reluctance to fight, resulting in a general *sauve qui peut* psychology which broke the French organization into pieces. The enthusiasm, the patriotism, the will to win and willingness to sacrifice of 1914 were absent in 1940 and the only thing Pétain could do was to try to pick up the pieces, to assume responsibility for the armistice and provide the leadership and authority which the crisis demanded. Ultimately, by providing a scapegoat in his person, he could help his people rationalize their breakdown and restore their pride.

13

Denouement

When the French armies crumbled before the German onslaught in May 1940, Pétain was serving as Ambassador to Spain. Premier Reynaud, desperately trying to strengthen his government in the face of the tragedy, sent General Pujo, one of his aides-de-camp and an officer in the War Ministry, to persuade the Marshal to return to France to take part in the government. Pétain agreed, receiving the designation of Vice-President of the Council and Minister of State.

This designation was intended to make the most of Pétain's presence, for prestige purposes, while leaving him little in the way of administrative function to perform. His great age seemed to preclude any activity other than a purely formal one, although Reynaud apparently intended to rely on him for personal military advice. The Marshal himself recognized that he was too old for government service. In April, 1939 he had firmly and categorically put a stop to a movement by friends in government who were proposing his candidacy for the presidency of the republic. He also resisted other suggestions that he enter government as a cabinet member or as president of the council, pleading that he no longer had the vigor to fulfill such demanding functions.

The entry by the eighty-five-year-old Marshal into the government was received by the country at large, as well as by the members of the parliament of all political shades, with acclamation and expressions of relief. It was thought that perhaps the saviour of Verdun and hero of the first World War could restore the military situation.

This pathetic reliance upon memories of the past is an indication of how far past hope the situation really was.

On his first day as a member of Reynaud's cabinet, May 18, Pétain and the Premier went together to the headquarters of General Georges. There the military situation was outlined to them by a shaken commander who seemed already defeated. Pétain's worst fears were confirmed. Even while he was in Spain, before the German offensive, he knew that the French army was not a strong force. He did expect that the active divisions would be able to stand their ground but he had few illusions about the reserve divisions which constituted the bulk of the army. He thought too that the government was incompetent because it was a reflection of the parliament that issued from the Popular Front electoral victory of 1936.

From Georges' headquarters Pétain and Reynaud went to see Gamelin at Vincennes. Gamelin gave them what information that he could but it was evident that he had been overtaken by events and was stunned by the collapse of his plans. Little time was lost in fruitless recriminations but Pétain was angry at Gamelin's handling of the Belgian maneuver. He thought that they should have maintained contact with their fortifications and used them as a base for maneuver, instead of launching the best part of the army deep into the Low Countries. Gamelin's advance to the line Antwerp-Namur—an operation, in general, hinging upon the western end of the Maginot Line—could have been successful only if the conditions preconceived for such a move had been met: that there would be time to organize the new positions, and that the Belgians would have established prepared positions and otherwise have created a line of defense. Without those conditions being met they should not have advanced beyond the Escaut (Scheldt).

Gamelin's Belgian maneuver to a large extent went counter to the military philosophy of the French army which had developed since 1914–18, that "battles of encounter" should be avoided at all cost and that enemy attacks should be met in well-prepared positions. All their pre-1940 instructions reveal this preoccupation. It is idle to say that Pétain was responsible for this defensive mentality, although he did subscribe to it fully. Even if he had not existed, the French army of 1940 would have been the same. The experiences of World War I, and the militia-like army provided by the army organization laws of 1927–28, plus the pacifist and anti-militaristic sentiment so prevalent in France during the inter-war period, bred a fighting force which had to be eased into combat under the most favorable conditions.

French military leaders recognized the deficiencies of the men under their command, deficiencies which were soon apparent when active operations began. In Norway the young German Nazi soldiers exhibited fighting qualities which the soldiers of the democratic nations found difficult to match. It is not excessive "defensive mindedness" for commanders to judge the quality of their troops and to formulate their plans of operations accordingly. Gamelin attempted too much and he attempted it with the best part of the forces under his command, so that when he failed he had compromised the whole French military position.

Reynaud told Pétain that he had summoned General Maxime Weygand from Syria to replace Gamelin, and the Marshal approved. The appointment of the seventy-three-year-old former assistant to Foch to command the armies was, like that of Pétain, expected to conjure up shades of past plory. When the Premier announced to the Senate the appointments of the two old men he was loudly acclaimed, amid shouts of "At last!" and "It's a little late but they are here."[1]

The military situation indeed was one that would require the assistance of ghosts of the past, for it was beyond the means of the French army. The German breakthrough at Sedan and Dinant, and the subsequent encirclement of the best part of the allied armies in the north, had left the French army with greatly reduced effectives to hold a line resting on the Somme and the Aisne, a line longer than the line resting on Antwerp had been. When the battle on the Aisne and the Somme began on June 5 the allies had already lost approximately one-third of their divisions, not counting the Belgians, along with most of their modern equipment. Above all, the rank and file had lost hope; despair gripped the army and events moved too fast for them to get set, to brace themselves, to recover their shattered morale.

Weygand assumed command on May 19, and after visiting Georges and Gamelin at their respective headquarters—the two-headed command organization which had cost France so much—he reported to Reynaud and Pétain that the enemy had a firm grasp on the initiative and that the French had no control over the conduct of the battle. They could only attempt to parry the German attacks. In accepting the command Weygand warned that he could not promise success. Every day thereafter he reported to Reynaud and Pétain at 11:00 A.M. and every day the situation became progressively worse.

---

[1] Paul Reynaud, *Mémoires* (Paris, 1963) , II, 362.

He at first attempted to reestablish contact between the isolated 1st Army Group and the main armies, by coordinated attacks from the north and south, but the armies were not able to make the necessary effort and the withdrawal of the British toward the sea ended any chance of joining the separated forces. From then on, the end was only a question of time.

If Pétain's participation in the Council of Ministers was a boost to the morale of the nation, it was hardly a tonic to the government leaders. At meetings of the Council he remained silent and contributed nothing. When asked for his opinion he would respond, "I have nothing to say."

His rare utterances were sometimes disastrous. At one meeting President Lebrun asked him his explanation for the unprecedented military debacle. Members of the cabinet leaned forward, to hear what France's foremost military leader would say. They were stunned to hear him respond, in the measured, hollow tones of an old man, soon to become familiar to the country over radio Vichy, that the army perhaps had put too much reliance on modern communication systems, which had broken down in the general retreat. He thought that the old carrier-pigeon service had been discontinued prematurely and he suggested that pigeon-coops be set up at General Headquarters to restore communications. After that his opinion was not again solicited.

The lack of substantial ground forces by the British in France was a sore point with Pétain. At a War Committee meeting on May 25, when the point was made that in any discussion of an armistice there must be agreement between France and her ally, he declared that the question of reciprocity of duty to one's ally should be in direct proportion to the aid or effort which each had contributed, and since France had eighty divisions fighting to Britain's ten, the consideration that France should pay to Britain should be in that proportion. Further, he pointed out, the comparison should not only be in proportion to the military effort made by each country but should also consider what the relative sufferings would be for each country as a result of whatever action France should take. In other words, France would suffer most by continuing the war and should therefore consider her own interests paramount in making her decisions.

On May 26 Weygand ordered the army to adopt new tactics, in a desperate attempt to hold the Somme-Aisne line. To counter the enemy panzer tactics the French troops were not to retreat or surrender when bypassed or cut off; they must meet infiltration with infiltration. They were to form strongholds of resistance and continue to fight in the German rear. He ordered that the troops should fight and die in place rather than retreat, and officers must set the example. Officers should exercise their right to enforce obedience on the men—or, in other words, to shoot them if necessary. Pétain reproached him for the latter measure but Weygand was obdurate, having received information that the troops were weakening and that discipline was breaking down.

On June 11 the Germans were approaching Paris and Weygand informed Reynaud and Pétain that he was going to declare it an open city, to save it from damage. Both Pétain and Reynaud accepted this development without comment; they had already reconciled themselves to the loss. There could be no battle of the Marne in 1940.

On the same day a meeting of the Supreme Allied Council was held at Briare, which was attended by Winston Churchill, Reynaud, Pétain, and Generals Weygand, Georges, and de Gaulle. Churchill attempted to hold out some hope of military success by evoking memories of March 1918 when the situation of the allied armies also looked bad. Weygand pointed out the differences between the present situation and that of 1918. In March 1918 Britain had a large army in France, France herself had more troops than she had in June 1940, and the Americans were arriving in some force. Pétain said that there was little analogy between the present situation and that of 1918; during the German offensive of March 1918 he was able to send immediate assistance to the British Fifth Army in the form of twenty divisions and several days later he could send twenty more, the total of forty divisions coming from his reserves. At the present time there was no general reserve from which divisions could be taken.

Churchill then suggested that perhaps the French armies, if unable to continue a coordinated defense, might carry out a guerrilla warfare in various regions of France and thereby oblige the Germans to disperse their forces to cope with this activity. Both Weygand and Pétain vigorously rejected this suggestion, which they said would mean the destruction of the country. It would be years before Britain and the United States could intervene effectively, if indeed they ever would, and in the meantime France would be destroyed.

It was at this meeting that Churchill was asked for the support of the fighter aircraft which were based in Britain. The British Prime Minister indicated that his government could not give up their aircraft, which they needed so vitally themselves, to support a cause almost already lost.

On June 12 the Council of Ministers met at the chateau of Cangé at Tours. A report on the state of the army revealed an alarming picture. The Germans had broken through everywhere and the French units left in the field—about 400,000 or 500,000 men remained in intact formations—were in full retreat, withdrawing in different directions, having lost most of their artillery. Weygand reported that most of the men no longer fought, many of them having thrown away their rifles. He demanded an armistice to end further useless hostilities, and Pétain associated himself solidly with Weygand's views.

It was at this meeting that Pétain declared that under no circumstances would he leave metropolitan France. If the government should flee the country, it should do so without him. This uncompromising attitude he maintained to the end. President Lebrun later said that the Marshal had an *idée fixe* about never leaving France, for in June 1940 he uttered this intention repeatedly, whenever the question arose.[2]

Was this the result of old age, a senile fixation? Pétain had seldom in his long lifetime left French soil; he had not even served in the colonies during his early military career. In a way he was the victim of his own image; the protector and savior of the *poilus* of World War I had become the grand old father of his people. He was resolved to stay with the people of France to share their misery and to do what he could to alleviate their suffering. In June 1940 it was not generally considered the part of honor to flee the country. That was considered by many to be the easy way out. For example, the members of the parliament who embarked from Bordeaux on the Massilia were referred to as "runaways." Only time and subsequent events changed attitudes so that those who fled became heroes.

The rapid German advance forced the government to flee once again farther southward, and they arrived at Bordeaux on June 15. From June 12th to the 16th the main point at issue in the Council was whether to request an armistice or to remove the government from metropolitan France to the colonies to continue the fight there. Pétain and Weygand insisted upon an armistice and refused, for their part, to quit France.

The idea of continuing the war from North Africa was considered militarily infeasible by the two military chiefs. North Africa had already been stripped of her first-quality troops to support the fighting in France—the only two active divisions in North Africa had just been shipped to France as reinforcement for the crumbling front. There were no factories or industry in North Africa to manufacture war matériel and there was no heavy artillery there.

---

[2] *Commission chargée d'enquêter sur les événements survenus en France de 1933 à 1945* (Paris, 195?) , IV, 1006.

Weygand pointed out that normally it took eight days to transport one division across the Mediterranean. The Germans were not likely to allow the leisure or the undisturbed embarkation conditions to effect a movement in a fraction of that time. An operation of that nature would require that the armies hold the front while selected units were disengaged to be embarked for overseas. Under the existing circumstances that was impossible. The front was not holding; there were no reserves; all surviving units were heavily engaged and it was impractical to disengage them.

The Minister of Merchant Marine in 1940, Alfonse Rio, one of the cabinet members opposed to the armistice and therefore one whose testimony is significant, later pointed out that although there were 600,000 tons of shipping available in southern ports, the evacuation of substantial forces was impractical. When the question was broached in June 1940 the Germans were at Tours with nothing holding them and could have been at Marseilles in a few days. What would they evacuate? he asked. Disbanded and disorganized troops? There was no longer any order in the conduct of affairs and time was lacking.[3]

Pétain considered that an armistice was inevitable and that the longer one waited the worse the French bargaining position would be. Better to end hostilities while something of France's territory and military force was left, he thought.

At a meeting of the Council on June 16 the Marshal threatened to resign unless an immediate armistice was sought but he was persuaded to withdraw his intention for the time being. His gesture was merely a means of putting pressure upon the government, an unfair gesture perhaps, in that moment of crisis. The government had enough problems without being undermined in public opinion by the resignation of the most respected man in France. If Pétain had wanted to employ resignation as a tool to influence government policy he might better have used it long ago, perhaps in 1927 to show his disapproval of the new army organization and recruitment laws.

A way out of the impasse had been suggested by a member of the Council, Camille Chautemps, the day before and was now brought up again—after a desperate telegram to President Roosevelt had brought no tangible results. Chautemps suggested that they ask the Germans what their terms would be as a basis for an armistice. If the terms proved too harsh they could continue the fight, pointing out to the French people the necessity for prolonging the war. A majority of the Council favored this proposal and Reynaud, finding himself in the minority, resigned.

[3] *Commission chargée d'enquêter . . . ,* V, 1323.

Reynaud was outspokenly opposed to a request for terms but his attitude was a curious one. He had been an advocate of continuing the war and when he found himself in the minority he resigned, recommending Pétain to the President of the Republic as his successor, since the Marshal represented a majority in the government. It seems apparent that he was aware that the war must come to an end but that he would not accept the onus for officiating over the defeat. He was further embarrassed by the fact that it was due to his initiative that on March 28, 1940, an agreement had been signed between the French and British governments pledging each not to sign any armistice separately.

By requesting that Pétain form a new government on June 16 Reynaud was getting out of a difficult situation at little cost to himself. He knew that Pétain was in favor of requesting an armistice and that he would unquestionably try to get one if he came to power. Why then propose Pétain as the head of a new government if he, Reynaud, did not feel that a cessation of hostilities was inevitable? By giving the new government a Marshal of France as its chief he ensured that the onus of seeking peace from the victorious enemy would be upon the military.

Reynaud all along had sought to convince Weygand to capitulate in the field, a step which Weygand, supported by Pétain, obstinately refused to take. By resigning and giving way to the Marshal, Reynaud circumvented Weygand and gave the task of concluding a military collapse to the army, something that the German generals of 1918 had been able to avoid. Thus in France the "stab in the back" cry was to come from the civilian government—the military had betrayed the republic.

It is this old question of animosity between politician and soldier in France which explains much behind the events of June 1940. The politicians, traditionally afraid of the military menace to the republic, and the military, traditionally contemptuous of politicians, were each determined that the other should accept the responsibility for the defeat.

The conflict is illustrated by Reynaud's calling upon Weygand to surrender the army to the Germans—leaving the civilian government's hands clean to carry on the government abroad if necessary. On this question of capitulation versus armistice the military were adamant. They said that it was contrary to the honor of the army and, in fact, contrary to law: article 234 of the Military Code of Justice prescribed the death penalty and military degradation for the commander who capitulated in the field. A generation of old officers had memories of

Marshal Bazaine and Metz. The attitude of the military leaders was that the government had declared the war and it was the government who should end it, although there was something unrealistic in Weygand's protests regarding the "honor of the colors" when the French army was, at that moment, little better than a mob of fugitives.

Even assuming that the Premier could cover the army by ordering it to cease hostilities, thus assuming responsibility, as Reynaud offered to do, the military leaders still refused to capitulate. If they surrendered in the field and the government made good its escape abroad, as had happened in the Netherlands, the consequences for France would have been far worse, they thought, than they were under the terms of the armistice. At least with the armistice, harsh as the terms were, they had a convention limiting the powers of the victor. Military capitulation would have meant the whole army, the manhood of France, in German prison camps instead of the half of it captured before the armistice. It would have meant the complete occupation of France, to be administered by the Germans, just as in Poland or other occupied countries.

One of Pétain's first acts upon becoming chief of state had unfortunate repercussions on the army still at grips—loosely speaking—with the enemy. He made a radio broadcast on June 17 announcing that he had assumed direction of the French government and that France must seek an armistice. Most of the soldiers who heard of the message were greatly relieved by it and some troops units took it to mean that they could surrender without authorization. Weygand had to issue a general order stating that hostilities had not ended and that the fighting must continue.

On the same day Pétain, through the Spanish ambassador, asked the Germans for terms. On June 20 the French armistice delegation, under General Huntziger, was sent to meet with the enemy. Pétain instructed them to break off negotiations if the Germans should demand the delivery of all or part of the fleet, or the occupation of any portion of French overseas possessions. As it turned out, neither of these demands was made by the Germans. Despite the understandable fears of the British (and the United States) he had no intention of giving over any part of the fleet to the enemy. The fleet would have been scuttled before any accession to such a request. In fact, the fleet units at Toulon, which the Germans attempted to seize when the allies invaded North Africa in 1942, were scuttled to keep them out of German hands.

Through the armistice Pétain kept a 100,000 man army plus the troops in the colonies. His government kept sovereignty over part of

France. He kept the fleet and he kept the colonies, thus providing a North African springboard for the allied forces later in the war, although that was not necessarily his intention. He was able to some extent to protect part of the French people from the miseries of occupation such as were inflicted by the Germans elsewhere in Europe, at least until late in 1942 when the Germans occupied all of France in answer to the allied invasion of North Africa.

Some German leaders, among them Goering, Keitel and Guderian, said, at the Nuremberg trials or elsewhere after the war, that Hitler made a serious error in conceding the armistice to France in 1940, in leaving her the navy, the colonies, and creating a nonoccupied zone in southern France. They claimed that it would have been better to push on to the Mediterranean, to have taken Gibraltar, to go into French North Africa. If this had been done, Egypt and the Near East could have been taken.

Pétain was able to mitigate the sufferings of the French people, something a government in exile could not do; and the misery which he could not prevent he shared, which a government in exile could not do.

The military situation was hopeless and all France knew it. The vast majority of the French people were in full accord with Pétain's determination to effect an armistice. The American ambassador to France, Anthony Biddle, advised his government that Marshal Pétain was the only man who could have led the country at that critical moment, to prevent a possible revolution and to accept what were expected to be stiff armistice terms.[4]

Meanwhile the French armies were at their last extremity. On the same day that Huntziger was sent off, General Georges wired Weygand that the Third, Fifth, and Eighth Armies had almost run out of supplies and munitions and he asked what their conduct should be. Weygand told them to keep fighting as long as possible, until their supplies and munitions were gone, and then to ask for a cessation of hostilities with the honors of war.

With or without the formality of an armistice—it was concluded on June 22—the war was over for France. Any discussion as to the necessity for an armistice, or the wisdom thereof from a military point of view, is academic. The Germans had already conquered four-fifths of French territory and could easily have occupied the rest in a few days.

On July 10, 1940, the National Assembly met practically in its

---

[4] William L. Langer, *Our Vichy Gamble* (New York, 1947), 41, footnote cites Biddle's telegram of June 16, 1940 and his memorandum of July 1, 1940.

entirety, despite the transportation difficulties, and voted overwhelmingly, 569 for and 80 against, to give Pétain full powers. This was
deemed necessary in view of France's tragic circumstances. Even
among the 80 deputies who voted "against," many favored the Marshal
as chief of state but objected only to altering the Constitution. It was
easy for the man who had once told President Poincaré that he did
not "give a damn about the Constitution" to accept full powers and
to see himself as the savior of his country, particularly when it was
generally agreed that he was the only figure about whom the country
could unite. As Commandant Loustanau-Lacau, a fine Frenchman who
had no reason to love Pétain, said of him during the Vichy days, "The
Marshal is a symbol. If he should die, we would have to stuff him."[5]

The French in the summer of 1940 were in a state of shock. In 1914
France was able to recover from the initial defeats and to hold the
Germans at bay for four years but in 1940 she had succumbed to the
first blows. What was the reason for this difference? An important
reason was the absence of an ally in the east in 1940, to force the Germans to divide their efforts and their forces, as the Russian armies
did in 1914.

By the time war broke out in 1939 French foreign policy, determined
largely by an internal political situation bordering on the chaotic, had
led France into a position so strategically unfavorable that it would
be difficult to conceive of a worse one. In 1914 French military leaders
had only to concentrate on the northern and northeastern fronts,
reasonably certain that the frontiers on the Pyrenees and Alps were
secure, while Germany had to fight a two-front war. It was only this
factor which saved France from defeat in the early days of the war in
1914. But in 1939 a hostile Italy menaced the Alpine frontier, while
across the Pyrenees a fascist government, owing its existence to German and Italian support, threatened the French rear. Germany was
secure in her rear and free to devote her entire strength to a knockout
blow on the western front. In the 1930's a military alliance with the
Soviet Union was prevented in France by bitter right-wing opposition,
among which Pétain must be numbered, while the political left wing
prevented an agreement with Italy and drove that power into the arms
of Hitler's Germany. Ideology ran rampant and nationalism came in
a weak second.

Another important reason for the disaster was the low state of
morale in the French forces of 1940 and, indeed, in the French nation
as a whole. The enthusiasm, the fiery patriotism, the will to win, the
willingness to sacrifice were all less apparent in 1940 than in 1914.

---

[5] J.-R. Tournoux, *Pétain et de Gaulle* (Paris, 1964), 224.

With the flank of their Maginot Line carapace turned, the French suffered the psychological shock of the turtle divested of his shell, brusquely and unexpectedly deprived of the protection upon which he was accustomed to rely.

In a moment of objectivity Paul Reynaud accused the French of looking throughout their history for a "scapegoat in order to escape from their own collective responsibilities" after each defeat.[6] In 1871 it was Bazaine, although the causes of the defeat in that war lay elsewhere, and after World War II it was Pétain.

Before World War II the French wanted to be told that a defensive military doctrine was the best one; they were pleased when they were told that they could fight from behind concrete. Major retreats in foreign policy like the Munich settlement were accepted, and even demanded, by them. But, as Reynaud said, the people were sovereign and the errors were theirs.

Pétain was partly senile by 1940 but he was lucid enough to know what his sacrifice entailed, a sacrifice which he voluntarily accepted. When he declared at Bordeaux in 1940 that he made a gift of his person to France, apparently he meant this quite literally. Later, through his disgrace, the French people did recover their pride. He has been accused of a great egotism; perhaps in his messianic urge he justifies that criticism.

In 1940 the condition of the people of France was one of surprise, shock and bewilderment following the brutal handling which they had received. In times of crisis a society, a living organism, takes to itself a leader who expresses within himself the temper, the fears, and the aspirations of the mass of the people who compose the society, and whom they feel will best ensure their survival. Not only in a democracy is the government no better than its people but in any society the form of government usually represents the character and dominant desires of those who make up its mass and upon whom it rests.

Given the temper of the French people after the catastrophe of the German victory, and taking into consideration their bewilderment under the blow they had suffered—its very swiftness and completeness the determining factor—it seemed that the German force was invincible and destined to achieve, at least, a European hegemony. What else to do then, than to find shelter behind the great figure of le Maréchal, who would work out some modus vivendi with the conqueror?

And when that conqueror had been in turn conquered, when the pall of defeat had been lifted and the spirit again revived, what better way to erase the bitterness and shame of the defeat, to wipe out

---

[6] *Commission chargée d'enquêter* . . . , Supplement, I, 118.

the memory of national weakness and humiliation, than to sacrifice the leader whom they had chosen in the depths of their discouragement, to heap upon him their sins and to chastise themselves in him? He had offered his person to the French people; they took it and used it.

Pétain served his country's interests during the Vichy period, not gloriously but in filling a function. He did stand between his people and the most ruthless conqueror of modern history and his conduct of affairs did spare them physical suffering, but his actions could not restore their pride. There was no question of a "double game" in his Vichy foreign policy. If Germany won the war, he was prepared to live with her, and if the allies won, he hoped to accommodate himself to them too. He cared only about France and his whole policy, however misguided at times, was designed to further the interests of his country.

The French supported the Marshal until it became evident that Germany was not going to win the war. When Hitler failed to defeat Russia, and when the United States entered the war, the tide turned and de Gaulle's lonely voice from London began to win a significant number of adherents. The French Resistance movement grew in strength when the Vichy government, after Pierre Laval took the reins of leadership from Pétain's impotent hands in 1943, began to send French young men as laborers to Germany. The men who fled those manpower requisitions formed, in the hills and fields, a substantial segment of the underground movement, which grew as the allied cause advanced. As liberation came closer, opposition to Vichy increased. By 1945 France had turned full circle as far as Pétain was concerned and could try him for conspiring against the state and for intelligence with the enemy; the latter crime constituted treason.

The chief of the Provisional Government, Charles de Gaulle, who once had boasted of his close association with the Marshal in order to further his own career and later became his former benefactor's bitter enemy, commuted the death penalty to life imprisonment. The sentence was executed on the lonely little Isle d'Yeu, off the Vendean coast, where a tired old man lived out his final years, his humiliation only dimly felt through the veil of his failing mental powers.

Marshal Pétain died in his ninety-sixth year, on July 23, 1951. He rests in the little cemetery of Port-Joinville on the Isle d'Yeu, in the Bay of Biscay. His wish that he rest someday among the fallen of Verdun in the national cemetery at Douaumont has as yet been denied him.

Index